Earthly Politics

Politics, Science, and the Environment
Peter M. Haas, Sheila Jasanoff, and Gene Rochlin, editors

Earthly Politics
Local and Global in Environmental Governance

edited by Sheila Jasanoff and Marybeth Long Martello

The MIT Press
Cambridge, Massachusetts
London, England

Set in Sabon by The MIT Press. Printed and bound in the United States of America. Printed on recycled paper.

Library of Congress Cataloging-in-Publication Data

Earthly politics : local and global in environmental governance / edited by Sheila Jasanoff and Marybeth Long Martello.
p. cm. — (Politics, science, and the environment)
Includes bibliographical references and index.
ISBN 0-262-10103-3 (alk. paper) — ISBN 0-262-60059-5 (pbk. : alk. paper)
1. Environmental management—International cooperation. 2. Environmental policy—International cooperation. I. Jasanoff, Sheila. II. Martello, Marybeth Long. III. Series.

GE300.E23 2004
363.7'0526—dc22

2003060622

10 9 8 7 6 5 4 3 2 1

Contents

Acknowledgments

This book is an outgrowth of many interactions; correspondingly, it owes debts to a number of important supporters. The biggest debt is to the Global Environmental Assessment Project (GEA), an international, interdisciplinary effort funded by the National Science Foundation and housed at Harvard University's John F. Kennedy School of Government. Over a five-year period, beginning in 1995, GEA brought together many of the volume's authors with the aim of exploring the roles played by scientific assessments in multilateral environmental policy. We are extremely grateful for the resources GEA provided and for its important community-building role among the book's authors. We extend our thanks to all GEA participants, most particularly to William C. Clark and Nancy Dickson for their generous intellectual, administrative, and financial support throughout the project.

Funding for the research that led to this volume came from a number of sources. Initial support for research by the co-editors, and by Clark Miller, came from National Science Foundation's Sustainable Knowledge about the Global Environment grant (SBR-9601987). Support for the GEA Project was provided by a grant from the National Science Foundation (SBR-9521910) to the Global Environmental Assessment Team. Supplemental support came from the National Oceanic and Atmospheric Administration, the Department of Energy, the National Aeronautics and Space Administration, the National Science Foundation, and the National Institute for Global Environmental Change. Additional support was derived from the Research and Assessment Systems for Sustainability project, funded by National Science Foundation grant BCS-0004236 with contributions from the National Oceanic and Atmospheric Administration's Office of Global Programs.

The ideas for the book originated in a weekly research seminar led by Sheila Jasanoff at the Kennedy School in fall 1999 and spring 2000. Seminar participants included graduate students from MIT, Harvard, Cornell, and Yale, as well as postdoctoral research fellows and faculty from the Kennedy School. The seminar explored the meanings, uses, and implications of "local knowledge," while linking the empirical work done by GEA participants to theoretical work in science and technology studies and international relations. The insight that local knowledge is not merely place-based but is constituted within particular communities, histories, institutional settings, and expert cultures emerged from discussions in this seminar.

These ideas were further refined through two workshops held at Harvard. The first, titled Local Knowledge and Its Global Consequences: New Perspectives on Environment and Development, took place in spring 2000. Organized by Sheila Jasanoff, Marybeth Long Martello, Clark Miller, and Charis Thompson, it received support from the GEA project. The second, titled Localizing and Globalizing: Knowledge Cultures of Environment and Development, was held in spring 2001. Organized by Jasanoff and Long Martello, it received support from the GEA project and from the NSF Sustainable Knowledge grant.

Several individuals were extremely important to the book's production. Peter Sedlak played an invaluable role in organizing both workshops. Kristen Eddy was an enormous help in providing web resources for the second workshop and making the papers electronically available to participants. Seth Kirshenbaum's help was indispensable in the final stages of manuscript preparation. We are also grateful to several anonymous reviewers for The MIT Press and to Clay Morgan and the series editors for their constant encouragement. Finally, we wish to thank the authors for their tireless and good-natured work through many revisions.

Earthly Politics

Introduction
Globalization and Environmental Governance

Marybeth Long Martello and Sheila Jasanoff

The Shape of the Future

The world today is in the grip of globalization. Networks of economy, technology, politics, and ecology have encircled the Earth, weakening the historical claims of nation-states, sovereignty, and cultural identity. With the end of the Cold War, worldwide trade liberalization, and the growing influence of multinational corporations, economic waves originating in one region flow out to others, sometimes with tidal force. Information travels instantaneously around the globe through phones, faxes, television, e-mail, and the Internet. As transportation and communication technologies develop, an expanding world population feasts on an increasingly homogeneous diet of fast food (Schlosser 2001), logoized consumer goods, blockbuster movies, international best-sellers, and the culture-defying strains of global popular music. The planet itself, as a self-contained orb, a biosphere of limited resources, challenges human beings to find communally sustainable ways of life, now and in the future (WCED 1987).

Sometimes, an event brings into fleeting focus an image of relative global harmony. The turn of the millennium was one such occasion. A huge, day-long spectacle, in which tens of millions participated from the privacy of their living rooms, focused the world's gaze upon itself as never before. The show began on a small and uninhabited outcrop of land in the Pacific Ocean, newly renamed Millennium Island, in the tiny Republic of Kiribati. Some 70 Micronesian dancers, splendidly attired in natural materials (grass skirts, headdresses, bold ornaments), transported there for the occasion from Kiribati's capital Tarawa, staged for the eyes of the global media a "traditional" ceremony to mark the birth of the new millennium. In succeeding hours, celebration moved from obscure Kiribati to Tonga,

Auckland, and Sydney; across Asia, heedless of competing local calendars (Joerges 2003), to Tokyo, Beijing, Jakarta, New Delhi; thence to Moscow, Berlin, Paris, and London, linking Europe's capitals in bursts of light; then across the Atlantic to New York's jubilant Times Square and on to Hollywood, before coming to rest in Honolulu, the occident's final outpost. For masses of people still nervously waiting for a "millennium bug" to trigger disastrous computer breakdowns, this ephemeral collage of the ancient and the modern, the real and the virtual, the natural and the artificial, the marvelous and the threatening fittingly captured the restless spirit of globalization.[1]

Other times, images of discord and disunity dominate our consciousness. As was horrifically demonstrated by the events of September 11, 2001, globalization can be as much a catalyst for conflict as an incentive for living harmoniously together on a bounded planet. Often inarticulate and unfocused, the anti-globalization movements of the turn of the century nonetheless reflect a deep-seated antagonism toward emerging world institutions and the shape of the future they allegedly represent. Prospects for a consensual world order remain distant, whether or not one accepts the political scientist Samuel Huntington's (1996) prognosis that we are bound for a period of sustained clashes among civilizations. Finding common ground on a planetary scale is not outside the realm of imagination, but the way forward lies across uncharted ideological and political minefields.

Whether consensual or conflict-ridden, rising interchange among citizens and societies has generated demands for new forms of governance. A word of ambiguous meaning but growing popularity, "governance" lies in the conceptual gray zone between electoral politics and administrative rule making. It has been defined most neutrally as "rules and institutions for the authoritative organization of collective life" (Donahue 2002, p. 1). In European usage, it refers to methods or mechanisms for "dealing with a broad range of problems/conflicts in which actors regularly arrive at mutually satisfactory and binding decisions by negotiating and deliberating with each other and cooperating in the implementation of these decisions" (Schmitter 2001, p. 8). Equally normative is the definition adopted by the European Commission (EU 2001, p. 8): "'Governance' means rules, processes, and behavior that affect the way in which powers are exercised at European level, particularly as regards openness, participation, accountability, effectiveness, and coherence."

Not only does the word "governance" point to the rise of intermediate governing structures supplementing states and markets, but it also signals a growing role for decision-making bodies that are neither domestic nor international (i.e., representing nation-states). As "world" institutions proliferate—consider only the World Bank, the World Trade Organization, the World Intellectual Property Organization, and the World Economic Summit—the word "international" seems at times almost a relic of a forgotten age. The institutions and processes designed to manage the world system not only accommodate diverse national interests and facilitate cooperation; they help to construct a politics that at once crosses geopolitical borders and transcends them. Forums such as these are creating supranational norms and regulations and, in the process, helping to redefine agency, authority, leadership, and even citizenship in a new domain of supranational politics. So powerful and ineluctable do these forces appear that some have spoken of the coming of a new global empire (Hardt and Negri 2000). Yet it seems clear that global governance in coming decades will have to accommodate profound differences of religion, culture, property, and aspiration even as it obliterates distance and enforces economic and social togetherness. Global actors will have to tolerate, respect, or even defer to many aspects of the local while crafting institutions that seek to avoid the risks and errors of rampant localism.

Over the past 30 years, some of the most interesting balancing acts between the global and the local have come from the domain of environmental governance. The willingness to seek global solutions to problems of the human environment is one of the big—and as yet only partly told—stories of the late twentieth century (Miller and Edwards 2001). Starting in the 1970s, nations rallied together around such issues as acid rain, ozone depletion, hazardous wastes, marine pollution, biodiversity loss, desertification, and climate change. These efforts preceded the widely discussed globalizing effects of the Internet, trade liberalization, and the marketization of socialist economies at end of the Cold War. Environmental initiatives revealed, often for the first time, emergent aspects of transnational politics that will only grow in significance in this century: the increasing interaction between scientific and political authority, highlighting fault lines in each; the salient role of non-state actors in both knowledge making and politics; the emergence of new political forms in response to novel conjunctions of actors, claims, ideas, and events that cut across national boundaries; and, of greatest interest here, the reassertion of local knowledge claims and local identities against the simplifying and universalizing forces of global science, technology, and capital.

In a time when national particularities are under pressure from many directions, it is of no small interest that the idea of the local has emerged as a salient topic in the policy discourses of environment and development. While seeking to establish common transboundary approaches to issues of sustainability, a remarkable variety of international regimes have recognized and accommodated knowledges and perspectives that are tagged as local. This juxtaposition of global and local, universal and particular, serves as the entry point for the work presented in this volume. We confront here a twofold puzzle. On the one hand, it is notable enough that environmentalism, so long associated with place-specific political phenomena such as the NIMBY ("not in my back yard") syndrome, has become global at all. On the other hand, it is equally striking that the implementation of the global environmental agenda should so quickly and on so many levels have led to a rediscovery of the local.

Our aims in exploring these puzzles are both theoretical and pragmatic. On the theoretical front, we draw upon recent experiences in the field of environment-development politics to enrich our understanding of the phenomenon of globalization and its political ramifications. We are persuaded that the reappearance of the local within the discourses and practices of global governance is no passing fad—comparable for instance to global brand-name manufacturers deciding, after September 11, 2001, that business would improve through the incorporation of local style features into their blandly standardized luxury goods. Localism and globalism are far more problematic concepts for us than they appear to be for these suppliers of "glocal" mass markets.[2] The studies in this volume begin by asking what is *meant* by "global" and "local," and how the meanings of these words connect to political struggles around varied environmental regimes. Each chapter examines how the dynamics of localization and globalization relate to different ways of knowing and evaluating environmental phenomena, as well as to the norms, beliefs, practices, and artifacts through which environmental knowledges gain power in political domains. Issues of this complexity can only be grasped by bringing together perspectives from several disciplines. Most of the contributors draw on more than one field that adds depth and texture to their analysis of environmental globalization. Insights from science and technology studies (S&TS) provide the intellectual backbone of the project as a whole, but the chapters are also informed by approaches from such fields as anthropology, sociology, law, political science, and political ecology.

Our pragmatic aims center on the design of institutions and processes of global environmental governance. The cases examined in succeeding chapters tell us much about what it will take to forge robust institutions to address problems that will in the future increasingly refuse to remain encapsulated within national boundaries. Three strong and interrelated themes emerge from these cases:

• Global solutions to environmental governance cannot realistically be contemplated without at the same time finding new opportunities for local self-expression.

• The construction of both the local and the global crucially depends on the production of knowledge and its interaction with power. How we understand and represent environmental problems is inescapably linked to the ways in which we choose to ameliorate or solve them (Jasanoff 2004). And which issues are defined as meriting the world's attention has everything to do with who has power and resources, including scientific ones, to press for them.

• Effective governance requires constant translation back and forth across relatively well-articulated global and local knowledge-power formations. This, in turn, calls for procedural innovation in science, politics, governance, and the interactions among them.

By presenting and analyzing a variety of such experiments, the chapters in this book enlarge our capacity to imagine more flexible, just, and effective approaches to global governance.

In the sections that follow, we first review several global environmental regimes that have established formal niches for local knowledge and politics. We next turn to different ways of theorizing the global and the local in the context of contemporary environmental politics. Drawing on several analytic literatures, we show that there is a need to integrate ethnographic and micro-focused accounts of local institutions and cultures with more systemic and macro-focused perspectives on globalization. This section also elaborates on the central role of knowledge in the formation of local-global relationships and draws out some themes that cut across subsequent chapters. We conclude by presenting an outline of the remaining chapters and showing how they relate to the main concerns of the book.

Recovering the Local in Global Regimes

The discourse of globalization has figured importantly in the framing and dynamics of environmental action since the early 1970s. Satellite images of the "pale blue dot" (Sagan 1994) gave rise to a rhetoric of the Earth's fragility, finiteness, and ecological interconnectedness, as well as a new concern for preserving the biosphere's shared and limited resources (Miller and Edwards 2001, particularly Jasanoff in that volume). Concurrently, *Only One Earth* (Ward and Dubos 1972) and *Our Common Future* (WCED 1987) helped to translate these ecological and ethical ideas into political action. Nations of the North and the South, both developed and developing, were urged to unite in a project of global environmental stewardship.

The terms "sustainable development" and "intergenerational ethics," though vague and imprecise, nonetheless facilitated global negotiations about environmental goals and how to achieve them (Weiss 1989; Litfin 1994). Environmental science, too, became global in its ambitions, identifying new processes and objects for collaborative investigation. The proliferation of multilateral environmental agreements in the last quarter of the twentieth century attests to the wholesale adoption of shared environmental ontologies among the nations of the Earth: the ozone hole, shrinking habitats, biodiversity loss (Takacs 1996), and climate change, among others, were recognized as "real" problems, giving proof, if any were needed, that the severest environmental threats are politically borderless.

Institutional change followed quickly. For the environment as for the economy, mega-institutions such as the United Nations and the World Bank took up the task of management on a global scale. Just as modern states had done in the twentieth century (Price 1965; Mukerji 1989; Ezrahi 1990; Jasanoff 1990; Solingen 1994; Rueschemeyer and Skocpol 1996), and colonizing empires in the century before (Cohn 1996; Drayton 2000), these global bodies soon discovered the need for reliable knowledge to support their administrative and political authority. Producing shared cognitive foundations for global environmental regulation required further institutional innovation, and the new environmental regimes were fitted out with a panoply of scientific and expert bodies, such as the Intergovernmental Panel on Climate Change (IPCC) and the Subsidiary Body for Scientific and Technological Advice (SBSTA) attached to the UN Framework Convention on Climate Change (UNFCCC). Non-governmental organizations (NGOs) with global missions, such as Greenpeace and the Worldwide Fund for Nature, followed suit, creating their own resources of expertise, or often *counter*expertise. All these actors took up the business of producing for a global audience universally acceptable facts, ideas, and messages about phenomena such as "species protection," "biosafety," "risk assessment," and "precaution." They thus emerged as knowledge brokers for the world, although their political priorities and strategies remained, of course, markedly diverse.

It seems inevitable in retrospect that this vast project of integration—offering some of the starkest evidence, in Hardt and Negri's (2000) terms, of the dawn of "Empire"—could not have unfolded without meeting resistance on many fronts. Environmental politics, as we have already noted, has historically been a politics of the local. It derives emotional force from people's attachment to particular places, landscapes, and livelihoods, and to an ethic of communal living that can sustain stable, long-term regimes for the protection of shared resources (Ostrom 1990). Homely sayings such as "think globally, act locally" and "getting down to earth" point to the continued importance of local self-sufficiency and place-based identities. Not surprisingly, then, as some decision makers, experts, and publics confronted global articulations of environmental problems, it also became evident that other relevant actors, as well as their understandings of nature, could be integrated into environmental governance only at scales much more modest than the planet as a whole.

The paradoxical rediscovery of the local can be readily observed in the science and politics of climate change. Experts in the (global) IPCC and the (national) US government, for example, began to regionalize or localize their studies of climate impacts. Early work on sea level rise, extreme weather events, and crop yields tended to focus on how changes in climate parameters would affect ecological and social systems on global or near-global scales. Newer analyses, by contrast, examine the vulnerability and adaptability of particular social groups and ecological systems—in the Great Plains of the United States, for example, or on small islands such as Samoa. Acting under a 1990 law, the US government in 2000 completed its own assessment of the national consequences of climate variability and change (USGCRP 2000). The process involved stakeholders from all major geographical regions, as well as groups whose interests could not be physically localized; native peoples and their homelands received an entire chapter in the final overview report, reflecting the quasi-sovereign status and political voice of this 1 percent of America's population.

Similar trends were evident in the politics of development. Thirty years ago, development organizations committed to the Green Revolution disseminated science-based agriculture to developing countries. Their aim was to increase productivity and enhance capacity according to a template of progress then deemed universally valid (Jasanoff and Wynne 1998). These efforts were only partly successful. Reprieve from hunger brought with it many disruptive changes in land tenure, wealth accumulation, and class relations. It aroused from the poor a covert resistance, using what James Scott (1985) has aptly termed the "weapons of the weak." The ecological costs were also considerable and not well accounted for in advance. The new grain varieties need such high inputs of water and fertilizers to "succeed" that some critics call them "high-response varieties" instead of "high-yielding varieties" (Shiva 1993, pp. 39–49).

Today, environmental regimes such as the Convention on Biological Diversity and institutions such as Canada's International Development Research Center recognize the need for more "culturally appropriate" technologies. In other words, even global actors have admitted the need to mobilize indigenous knowledge and promote community participation so as to improve people's lives in the developing world. No longer seen as merely victims of ecological breakdown, local communities and groups are instead assumed to hold some part of the solution to these problems.

International programs for biodiversity loss and forest preservation, for example, advocate participatory approaches, in which individuals—not state-like agencies—are given the opportunity to design, conduct, and evaluate environmental programs. The Convention to Combat Desertification similarly rests on a bottom-up strategy aimed at engaging women, communities, and NGOs in a common fight against dryland degradation. While the UNFCCC has not embraced a particularly populist management style, debates around global warming have catalyzed the formation of unlikely actor coalitions at far below global scales. One example is the Alliance of Small Island States (AOSIS), a group of 42 countries from around the world with disparate governments, economies, and social priorities. They are united only by a common vulnerability—the threat of extinction from sea-level rise. Armed with the strongest of normative claims, the right to live, this odd association emerged in the 1990s as one of the staunchest advocates of policies to mitigate climate change.

Equally noteworthy is a shift from "science" as the primary cognitive resource for addressing global-scale social and ecological challenges to the broader category of "knowledge." International environmental regimes increasingly admit that local, traditional, and indigenous knowledges may serve as useful instruments for sustainable development and for connecting with "on the ground" political constituencies. Some global institutions, including the World Bank, have even sought to standardize these resources, collecting and disseminating local knowledges through centralized databases. The desertification regime has sponsored workshops for sharing traditional and local knowledges and established a Panel of Experts on Traditional Knowledge. Similarly, the Convention on Biological Diversity established an Ad Hoc Working Group for the protection and application of local and traditional knowledge and practices (Martello 2001). Table 1 summarizes these and related provisions.[3]

In one sense, this move runs counter to the suggestion, made by Haas (1990) and others, that progress on regional and possibly global environmental accords would most likely come about through transnational "epistemic communities"—coalitions of professionals sharing a common causal explanation for perceived problems and an associated normative basis for allocating the costs of prevention and mitigation. The turn to local knowledge seems to make room instead for more fragmented and multiple visions of what is wrong with the environment, what values are stake, and above all what should be done about perceived harms and threats.

How should we account for the embrace of "knowledge" as a supplement to "science" in so many environmental regimes? We note to begin with that framings of environmental problems became increasingly more complex and systemic in the final decades of the twentieth century. Endangered species gave way to the ecologically sounder concept of biodiversity loss, encroaching deserts to land degradation, and the linear notion of global warming to the more turbulent concept of climate change. One consequence of these shifts is that policies for mitigating or managing environmental change must be spread across more numerous and diverse actors. Efforts to combat stratospheric ozone depletion, for example, could reasonably focus on the control of a small class of hazardous chemicals, whose properties could be scientifically studied, and on their manufacturers, many

Table 1
Traditional knowledge policies and programs (adapted from Martello 2001).

Treaty or organization	Provisions or actions concerning traditional, local and indigenous knowledge
Agenda 21 (1992)[a]	Traditional knowledge is important for promoting sustainable development and "capacity building."
	Improvements are needed in understanding and applying indigenous environmental knowledge.
	Consultations with indigenous people are important for integrating their needs, values and practices into national policies and programs.
Convention on Biological Diversity (1992)	Respect, preserve, maintain, and apply indigenous, local and traditional knowledge, innovations and practices relevant for the conservation and sustainable use of biological diversity with the approval and involvement of knowledge holders.
	Protect and encourage biological resource use in accordance with traditional practices that are compatible with conservation or sustainable use.
	Facilitate exchange of indigenous and traditional knowledge relevant to biodiversity conservation.
	Encourage development and use of indigenous and traditional technologies.
Forest Principles (1992)	National forest policies should support the identity, culture and rights of indigenous people and their communities.
	Integrate indigenous capacity and local knowledge into programs.
	Equitably share benefits from the utilization of indigenous knowledge.
Convention to Combat Desertification (1994)	"Protect, integrate, enhance and validate traditional and local knowledge, know-how and practices," and ensure equitable sharing of benefits.
	Parties shall, subject to national legislation and capabilities, promote, use, disseminate, adapt and make inventories of relevant traditional and local technology, knowledge, know-how and practices and their use.
	Integrate such technology with modern technology, as appropriate.
World Bank (1998)	Indigenous knowledge is embedded in practices, institutions, and relationships, and is "essentially tacit and not easily codifiable."
	The sharing and exchange of indigenous knowledge and its integration in assistance programs can help to reduce poverty.

Table 1 (continued)

Treaty or organization	Provisions or actions concerning traditional, local and indigenous knowledge	
World Conference on Science (1999)	Declaration on Science and the Use of Scientific Knowledge	Traditional and local knowledge systems are dynamic expressions of perceiving and understanding the world.
		Preserve, protect, research and promote traditional and local knowledge.
		Bring together scientific and traditional knowledge.
	Science Agenda— Framework for Action	Countries should develop their strengths regarding "local knowledge, know-how and human and natural resources."
		Environment-related science education should utilize traditional and local knowledge.
International Council for Science (ICSU)	Cairo Meeting 1999	Undertook a study of the concept of "traditional knowledge" because of member concerns about the potential support for 'anti-science' ideas. (Dickson 1999).

a. References to indigenous and traditional knowledge appear in several chapters of Agenda 21. Excerpts in this table are from chapter 26.

of whom were concentrated in developed nations (Benedick 1991). By contrast, policies for coping with climate change must reach into a broad range of economic and social activities whose impacts and interconnections are at best poorly understood, from subsistence agriculture and forestry to sophisticated forms of industrial production. Controls on greenhouse gas emissions are unthinkable without enrolling a far larger cross-section of the world's population, and if possible their knowledges, into management initiatives. Similar observations could be made about many other regimes.

For many of the newer issues, too, ideas of physical and biological causality can scarcely be separated from normative presumptions about the agents and behaviors responsible for environmental harm. Anil Agarwal and Sunita Narain of India's Centre for Science and Environment made this point most forcefully in connection with calculating the warming potential of greenhouse gases. They observed that treating all emissions alike, regardless of their source, would penalize "subsistence" activities just as severely as "luxury" ones; farmers producing greenhouse gases from rice paddies would be held accountable for warming the Earth on exactly the same scale as car-owners driving to the beach for their summer holidays. The superficial egalitarianism of a scientific calculation, they argued, concealed a profoundly political intention *not* to distinguish among different types of resource consumption or different historical trajectories of development (Agarwal and Narain 1991). Bringing diverse knowledge holders into global deliberations offers a means of counteracting potentially explosive value choices of this kind that often underlie apparently scientific formulations of environmental problems.

Attempts to draw systematically on local knowledge, however, may entail major political adjustments. Unconventional forms of expertise cannot be accommodated in global environmental regimes without renegotiating basic rules of modern technical decision making. New participatory forums must be devised, because local knowledge resides, when all is said and done, in people, not places. Claims to the specificity, even superiority, of local epistemologies are frequently tied to the recognition of new rights for previously marginalized peoples; further, as we will see in succeeding chapters, "common" environmental resources may not be perceived or reliably managed as such unless they are coupled to processes of group identification and self-identification, so that people accept the resource as "theirs" to have, hold, and be responsible for.[4]

The concept of traditional knowledge, at any rate, has become a rallying point for indigenous groups around the world who wish to exercise voice in global forums. The "holder of indigenous and traditional knowledge" has emerged as a new actor in international discourse, with legally recognized claims to sit at international bargaining tables. Translocal actor coalitions have become increasingly prominent players at United Nations meetings and conferences, where they fight not only for their cultural and political rights, but also for the recognition of their knowledges and environmental practices. Constituted by and through their experiences of the environment, such groups have acquired new standing as experts. In desertification negotiations, for example, NGOs that once portrayed themselves as people's advocates now also pattern as possessors of local expertise, with the capacity to provide practical solutions for dryland degradation.

By making room for local or indigenous knowledge, then, global environmental regimes have opened the door to experiments in politics and governance that will occupy us in succeeding chapters. There is, however, a further point that needs to be emphasized in this introduction. While broadening the epistemological spectrum from "science" to "knowledge," international regimes have continued to invoke, and so to reinforce, the boundary between science and other forms of knowledge; only knowledge that cannot and does not aspire to the status of science is labeled local or indigenous, as against science itself, which remains putatively universal and free from local coloration. The contributors to this volume adopt a more symmetrical position with regard to science and other knowledge,[5] arguing that both can be seen as local—or, to borrow a term from the feminist historian of science Donna Haraway (1988), *situated*. Haraway and others have shown that communally accepted knowledge derives its robustness not from a free-floating universalism but from its attachment to particular ways of knowing. The authors in this volume argue that it is the *situatedness* of environmental knowledge that gives it force in decision making, whether the knowledge is scientific or of any other kind. The boundary between science and knowledge, moreover, is not given in advance but is constituted through social and political processes (Gieryn 1999; Jasanoff 1990). A major question addressed throughout this volume is how certain cognitive positions and technical skills achieve the privileged status of science, and what it means to attach the label "science" to particular ways of making sense of the world. We hope to show that the practices through which scientific and non-scientific knowledge are assessed, combined or differentiated form an essential component of contemporary environmental governance.

Knowing and Being: The Localisms of Modernity

In everyday speech, "local" connotes belonging to a particular place, a well-defined subunit of a larger geographical or political space, such as a region or a nation-state. A New York accent is local, as are Cajun cooking and Yankee ingenuity; so too are British humor, Italian elegance, and Arab hospitality. The localisms that have sprung up within the perimeter of the global, however, are different in kind. They are, to begin with, not necessarily tied to places. In the context of policies for environment and development, "local" has acquired richer meanings, associated not only with geographic locations but also with particular communities, histories, institutions, and even specialist expert bodies. What is interesting about the local in all these senses is how it comes into being, sustains itself, competes with other localisms, and sometimes—as in the case of India's famed Chipko movement (Gerlach 1991)—moves beyond the constraints of spatial or cultural particularity.

We argue in this book that the modern local is importantly constituted through its methods of producing situated knowledge; communal affiliations arise and are sustained by knowing the world in particular ways. This argument points to a need to supplement traditional social-science analyses of environmental globalization with perspectives from S&TS. It also underscores the centrality of knowledge making as a site of political engagement.

Between Knowledge and Information: An Analytic Deficit

As yet, the social sciences have not done justice to the resurgence of local epistemologies and their associated politics in the context of globalization. There are several reasons for this neglect. First, the local and the global have tended to be investigated by different disciplines in isolation from one another, thereby overlooking the ways in which they are related and the means by which each participates in the definition of the other.[6] Second, conventional approaches to globalization tend to reinforce simple dualities, such as "modern" versus "traditional" and "Western" versus "non-Western"; the local comes to be seen in this context as pre-scientific, traditional, doomed to erasure, and hence not requiring rigorous analysis. Third and related, since much of the academic literature on environment and development accepts globalization as inevitable, localization is not recognized as a phenomenon deserving attention. Finally, much relevant work presents a static vision of local and global, as if these categories were fixed in meaning for all time rather than fluid and subject to strategic reinterpretation.

Interestingly, the theme of knowledge has figured more prominently in the scholarship of the local than the global. Localism, as we know from important works of twentieth-century cultural anthropology, is concerned as much with particular ways of knowing things as with being in particular places (Douglas 1970). Today, knowledge deficits are often adduced as an explanation for localisms, such as resistance movements, that hinder the spread of global technologies. Any deeper understanding of modern localism, however, has to liberate itself from the framework of "us" and "other" and from the implicit power relations between subject and object that characterized older ethnographic traditions. Clifford Geertz's 1983 book *Local Knowledge* took a long step away from assuming the superiority of the observer's position to that of the observed. He advocated a special responsibility on the analyst's part to understand local ways of life within their own logics and frames of reference, and so break down the subject/object divide. But Geertz's work, too, has been criticized for adopting too essentialist a concept of local culture and privileging the eye of the beholder (Clifford and Marcus 1986). For similar reasons, some feminist theorists of science have advocated replacing local knowledge with the less loaded concept of situated knowledge (Haraway 1988). The discussion of new localisms throughout this volume is informed by this more reflexive and critical stance.

Recently, too, an impressive body of research has begun to challenge the assumption latent in many big development projects that local ways of knowing and relating to the natural world are invariably inferior to scientific knowledge and science-based technological practice (Brokensha et al. 1980; Escobar 1995; Fairhead and Leach 1996; Grillo and Stirrat 1997). Based on field studies in Africa, Latin America, and elsewhere, these works contend that practices of indigenous farming, livestock management, and water resource use can be more logical, effective, and fair than imported scientific methods of intervening in socio-ecological processes. James Scott (1998), for example, concluded that many large-scale twentieth-century development schemes failed because they did not incorporate local knowledge or forms of life. From a developing country perspective, Vandana Shiva (1993) has levied comparable charges against scientific forestry and agriculture, which are driven in her view by Western productionist ideologies and may have devastating consequences for local cultures and economies. In a similar vein, though in an altogether different context, Brian Wynne (1989; see also Irwin and Wynne 1994) showed how official UK scientific investigations of Chernobyl's effects ignored to their detriment the Cumbrian farmers' complex knowledge of their local environments and livestock management practices.

Globalization has become a prominent theme in the quantitative and predictive social sciences over the past decade, but as yet this work displays little of the engagement with epistemological issues that we observe in cultural anthropology and development studies, let alone in science and technology studies. "Information" is the word that comes closest to knowledge in the globalization literature, but, black-boxed and unproblematized, information is ordinarily treated as just another commodity flowing—along with goods, money, people, and pollution—through dense networks of communication, trade, and transport that are shrinking space, compressing time, and melding cultures (Keohane and Nye 2001; Castells 2000; Giddens and Hutton 2000; Held et al. 1999; Cvetkovich and Kellner 1997; Appadurai 1990). To the limited extent that the local appears in these accounts of global movement, it is often portrayed as a vanishing social form—lodged in peoples, knowledges, and ways of life that are appropriated, threatened or deservedly overtaken by the liberating forces of the global.[7]

Most works on globalization dwell instead on the novel interdependencies that are created by global flows and networks: upturns and downturns rippling across financial markets; borderless environmental threats such as climate change and transboundary air pollution; migration of people in an increasingly mobile world; non-localizable "cyber crimes" requiring international systems of law enforcement; and the building of a worldwide coalition of nation-states against terrorism. But how do societies undergoing such massive transformation *know* things? Where do they turn for credible information, and what even counts as information in today's complex and noisy networks of communication? How do widely dispersed actors, with no common experiential base, acquire shared knowledge, and what happens when they disagree about the immensely varied facts that are relevant for their survival? These questions, so critical to the success of global governance, have remained unasked and largely unanswered.

The contributors to this volume avoid these limitations in several ways. First, they approach the local and the global not as fixed in advance but as constituted through the beliefs, actions, and normative commitments of relevant social actors. This orientation is particularly consistent with the aims of STS, a field centrally concerned with the production of authority structures in scientifically and technologically advanced societies. Drawing on STS perspectives, the authors start from the tenet that *all* knowledge, including the "hardest" scientific facts, originates in some sense as local or situated. From this standpoint, the spread of science is something to be accounted for rather than taken for granted. It is well established, for example, that considerable simplification is needed to wrest scientific knowledge from its chaotic and often unreadable contexts and to make it intelligible to varied audiences (see Lachmund, this volume). Indeed, one way to understand the nature of scientific production is to see it as a series of progressive translations from "wild" and excessively signal-rich contexts to the tamed but interpretively constrained currency of representations and publications (Latour 1999).

To such micro-focused accounts of "science in action" (Latour 1987) may be added the perspectives of development critics who stress another kind of reductionism: the displacement of heterogeneous local sensibilities through the particular highly successful local vision that goes by the name of "science"—producing what Vandana Shiva (1993) has provocatively called "monocultures of the mind." Science, for our purposes, is not automatically exempted from the attributes of parochialism. Localism, correspondingly, is confined neither to remote villages nor to sophisticated laboratories and scientific workplaces, but can appropriately be observed in any site that produces authoritative knowledge. Localness in this sense is just as readily found in United Nations negotiating bodies and international scientific committees as in colonial South Africa or Native American tribal organizations.

Second, and related, our understandings of both local and global include but are not limited to geographic conceptions. Other ways of bounding the processes and preserves of knowledge making turn out to be equally significant for environmental governance: for example, the word "local" can be used to describe residents' knowledge of a nature conservancy, users' understanding of a technological system, the conclusions of a policy-making agency, or the practices developed by a scientific discipline or advisory body. By finding the local in such a diversity of sites, the contributors to this volume resist the tendency to equate "global" with progress or inevitability and "local" with tradition or resistance. Accordingly, a third concern of our contributors is to explore the complementarity between the local and the global. How, for example, do different conceptions of the local help to authorize the turn to the global, or vice versa? The answers open up news ways of thinking about what it means to embrace local as against global habits of thought when confronting environmental challenges. It is the mutually constitutive relationship between these allegedly opposing forms of life that commands the greatest interest. Thus, international debates about biodiversity conservation weave into a city's urban wasteland experiments (Lachmund); assertions of community identity and expertise help to counter corporate notions of universal technical knowledge

(Iles); and international institutions attempting to produce shared meaning around ostensibly global concepts such as biosafety or climate change, reveal that to "assess" environmental risk globally is to take on board a host of locally significant normative and distributive questions (Fogel, Goldman, Gupta).

Finally, all the authors challenge static notions of local and global. They deal in one or another way with processes, be they processes through which scientists and communities negotiate over nature preserves in Berlin, citizens gain access to chemical companies, or plants from South America are translated into biodiversity information for US corporations. By treating local and global in these terms, the authors illuminate the intensely political character of local-global interactions. They call attention to the mechanisms through which ideas, communities, practices, economies, and knowledges acquire power and achieve currency. This dynamic approach also brings into relief crucial questions about institutional design: Who decides what counts as local or global, and by what criteria; and what weight is accorded to local concerns in translocal forums? Who speaks for the local and the global, and on what authority? How do knowledges, people, and technologies circulate (or fail to do so) in and across local and global arenas? How are these arenas shaped by, and in turn how do they shape, additional knowledge claims and technological developments? And in what ways do new configurations of the local and the global transform the processes of environmental knowledge making, technological innovation, and political action?

What Is at Stake?

Changing notions of locality and globality, then, are more than mere academic curiosities. They have important consequences for the configuration of power and the efficacy of governance in environment and development contexts. They also have far-reaching implications for the production of knowledge acceptable to an emerging global polity. As the chapters in this volume demonstrate, there are myriad ways in which processes of localizing and globalizing bear on the creation of laws and institutions, the allocation of resources, the provision of access to scientific or political forums, and the wielding of voice in public debates. The interplay of the local and the global influences the kinds of knowledges about the environment that are discovered, accepted as authoritative, and put to use in decision making. For now, we restrict ourselves to a few general observations about the political implications of our analysis; we will return to a more detailed evaluation in the concluding chapter.

Environmental science, as we noted earlier, can be either local or global, situated or portable. Scientific knowledge production begins at one level as a deeply local activity. It takes place in field sites, laboratories, and at computer screens; equally, its production is embedded in particular traditions of securing social trust and credibility. But, as the sociologist of science Bruno Latour has shown in a series of influential works (1987, 1990, 1999), observations that achieve the status of "science" are able to circulate globally through journal articles, mathematical equations, maps, and charts, and through the interactions of international scientific communities. Claims that fail to circulate in these ways are not considered science, which continues to be seen as the only universally valid source of knowledge. Yet studies of environmental management have called into question assumptions about the adequacy, universality, and superiority of much scientific knowledge. The coming together of disparate cultures in international environment-development forums reveals important differences in ways of knowing throughout the world, even among scientifically advanced societies.

Globalization processes, as we have seen, have paradoxically helped to diversify the types of knowledges recognized and used in environment-development policy. Global regimes have not neutralized the politics of knowledge by consolidating all claims under one big, hospitable, relativizing tent, but rather have channeled scientific and political activity in specific directions. Thus, the dominance of computer modeling in an area such as climate change may discourage the use of more locally or regionally oriented methodologies such as forecasting by analogy (Glantz 1988). Sidelining the latter sorts of techniques may, in turn, disfavor framings of climate change that are most directly relevant to place-bound communities such as farmers and natural resource managers.

But it is not only such basic epistemological divisions that have come to light through the globalization of environmental problems; at stake as well is whose knowledge counts when views conflict. The emergence of local knowledge as a resource for achieving sustainable development has, in some cases, broadened the definition of "expert" to include non-scientists and caused expert committees to become more diverse and inclusive. And the resurfacing of local knowledge has also helped to redraw the meanings and goals of capacity building. Early development programs sought to build capacity in the image of Western know-how by providing local peoples with modern technologies and analytic techniques deemed to be advantageous in all contexts. The new respect for local forms of knowledge and action recognizes the flaws in that approach. It has the potential to transform capacity-building by strengthening and enabling existing, in-situ capabilities among recipients of development assistance. These points are taken up repeatedly in the volume.

Sites of Localization: An Outline of the Volume

Each chapter in this volume takes up most of the themes and issues outlined above. It is thus important to emphasize the synergies among them. At the same time, the various chapters also deal with some recurrent forms of local-global negotiation that deserve recognition. The chapters are therefore organized so as to capture the interplay between the local and the global at three levels of governance: international institutions and their standardization of knowledge; national responses to environmental globalism; and environmental knowledge and cultural identity in communities other than nation-states.

In "Heaven and Earth," Sheila Jasanoff introduces many of the volume's principal themes. She connects the origins of the global perspective on the environment to the history of the US manned space program and notes that the resulting vision of the biosphere as a limited, ecologically interconnected space is not uniformly accepted across the world. In India, for example, environmental needs and values are related to visual representations that are remote from the totalizing image of the Earth floating in space. The adoption of the global view, Jasanoff suggests, entails the overriding of local sensibilities and commitments, without necessarily acknowledging the political consequences at stake.

In part I, Michael Goldman, Clark Miller, Cathleen Fogel, and Aarti Gupta examine how development processes managed by suprastate bodies, under the heading of modernization, produce demarcations between local and global. These accounts illustrate how global scientific rationality, operating as a leveler of difference, encounters and deals with local specificity. As well-intentioned analysts seek to develop common languages and create portable claims and artifacts, they often over-simplify or ignore complex local ways of life. In response, local constituencies are increasingly demanding voice and agency, not only in the forums that develop multilateral policies, but also in processes that generate knowledge about global environmental change. Transnational negotiating forums have emerged in consequence as producers of local knowledge as well as global regulatory concepts.

Goldman examines the World Bank's social and environmental assessment practices following the protracted Narmada Dam controversy in India. The Bank, in Goldman's account, functions much like a reductionist planning state, translating local peoples and their complex life worlds into abstract knowledge and data that can circulate globally. Newly devised assessment and consultation procedures ostensibly serve as tools for avoiding the "Narmada effect" by promoting environmental sustainability and creating transparency. In employing these tools, however, the Bank reverts to its old habits and does more to simplify and even erase "local" subjects than to empower them.

Along similar lines, Miller, in his analysis of the International Research Institute for Climate Prediction (IRI), emphasizes the lack of accountability in the scientific expertise and predictive technologies undergirding some international institutions, and he suggests that many of globalization's discontents stem from this weakness. Reviewing IRI's attempts to make El Niño-Southern Oscillation (ENSO) forecasts available worldwide (in Peru in particular), he pleads for greater attention to the ways in which such institutions remake, or attempt to remake, the localities in which they intervene.

Fogel takes forest management as her focus and analyzes the activities of the Intergovernmental Panel on Climate Change and the Kyoto Protocol regime in constructing the identities and roles of indigenous peoples. As Scott (1998) and Shiva (1993) did, Fogel shows how the IPCC's scientific forest assessments have tended to overlook the people who use forests. Indigenous groups, however, have reinserted themselves in climate change negotiations, where they present their own ways of understanding and relating to forests and argue for greater attention, on the part of scientists and policy makers, to peoples and places served by global forest resources.

In partial contrast, Gupta's analysis of the Biosafety Protocol negotiations suggests that a conceptual framework such as biosafety can function as both globally compelling and locally contingent. At one level, negotiators from participating countries appear to be talking about the same thing when referring to biosafety. Yet when they attempt to give the concept a universal meaning, they run into problems because the scientific principles on which biosafety is allegedly based turn out in reality to be highly contested and culturally variable.

In part II, Myanna Lahsen, Silke Beck, Tim Forsyth, and Astrid Scholz deal with the uptake and redefinition of global knowledge-power settlements in national contexts. The authors ask how knowledge is traded, interpreted, and institutionalized across different levels of governance, and how these exchanges shape the politics of centers and peripheries. When national-level actors confront transnational problems such as climate change, they often discover incongruities between globally constructed framings of environmental phenomena and their own histories, political cultures, and priorities. And while global institutions may operate on the assumption that local groups speak for the disenfranchised, national-level experiences sometimes reveal a different reality. These chapters point to the dangers of stereotyping the local or the global. They illustrate the everyday challenges that people (including indigenous peoples and developing country scientists) face in traversing and mediating between the national and transnational settings in which environmental science engages with politics and ideology.

Lahsen's analysis of climate scientists in Brazil explores the contradictions of leading an active scientific life in both local and global arenas. Climate scientists are supposed to belong to a unified international research community, but Lahsen's ethnographic investigations reveal a more complicated reality. From a scientific standpoint, climate change is a global problem demanding a unified response from science; yet the consequences of climate change are not evenly distributed around the world, and the politics of knowledge making and knowledge interpretation vary by region and state. Thus, while participation in international forums confers professional rewards, Lahsen's Brazilian scientists realize that these forums also support research and policy agendas at odds with Brazilian needs and priorities.

Beck draws on theories of political culture in examining the appearance of climate change as a national policy issue in Germany. Looking at the work of two parliamentary commissions, she shows that each translated concerns about the climate into a political idiom consistent with German views about the nature of expertise, the role of dissent, and the norms of environmental responsibility. Beck argues that institutions, scientific enterprises, and policy processes put in place to deal with climate change at the international level are founded on unrealistically monolithic visions of the problem and its management. Not surprisingly, such approaches tend to overlook the national particularities that make international coordination on this issue so difficult to achieve.

Turning to Thailand, Forsyth takes issue with the idealistic view that associates environmental NGOs with the elevation of local knowledge and democratization. Environmental social movements, he observes, are not classless resistance movements, but are themselves tied to particular socio-economically and culturally inflected visions of the environment. NGOs thus may propagate erroneous or ill-considered scientific doctrines, ignore systematic environmental abuses, propagate falsely romantic views of the "local" or ally themselves with repressive policies. In Thailand, he further suggests, environmental social movements have been largely middle class enterprises. Far from representing the voices or knowledges of the poor or marginal, they have more often repressed them.

Scholz tells a more optimistic story about the dynamics of localization and globalization in the emerging field of natural products chemistry, where important relationships between knowledge and power are again at stake. Scholz compares a project of the International Cooperative Biodiversity Group (ICBG) in Panama with its sister projects elsewhere in the program. The Panama program successfully produces natural products for the world, but also gives back resources, knowledge, and technologies to the localities from which the products are derived. Elsewhere in the ICBG program, the delocalization of biodiversity and local knowledge has proceeded without comparable local payoffs.

In part III, Jens Lachmund, Marybeth Long Martello, Alastair Iles, and Stacy VanDeveer examine the intricate links between knowledge making and identity formation in the context of environmental politics and explore how knowledge is mobilized in support of local forms of life that gain their power partly by contesting or dissociating themselves from global environmental regimes. Strategies of localization and globalization have proved to be important resources for scientists, Native Americans, citizens, corporations, and regional communities as they work out their own identities; their definitions of nature, expertise, and place; and their roles in environmental governance. In discussing these examples, the authors ask what it takes to establish or extend the power of knowledge produced in various local settings, be they nature reserves or new scientific disciplines.

Lachmund's analysis of a nature park in Berlin offers fascinating insights into the tenacity of local practices, both symbolic and material, in a globalizing world. Tracing the development of urban ecology in West Berlin, Lachmund describes how ideas about human-nature relationships co-evolved with new conventions of ecological research, and how the results achieved both cognitive and political viability in the unique environment of Germany's once and future capital city. "Living ecologically" and adapting to "global change," in his account, were not scientifically defined endpoints; rather, they were performative goals that allowed both lay and expert actors to participate in determining what should count as natural and how nature should be studied and protected.

Martello looks at the strategic deployment of rhetorics of localization and globalization in the debate over whether the Makah tribe of the Pacific Northwest should be allowed to hunt gray whales. The Makah's very existence as a community depended in this case on their ability to assert unique claims about their relationship to the environment. Exchanges between the Makah and the anti-whaling activists centered on who (if anyone) has the right to define "global nature" on their terms, and on what (if anything) counts as authentic "local" culture, entitled to retain its distinctive environmental practices in a globalizing world.

Iles turns to the corporate sector as a locus of knowledge and identity formation and examines how the American chemical industry reinterpreted the notions of "local" and "expert" in implementing global standards. This quintessentially modern industry once equated the local with notions of inferior, parochial, non-expert, and lay; today, however, a new vision is emerging in which the local is recognized as a source of power, voice, and specialized knowledge. Even the chemical industry has begun to view so-called local people as potential experts and as reliable partners in chemical plant oversight, thus laying the basis for a new, transnational culture of regulatory cooperation.

VanDeveer uses examples from the European Union and eastern Europe to illustrate the emergence of "regions" as a new unit of environmental governance. The identity and autonomy of regions, he suggests, results from the interaction of knowledge about nature and visual representations of nature, such as maps, with associated forms of politics. In a global context that is otherwise largely governed by national entities, regions function as an interesting kind of locality, with power to foster politics and even identity formation on the basis of shared conceptions of environmental problems.

In a brief concluding chapter, we summarize the insights gleaned from the preceding chapters and their implications for policy institutions and processes. We indicate which kinds of accommodations between the global and the local are most likely to lead to political impasse and injustice, and which by contrast can be expected to produce more balanced, interactive, and knowledge-enhancing relations in future environmental governance.

Notes

1. Others have noted the weaving together of local and global themes and images during the millennium celebrations. We are particularly indebted to Clark Miller for related insights and comments.

2. The words "glocal" and "glocalism" have attained currency in journalistic and popular writing (Ball 2002). They imply that there are ready-made spheres of the global and the local and that the challenge of marketing or governance is simply to hybridize them. The authors of this book resist any such implication.

3. The table does not claim to present an exhaustive account of all transnational initiatives on local, traditional, and/or indigenous knowledge. Agreements and organizations that address traditional knowledge but are not included in the table include the International Undertaking on Plant Genetic Resources, the World Intellectual Property Organization, the General Agreement on Tariffs and Trade, and the Trade-Related Aspects of Intellectual Property Rights Agreement.

4. The co-construction of norms and identities around natural resources has not been sufficiently stressed in the extensive and widely cited literature on common pool resources (e.g., Ostrom 1990). Written from a realist perspective on the natural world, this literature generally takes the "commonness" of natural resources for granted. Particularly in the context of globalization, however, we need to consider how planetary resources come to be seen as held in common and demanding shared stewardship.

5. This methodological approach is consistent with the strong program in the sociology of scientific knowledge, which invites analysts to explore through social scientific means how certain facts and claims acquire or maintain the status of science while others do not (Bloor 1976).

6. For exceptions, see Robertson 1995 and Cvetkovich and Kellner 1997.

7. Roland Robertson (1995) uses the word "glocalization" in calling for sociological analyses that examine the interactions of homogenization and heterogenization that have been part of so much late-twentieth-century life. Robertson argues that focusing exclusively on globalization as a process that overrides the local neglects the role of the trans-local and the super-local in constructing the local and overlooks weaknesses in notions of "universal time" and "particularistic space."

References

Agarwal, Anil, and Sunita Narain. 1991. *Global Warming in an Unequal World*. New Delhi: Centre for Science and Environment.

Appadurai, Arjun. 1990. "Disjuncture and Difference in the Global Cultural Economy." In *Global Culture*, ed. M. Featherstone. Sage.

Ball, Deborah. 2002. "Global—with a Touch of Local." *Wall Street Journal Europe*, June 7–8.

Benedick, Richard E. 1991. *Ozone Diplomacy: New Directions in Safeguarding the Planet*. Harvard University Press.

Bloor, David. 1976. *Knowledge and Social Imagery*. University of Chicago Press.

Brokensha, David, D. M. Warren, and Oswald Werner, eds. 1980. *Indigenous Knowledge Systems and Development*. University Press of America.

Castells, Manuel. 2000. *End of Millennium*. Blackwell.

Clifford, James, and George E. Marcus. 1986. *Writing Culture: The Poetics and Politics of Ethnography*. University of California Press.

Cohn, Bernard S. 1996. *Colonialism and Its Forms of Knowledge*. Princeton University Press.

Cvetkovich, Ann, and Douglas Kellner. 1997. "Introduction: Thinking Global and Local." In *Articulating the Global and Local*, ed. A. Cvetkovich and D. Kellner. Westview.

Dickson, David. 1999. "ICSU Seeks to Classify 'Traditional Knowledge.'" *Nature* 401 (6754): 631.

Douglas, Mary. 1970. *Natural Symbols: Explorations in Cosmology*. Pantheon.

Donahue, John. 2002. "Market-Based Governance and the Architecture of Accountability." In *Market-Based Governance*, ed. J. Donahue and J. Nye. Brookings Institution.

Drayton, Richard. 2000. *Nature's Government: Science, Imperial Britain, and the "Improvement" of the World*. Yale University Press.

Escobar, Arturo. 1995. *Encountering Development: The Making and Unmaking of the Third World*. Princeton University Press.

European Union. 2001. European Governance: A White Paper. Brussels: Commission of the European Communities, COM(2001) 428 final.

Ezrahi, Yaron. 1990. *The Descent of Icarus: Science and the Transformation of Contemporary Democracy*. Harvard University Press.

Fairhead, James, and Melissa Leach. 1996. *Misreading the African Landscape: Society and Ecology in a Forest-Savanna Mosaic*. Cambridge University Press.

Geertz, Clifford. 1983. *Local Knowledge: Further Essays in Interpretive Anthropology*. Basic Books.

Gerlach, Luther. 1991. "Global Thinking, Local Acting: Movements to Save the Planet." *Evaluation Review* 15, no. 1: 120–148.

Giddens, Anthony, and Will Hutton. 2000. "In Conversation." In *Global Capitalism*, ed. W. Hutton and A. Giddens. New Press.

Gieryn, Thomas F. 1999. *Cultural Boundaries of Science: Credibility on the Line.* University of Chicago Press.

Glantz, Michael H., ed. 1988. *Societal Responses to Regional Climatic Change: Forecasting by Analogy.* Westview.

Grillo, R. D., and R. L. Stirrat. 1997. *Discourses of Development: Anthropological Perspectives.* Berg.

Haas, Peter M. 1990. *Saving the Mediterranean: The Politics of International Environmental Cooperation.* Columbia University Press.

Haraway, Donna J. 1988. "Situated Knowledges: The Science Question in Feminism as a Site of Discourse on the Privilege of Partial Perspective." *Feminist Studies* 14, no. 3: 575–599.

Hardt, Michael, and Antonio Negri. 2000. *Empire.* Harvard University Press.

Held, David, Anthony G. McGrew, David Goldblatt, and Jonathan Perraton. 1999. *Global Transformations: Politics, Economics and Culture.* Stanford University Press.

Huntington, Samuel P. 1996. *The Clash of Civilizations and the Remaking of World Order.* Simon and Schuster.

Irwin, Alan, and Brian Wynne, eds. 1994. *Misunderstanding Science? The Public Reconstruction of Science and Technology.* Cambridge University Press.

Jasanoff, Sheila. 1990. *The Fifth Branch: Science Advisers as Policymakers.* Harvard University Press.

Jasanoff, Sheila, ed. 2004. *States of Knowledge: The Co-Production of Science and Social Order.* Routledge

Jasanoff, Sheila, and Brian Wynne. 1998. "Science and Decisionmaking." In *Human Choice and Climate Change*, volume 1, ed. S. Rayner and E. Malone. Batelle.

Joerges, Bernward. 2003. "Metropolitan Time: Reflections on the Millennium, Calendars, and Gregorian Hegemony." In *Social Studies of Science and Technology,* ed. B. Joerges and H. Nowotny. Kluwer.

Keohane, Robert O., and Joseph S. Nye Jr. 2001. *Power and Interdependence.* Longman.

Keohane, Robert O., and Joseph S. Nye Jr. 2000. "Introduction." In *Governance in a Globalizing World*, ed. J. Nye and J. Donahue. Brookings Institution Press.

Latour, Bruno. 1990. "Drawing Things Together." In *Representation in Scientific Practice*, ed. M. Lynch and S. Woolgar. MIT Press.

Latour, Bruno. 1999. *Pandora's Hope: Essays on the Reality of Science Studies.* Harvard University Press.

Litfin, Karen. 1994. *Ozone Discourses: Science and Politics in Global Environmental Cooperation.* Columbia University Press.

Martello, Marybeth. 2001. "A Paradox of Virtue?: 'Other' Knowledges and Environment-Development Politics." *Global Environmental Politics* 1, no. 3: 114–141.

Miller, Clark A., and Paul Edwards, eds. 2001. *Changing the Atmosphere: Science and the Politics of Global Warming.* MIT Press.

Mukerji, Chandra. 1989. *A Fragile Power: Scientists and the State.* Princeton University Press.

Ostrom, Elinor. 1990. *Governing the Commons: The Evolution of Institutions for Collective Action.* Cambridge University Press.

Price, Don K. 1965. *The Scientific Estate.* Harvard University Press.

Robertson, Roland. 1995. "Globalization and Glocalization." In *Global Modernities,* ed. M. Featherstone et al. Sage.

Rueschemeyer, Dietrich, and Theda Skocpol, eds. 1996. *States, Social Knowledge, and the Origins of Modern Social Policies.* Princeton University Press.

Sagan, Carl. 1994. *The Pale Blue Dot.* Random House.

Schlosser, Eric. 2001. *Fast Food Nation: The Dark Side of the All-American Meal.* Houghton Mifflin.

Schmitter, Philippe C. 2001. "What is there to legitimize in the European Union . . . and how might this be accomplished?" No. 75, Political Science Series, Institute for Advanced Studies, Vienna.

Scott, James C. 1985. *Weapons of the Weak: Everyday Forms of Peasant Resistance.* Yale University Press.

Scott, James C. 1998. *Seeing Like a State: How Certain Schemes to Improve the Human Condition Have Failed.* Yale University Press.

Shiva, Vandana. 1993. *Monocultures of the Mind: Perspectives on Biodiversity and Biotechnology.* Zed Books.

Solingen, Etel. 1994. *Scientists and the State.* Ann Arbor: University of Michigan Press.

Takacs, David. 1996. *The Idea of Biodiversity: Philosophies of Paradise.* Baltimore: Johns Hopkins University Press.

United Nations. 1992a. Agenda 21: The United Nations Programme of Action from Rio. United Nations Department of Public Information.

United Nations. 1992b. Convention on Biological Diversity. Geneva: Interim Secretariat for the Convention on Biological Diversity.

United Nations. 1994. United Nations Convention to Combat Desertification in Countries Experiencing Serious Drought and/or Desertification, Particularly in Africa. Nairobi: UNEP.

United Nations Conference on Environment and Development (UNCED). 1992. Non-Legally Binding Authoritative Statement of Principles for a Global Consensus on the Management, Conservation and Sustainable Development of all Types of Forests.

US Global Change Research Program. 2000. *Climate Change Impacts on the United States: The Potential Consequences of Climate Variability and Change: Overview*. Cambridge University Press.

Ward, Barbara, and Rene Dubos. 1972. *Only One Earth: The Care and Maintenance of a Small Planet*. Norton.

Weiss, Edith Brown. 1989. *In Fairness to Future Generations: International Law, Common Patrimony, and Intergenerational Equity*. Transnational Publishers and United Nations University.

World Bank Knowledge and Learning Center, African Region. 1998. Indigenous Knowledge for Development: A Framework for Action.

World Commission on Environment and Development (WCED). 1987. *Our Common Future*. Oxford University Press.

World Conference on Science (WCS). 1999a. Declaration on Science and the Use of Scientific Knowledge.

World Conference on Science (WCS). 1999b. Science Agenda—Framework for Action. Text adopted by the WCS, July 1.

Wynne, Brian. 1989. "Sheepfarming after Chernobyl." *Environment* 31: 11–15, 33–39.

1

Heaven and Earth: The Politics of Environmental Images

Sheila Jasanoff

Environmentalism without Borders

The year 2002 featured several important anniversaries for global environmentalism. On September 2–11, Johannesburg hosted the World Summit on Sustainable Development, a ten-year retrospective on the 1992 United Nations Conference on Environment and Development (UNCED) in Rio de Janeiro. Widely billed as the year of "Rio Plus Ten," 2002 marked the end of a decade that propelled the environment into an issue of global significance, inextricably linked it to development, and energized non-governmental organizations around the world to play a more active, participatory role in environmental governance. It was 15 years after the publication of *Our Common Future* (WCED 1987), the report whose commanding title and insistence on the idea of sustainability achieved a resonance beyond anything contemplated by the international committee that authored it. It was 30 years since the 1972 United Nations conference in Stockholm, which, arguably for the first time, placed the environment on the international policy agenda. That event, in turn, followed by just one year the 1971 Earth Day demonstrations that framed the environment as a people's cause and established April 22 as a date to remember on the calendar of an emerging global civil society. And it was 40 years since *Silent Spring* (Carson 1962) began the consciousness-raising work that many now credit with the birth of environmentalism as a social movement in America.

Among the achievements leading to this year of multiple anniversaries, few are so remarkable as the world community's apparent willingness to see the environmental dilemma as a truly planetary problem, calling for concerted action on an equally expansive scale. In just a generation, the idea that there is "only one Earth" seems to have lost its sloganeering quality and been accepted as reality by activists and policy makers, the media, and the public. How this happened, how far this reality has influenced belief and action, and whose realities have been ignored or sidelined along the way are the primary topics of this chapter.

Citizens of postmodern times need few reminders of the multiplicity of human responses to the world. Relativism has been a recognized strain in humanistic and social thought since the early decades of the twentieth century, when people of different cultures and conditions first confronted "the other" through technological achievements in transport, communication, and military conflict. (See, for example, Fussell 1975.) We may still fight wars to settle ideological conflicts, but the fact of cultural difference no longer threatens in and of itself; indeed, within certain limits, rights to be different and to behave differently have been significantly expanded. It has become an axiom of critical theory that one's perception of the world legitimately reflects the position from which one looks at it, whether in politics, in culture, or in law (Said 1978; Guha and Spivak 1987; Kelman 1987). Even scientific knowledge, built up over centuries as the one domain of human experience that is independent of personal and cultural biases, is now widely, if still controversially, acknowledged to be a social achievement (Kitcher 2001; Jasanoff et al. 1995; *contra* see Gross and Levitt 1994). Today's puzzles, for academics and activists, are less about why difference exists and more about how people can overcome their positional differences and come together on issues of common concern.

The rise of global environmentalism in the latter decades of the twentieth century promises much illumination, then, as a case study of global norms-making. If the environment is a space of thought and action in which the people of the world have learned—however partially—to set aside their differences, then understanding how and why this happened is of paramount importance. Environmentalism can take its place beside a few other emerging global norms (human rights, nuclear non-proliferation, anti-terrorism) that are, with luck, laying the basis for supranational governance in the twenty-first century. Environmental action can be seen in this sense as part of a larger process of global constitution making (Jasanoff 2003). Unlike norms against biological weapons or chemical warfare, moreover, environmentalism has grown as much from the bottom-up politics of civil society (Keck and Sikkink 1998) as from the top-down interventions of policy makers and technical experts. It is, in this respect, a particularly appealing model for global democracy.

I hope to show in this chapter that global environmentalism is a more complex, incomplete, and heterogeneous construct than some of its most ardent celebrators have suggested. To do this, I concentrate on one aspect of environmental discourse—the visual repertoire of environmentalism—that has not received as much analytic attention as more formal developments in environmental science, law, and politics. Using the examples of the United States and India, I suggest that the Earth is imaged and imagined in strikingly different ways by different polities around the world, with consequences that matter for all aspects of environmental action, from scientific research to political campaigns. The concept "global" in contemporary environmentalism remains in this respect as essentially contested as are "liberty" and "accountability" in democratic politics. This lack of agreement, however, need not be a cause for despondency. For now, the struggle to define "global" may be one of the best avenues we have for engaging in a meaningful politics of globalism.

The Politics of Global Environmentalism

Three well-known theories of convergence have been applied to the global environment, but each has flaws. The simplest is the model that attributes social change either to exogenous events that everyone can see (e.g., new scientific findings, crises, disasters) or to the work of entrepreneurial individuals and institutions determined to elevate their private scientific or moral concerns into wider political causes. Environmentalism, according to this way of thinking, fits into a well-established linear and positivist explanation of why issues appear on social and political agendas. This approach is enshrined in the work of political analysts such as John Kingdon (1984) and ratified by a long commitment to scientific and technological determinism in American thought (Ogburn 1923; Smith and Marx 1994).

Others have recognized that the ideas shared by transnational alliances do not travel in and of themselves, independent of human agency. A second line of theorizing therefore attributes environmental policy change to the work of transnational "epistemic communities": groups of professionals and policy makers who are motivated by both technical and normative commitments to pursue programs of international coordination (Haas 1990, 1992). Similar arguments have been offered by scholars who stress the role of advocacy coalition frameworks in policy making (Sabatier 1999, pp. 117–166). A related body of work argues that the power to mobilize rests not only with policy elites, as in much of the epistemic community literature, but also with networks of activist citizens. In a detailed elaboration of this position, Margaret Keck and Kathryn Sikkink (1998) suggested that non-governmental organizations succeed in promoting transnational social agendas such as environmentalism through a mix of communicative strategies, one of which is the exchange of information.

A third body of analysis has stressed the importance of discourses rather than actors in building consensus on environmental issues, especially across national boundaries. In a study of the Montreal Protocol on ozone-depleting chemicals, Karen Litfin (1994) argued that nations came together through a common discourse of prevention, even before a definitive cause-effect relationship was established between the discharge of chlorofluoro-carbons and the destruction of the stratospheric ozone layer. Cooperation occurred simply because the fact of the "ozone hole" was widely accepted and there were no plausible non-anthropogenic causes for the phenomenon. A contrasting perspective, championed for example by Maarten Hajer (1995) in his work on the European politics of acid rain, takes issue with the idea that activists simply find or generate knowledge and instrumentally use it to advance preconceived positions. Rather, Hajer suggests, actors' cognitive and moral sensibilities are shaped by their own discourses, rendering them more or less inclined to interpret facts, evidence, and the credibility of scientific findings in particular ways. The spread of a given discourse (precaution, for example) thus promotes accord on previously contested claims.

Research in the sociology and politics of scientific knowledge has rendered problematic both the knowledge-centered and the actor-centered approach to global environmental cooperation. In the linear model of policy formulation, citizens and society at large are implicitly cast as passive entities, easily led by charismatic leaders and untoward events, seemingly without independent will, purpose, cognition, or imagination of their own. The public is granted agency only when its responses diverge from expert technical judgments, as for example in the resistance to nuclear power in the 1970s, to environmental chemicals in the 1980s, and to agricultural biotechnology in the 1990s. In these cases, the public is often characterized as a collectively irrational entity that either is ignorant of the facts or has been misled by the press and politics and that hence does not understand how to act in its own best interests (Breyer 1993).

Empirical research has increasingly called into question the adequacy of these explanations. Pioneering work in the sociology of scientific knowledge has shown that social factors can be invoked to explain true as well as false beliefs (Fleck 1979 [1935]; Kuhn 1962; Bloor 1976). We have learned to see scientific knowledge making as an activity deserving every bit as much analysis as, say, the manufacture of paintings, novels, or widgets. Science is a form of organized work, a site of politics, a marketplace of ideas, an exercise in meaning-making, and an instrument of power. Therefore, when studying the role of science and technology in policy or in politics, it no longer suffices to say that facts or inventions simply drive responses and outcomes. We have to ask a series of deeper questions: How did people recognize some facts as salient or as relevant to their problems? Whose knowledge was deemed important? How were uncertainties and disputes resolved? Who participated in their resolution?

There is too the problem of science's translation to new audiences. Given increasing specialization within the sciences, even experts in one or another scientific domain pattern at best as semi-educated lay persons when confronted by findings in fields outside their own. A mathematician can no more knowledgeably take sides in disputes over climate science than a geneticist can convincingly elaborate the "laws" of game theory. Public trust in science is even less a given. Why then do people believe assertions based on science? What are the sources of science's special claim to credibility (Shapin 1994), and how is that credibility maintained even when the public sees only heavily mediated representations of scientific reality? To get to the bottom of these questions, we must interrogate the role of science and technology in constructing collective beliefs. Instead of assuming that science compels belief simply through its correspondence with the truth, we have to undertake more situated, localized investigations, asking how science's claims are interpreted within particular institutionalized frameworks for making sense of the world.

The actor-centered and discourse-centered approaches to understanding collective environmental action seem at first to avoid the deficiencies of the deterministic, knowledge-centered model. By putting forms of human agency at the center of analysis, these approaches at least recognize that facts about the environment are embedded in social contexts; without human actors to mobilize them, even scientific claims have no power to move others. Yet even when, as in the epistemic community framework, allegiance to a shared episteme is at the heart of the theory, issues of persuasiveness and credibility remain curiously outside the analysts' purview. (For a more extended critique, see Jasanoff 1996.) That scientific claims may be uncertain, controversial, or interest-ridden, let alone historically and culturally situated, has received little acknowledgment in the work on advocacy coalitions and social movements. The boundary between science and political action (Gieryn 1999) is mostly taken for granted in such work. Keck and Sikkink, for example, distinguish "information politics" from "symbolic," "leverage," and "accountability" politics. The implication is that the standard resources of politics—language, symbols, interests, legitimacy—are not influenced by the production of information, or vice versa. This view is profoundly at odds with fundamental observations in the sociology of knowledge.

Discourse analysts are more attuned to the notion that so-called facts are always interpreted within pre-existing hermeneutic traditions. How else can we explain the rifts that repeatedly occur about the meanings of particular scientific observations? The discursive approach also helps us understand how gaps in scientific knowledge can be repaired or rendered invisible in the course of building political coalitions. In foregrounding discourse, however, this framework downplays the role of material instruments and that of human interpretive faculties other than language (most notably the power of seeing and witnessing). It also pays more attention to the high culture of environmentalism—the formal discourses of policy and law—than to the vernacular traditions of television, advertising, cartoons, or popular art. Yet if environmental norms are changing to accommodate a truly global perspective, then it is precisely in the interplay of high and low, elite and vernacular, that we should find evidence of this swing.

Making Planet Earth: Destiny Manifested

In the middle of the twentieth century, we saw our planet from space for the first time. Historians may eventually find that this vision had a greater impact on thought than did the Copernican revolution of the 16th century, which upset humans' self-image by revealing that the Earth is not the center of the universe.

From space, we see a small and fragile ball dominated not by human activity and edifice but by a pattern of clouds, oceans, greenery, and soils. Humanity's inability to fit its activities into that pattern is changing planetary systems fundamentally. (WCED 1987, p. 308)

This exceptionally eloquent statement from the report of the World Commission on Environment and Development set forth some of the major themes of global environmental discourse during the final decades of the twentieth century. The commission linked the image of the whole Earth as seen from outer space to a moment of changed awareness, similar to a scientific revolution or paradigm shift (Kuhn 1962). The effect of this image, the commission implied, was to unseat human beings from the center of environmental analysis and to replace the humanistic gaze with an ecological one, focused on "a pattern of clouds, oceans, greenery, and soils." The Earth, seen as a "small and fragile ball," needs human stewardship, the commission suggested, but it also indicated that the concerns of humankind might have to be backgrounded in favor of more systemic, less human-centered understandings of environmental phenomena.

The commission offered at one level a newly thought out message about the obligations of environmental ethics, but its message could also be read as deeply political. Without much of a stretch, one can see the WCED as advocating a new kind of globalism transcending the old nationalisms of the past two centuries. This imagined global polity is held together in the commission's view through a shared custodial responsibility for the Earth, symbolized by an image that dramatically subordinates "human activity and edifice" to the dynamics of large natural systems.

In *Imagined Communities* (first published in 1983), the political theorist Benedict Anderson called attention to the pull that nation-states exercise on the imagination of their citizens. It is a force strong enough to make people die for an object that has no tangible reality and may not even occupy a piece of contiguous space upon a map.[1] At first, Anderson credited mainly print capitalism with the power to commandeer people's imaginative faculties in this way, but he later turned to other forms of representation that have also played their part in cementing the identity of newly emerging nations, such as the census, the map, and the museum. The power of the map, in particular, derives from its ability to project what Anderson called a "logoized" image of political space, erasing differences that exist within the depicted national boundaries. The planetary image, as described by the

World Commission, serves just such a function: it unites the Earth by making invisible the divisions within it.

But is it so simple? Unquestionably, the image of Planet Earth captured by the Apollo 17 astronauts in December 1972, on the last manned flight to the moon, has achieved an iconic status reserved for very few images in our visual culture (Jasanoff 2001; Sachs 1999). It appears everywhere. Often, it is tied specifically to environmental causes and messages, as when the image is used to advertise books, conferences, organic foods, and, increasingly, environmental organizations on the Internet. In these contexts, it stands not only for a global associationism, but also for an awareness of the Earth's environment as an integrated system. At other times, the image conveys more a sense of dissolving boundaries, implying that physical and social borders do not matter, as when the image is appropriated by a credit-card or a telephone company, by CNN or Barnes and Noble, or by an airline. It is also used in odd juxtapositions that attest to its "found" or vernacular character, as in an advertisement for pet food showing a dog and a cat gazing up at the planetary image. In these displacements and relocations, the Earth image resembles nothing so much as the inscrutable face of Mona Lisa, on which artists and pranksters have inscribed their personal readings for the past hundred years.

Even celebrated icons, however, are made, not born, and the most familiar image of Earth ever created is no exception. It can be tied to three successive phases of meaning-making: first as an extension of the military adventures of twentieth-century superpowers, second as a symbol of environmentalism, and third as a foundation for scientific investigations of the global environment.

In the Beginning: The Earth from Space

Neil Armstrong's first footsteps on the moon are often cited as the beginning of a new era in human self-perception, as revolutionary in its way as the Copernican revolution (see, for example, WCED 1987, p. 308; Sachs 1999, pp. 110–111; Jasanoff 2001). That moment is said to have reversed the direction of the ordinary human gaze *toward* the Earth rather than always looking up from it. Yet the human mind "saw" the Earth from space long before we as a species acquired the technological capacity for flight. There is in the British Library's map collection a complete copy of the most famous celestial atlas of the seventeenth century, Andreas Cellarius's

Harmonia Macrocosmica (1660). In its elaborate, beautifully engraved pages, the German-Dutch cosmographer Cellarius depicted the Earth from all kinds of perspectives, both spatial and scientific. The plates illustrate the planet's position in the solar system according to the astronomical theories of Ptolemy, Copernicus, and Tycho Brahe. They show the equatorial view as well as the views from both poles. One plate displays the old world, with its meridians, its climate zones, and the dwelling places of its distinctive races. One, as described on the British Library's web site, "presents a novel view of the Earth, the Pacific and Antarctic regions, as if seen through the starry sphere from a deep point in space"; though "ingenious," the caption asserts, this view was of doubtful practical utility to astronomers. In several engravings, the Earth appears suspended within concentric circles representing the motions of various celestial bodies; the planet in these images is small, blue, distant, and beautiful.

Modern warfare brought another kind of utility to images from points in the sky, if not yet from space. When aerial combat became a reality in World War II, the US government acknowledged the altered topography of national vulnerability by producing new maps. The view from the North Pole figured prominently in the Air Force's and the government's calculus of where the threats to the nation's security would originate in the future. A report sponsored by the Council on Foreign Relations in 1947, for example, copied the polar perspective from an official chart used by the Air Force. The map cuts off the Earth below the 30th parallel, showing only the northernmost regions of Africa, Iran, and India, and nothing of Latin America. The missing parts of the world were neither visually nor strategically important. The report observed that "strategists term the area between the 30th and 65th parallels the key zone since all modern wars have started there" (Baldwin 1947). Appropriately for the beginning of the Cold War, the land masses of North America and the former Soviet Union almost entirely dominated the frame.[2] It is instructive to compare this apparently natural, geopolitically bipolar representation with the roughly contemporaneous United Nations flag, officially adopted in December 1946. That flag also shows the Earth from the North Pole, but it is an inclusive image, with the globe flattened out so as to take in most of the southern hemisphere, including the Australian continent.

Sputnik initiated another new age in Earth viewing. On October 4, 1957, the Soviet Union announced that it had launched a satellite into space,

thereby confounding US expectations of being the first in space and causing near panic among American defense experts and policy makers. While
people tried to digest the meaning of this event, some even belittling the
Soviet achievement because of the satellite's small size (a mere 184 pounds),
a second, much larger satellite was launched on November 3, 1957, with a
dog on board. At 1,120 pounds, Sputnik 2 was large enough to be a
weapon, and its ability to circle the Earth, crossing all national boundaries,
contributed to a sense of deepening crisis and insecurity. Within days, the
outlines of a US space program were under discussion, culminating under
the leadership of Senate Majority Leader Lyndon B. Johnson in the passage
of the National Aeronautics and Space Act of 1958. In retrospect, many of
the experts who guided the legislation agreed that the US response was more
ambitious and sweeping than it would have been in the absence of Sputnik.
With confidence in the nation's educational system shaken, congressional
leaders opted for a program to claim back the lead in every aspect of space
science and technology (NASA 1998).

But more was at stake than national defense. The idea of space conjured
a different vision. George Reedy, press secretary and senior adviser to
Johnson, recalls how he was talked into taking the space program seriously.
Charles Brewton, an experienced Democratic staff assistant in the Senate,
came to see him in Texas about two weeks after Sputnik 1:

He insisted we drive out of Austin and out into the hill country right around Austin.
We found a little mound where we could look and see hundreds of miles of practically nothing. He began to talk about the space program; that man had really
mastered the drift of it, the poetry. He didn't know very much about outer space,
but he had grasped immediately that this was something that could change the
whole way that we lived; it could change our nation. He convinced me. I remember going back that night. My mind was just full of it. (NASA 1998, p. 1)

Mission, catharsis, and radical transformation—themes that would be
sounded by the World Commission 30 years on in *Our Common Future*—
were already germinating here. Important, too, is the imagery of distance
and altered perception. Space for Brewton and Reedy meant the erasure of
ordinary visual signals, replaced by the grandeur of "hundreds of miles of
practically nothing," until one's mind was "just full of it."

Features that loom large on Earth vanish when seen from space. Lines
that do not correspond to physical demarcations, like most political boundaries, disappear entirely. What looms as monumental is the form of the
planet itself, brightly outlined against the dense blackness of space. Perhaps

for this reason, in spite of its roots in military competition, the thought of space was coupled early on with ideas of human cooperation, especially in the thinking of some noted liberals of the 1960s. Barbara Ward, a distinguished British economist and an early proponent of global environmentalism, speculated that the flights of the Soviet and American astronauts would build solidarity between the superpowers:

When the astronauts spin through more than a dozen sunrises and sunsets in a single day and night; when the whole globe lies below them with California one minute and Japan the next; when, as they return from space, they feel spontaneously, with the first Soviet spaceman: "How beautiful it is, *our* Earth"; it is inconceivable that no modification of consciousness or imagination occurs, no sense that quarrels are meaningless before the majestic yet vulnerable reality of a single planet carrying a single human species through infinite space." (Ward 1966, p. 146)

For Ward, seeing the same Earth, and seeing it whole, could not but obliterate differences among human beings. How could such a sight fail to produce a new political imagination, transcending national rivalries and centering on the future of the entire species?

By the time the Apollo program began producing its unforgettable images, the groundwork had thus been laid for interpreting the planet as a space without political boundaries, or at least a place in which old political distinctions lost their meaning. Carl Sagan, the astronomer who did more than anyone else to make space accessible to millions on Earth, followed in the tradition of Ward and others in seeing the space program as a negation of standard geopolitics. Sagan (1994, pp. 5–6) suggested that the Apollo 17 picture of the full Earth undermined the very basis for nationalism: "We are too small and our statecraft too feeble to be seen by a spacecraft between the Earth and the Moon. From this vantage point, our obsession with nationalism is nowhere in evidence." Ironically, the image that triggered this observation showed parts of the world—Africa and the Arabian peninsula—where vigorous nationalisms still flourish, wars are fought, and heavy penalties are exacted in maimed lives, destroyed environments, and wrecked economies.

Spaceship Earth

The moon voyagers of the Apollo program were not, as a rule, a gregarious lot. Only a few of the astronauts who journeyed to the moon recorded their experience in identifiable voices. Among them was William Anders, one of the first three men to circle the moon on Apollo 8 and the first to see an Earthrise. Recorded on color film with a hand-held camera in an unscheduled photographic session, the resulting image is one of the most widely diffused products of the Apollo program. The spectacle left Anders and his fellow crew members with an overwhelming impression of Earth's beauty and frailty. Later, Anders compared the planet to a fragile Christmas tree ornament. It remained, in retrospect, the most vivid legacy of his voyage. "We came all this way," Anders observed, "to explore the moon, and the most important thing is that we discovered the Earth." (Chaikin 1994, p. 119)

The environmental philosopher Wolfgang Sachs (1999) has called attention to the not entirely innocent character of this "discovery." Sachs is aware that images have the power not merely to represent the Earth but to construct it. He is sensitive to the ontological function of photography, its ability to render things visually and cognitively graspable from angles and perspectives not available to unaided human sight. What are the salient features of the Earth's iconography as read from space? First, there is the very ability of the depicted object to lay claim to physical reality, in a way that Cellarius's images either could not do or, embellished by intricate borders and mythological creatures, chose not to. Second, it is the demarcation of Earth from space that matters; all other boundaries and features are subordinated. Blue or silver against black, the spherical shape possesses a thoroughly monumental quality. Third, the image makes the Earth seem small, a feat that Sachs argues calls forth contradictory sentiments of stewardship (it needs our care) and aggrandizement (we can manage it). Fourth, the view is synoptic, providing spurs to systemic thinking and undermining, Sachs suggests, progressive ideals associated with ideas of frontiers still ahead. Finally, quoting Susan Sontag (1977), Sachs suggests that imaging the Earth produces a probing, measuring, and instrumental response to it, because there is no longer anything about it that should not be seen and recorded.

Themes of the planet's small size and the systematicity of its environmental dynamics, along with ideas of management and control, were already circulating in the environmental discourses of the 1960s, before the production of the Earth as a modern icon. These discussions provide some support for the view that the Apollo images brought about something of a change in consciousness. Particularly interesting is the image of "Spaceship Earth," coined by the inventor and engineer R. Buckminster

Fuller, who imagined the planet as a beautifully designed spacecraft lacking only an intelligible operating manual, a gap he promptly proceeded to rectify (Fuller 1969). It was a catchy idea, but it took on very different connotations in other people's minds. The economist Kenneth Boulding read it as a sign that an economy of unbounded consumption would have to give way to a new "spaceman economy," marked by constraints and concern for future generations (Boulding 1966). Adlai Stevenson, in a speech at the United Nations shortly before his death, gave the notion a characteristically normative spin, Lincolnesque in its portrayal of socioeconomic inequality:

We travel together, passengers on a little spaceship, dependent on its vulnerable resources of air and soil; all committed for our safety to its security and peace; preserved from annihilation only by the care, the work, and I will say, the love we give our fragile craft. We cannot maintain it half fortunate, half miserable, half confident, half despairing, half slave—to the ancient enemies of man—half free in the liberation of resources undreamed of until this day. (Stevenson 1972, volume 8, p. 828)

Before the end of the decade, the distinguished environmentalist René Dubos, both alone and as co-author with Barbara Ward, had also picked up on the image of humanity on Spaceship Earth (Dubos 1970; Ward and Dubos 1972). But in Dubos's writing the metaphor became identified with caution and humility rather than management. While admitting a place for human agency, Dubos represented the human condition as dire, threatened, and likely to be overtaken by events unless there was a fundamental reorientation in the uses of human science and reason. If Fuller's spaceship had a rational human hand confidently at the helm, Dubos's craft was under far less competent control. It was headed for virtually certain ruin under scenarios that would soon be modeled, but also heavily critiqued, by the first great classic of world modeling, the Club of Rome's commissioned study *Limits to Growth* (Meadows et al. 1972).

In all these accounts of the Earth in space, humanity occupies a place, although an ambiguous one. Human overconsumption may be polluting land and water, human cities be fostering violence and anomie, and human carelessness be exacerbating the gaps between rich and poor. But the Spaceship Earth of the 1960s is still a vehicle with direction and forward thrust, guided by energetic, well-informed operators toward brighter destinations than the bleak ones foretold by predictive models. In Sachs's iconography of the 1990s, by contrast, planet Earth hangs isolated in space, blue, beautiful, and infinitely remote from human intervention. Humanity, in turn, is reduced to the status of detached observer, situated outside and at a great distance from the silent representation of its own abode, rather than in the control room of a throbbing machine, at the nerve center of thought and action.

Earthly Knowledge: The Sciences of Earth

Just as cartographers and cosmologists began to "see" Earth from space long before there were technological means for physically situating themselves at external points of vision, so scientific efforts to comprehend global phenomena were well underway before the capacity existed to collect and record data on a global scale. Large-scale understandings of natural phenomena can be built up in several ways: through the compilation of discrete, site-specific observations, collected into maps or charts and, now, computerized databases; through instruments that can observe phenomena on scales beyond the reach of individual recorders; and through computerized modeling and simulation that aggregate data and build scenarios of possible future events. The first approach relies on social coordination to achieve results that are taken over by machines and instruments in the latter approaches. Historically, that is how global modeling of the environment began, but the process has changed.

One important effort was the International Geophysical Year (IGY), spanning 1957 and 1958. The project allowed scientists from various parts of the world to participate in coordinated efforts to observe various geophysical phenomena on a global scale. Modeled on the International Polar Years of 1882–83 and 1932–33, IGY began with 46 participating countries and ended with 67. Two years before the beginning of IGY, in the summer of 1955, both the United States and the Soviet Union announced that they would launch a scientific satellite during IGY. One source close the US space program observes that no one took the Soviet plan seriously or believed that the USSR would be the first to reach the goal. That complacency made the launch of Sputnik all the more dismaying when it happened. (See comments of Glen P. Wilson, NASA 1998, p. 49).

By the 1960s, computing power had grown, and mathematical techniques for modeling all kinds of complex phenomena were on the rise (Kwa 1994). Side by side with the production of the Earth as a new political space, scientific characterizations of environmental change also went from local or regional to global, and in some cases back again (Miller and Edwards 2001). These transformations have had many noteworthy consequences for the nature of scientific work, the building of institutions, and the framing of policy responses.

For the earth sciences, the availability of new instruments, sometimes energetically propagated by government agencies, altered fundamental theoretical framings and methodological approaches. One field particularly affected by satellite-based imaging techniques was Northern ecosystems ecology, whose practitioners turned increasingly from close investigation of small plots of land and specific types of vegetation to using remote sensing as a tool for looking at global change. In this process, ecology became more interdisciplinary and useful, because its findings were needed by climatologists and oceanographers for purposes of predicting the impacts of climate change. Yet this is a field that does not "scale up" so easily, since knowledge gained from one type of ecosystem does not necessarily allow for more general claims-making at larger scales (Kwa, forthcoming). It is as if the process of seeing the Earth whole produced pressures on ecology to generate a kind of "legibility" (Scott 1998) that the field could deliver only at the cost of losing the local specificity associated with its earlier disciplinary traditions.

Producing facts on a planetary scale requires not only scientific instruments and work, but also institutions capable of interpreting and disseminating knowledge. The IGY and the more ambitious International Geosphere-Biosphere Program (IGBP), begun in 1986, are examples of social technologies developed by global change scientists to record the Earth at such a scale. Other institutions, too, arose to produce simulations and statistics about the Earth that could more readily serve as a basis for global policy. These bodies straddle the worlds of science and governance by hybridizing knowledge and power. For example, the Intergovernmental Panel on Climate Change (IPCC) added an important layer of support to the global framing of environmental change through its periodic assessments of the nature, impacts, and policy implications of climate change. These assessments also provided a framework within which the conceptual underpinnings of global environmentalism (e.g., sustainability, equity, vulnerability) were given a newly "scientific" reading.

No Other Worlds? A Southern Perspective

If global environmentalism since the 1960s has been achieved through certain kinds of erasure—the elimination of people, places, and political boundaries—the spread of this framing has not been uniform by any means. Representing the environment in many quarters of the world involves bringing places back in, along with the people who inhabit them, their communities, their lifestyles, and not least their histories and memories. A brief contrasting case of visualizing and modeling the environment, from India, helps make this point.

Down to Earth

The Centre for Science and Environment (CSE), one of India's most prominent environmental organizations, has been occupied since the mid 1970s with trying to raise the nation's environmental awareness. CSE has also emerged as a leading Indian voice on global environmental change (Agarwal et al. 1999). Its representatives are involved in shaping not only the Indian government's position on many topics, but also those of the G77, the group of "Southern" or "developing" nations that has formed a relatively stable negotiating bloc on issues from climate change to biodiversity.

CSE's representational strategies are, for the most part, resolutely place-based, and they combine the visual, the normative, and the discursive modes in quite different ways from those adopted in the United States. Elements of CSE's approach emerged in 1991, when the organization's leaders Anil Agarwal and Sunita Narain issued a slim report entitled *Global Warming in an Unequal World* (Agarwal and Narain 1991). In it, they argued that the basis on which Northern nations were allocating responsibility for greenhouse gas emissions was fundamentally flawed because it failed to deal with history and equity. History, in the Indian context, meant colonialism and its aftermath. According to many Indian intellectuals, colonialism did not end with the formal handing over of the symbols of power at the moment of national independence. Rather, the forces of hegemony persist as former colonizers continually reassert their power to shape Indian circumstances through multiple, invisible pathways. The global environment, Agarwal and Narain argued, is one site where these rituals of dominance are being reenacted; they translated their claim into discourses, images, and action.

At the discursive level, CSE and its allies not only deploy overtly polemical language, such as "environmental colonialism," but also, more interestingly, a variety of hybrid concepts that purposefully blur the line between facts and values or that between science and equity. In their global warming report, for example, Agarwal and Narain rejected the proposition that greenhouse gases should be accounted for in the same way regardless of their sources and origins. Instead, they proposed to divide the basket of greenhouse gases into "subsistence emissions" and "luxury emissions": the former generated by the poor to meet their basic needs, the latter produced through the needless consumption of the wealthy.

Images used by Indian activists have consistently sought to depict environmental degradation as a problem of the poor. One ghastly CSE cartoon shows a dying African child lying close up to its mother. "Mummy," the caption reads, "I wish we were whales." Another widely disseminated image, used on the cover of CSE's global warming report, shows a large man in a Hawaiian shirt and sunglasses, an obvious American, pulling up in a smoke-belching pick-up truck beside a small, skinny figure with an axe, standing beside a tree with a donkey at his side. The man from the developed world calls out, "Yo! Amigo!! We need that tree to protect us from the greenhouse effect!"[3] These images intertwine with action. CSE and other activists have mobilized Indian environmental law to draw the boundary between humans and nature differently from US law in numerous ways, recognizing for instance that urban environments need legal protection as much as wildernesses or endangered species; access to clean water for a pavement dweller in Mumbai could be, from this perspective, an essential environmental right.

In this political context, what becomes of Planet Earth? Even when Indian environmentalists represent the whole Earth, it is not the space-age icon, Carl Sagan's "pale blue dot," that occupies their imagination. Rather, it is an altogether more ancient and mundane representation, the globe not the planet, recognizable most often from the circles of latitude and longitude that are clearly inscribed on its spherical form. Often, too, the signs of human habitation, such as houses and trees, remain very much part of cartoon representations. To the extent that there is an image whose deployment signals India's particular environmental predicament, it is significantly not the Earth of Apollo 17. It is the picture of the Earth in drought, the land as it looks before the life-giving monsoon, cracked and parched, a place where nothing grows. It is one of the images that CSE selected for the millennial cover of its appropriately named journal, *Down to Earth*. It gave its name to a book on Indian environmental history, *This Fissured Land* (1992), by two of the country's foremost environmentalists, Madhav Gadgil and Ramachandra Guha.

Gadgil and Guha are Western-trained, cosmopolitan scientists, fully conversant with recent trends in ecology and in the social and human sciences. Yet they have interpreted the post-space age environmental order differently from the global ecologists participating in the climate change program. Instead of taking the globe image as the dwelling place of a single, faceless "humanity," Gadgil and Guha emphasize three radically different social orders that persist in the era of globalism. More than half of India's huge population, a group they characterize as "ecosystem people," live today without any of the benefits of globalization. They "must scratch the earth and hope for rains in order to grow their own food, must gather wood or dung to cook it, must build their own huts with bamboo or sticks of sorghum dabbed with mud and must try to keep out mosquitoes by engulfing them with smoke from the cooking hearth. Such people depend on the natural environments of their own locality to meet most of their material needs." (Gadgil and Guha 1995, p. 3) Only one-sixth of India's people belong to the same class as the bulk of those in the North, reaping the material and social rewards of globalization; the rest are displaced, as ecological refugees.

This threefold classification of India's human ecology, with its hybrid scientific and normative categories, challenges the epistemology of Western global environmentalism in interesting ways. Let us note only the most significant of these. Whereas Western globalism has sought to override old categories of social analysis with new terms (e.g., sustainability, vulnerability, security), and sought to make them scientifically meaningful, Gadgil and Guha suggest that ancient ills of poverty and class persist in a country like India, perhaps exacerbated by the new global affiliations of the twenty-first century. The former tradition produces a global ontology by making people either fungible or invisible; the latter produces legibility by reinvesting ecological categories with humanistic and normative content.

Conclusion

In a secular, multicultural age, the image of Earth is the nearest thing we have to an icon, a universal common property with shared meaning and, for many, spiritual resonance. It has been appropriated by environmentalists as *their* image. At the same time, it is an image which, as I have tried to show, sets up an unresolved dialectic between those who wish to approach environmental problems on a global scale, with gaze averted from the particularities of culture or place, and those who believe that the work of saving the planet must begin with more down-to-earth considerations, in the realities of lived experience, with questions about the kinds of lives people want to forge for themselves, their communities, and their descendants.

These contradictory pulls should not astonish us. Although the image may have attained universal currency, the means of producing and reproducing it, as well as the ability to translate the mandate to "think globally" into science and action, are unequally distributed around the world. The space-based view of Earth remains a uniquely American achievement, born of a conjunction of wealth, pride, and insecurity, and a culture of separating science from values, not shared by most other nations. The image's meanings are secured, I have suggested, through multiple iterations of interpretive practice, both scientific and social. When people from other countries and cultures look at the Earth, unsurprisingly they do not perceive it in the same way.

Where then should we look for collective solutions to earthly problems? Nearly 500 years ago, John Donne wrestled with the right place to seek for atonement. The seventh of his Holy Sonnets begins with the magnificent line, "At the round earths imagin'd corners, blow your trumpets, Angells." Immediately, we are back on the pages of Cellarius, with the image of Earth in its roundness fitted within the four corners of the printed page, rich with angels, cherubs, and figures invoking the order of the pre-modern, pre-Copernican world. But although Donne contemplates the rising up of "numberlesse infinities of soules" to see God, he turns back to earth for his personal work of salvation: ". . . here on this lowly ground, teach me how to repent." The growth of interest in local knowledge and local environmental action today suggests that much of the rest of the world is inviting the United States (and perhaps the North more generally) to supplement its detached planetary gaze, and the global sciences of sustainability that it has usefully fostered, with a more situated, historical, and ethical understanding of human-nature relationships. Can today's environmental globalists meet the rest of the world halfway without catering to the sometimes divisive selfishness of local particularism? Sustainability in the twenty-first century will depend on finding ways.

Acknowledgments

This chapter was originally prepared for presentation at the Yale University seminar in Agrarian Studies in 2001. I would like to thank James C. Scott and the seminar participants for valuable comments on an earlier draft. I would also like to thank NASA's History Office for permission to use its archives.

Notes

1. Shakespeare's Hamlet was Anderson's intellectual precursor. Hamlet speculated on the enigma of sacrifice for a national project when contrasting his own indecision with the decisiveness of Fortinbras. The followers of Fortinbras, Hamlet mused, were ready to die for a nothing, a plot of land not large enough to hold the tombs of the dead, and all for "a fantasy and trick of fame."

2. The association with Cold War politics gave the image wider currency. The same projection appears as a logo on publications of Harvard University's Belfer Center for Science and International Affairs. Created in the 1960s during a period of intense bipolar politics, this security studies group developed its geopolitical imagination in ways congruent with looking down on Earth from the North Pole.

3. Created in 1989 by Scott Willis of the *San Jose Mercury News*, this cartoon has entered the lexicon of global environmental images. It is reproduced in *Managing Planet Earth* (Freeman 1990).

References

Agarwal, Anil, and Sunita Narain. 1991. *Global Warming in an Unequal World*. New Delhi: Centre for Science and Environment.

Agarwal, Anil, Sunita Narain, and Anju Sharma. 1999. *Green Politics*. New Delhi: Centre for Science and Environment.

Anderson, Benedict. 1991 [1983]. *Imagined Communities*. Revised and expanded second edition. Verso.

Baldwin, Hanson W. 1947. *The Price of Power*. Harper.

Bloor, David. 1976. *Knowledge and Social Imagery*. University of Chicago Press.

Boulding, Kenneth E. 1966. "The Economics of the Coming Spaceship Earth." In *Environmental Quality in a Growing Economy*, ed. H. Jarrett. Johns Hopkins University Press.

Breyer, Stephen. 1993. *Breaking the Vicious Circle: Toward Effective Risk Regulation*. Harvard University Press.

Carson, Rachel. 1962. *Silent Spring*. Houghton Mifflin.

Cellarius, Andreas. 1660. *Harmonia Macrocosmica*. Amsterdam: Johannes Janssonius.

Chaikin, Andrew. 1994. *A Man on the Moon*. Viking.

Dubos, René. 1970. *Reason Awake: Science for Man*. Columbia University Press.

Fleck, Ludwik. 1979 [1935]. *Genesis and Development of a Scientific Fact*. University of Chicago Press.

Fuller, R. Buckminster. 1969. *Operating Manual for Spaceship Earth*. Southern Illinois University Press.

Fussell, Paul. 1975. *The Great War and Modern Memory*. Oxford University Press.

Gadgil, Madhav, and Ramachandra Guha. 1992. *This Fissured Land: An Ecological History of India*. Oxford University Press.

Gadgil, Madhav, and Ramachandra Guha. 1995. *The Use and Abuse of Nature in Contemporary India*. Routledge.

Gieryn, Thomas F. 1999. *Cultural Boundaries of Science: Credibility on the Line*. University of Chicago Press.

Gross, Paul R., and Norman Levitt. 1994. *Higher Superstition: The Academic Left and Its Quarrels with Science*. Johns Hopkins University Press.

Guha, Ranajit, and Gayatri Spivak, ed. 1988. *Selected Subaltern Studies*. Oxford University Press.

Haas, Peter M. 1990. *Saving the Mediterranean: The Politics of International Environmental Cooperation*. Columbia University Press.

Haas, Peter M., ed. 1992. *Power, Knowledge, and International Policy Coordination*. International Organization 46.

Hajer, Maarten A. 1995. *The Politics of Environmental Discourse*. Clarendon.

Jasanoff, Sheila. 1996. "Science and Norms in International Environmental Regimes." In *Earthly Goods*, ed. F. Hampson and J. Reppy. Cornell University Press.

Jasanoff, Sheila. 2001. "Image and Imagination: The Formation of Global Environmental Consciousness." In *Changing the Atmosphere*, ed. P. Edwards and C. Miller. MIT Press.

Jasanoff, Sheila. 2003. "In a Constitutional Moment: Science and Social Order at the Millennium." In *Social Studies of Science and Technology*, ed. B. Joerges and H. Nowotny. Kluwer.

Jasanoff, Sheila, Gerald Markle, James Petersen, and Trevor Pinch, eds. 1995. *Handbook of Science and Technology Studies*. Sage.

Keck, Margaret E., and Kathryn Sikkink. 1998. *Activists Beyond Borders: Advocacy Network in International Politics*. Cornell University Press.

Kelman, Mark. 1987. *A Guide to Critical Legal Studies*. Harvard University Press.

Kingdon, John W. 1984. *Agendas, Alternatives, and Public Policies*. Little, Brown.

Kitcher, Philip. 2001. *Science, Truth, and Democracy*. Oxford University Press.

Kuhn, Thomas. 1962. *The Structure of Scientific Revolutions*. University of Chicago Press.

Kwa, Chunglin. 1994. "Modelling Technologies of Control." *Science as Culture* 4, no. 20: 363–391.

Kwa, Chunglin. Forthcoming. "Local Ecologies and Global Science: Discourses and Strategies of the IGBP."

Litfin, Karen T. 1994. *Ozone Discourses: Science and Politics in Global Environmental Cooperation*. Columbia University Press.

Meadows, Donella H., et al. 1972. *The Limits to Growth*. Universe Books.

Miller, Clark, and Paul Edwards, eds. 2001. *Changing the Atmosphere: Expert Knowledge and Environmental Governance*. MIT Press.

National Aeronautics and Space Administration. 1998. *Legislative Origins of the National Aeronautics and Space Act of 1958*. Monographs in Aerospace History No. 8.

Ogburn, William Fielding. 1923. *Social Change with Respect to Culture and Original Nature*. Huebsch.

Sabatier, Paul A. 1999. *Theories of the Policy Process*. Westview.

Sachs, Wolfgang. 1999. *Planet Dialectics: Explorations in Environment and Development*. Fernwood.

Sagan, Carl. 1994. *The Pale Blue Dot: A Vision of the Human Future in Space*. Random House.

Said, Edward. 1978. *Orientalism*. Pantheon.

Scott, James C. 1998. *Seeing Like a State*. Yale University Press.

Shapin, Steven. 1994. *A Social History of Truth*. University of Chicago Press.

Smith, Merritt Roe, and Leo Marx, eds. 1994. *Does Technology Drive History?* MIT Press.

Sontag, Susan. 1977. *On Photography*. Farrar, Straus and Giroux.

Stevenson, Adlai. 1972. *The Papers of Adlai E. Stevenson*, volume 8, ed. W. Johnson. Little, Brown.

Ward, Barbara. 1966. *Spaceship Earth*. Columbia University Press.

Ward, Barbara, and René Dubos. 1972. *Only One Earth: The Care and Maintenance of a Small Planet*. Norton.

World Commission on Environment and Development. 1987. *Our Common Future*. Oxford University Press.

I
Knowing and Ruling

2

Imperial Science, Imperial Nature: Environmental Knowledge for the World (Bank)

Michael Goldman

In 1990, on Christmas Day, 5,000 villagers threatened by forced resettlement and their supporters set off on a long march to a dam site in India's Narmada River valley, hoping to close down the Sardar Sarovar dam construction project (McCully 1996; Baviskar 1995; Udall 1995). Eight days into their walk, police blocked their passage, many were beaten, 140 were arrested, and eight began a hunger fast on the side of the road. Twenty-one days later, with the local police and the national government refusing to budge, the dam's financier in Washington—the World Bank—agreed to commission its first-ever Independent Review Panel (the "Morse Commission"). Although the marchers never reached the dam site just a few miles away, they reached a more significant site of contestation, the heart of the World Bank. In doing so, they helped fuel a growing transnational movement that challenges the legitimacy of this powerful global institution. This movement has focused in part on the Bank's knowledge-production practices.

The deputy chairman of the Bank's Independent Review Panel, the Canadian jurist Thomas Berger, described his experience with these practices as follows:

When we first arrived in New Delhi, we had local hydrologists presenting us papers that showed that drinking water would never get to the two drought-prone regions. We had reports that showed whole fisheries would be lost. Scientists came forward with testimony that the irrigation schemes wouldn't work. Our team hydrologist found 15-year-old engineering reports buried in Bank file cabinets that said these schemes weren't feasible. None of this was made available to us by the Bank. In all the information made available to us by the Bank, all of the downstream consequences were omitted.[1]

For Berger, the contrast between the scientific data he received from the Bank to do his evaluation and the evidence given to him by people in India was shocking. "People would stand outside my hotel door in Delhi ready to hand over yet another report. Retired civil servants showed us their studies, community members spoke up—it became an incredible exchange of information and ideas." Yet none of this "free exchange" occurred between the Independent Review Panel and the Bank staff assigned to it by the Bank's president.

Between the panel's report and the social movement pressure that brought it about, the Bank's Executive Directors (EDs) had little choice but to vote to pull out.[2] This episode was significant not only to social activists around the world who could now see their potential power, but for the World Bank itself. The "Narmada effect," as it has come to be called, gets invoked regularly inside the Bank, and reminds staff of how the Bank must "reform or die."[3] In 1995, the first action of the incoming Bank president, James Wolfensohn, was to single-handedly cancel a large dam in Nepal, Arun 3, because of claims that the feasibility studies conducted on it failed to account for the likelihood of extremely negative ecological and social effects. He did so before any full hearing or, more importantly, before a social protest movement could fully ignite.[4] Wolfensohn's move sent chilling reverberations through World Bank headquarters, putting staff on alert that any project without rigorous scientific support could evaporate under social movement pressure or presidential fiat. After this event, the World Bank started doing business differently. As Bank staff are instructed in staff training seminars on environmental assessment in Washington: "Don't get zapped by the *Narmada effect*, do your EIAs (environmental impact assessments)!"[5]

This was the context in which, at the suggestion of a senior environmental advisor at the World Bank, I traveled to the Lao People's Democratic Republic (Laos) to observe the newly reformed World Bank *in situ*. Under the combined force of the "Narmada" and "Arun" effects, he explained, I would find that Bank projects follow a new scientific protocol with environmental and social standards. These changes are reflected in one of its biggest Mekong river investments—the Nam Theun 2 dam project.[6]

Indeed, Nam Theun 2 has become an effective litmus test for the Bank's ability to respond to its critics. The project, from the beginning, was not merely a hydroelectric dam project, as it would have been designed by the *pre-green* World Bank of the 1980s, but a national project that consumes most of the government's resources to finance a wide range of components including new regimes of law, regulation, and management of both the country's natural resources (its rivers, minerals, forests, wildlife) and the people whose livelihood directly depends upon these natural resources (more than half of the country's population). As preconditions for this dam project, national laws have been rewritten, government agencies have been restructured and retooled, and the use of the government's budget has been redefined.

Since the country is one of the most heavily indebted in the world, owing most of its external debt to the World Bank and its colleague the Asian Development Bank, its creditors have now taken over the traditional role of the government by financing these institutional changes, and hiring Northern consultants to do the work. Laos's creditors are introducing a new scientific protocol into the country, one that has begun to permeate three prominent spheres of Lao society: the capital-intensive, national project of "development"; new national regimes of law and regulation; and retooled government agencies, especially the Ministry of Agriculture and Forestry (more than half of Laos is under forest) and the government's primary environmental agency, STEA. This new scientific protocol and milieu are the focus of this chapter.

Whereas in the 1980s World Bank officials insisted that a strong environmental stance would shrink worldwide demand for its capital and services, today the Bank finds itself in the enviable position of having an expanding loan portfolio *and* a globally adopted environmental agenda, which it calls environmentally sustainable development. Simply put, the Bank has transformed an "anti-development" environmentalist agenda into one that works in its favor in many of its borrowing countries. To understand best the milieu in which the scientists hired for this agenda work, it is important to see this world *not* in simple developmentalist terms detached from the workings of the global political economy, i.e., a technical project administered by the "haves" transferring capital, knowledge, and technology to the "have nots" to help them catch up. The World Bank, as the primary financier and designer of what we can call "the development world," is a more complex institution (Escobar 1995; Crush 1995; Watts 1995; McMichael 2000). From this perspective, the World Bank functions by borrowing capital from a global bond market (that it helped to create), lending it to governments which are deemed as in need, and then requiring these governments to spend a substantial percentage of these loans to procure goods and services from firms of the "Big Five" creditor countries, i.e., the

United States, Japan, Germany, France, and Britain (George and Sabelli 1994; Kapur et al. 1997; World Bank 2002; Goldman 2003). Fifty-five years of this asymmetric triangular relationship among the Bank, its borrowers, and Northern firms has left borrowing countries highly in debt from its net capital transfer to the North. This bind gives the Bank a particular authority within countries, which it has mobilized today in order to restructure a broad array of in-country institutions and social realms according to its latest political rationality, neoliberalism. One of the more transformative arenas in which the Bank works—an arena ignored by the rich scholarship on the Bank—is the seemingly mundane area of scientific knowledge production. The question posed here is: To what extent does the World Bank's political economy of capitalist development affect, as well as get shaped by, its production of authoritative knowledge?

In answering this question, this chapter invokes Michel Foucault's arguments on relations of power, right, and truth (Foucault 1994; Rose 1999; Burchell et al. 1991). Rather than pose the traditional question on power and knowledge (i.e., what discourse of truth fixes *limits* on power?)—which assumes that the exercise of power is always repressive and negating—we can ask the alternative question posed by Foucault: What regimes of truth are endowed with potent effects that help *generate* the laws, *shape* subjectivities, and *drive* people to exercise power? That is, what enables the exercise of power *through* social bodies rather than merely against them, compelling them to act and to act in ways defined in the process of "the production, accumulation, circulation, and functioning of a discourse" (Foucault 1994)? In this chapter, it is useful to think about Foucault's triangle of power, right, and truth in the context of how societal rules are written (or removed), rights bestowed (or denied), and truths constructed (or deemed illegitimate), and how these are generated through the practices of many different types of actors in this world called development.

Although it appears that the World Bank is the new global sovereign prince, in fact many networks of actors have joined in the production of development knowledge, and have embraced the concepts of sustainability and sustainability rights. The focus here is on the knowledge production process that has become so inclusive and integral to large capital projects. In today's climate of vigilant social activism around World Bank interventions, there cannot be an acceptable plan for investment without a strong sense of the ecological and social. Since the World Bank cannot do the enormous task on its own (in Laos as well as its other 170-plus borrowing countries), it requires a growing network of translocal scientists, technocrats, NGOs, and empowered (or "responsibilized" [Rose 1999]) citizens to help generate the data and construct the discursive strategies of sustainability. In this case, the production of truth entails the birth of new experts, new subjects, new natures, and a new science of sustainable development, without which power could not be so fruitfully exercised.

Green Knowledge Production in Laos

Just as its latest self-proclamation as *the* global knowledge bank suggests (World Bank 1999b, 2002), the World Bank is the source for cutting-edge knowledge of global significance. During the 1990s, the Bank carved out its own *green agenda*, producing policies, financing, tools and data for an applied global environmental science, training thousands of professionals in borrowing countries—including Laos—to implement and indigenize versions of it.

Nam Theun 2 (NT2) represents the global flagship of the Bank's green incarnation, a model for other projects in the Bank's portfolio. At the heart of the project is a large dam to produce hydroelectricity for Thailand, which—until its recent economic crisis—had been experiencing a period of sustained economic growth undergirded by rapid industrialization. Associated with the dam, and reflecting the Bank's new concern with environmentally sustainable development, is a state-of-the-art suite of linked projects that includes investments for a Forest Conservation and Management Project, Wildlife and Protected Areas Management Project, indigenous peoples' extractive reserves, irrigated and modernized agriculture with experimental farms, electricity and new roads, mega-fauna running corridors and eco-tourism, sustainable logging and tree plantations, and new housing settlements. To help understand the potential impacts of NT2, a series of detailed environmental and social assessment studies have been conducted. Because of the controversial nature of the Bank's large-scale projects, two independent evaluation teams have been set up to ensure that this project unfolds according to the Bank's new environmental directives: the International Advisory Group, which looks at large dams internationally, and the Panel of Experts, which looks at NT2 specifically. A recent World Bank annual report (World Bank 1999a, p. 51) expressed the uniqueness of its "Laos model" of sustainable development, explaining that "an unprecedented program of international oversight and local consultation is accompanying environmental and social impact assessment studies" for Nam Theun 2.

Given the scope of the proposed project—costing more than the country's annual budget and covering substantial territory—and the small domestic professional class capable of meeting the scientific-technical demands ("standards") of multilateral aid conditionalities, the Bank has allocated money to support a wide range of state-oriented activities related to NT2, including state capacity and institution building, a thorough review of government policies, and environmental law reform. Because neither the World Bank nor the government of Laos has the in-house capabilities to study the feasibility and social and environmental impacts of the proposed investment, the Bank has enlisted an army of Northern consultants to do these studies. In what follows, I describe how the practices for hiring these consultants and the conditions under which they work reflect shifts in development under the Bank's greening.

The Hiring of Project Evaluators
The old system of hiring consultants to evaluate a proposed project was efficient, cost-effective, and mutually beneficial for the major players involved. Typically, the World Bank would hire familiar Northern engineering firms that had often worked with the proposed contractors—that is, the firms who were expected to build the infrastructure, be it a dam, power plant, or irrigation system—to collect and analyze data to assess a project. More often than not, the engineering firms would find that indeed the project was feasible (or would be, with certain modifications) and that its negative impacts could be mitigated through some additional investment—for example, a drainage system might be added to resolve a potentially leaky irrigation system. As long as the project was not shown to be *in*feasible (a highly unusual occurrence), these impact assessments could lead to an increase in the size of a loan and the work for engineering firms and builders. In some parts of the world, the World Bank uses the same firms for all its projects, creating an enduring and comfortable relationship between the loan managers and the projects' reviewers.[7]

This is precisely what happened, at least initially, with the Nam Theun 2 project in Laos. In 1990, the World Bank contracted an Australian engineering firm, Snowy Mountains Engineering Company, to conduct its feasibility study for Nam Theun 2.[8] Snowy Mountains has worked with the largest stockholder of Nam Theun 2, Transfield Holdings Ltd. of Australia,[9] in the past. The feasibility report that Snowy Mountains produced was quite positive overall; on this basis, the government of Laos, the World Bank, the dam investment consortium (NTEC), and the Bank-appointed Panel of Experts recommended that the project be funded.

After NT2 got the official green light, the international NGO community did its own evaluation of the report and made a strong case that it was seriously flawed. In the end, the Bank was forced to admit that the environmental impact assessment (EIA) and social impact assessment (SIA) were inadequate, and that the required "study of alternatives" was missing (e.g., studying alternative scenarios such as smaller dams or energy conservation). It then contracted with another engineering group to do the job, the Thai-based TEAM firm, another old-time Bank consultant. Its environmental impact assessment for Nam Theun 2 met a similar fate, and was ultimately dismissed by the World Bank when challenged by international activists.

In 1995, a *third* round of feasibility studies was commissioned, with some responsibilities contracted out to two long-time Bank consultants, the German firm Lahmeyer International (the study of alternatives) and the New Jersey-based firm Louis Berger International (economic analysis). Representing a dramatic shift for the Bank, however, the environmental and social assessments were contracted out to two international NGOs: the IUCN (World Conservation Union) and CARE International. The decision by the World Bank to incorporate NGOs into the process reflected a highly conscious sense within the Bank of the need to work *with* its critics if it hoped to transform them from critical observers into constructive participants who could help expedite and expand its efforts.

Knowledge under Contract

As NGOs and private consultants have been incorporated into the project assessment process, the process has the appearance of being more open and less subject to conflicts of interest. Yet even for the independence of these groups and individuals, important institutional factors shape the knowledge production process. The most general are the "terms of reference" (TORs) under which hired consultants must work. In exchange for high salaries, unique research opportunities, and unusual access to what were formerly impenetrable research sites, the Bank specifies exactly what kinds of information is needed, a time frame in which the research must be completed (and by implication, how long the researcher can be in the field), and by when it will be written up. Ownership and circulation are also important dimensions of the TOR: the direct contractor—be it the Bank, the borrowing government, an engineering firm, or an NGO—is given exclusive right of ownership over the product as well as the raw data. Legally, one cannot use the data for one's own research, or distribute one's findings without permission from the contractor.

By far the biggest pressure comes from the stringent time constraints placed on those carrying out research for the Bank. Because social and environmental assessments are not stand-alone projects but pre-conditions to a loan process with its own set of temporal imperatives, the amount of time allocated for data collection and analysis is extremely limited. As a result, the method of development-related social and environmental research that has come to be most widely accepted is "rapid rural appraisal," a form of applied research that well suits the World Bank's constrained timeline for loan processing. Rapid rural appraisal (RRA) is "a systematic means of quickly and cost effectively gathering and analyzing information. The method has an *extractive* purpose in which *outsiders learn about local situations* . . . an iterative process of rapid and progressive learning from respondents and secondary data" (IUCN 1998, p. A-9, emphasis in original in the first case and added in the second). Particularly notable here is the emphasis on speed.

Those who do social and environmental impacts studies for Nam Theun 2 are powerfully affected by the fast pace of Bank projects. One consultant for the most recent socio-economic study of the Nakai Plateau people (the group that will be most directly affected by the dam and its standing reservoir) described his team's working conditions in the following terms:

At first, we asked if we could get three days for every two villages in the plateau and another four to six days time for write-up—7–9 days per two villages—so the data wouldn't get confused in our minds. We figured it would take up to three days just to hike into a village. That's the very least we asked for. But the project was on a very tight schedule, as the World Bank needed the report soon [in order to push the project forward].

It's not easy work, and we were working in completely new terrain. [My partner, an ethnolinguist] discovered at least two previously unknown languages. We were trying to cope with new languages, cultures, lifestyles, and trying to interpret it, all within a very short time period.

Because so much time was being consumed by the arduous task of getting from village to village, covering hundreds of miles of very dense jungle, his team was transported by military helicopter, at the cost of US$1,100 per hour.[10]

The helicopters saved us some time. But everything else about working in the jungle takes time. We brought in our own food, which we cooked on our own, and we'd set up camp. We were left with very little time to enter a village, explain who we were, and learn about their lives, only to turn back, return the helicopter, and write it all up in Vientiane.[11]

A similar pressure to do research quickly was noted by several ichthyologists who were hired to assess the effects of a set of proposed projects on the Mekong fisheries. According to these scientists, the task of studying the Mekong fisheries is enormous, and requires a large, interdisciplinary team to gather data all along the river and its tributaries. At the very least, they believe, data should be collected over several years. One consultant explained:

Everything is geared to the annual flood-dry cycle. Different species appear at different places and different times of the year to carry out critical life-cycle events (spawning, feeding, refuge during the dry season). Migration enables these habitat shifts to take place and is of course the fundamental reason why any migratory animal needs to make regular seasonal movements.

In addition, researchers need to collect data on fish movements at multiple sites, because these fish do not migrate in straight lines, and the Mekong is not a single river but a whole system of rivers, with numerous arteries that house their own diverse fish species. The problem is further complicated by the fact that these rivers are not clear trout streams, but are deep, dark, and characterized by dangerous currents.[12] The Bank's approach, however, has been to hire consultants on several different occasions to do the job in three to five months.

The fish biologist who told me the preceding story took care to distinguish these "jet-setters" from "fish-heads" like himself, who prefer to go to a village and work with local fisher folk who have generations of experience with the river. He was asked to study the downstream effects of the recently completed Theun-Hinboun dam adjacent to the Nam Theun 2 site (AMRC 2000). (International activists and local villagers protested that the fisheries were being destroyed, which the government, lenders, and builders strongly denied; consequently, he was hired to conduct a study.) Hired on a "4-day input per month" schedule, he found it impossible to do what his contract directed: to study the bypass flows at this post-impoundment stage of the finished dam. He took the view in his report that a whole team of scientists was needed to study the dam's effects on the river, over a substantial period of time and space.

Yet, he also emphasized, one did not need to be a biologist to understand that if there should be between 45 and 60 cumecs of water passing the dam site and only 5 cumecs were passing through, this will cause problems for downstream biota. "If the 45 to 60 cumecs represents a loaf of bread necessary to maintain the system, then the 10 cumecs represents a slice and the 5 cumecs just crumbs." In other words, the more water the dam held back to produce electricity, the more the downstream fisheries would be destroyed, as the downstream villagers were experiencing. His immediate recommendation was to increase the minimum dry-season bypass flows from 5 to 10 cumecs, which he noted would result in the loss of electrical sales of US$1 million but would save at least some of the fisheries in the short term. In spite of public promises to post the report on its web site, the Asian Development Bank chose to suppress it, claiming there were no "clear recommendations" in the report.[13]

This incident of suppression is not unique; in fact, it is common practice.[14] Tyson Roberts, an ichthyologist well-known for his work on the Mekong fisheries, was hired to do a fishery study for Nam Theun 2. Like a number of his peers, Roberts cautioned the Bank and government against making any rapid assessments without first gathering extensive data on fish migration.[15] But, midway through his consultancy, he was fired and his visa was taken from him.

My (legally contracted) EIA work on Nam Theun 2 was suppressed by the Lao Hydropower Office, probably in collusion with the Nam Theun 2 project sponsors (NTEC). World Bank policy of only employing EIA consultants approved by the World Bank and the host country (thereby assuring the sponsoring company can influence the selection [since they are the ones generating the revenues for the host]) is totally against any honest concept of EIA.[16]

Meanwhile, Roberts and his colleagues have documented more than 85 different species on the Theun river, and he suspects that several are endemic to the river and will become threatened with extinction if the dam is built.[17]

After he was fired and forced to leave the country, the government, the World Bank, and NTEC hired another Northern scientist to conduct the rapid appraisals they needed to move the project along.[18]

Although the reason for particular acts of suppression varies with context, the most general motivation is that problematic EIAs and SIAs can delay, or, even worse, prevent a project's approval. The whole process of having to do these assessments is strongly disliked both by Bank staff whose job it is to make loans, and by borrower government staff, who often have strong political and economic interests in the kind of large infrastructural projects the Bank funds. As one veteran environmental advisor at the World Bank explained to me, it is never easy to get support for a long-term study unless investors (i.e., multilateral banks, private foreign capital, and governments) are certain there will be a project at the other end.[19] In other words, project investors wag the scientific tail. Since there can be no "guarantee" by the World Bank for a project investment without the requisite environmental assessments—a direct result of social movement pressure—EIAs are being done, but the process is neither disinterested nor apolitical. For Bank loan officers, the primary concern is to promote their portfolio and avoid getting burned by activists who are closely monitoring their studies.

In another incident involving the socioeconomic study mentioned above, certain research findings were suppressed although neither the Bank nor the Lao government was directly responsible. As one of the researchers (an anthropologist) explained, what he and his partner found did not please their contractor, the world's largest international conservation group, IUCN, which had its own reasons for wanting the dam project to move forward: It was negotiating a $60 million contract with funders to design and run a series of National Biodiversity Conservation Areas (NBCAs) that would enclose more than 15 percent of the nation's territory. The anthropologist recalled that what they found in the field was deemed too controversial to publish:

We found that people on the plateau (near the dam site) survived on tubers and foraging, hunting and trapping, rice and corn cultivation, and animal raising. People in Vientiane (the capital city) had warned that there was famine in these places where rice crops had failed. But we saw that the people survived fine on non-farm activities. This would be impossible if the people living in the surrounding areas were to be forced out of their villages and into new places to only cultivate rice. If they were left only with sedentary agriculture and not allowed to forage, hunt, and fish, as current plans call for, they might not survive.

We also knew what happened to other ethnic minorities who have been resettled from the hills to the plains, as the government has tried with others from the hills. . . . Almost half the resettled population had died within the first few years. You know, it takes more than three years to adjust to grow rice or adjust to the new environment and lifestyle. Many just can't adjust fast enough to survive, so they die, and are listed officially as famine victims. That's why we made the case that the government and the Bank needed to take this whole resettlement plan slowly.

My partner wrote the section of the report saying that these people should not be classified as "ethnic minorities" but as "indigenous people." But that opened a whole can of worms with IUCN. . . I myself pushed another line that they hated equally. I said instead of moving them out, the best thing for these people are health clinics, schools, and agro-ecosystem support to keep them going. But IUCN felt it would make the plateau such a livable place to be that others would migrate in and destroy their project of developing the non-inundation parts of the Plateau into one large NBCA (National Biodiversity Conservation Area).[20]

The anthropologists found themselves in a struggle with IUCN staff, who disliked their findings and demanded that they rewrite their final report. In particular, IUCN staff in Vientiane did not want the term "indigenous people" used at all, for fear that the classification would require that the project fall under the Bank's Operational Directive on indigenous people, which could further postpone it. The delay threatened to affect IUCN and its negotiations to oversee the NBCA system in Laos. These NBCAs would be largely financed by a percentage of the government's share of the revenues from the Nam Theun 2 dam, and the Bank planned to set up an international board of directors that would directly receive these revenues for conservation. In other words, groups such as IUCN were on the verge of a remarkable windfall as Laos is one of a number of sites where large conservation projects are being linked to controversial Bank investments.

In the end, IUCN decided to not circulate the report. NTEC, the consortium of private dam investors, subsequently hired a consultant from Norway to write up a new social action plan, which did not refer to the silenced study. In record time, he concluded that these ethnic minorities were in fact no different than many other groups living in Laos, and that all the peoples of the Plateau *could* be resettled without harm (NTEC 1997) and to great potential benefit. He specifically described the different ethnic tribes as a singular ethnic group, "as a whole, a melting-pot culture," which could survive and benefit from resettlement. This consultant is now the main anthropologist on the Nam Theun 2 project.

Instances of outright suppression and generation of research findings, such as those just described, are well known within the research community hired by the Bank and its contractors. But an equally significant, and invariably more subtle, shaping of knowledge occurs through the omission of information that is never written up by consultants nor formally circulated. Scientists whom I interviewed spoke at length about their research; yet much of what they discussed with passion and interest would never be written in their reports. What happened to these ideas, interpretations, and more nuanced understandings of the complex environmental and social realities they were studying?

The answer is suggested by a biologist who exhaustively described species interdependence and reproduction along the Mekong tributaries, as well as differences in social groups and their relations with different flora, fauna, and marine species.[21] He spoke to me about the people who depend at different times upon the river floods to revive the soils for harvesting rice, river flora for building materials, and harvesting snakes, fish, and frogs. When the river recedes, they hunt and gather in the forest. It was a startling image of complexity, reciprocity, knowledge, and interdependence that I had not come across in any official report on the Mekong. When I asked where in his report I could read about this complexity, he replied, "Nowhere." Why? Because the Bank had hired him only to explain the ability of the river to accommodate aquaculture aimed at the Tokyo fish market. The terms of reference did not permit an analysis of the intricate relationship between the river people and their natural environments. Instead, he responded to the question he was hired to answer: Can this particular Mekong river ecosystem hold up under the weight of a capital-intensive aquaculture investment? In this way, knowledges are selectively isolated and/or adapted into a larger truth regime (Foucault 1974; Burchell et al. 1991). It became clear through my conversations with both natural and social scientists that the most sophisticated expertise, analyses, data, observations, wisdom, and practices would never appear in formal scientific reports commissioned by development institutions *if* they conflicted with those institutions' larger purposes and preconceptions.

Of course with omission there is inclusion; for every framing, data set, interpretation, and recommendation that gets omitted or removed from reports, there are as many that fill the report, and circulate as science locally and oftentimes transnationally. In the case of the anthropologists and

IUCN, a new framework for understanding ethnic minorities (as a "melting pot" culture) is created. In the case of the fisheries study, what gets created is a scientific framework for rationalizing export-oriented aquaculture.

The Subjugation of Subaltern Knowledges

Along with privileging knowledge of "experts" (Northerners, locals, and translocals) is the subjugation of the knowledges of the "non-experts," the millions of people perceived as the object of study, and of development. Surveys typically construct and then characterize populations based on very simple (but enduring) social categories, classifying people as fisher, hunter, or swidden cultivator when many people can be all or none at different times of the year. Some studies define "downstream" as being just a few miles away from the dam or project and hence make invisible the ecological and social "downstreams" of large projects, which can include hundreds of miles and whole groups of people, such as the semi-nomadic, who remain absent from census data or outside of the "project's command area." While most people affected by Bank projects are accounted for through processes of census, classification, and project incorporation, they become legible and accountable only within the context of a specific capital investment and culture of development capital; hence, qualities that have little to do with commercial markets are ignored or defined as destructive to the unquestioned goals of (trans)national economic growth and sustainable development. The non-commodified realms of social interaction are considered to have value only within this context of development and become more easily comprehended when they do get incorporated within the project sphere. The effects are to normalize asymmetric relations between development experts and development "beneficiaries," and to make scientific stereotypes of the latter as "lacking," irrational, environmentally degrading, and in "need" of development at almost any cost.[22]

In a short time, the remote environments and societies of Laos—and scientific data, techniques, perspectives—have been judged in terms of their value to the proposed capital investment, and not the reverse. These formally noncommodified realms have been made legible, but only as new sites of scientific research, new objects for interrogation and betterment. Unknowns have been made knowable not just because the Bank has sponsored research, but also because these objects of knowledge have been translated through the epistemic discourse of development, and in its latest *green neoliberal* (con)version. In the Mekong, this has become the framing device through which authorities speak, and through which many become authorities. Some of the effects of power/knowledge production along the Mekong are the rise of new *subjectivities* of both the sustainable-development expert and the eco-rational citizen (e.g., "destructive" forest dwellers resettled as "ecological" and "productive" rice cultivators).

A small window into the relationship between the World Bank's consultants and its development clients is provided by the story of its public consultations on the Nakai Plateau. The Bank and its contractors have held numerous public consultations on the dam and its affiliated conservation projects with the people who will be most directly affected. The idea behind these interactions was that local people could—and should—help planners understand their needs and concerns, which would lead to project (and therefore stakeholders') "improvement." Indeed, public consultation has been honed to a new development science, especially since the issue of participation has become politically volatile for the Bank (Cooke and Kothari 2002). The Bank takes it so seriously that for Nam Theun 2, it hired an evaluation expert (another new development discipline) to evaluate formally the effectiveness of the Nam Theun 2 public consultations. According to her final report, while attending these meetings, the consultant noticed that most of the plateau people just stared at the presenters (Franklin 1997). Rightfully so, she wrote, as the presenters had described the dam project in a language "more appropriate to [a US] Army Corps of Engineers meeting." After the day-long sessions of PowerPoint presentations of maps, schemes, and diagrams, she interviewed the attendees—forest dwellers who had been brought down to the town to fill the consultation. She learned that a high percentage of them had absolutely no idea what the meeting was about. Of those who said they did understand the topic, most had no idea that these meetings were about moving them from their land and resettling them as rice farm entrepreneurs. In fact, some thought these men had come to present them with a simple but appreciated gift: not Laos's largest dam, but a village water well.[23]

Through these costly attempts, the Bank *fails* at the most direct form of information exchange with its "objects" of development, and yet it *succeeds* at formalizing, indigenizing, and replicating the new development rituals of participation, self-evaluation, and communication. Each round brings in a *more* scientific intervention, more actors, more feedback. Subsequent consultations brought in more local consultants who could better speak the language and explain the project. Nonetheless, as the consultation process improves (Rose 1999), the clear-felling of the forest for the dam reservoir is almost complete, project stakeholders have been identified and debriefed, rules rewritten, the project financing deal has been signed, and the retooled government agencies overseeing everything from electricity generation to people's resettlement put in place. The subaltern is finally able to speak (Spivak 1988), but mostly through the over-determined technologies of the development world, and not as decision makers able to control the trajectory of these powerful capital investments.

National Political Interests

These institutional forces shaping knowledge production converge with the political interests of the borrowing country government, in this case, the ruling party, the Pathet Lao. A top priority of the Pathet Lao government is to generate as much hard currency as possible, which the development of the country's hydroelectric power industry clearly facilitates. Hence the government's interest in getting the NT2 project funded, and its willingness to go along, however reluctantly, with most of the new green neoliberal conditionalities being placed upon it.

Yet it is not only the Lao government that is cooperating with the World Bank to make NT2 a reality; the World Bank is also cooperating with the government. For example, it has figured out ways to rationalize the Lao government's engagement in highly unsustainable logging practices—such as giving unlimited rights to log valuable native forests to the Chinese and Vietnamese militaries in exchange for past military support (TRP 2000; Walker 1996). The Bank has also ignored the government's ethnocidal "Laoization policy" of deploying the military to forcibly resettle 900,000 people, mostly non-Lao speaking minorities (of a population of 4.6 million), down from the forested mountains into the plains. Although countless studies have been contracted to analyze the "irrational" behavior of the "backward" peasant, no official studies have been conducted on the environmental and social impact of these massive national projects. Because the client state prefers no public scrutiny, the World Bank systematically sidesteps them, shifting its scientific gaze and logic of inquiry onto more acceptable practices.

Of course, corruption in the world's logging industry and bloody "nationalist" projects are nothing new, and this is not the first time the Bank has colluded with its borrowers. But the larger point is that there are institutional effects of this highly politicized knowledge production process: loans and grants are earmarked for a borrowing country's "development problems," as defined by the scientific work conducted to justify the investments. When the World Bank and its partners generate data for particular countries, and yet systematically leave out the most socially transforming and ecologically destructive nationalist projects, they are creating a powerful scientific protocol that underwrites a particular ideology of development.

From the money of bilateral and multilateral agencies, an accepted and widely utilized scientific protocol, or concretized set of practices, is emerging in Laos. The hiring practices, terms of reference, complexity of projects, institutional imperatives of the Bank and its partners, and the nationalist agenda of the state have all contributed to shaping this protocol. The "rapid rural appraisal" method of research, with its tremendous time-space constraints, plus the mechanisms that suppress, omit, and outright dismiss what are considered illegitimate or irrational forms of knowledge, represent the essence of this protocol. But the generative side is as impressive: tomes of reports, new categories, data sets, new actors, responsibilities, and conducts.

What percolates up from these practices on the ground? What *does* count as nature, society, and green scientific knowledge within these institutional constraints? How does this knowledge get reflected in new institutions and new subjects in the new Laos? It is to this that we now turn.

Subjectivities of Green Neoliberalism

In order to spread their particular approach to green science and environmentally sustainable development, Northern aid agencies and banks have invested in "capacity building" in borrowing countries. These funders have given birth to or helped to support research institutes, training centers, and national science and policy agendas. In this way green development knowledge has become entwined with processes of professionalization, authoritative forms of power, and disciplinary mechanisms. Enormous flows of money (relative to GDP) stream into borrowing countries to restructure and "modernize" state agencies and institutions. Consequently, the contentious, uncertain, and tentative process of knowledge production described above has become certain: institutionalized, normalized, and multiplied in local sites through which new forms of knowledge and power (or rather knowledge/power) now circulate.

In Laos, 50 foreign bilateral aid agencies, multilateral banks, and donors[24] contribute money annually to the Lao state. At a recent donor meeting ('the Roundtable Meeting for the Lao PDR") held not in Vientiane but Geneva, Switzerland, $1.2 billion was pledged directly to the Lao government for 1997–2000 (Government of Lao PDR [GOL] 1997a; United Nations Development Program [UNDP] 1997). In 1994, fully half of Laos's domestic revenue came from foreign grants, and a remarkably high 80 percent of the state's Public Investment Program came from foreign aid (GOL 1997a; UNDP 1997). That is, almost every public works project and every state agency (related to these large capital investments) is financed by foreign money.[25] Much of the funding actually goes to foreign consultants and firms who are hired to reform state institutions and to train a Lao professional class. Although the net capital outflow from borrowing countries is often greater than the capital inflows from multilateral banks and bilateral aid agencies (World Bank 1999a, 2002), artifacts do remain within the country; these include highways, transmission lines, a cultivated professional class, and discourses and forms of knowledge. These artifacts help localize transnational social networks, transnationalize the more effective practices emerging from the Lao experience, and accommodate potential foreign investors.

In the case of Laos, multilateral development banks and Northern agencies have tried to restructure the moribund and highly indebted socialist state into one that can accommodate better the needs of foreign agencies, banks, regulatory regimes, and corporations. In the past few years, many of Laos's property and natural resource use laws have been overhauled to reflect the prevailing ideology of its multilateral creditors, *green neoliberalism*. Many laws were written by Northern consultants hired by the Bank, bilateral agencies, and even NGOs. For example, Laos's new environmental protection law was written by consultants for UNDP; a US lawyer for IUCN wrote key forestry legislation, and Northern lawyers wrote the rules and regulations that will establish 20 National Biodiversity and Conservation Areas, projected to comprise some 15 percent of the nation's territory. Although these acts have been mediated and delayed by Lao state officials unhappy with such foreign interventions into the internal workings of the state, the *new regimes of rule* clearly reflect the *new truth regimes* on Lao nature and society generated by Northern experts.

The Forestry Department alone contains more than 50 separate foreign-funded projects that promote sustainable logging, tree plantations, forest conservation and more. The Ministry of Forestry and Agriculture, the Hydropower Office, and most state agencies overseeing natural resources in Laos are almost wholly financed, and their staff trained, by Northern agencies and their consultants. The National University's research arm, the Forest Training School and Training Centre, and the state's central environmental agency are all financed by foreign aid.

In the creation of these new resource use laws, new eco-zones, and new rules and regulations for forest access, a whole new lexicon has been introduced to Laos. Conservation, biodiversity, sustainable logging, environmentally sustainable development, and environmental economics are imbued with meanings derived from negotiations among these transnational agencies and experts. What counts as biodiversity in Laos is defined by actors other than the people who live there; the very idea of "biodiversity" is believed to be, according to Northern experts, a completely exogenous concept. In the mid 1990s, when the Wildlife Conservation Society (WCS) and IUCN described the state of the environment in Laos, they unambiguously stated that *no* conservation practices existed—indeed, one report (IUCN 1993) stated that the word did not exist in the Lao language.[26] Subsequently, Northern agencies funded the training of Lao professionals—often in courses overseas—so that they could properly identify Mekong species. These retooled experts return home to manage multi-pronged conservation projects within state and non-state agencies that are dependent upon financing from large capital-intensive development projects. It was the *untrained* forest dwellers who first guided Northern wildlife experts from IUCN, WCS, WWF, the World Bank, and GEF through the unknown Lao forests to reveal to them the world of exquisite "globally threatened species": the rare tigers, elephants, muntjacs, barking deer, gibbons, langurs, and warty pigs. They guided these curious experts down the inaccessible rivers so they could see the distinctive otters, white-winged ducks, and hundreds of diverse fish species, including the Asian cyprinid, known to locals for its remarkable ability to pluck monkeys off the river banks.

When human populations are scientifically isolated from their environments and categorized as slash-and-burn cultivators, poachers, illegal loggers, and failed rice farmers, and when new rules and regulations prohibit hunting, fishing, semi-nomadism, swidden cultivation, and forest use in large swathes of inhabited forest, these changes not only affect epistemic politics but also ontological and material realities. The new authoritative logic of eco-zone management that is carving up the Mekong region is designed to ensure that there will be ample high-value hardwood supplies for export, de-populated watersheds for hydroelectric dams, and biodiversity preservation for high-value pharmaceutical firms and eco-tourists.

In this way, the old nationalist Lao project to "Laoize" the ethnic minority forest populations (i.e., forcibly resettle them out of the forests and into the plains) has been transformed by the new transnational project of environmental sustainability, but in ways that further compel these minorities to get out of the forests and become *positive* actors in their society's development. For the more than 60 different ethnic minority communities incorporated into green-development processes, the effects promise to be enormous, and possibly devastating. Not only do these practices lead to the new subjectivity of the transnational eco-expert within the Lao professional class; it also reshapes the subjectivity of the subaltern forest dweller. By the time this green project is completed, most non-Lao forest dwellers may experience "sustainable development" in the forms of ethnicity-based oppression and expulsion from the forest.

Certainly, debates are taking place within the Lao ruling party on precisely how much power it should cede to foreign agencies, as government officials are taken aback by the onslaught of money and expertise, as well as these Northern actors' imperial nature. In one case, a state planning office wrote a critical conceptual paper on the origins of "the idea of poverty" in Laos (GOL 1997b), because Northern experts were asking the government to start using the concept in its policy work. The World Bank liaison officer in Vientiane explained to me that nothing changes in Laos unless a top official publicly says it is okay.[27] She said it wasn't until the recent Sixth Congress that a Lao official had ever used the term "poverty"; or, for that matter, "the environment" or even "regional integration"—all critical concepts for Bank-style rule of law. "It was only after that meeting that we could officially proceed on these issues," she noted. As an afterthought, she added: "They actually took the phrasing, word for word, from one of our reports."

Conclusion

The world of development and its proliferating—improving?—knowledge production practices are strategic sites of power in highly embattled North-South relations and in global capitalism. Within these entangled worlds sits the World Bank, a place currently under intense scrutiny due to the successes of growing anti-Bank and alternative-development social movements. This chapter has sought to explain the Bank's latest innovation in knowledge production and how it becomes authoritative, locally and transnationally. Such practices are best understood within the milieu in which they are being constructed, reproduced, and circulated.

In an attempt to overcome the charges of its critics and to regain (and sustain) the confidence of its investors, the World Bank at the turn of the millennium has pushed itself to become the world's "knowledge bank" (World Bank 1998). In part, this is a valid claim: the Bank *is* unique in its ability to access the world's most remote regions and most secretive governments and emerge with a surfeit of apparently reliable information. There are no equivalent institutions in the world. Knowledge is now its greatest asset, and it is generated and used in highly strategic ways in borrowing as well as in lending countries. As we saw in Laos, transnational actors (who now include the small professional class in Laos) are the ones who gather the data, decide their utility, and design the institutions to help indigenize (and hence *globalize*) particular norms. Moreover, the data collection process reflects the needs and limits of the large-scale capital investments and investors that motivate them in the first place. Finally, however contentious and uncertain the localized process of knowledge production may be (as Mekong scientists have described above), the stamp of the World Bank gives it (and the data it yields) tremendous global stability, legitimacy, and circulation (Jasanoff 1997). Professional economists, corporate leaders, policy makers, reporters, and professors in universities in the South and North are among the many that use the Bank's reports as authoritative sources of information, and the basis for action.

Besides being the world's main producer of concepts, data, analytic frameworks, and policies on the environment, the World Bank has also become the world's most powerful *environmentalist*, teaming up with prominent environment and development NGOs, scientific institutions, borrowing states, and Northern aid agencies. This is particularly ironic because the Bank was pushed into its greening phase by an extremely effective transnational social movement that demanded that it "reform or die." Up against the wall, the World Bank responded with fervor, ingenuity, and lots of capital. Consequently, the Bank's form of environmental knowledge production has rapidly become hegemonic, disarming and absorbing many of its critics, expanding its terrain of influence, and effectively enlarging the scope and power of its neoliberal agenda.

Acknowledgments

I would like to acknowledge the following organizations for their generous support of the research for this project: John D. and Catherine T. MacArthur Foundation's Peace and International Cooperation Fellowship; S.V. Ciriacy-Wantrup Postdoctoral Research Fellowship, University of California-Berkeley; and the Research Board at the University of Illinois. I would like to thank Rachel Schurman, Serife Genis, Yildirim Senturk, Tuba Ustuner, Michael Burawoy, Julian Go, Barbara Thomas-Slayter, participants in the fall 2000 Transnational workshop at Illinois and the Globalizing/Localizing Knowledge workshop at Harvard, and the excellent editors of this volume, for their intellectual support.

A different version of this chapter is published in *Ethnography* 2 (2001), no. 2.

Notes

1. Interview by the author, Vancouver, B.C., 1996.

2. In anticipation of a negative result, the Indian government kicked the Bank out before the directors' vote.

3. Interviews at World Bank Headquarters, Washington, 1995–1998, and at a World Bank staff training seminar in which I participated.

4. The principal bilateral donor, the German development Bank (KfW), described Arun 3 as the "best-studied development project ever undertaken by the German government." See Usher 1996, p. 62.

5. From my participation in a Bank staff training seminar on EIAs in April 1996.

6. Interviews (Washington, 1995–96; Vientiane, Laos, 1998).

7. Some of these engineering firms are actually subsidiaries of builders; others have worked alongside them for years.

8. The term "feasibility study" generally refers to a group of studies that assess the economic and environmental feasibility of a project, its potential social and environmental impacts, and how it measures up against possible alternatives.

9. In early 2001, Transfield sold off its shares of NT2 to a Chicago-based firm but is still heavily invested in energy production in the Mekong.

10. These military helicopters were landing in the same remote densely forested areas where the US led its largest bombing campaign ever, along the Ho Chi Minh Trail. These anthropologists were asking for more time in part to try to overcome the fear and silence that such helicopters and their presence might evoke.

11. Interview by the author, Vientiane, January 1998.

12. Interview by the author with a highly regarded US ichthyologist of the Mekong, May 2001.

13. A few weeks later, International Rivers Network's (IRN) Mekong campaigner wrote a pointed letter to the ADB director in charge demanding that the report be released and rebutting the Bank's claims that the report failed to produce any clear recommendations. The quotation in the text comes from the ADB's response to the hired scientist and to IRN. The scientist was told by a Lao official that his report was suppressed to keep the information from the "environmental lobby" such as IRN.

14. This observation is based on numerous conversations I have had with consultants doing research for the World Bank, as well as public and news reports.

15. The first major study on NT2 fisheries by Hill and Hill (1994, p. 42) argued that "the central problem with this evaluation, as well as other studies of the Mekong fisheries, is a lack of data and information."

16. Personal correspondence, July 2000. See Roberts 1999.

17. Independent of the dam EIAs, Roberts and his colleagues have methodically identified new and potentially rare species of fish and other river fauna. See Roberts and Baird 1995 and Roberts 1995.

18. He described the task at hand as extremely complex: "In the tropics, these are feeding migrations, and the fish move when an area dries up. But that includes much more than the big fish—the whole ecosystem packs up and moves with them. And there are absolutely no data on how the whole system holds together." (interview, July 2000)

19. Personal correspondence, July 2000.

20. Interview by the author, Vientiane, January 1998.

21. Interview 1997. He is now an official in the Mekong River Commission, Phnom Penh, a funder-driven research and policy institute.

22. For differing views on this project, see World Commission on Dams 2000, the report's web site, the IRN's web site, and the World Bank's web site.

23. Sources: Franklin 1997 and the author's interviews with people who attended the consultations.

24. These range from the ADB to bilateral aid agencies such as the Swedish SIDA to NGOs such as CARE.

25. See Goldman 2001.

26. By the early 1990s, large transnational conservation groups shifted their stance on the dam project, agreeing with the World Bank that the only way to "save" mega-fauna or biodiversity was to support the massive dam project and fight to ensure that a portion of the revenues goes for Western-style "conservation."

27. Interview by the author, Vientiane, January 1998.

References

Australian Mekong Resource Centre (AMRC). 2000. Accounting for Development: Australia and the ADB in the Mekong region—Conference Proceedings. Sydney University.

Baviskar, Amrita. 1995. *In the Belly of the River*. Oxford University Press.

Burchell, Graham et al., eds. 1991. *The Foucault Effect: Studies in Governmentality*. University of Chicago Press.

Corner House (Dorset). 2000. Exporting Corruption: Privatisation, Multinationals and Bribery. Briefing 19.

Crush, Jonathan, ed. 1995. *Power of Development*. Routledge.

Escobar, Arturo. 1995. *Encountering Development*. Princeton University Press.

Foucault, Michel. 1994. "Two Lectures." In *Culture/Power/History*, ed. N. Dirks et al. Princeton University Press.

Foucault, Michel. 1991. "Governmentality." In *The Foucault Effect*, ed. G. Burchell et al. University of Chicago Press.

Franklin, Barbara. 1997. A Review of Local Public Consultation for the Nam Theun 2 Hydroelectric Project. Report prepared for Government of Laos.

George, Susan, and Fabrizio Sabelli 1994. *Faith and Credit: The World Bank's Secular Empire*. Penguin.

Goldman, Michael. 2003. Imperial Nature: The World Bank and the Making of "Green" Neoliberalism. Manuscript, University of Illinois.

Goldman, Michael. 2001. "Constructing an Environmental State: Eco-govern-mentality and other Transnational Practices of a 'Green' World Bank." *Social Problems* 48, no. 4: 499–523.

Goldman, Michael, ed. 1998. *Privatizing Nature: Political Struggles for the Global Commons*. Rutgers University Press and Pluto Press.

Government of Laos PDR. 1997a. Socio-Economic Development and Investment Requirements, 1997–2000. Government report, Sixth Round Table Meeting, Geneva, Switzerland.

Government of Laos PDR. 1997b. The Concept of Poverty. State Planning Committee.

Hill, Mark, and Susan Hill. 1994. *Fisheries Ecology and Hydropower in the Mekong River: An Evaluation of Run-of-the-River Projects*. Bangkok: Mekong Secretariat.

International Rivers Network (Berkeley). 1999. Power Struggle: The Impacts of Hydro-Development in Laos.

IUCN (Vientiane). 1993. Improving the Capacity of the Lao PDR for Sustainable Management of Wetland Benefits.

IUCN (Vientiane). 1998. Environmental and Social Plan for Nakai-Nam Theun Catchment and Corridor Areas..

Jasanoff, Sheila. 1997. "NGOs and the Environment: From Knowledge to Action." *Third World Quarterly* 18, no. 3: 579–594.

Kapur, Devesh et al. 1997. *The World Bank: Its First Century*. Brookings Institution.

Khagram, Sanjeev. 2001. *Transnational Struggles for Power and Water*. mss. Harvard University.

McCully, Patrick. 1996. *Silenced Rivers*. Zed Books.

McMichael, Philip. 2000. *Development and Social Change*, second edition. Pine Forge Press.

Morse, Bradford. 1992. *Sardar Sarovar: The Report of the Independent Review*. Resource Futures International.

Nam Theun Electricity Consortium (NTEC) 1997. *Social Action Plan*. Vientiane.

Pincus, Jonathan, and Jeffrey Winters. 2002. *Reinventing the World Bank*. Cornell University Press.

Rich, Bruce. 1994. *Mortgaging the Earth*. Beacon.

Roberts, Tyson. 1999. "A Plea for Proenvironment EIA." *Natural History Bulletin of Siam Society* 47: 13–22.

Roberts, Tyson. 1995. "Mekong Mainstream Hydropower Dams: Run-of-the-River or Ruin-of-the-River?" *Natural History Bulletin of Siam Society* 43: 9–19.

Roberts, Tyson, and Ian Baird. 1995. "Traditional Fisheries and Fish Ecology on the Mekong River at Khone Waterfalls in Southern Laos." *Natural History Bulletin of Siam Society* 43: 219–262.

Rose, Nikolas. 1999. *Powers of Freedom: Reframing Political Thought*. Cambridge University Press.

Spivak, Gayatri. 1988. "Can the Subaltern Speak?" In *Selected Subaltern Studies*, ed. R. Guha and G. Spivak. Oxford University Press.

State Planning Committee, Government of Lao PDR. 1997. *Towards a Lao Definition of Poverty*. Vientiane, April.

Tropical Rainforest Programme (TRP). 2000. *Aspects of Forestry Management in the Lao PDR*. Amsterdam, April.

Udall, Lori. 1995. "The International Narmada Campaign: A Case of Sustained Advocacy." In *Toward Sustainable Development*, ed. W. Fisher. M.E. Sharpe.

UNDP. 1997. Report of the Sixth Round Table Meeting for Lao PDR. Roundtable Meeting for the Lao PDR.

US Treasury. 1994. *The Multilateral Development Banks: Increasing US Exports and Creating US Jobs*.

Walker, Andrew. 1996. "The Timber Industry in Northwestern Laos: A New Regional Resource Economy?" In *Development Dilemmas in the Mekong Subregion*, ed. B. Stensholt. Monash University.

Watts, Michael. 1995. "'A New Deal in Emotions': Theory and Practice and the Crisis of Development." In *Power of Development*, ed. J. Crush. Routledge.

World Bank. 1999a. *Annual Report*.

World Bank. 1999b. *World Development Report, 1998–1999*.

World Bank. 2002. *Annual Report*.

World Commission on Dams. 2000. *Dams and Development*. Earthscan.

3

Resisting Empire: Globalism, Relocalization, and the Politics of Knowledge

Clark A. Miller

In *Empire* (2000), Michael Hardt and Antonio Negri call attention to the emergence of a new global order, a new kind of sovereignty that transcends the nation-state. They call this new order an "imperial machine." Yet they seem strikingly inattentive to the sites of scientific and technological production in which the rules of this machine are being written: scientific and engineering laboratories, as well as institutions like the Internet Corporation for Assigned Numbers and Names, Britain's Human Fertility and Embryology Authority, weapons inspection teams, bioethics panels, and international technical committees. Empire, they seem to believe, is an essentially political project and must be traced in political institutions.

Contra Hardt and Negri, if Empire exists, its power resides in the construction of new systems for classifying, standardizing, organizing, and ordering knowledge and people on a worldwide basis. These systems—at once scientific, technological, social, and political—link together the inhabitants of far-flung networks, structuring the production and reproduction of identities, values, and bodies (Bowker and Star 1999). This was the fundamental insight of Foucault's work on the normalizing, disciplinary technologies of the prison and the sanitarium and the experts who designed their practices and architecture (see, e.g., Foucault 1973). Thus, as we seek to understand the constitutional foundations of global governance, we must turn not to the United Nations General Assembly—or even the Security Council—but rather to the Specialized Agencies, and to the growing array of public and private, formal and informal institutions of scientific, technical, and technological production and harmonization that lie outside the UN. It is in these institutions that Empire's regulatory and normative armature is being forged.

Globalism and Relocalization

The centrality of science and technology to emerging global order resides, I contend, in two factors: first, the growing tendency of people all over the world to frame policy problems in specifically *global* terms; and, second, the casting of actions in specifically *technical* terms as a strategy for bypassing traditional concerns with sovereignty in the world system. Consider, for example, the remarks of Egyptian president Hosni Mubarak at Davos in the aftermath of the Asian financial collapse: "Our global village has caught fire, from where we do not know. In the emerging world there is a bitter sentiment of injustice, a sense that there must be something wrong with a system that wipes out years of hard-won development because of changes in market sentiment." (Cowell 1999) The idea that capital markets form part of a "system" that spans the globe and determines everyone's fortunes reflects what I call a new *globalism* in political discourse. No longer do people imagine that the affairs of their own country are independent of the affairs of other countries around the world. Rather, national economies, cultures, and governing institutions are increasingly viewed as interdependent and undergoing further rapid globalization.

My definition of globalism differs markedly from that of many students of international relations. Keohane and Nye (2001) define globalism as "a state of the world involving networks of interdependence at multi-continental distance, linked through flows and influences of capital and goods, information and ideas, people and force, as well as environmentally and biologically relevant substances (such as acid rain or pathogens)." Globalism, for them, thus reflects material features of the world. In contrast, my own definition of globalism follows more closely Edward Said's (1978) notion of orientalism. I define globalism as the framing of particular features of nature or society as amenable to investigation, measurement, analysis, and response solely on a worldwide basis. Like orientalism (or the *nation* in Benedict Anderson's treatment of nationalism; see Anderson 1983), globalism is a creative product of human imagination, disciplined by techniques, skills, tools, schools of thought, institutions, and practices for producing knowledge. It is, to borrow further from Said, "the corporate institution for dealing with [the globe]—dealing with it by making statements about it, authorizing views of it, describing it, by teaching it," as well as regulating it, governing it, and protecting it (Said 1978, p. 3). My understanding of globalism thus contributes to the interpretive turn in international relations, which seeks to explain the role of ideas in world politics.

Experts and expert knowledge figure prominently in the emergence of globalism via their construction and dissemination of conceptual models of global systems. These models have helped build an ontology of global social problems. Whereas nature, society, and economy were perceived in the past as *local* or *national*, during the second half of the twentieth century, experts increasingly cast them in global terms, often developing elaborate computer simulations of planetary-scale processes and systems. (See Miller, forthcoming; Miller and Edwards 2001; Takacs 1996.) Today, the existence and recognition of the climate system, the ozone layer, biodiversity, global financial markets, global epidemics, and world trade underpin the authority of a growing array of international governing institutions.

In addition to globalism, these institutions derive authority from providing technical assistance to countries to help them understand the implications of globalization and integrate national policies with global expectations. The power of expertise to authorize international institutions stems not only from the construction and deployment of global imaginaries but also from their transmission, uptake, interpretation, and use in local contexts around the world. Technical assistance works as a two way street. Data collection networks developed by these institutions provide detailed information for increasingly sophisticated models of global systems and processes. At the same time, these networks help *relocalize* global knowledge in a variety of ways: (1) translating and extrapolating the outputs of global models into locally relevant information; (2) transmitting and transplanting this locally relevant information from sites of production to sites of consumption; and (3) helping recipients interpret and make sense of information in relation to local or national policy. If globalism constitutes the explicit framing of nature or society in global terms, relocalization combines processes of translation that make those ideas relevant to local circumstances with processes of social adaptation that occur as people in local contexts encounter such ideas, interpret them, and give them meaning in their daily lives and livelihoods.

Here again, experts shape the process of globalization, not only as bearers of knowledge (as in epistemic communities) but also as ostensibly objective or neutral agents, who merely collect and provide information, and thus circumvent the political concerns that otherwise face outsiders in local and national decision making. To describe this aspect of experts' role in buttressing the authority of international institutions, I adopt Yaron Ezrahi's use of the word "instrumentalism" to refer to "the appropriation of science and technology by modern liberal democratic ideology and politics as means for shaping and legitimating the uses of political power" (Ezrahi 1990, p. 9). Liberal democracies, Ezrahi argues, have been particularly concerned to find appropriate ways to deploy and constrain the use of political power, and science and technology have been prominent sources of inspiration in their efforts to do so. Instrumentalism refers to the ideological use of science and technology to depoliticize the use of power, particularly through the depersonalization of public action. In democratic societies, according to this view, science and expertise allow for the removal of arbitrariness, discretion, subjectivity, and judgment. (See also Porter 1995.) Social problems become the domain of expert analysis and solution. At the same time, instrumentalism (in Ezrahi's model) offers democratic publics a way to hold governments accountable for their actions by making those actions visible to attentive witnesses.

Instrumentalism has also found use as scientists, diplomats, and other policy makers have struggled to order international governance consistent with the sovereignty of individual nations (Miller 2001). IMF policies are not designed, so they argue, to redistribute wealth but rather to stabilize and regulate international capital markets. World Bank policies are meant to alleviate poverty and enhance development. The World Trade Organization seeks to increase and promote world trade by reducing barriers to the free flow of goods and services. The objective of the Framework Convention on Climate Change, as described in the treaty itself, is not to alter people's lifestyles but to "prevent dangerous anthropogenic interference with the climate system" (Article 2). Another aspect of instrumentalism is the oft-repeated mantra that, in offering advice to countries, international institutions merely provide information, presumably of a value-free sort. IMF reviews of countries, for example, are intended to convey objective advice about what countries need to do to adapt their economic policies to the demands of global markets. These ways of defending the authority of international institutions incorporate the notion that global actions can be depoliticized and made into technical problems and solutions, as well as the idea that international institutions can be held accountable on the basis of technical evaluation. Has the

World Bank alleviated poverty? Has the Framework Convention halted climate change? These, then, as opposed to alternative considerations, such as their commitment to democratic forms of decision making, are cast as the standards by which the world's citizens ought to evaluate global institutions.

Needless to say, relocalization does not always occur smoothly. Indeed, relocalization frequently results in deep-seated conflicts over meaning, identity, politics, and culture. In the rest of the paper, I turn to the specific case of the International Research Institute for Climate Prediction (IRI) at Columbia University's Lamont-Doherty Earth Observatory to illustrate how instrumental attitudes toward science and technology have exacerbated these conflicts. As we will see, IRI sells its services as an objective source of information on the future of the climate. Yet global and local are inevitably interdependent in the activities of international institutions. In the process of constructing global representations and categories of thought, and working out technical relationships between the "developed" and "developing" worlds, institutions like the IRI and IMF also construct, or, perhaps more accurately, *reconstruct*, local categories and representations.

The term "local knowledge" has acquired its greatest salience in just such conflicts. As many other authors in this volume demonstrate, "local knowledge" has become more than just a basis for competing knowledge claims; it is now also a tool for exercising voice in global politics. Demanding space for "local knowledge" thus functions as a form of boundary work designed to give value to practices and ways of interpreting nature and society that differ from those introduced by "forces of globalization."[1] By better understanding these conflicts over knowledge and expertise, this study suggests, like others throughout this volume, that we can strengthen our understanding of how to avoid the pitfalls of globalization.

Rethinking Instrumentalism

The International Research Institute for Climate Prediction is an excellent site for exploring the place of science and technology in the globalization of world affairs. Formally proposed in 1992, IRI was established in 1996 as "an innovative science institution working to accelerate the ability of societies worldwide to cope with climate fluctuations, especially those that cause devastating impacts on humans and the environment, thereby reaping the benefits of decades of research on the predictability of El Niño-Southern Oscillation [ENSO] phenomenon and other climate variations."[2] IRI scientists monitor the Earth's climate system and use computer models to forecast future climatic conditions for three to six months. IRI scientists then make their forecasts available to scientists and public officials in communities around the world, along with training in how to interpret the implications of rainfall, temperature, and other climatic factors for people's lives and livelihoods. IRI thus claims authority from both globalism—the ability of scientists to understand and predict the behavior of the Earth's climate system on time scales of a few months to a few years—and an instrumental form of relocalization—the ability to deliver those predictions to help communities make better decisions about the impacts of floods, drought, heat waves, and other climate-related events.

Few people have objected to IRI's globalism. Although for most people the link between scientific knowledge about the climate system and the day-to-day behavior of the weather in their own lives remains unclear, the idea that the atmosphere *is actually* a global system appears fairly uncontroversial. IRI's efforts to relocalize climate forecasts and apply them to community decision making have not been as lucky, however. Several of IRI's application projects have encountered difficulties of one sort or another. These challenges and the responses to them by IRI staff reveal a number of lessons about the limits of instrumentalism as an approach for conceptualizing the role of science and technology in world affairs.

IRI casts its application work primarily in informational terms. Climate scientists increasingly write not only about accurately forecasting ENSO events but also about the value of climate information to local policy (Philander 1999). Authors have linked ENSO events to myriad social and economic situations in which they believe forecasts would have helped avert or reduce the impacts of climatic variability. The following comments, culled from the scientific literature by a US National Research Council (1996) report on El Niño forecasting, exemplify common refrains:

El Niño is a natural phenomenon, and improved information about it could yield great benefits to those who choose to use it judiciously.

The potential for warning farmers in advance of drought and allowing them to prepare for it—not only in Zimbabwe, but in other regions of the world—brings science, literally, right down to the ground level.

Through appropriate planning of agriculture, water management, and health services, the region [Southern Africa] hopes to prevent disaster and the need for costly relief when drought next occurs. El Niño forecasts are central to this effort.

The advances made in the past decade in meteorological forecasting of the phases of the Southern Oscillation may help to predict areas at risk of malaria epidemics. . . . This offers possibilities for developing early warning systems that can facilitate epidemic preparedness.

Based on claims such as these, several governments instituted experimental research programs in the 1980s and the 1990s aimed at predicting El Niño events and linking predictions to decision making, including the United States, Japan, Australia, India, Peru, Brazil, and Ethiopia (National Research Council 1996). Growing out of these disparate efforts, IRI reflected the desire of governments to coordinate their activities and go beyond research to make operational forecasts of ENSO events and to distribute them worldwide to help reduce the impacts of climatic variability (Moura et al. 1992). As IRI reports describe it, the goal is to provide "end-to-end" assessments of global climatic variability, including the "production of forecasts of changing physical conditions such as temperature and precipitation; an assessment of the consequences of those changes for key regions and sectors; the delivery of useful information products which address specific decision making needs in those regions and sectors; and the maintenance of a continuous, interactive dialogue with users and the scientific community" (International Research Institute for Climate Prediction 1997). Through such assessments, a 1998 IRI promotional brochure observes, "IRI will provide the information societies need to adapt to extreme climate periods in order to save lives, reduce economic losses, and avoid suffering."

Use of the word "information" to characterize IRI's products exemplifies the adoption of an instrumentalist idiom, as noted above, to describe and defend its activities. In effect, IRI's forecasts and computer models are seen as instruments for translating between local and global perspectives in a non-political fashion. IRI scientists do not view their activities as making public policy choices; they merely provide facts and data useful to those who do make choices. Likewise, they portray the utility of climate models not in distributive terms, such as who is likely to win or lose from climatic variability, but rather as contributions to the general welfare or public goods. From this perspective, ENSO events are framed as a kind of natural disaster that, like forest fires, earthquakes, and tornadoes, generates uniformly negative outcomes for society. Any successful effort to predict such events thus provides positive value:

Even more with El Niño, we can now forecast six to nine months in advance when we're going to see an El Niño. So, we can help to reduce the human devastation. . . . I believe science is moving us in a direction where while we cannot avoid the disaster, we can be better prepared, we can reduce some of the human misery, and some of the economic costs, and the World Bank is working with many of our client countries, and we want to be there before the event, rather than after the event. (Watson 1998)

The claim that IRI merely provides information reflects both a strong normative position on the part of IRI staff and a principle of organization. In interviews, IRI scientists expressed their commitment that the Institute not become a player in local politics. IRI's organization and operations also reflect the model of "speaking truth to power" in which science develops information and provides it to policy makers. IRI is divided into a Scientific Division, located at the Scripps Institution—one of the world's foremost climatological laboratories—and an Application Division, located at Columbia University. Scientists at Columbia meet regularly with users of their data from around the world, provide them with training and information, and work with them to build applications of the information in their own countries. Their counterparts at Scripps, who develop and test IRI's climate forecasting model, do so far less frequently. In another important institutional feature, an expert advisory committee made up of prominent US and European climate scientists oversees IRI's scientific activities; no comparable advisory panel of developing country officials or users exists to oversee IRI's application activities.

The instrumentalist idiom does not fully capture the scope of IRI's activities, however. First, many of the issues IRI purports to address, such as famine, flooding, and droughts, cannot be fully (or possibly even partially) solved merely by providing information. Second, globalism and relocalization do more than simply provide information; they transform people's basic experiences of nature and, with this, their expectations of social behavior, relationships, and institutions. Third, the organization of knowledge production, validation, and use raises, in and of itself, political questions regarding who has voice in public decisions, what counts as legitimate knowledge, and who has the right to prioritize and review research. Fourth, and finally, the effort to transplant information from one context into another often bypasses consideration of the social institutions that help fit knowledge and techniques to the heterogeneities of power and nature in local contexts. I elaborate on each of these points below.

Is Lack of Information Really the Problem?

Hunger and famine are key issues for IRI. Nearly half of IRI's sixteen current application projects focus on agriculture. The logic behind this emphasis is straightforward: climatic fluctuations on time scales of months to years can significantly impact local harvests through floods, drought, temperature extremes, humidity, and other factors. If IRI could provide reliable climate forecasts to farmers, agricultural ministries, and agribusinesses, these groups could take actions to mitigate climate impacts, such as changing crops or cultivars, revising planting schedules, or modifying planted areas.[3] This would increase food supplies and thus avoid hunger and famine. In this line of thinking, effective communication to decision makers presents the major challenge (once accurate forecasts are available, of course).

In a recent *Science* article exploring famine in Ethiopia, however, two social scientists on the IRI's staff, Kenneth Broad and Shardul Agrawala, observe that the common assumption among climate forecasters—that better climate information will help avert famine and other natural disasters—may not always hold (Broad and Agrawala 2000). Referencing the Nobel-prize-winning work of Amartya Sen, they point out that famines result not from scarcity of food but from public and private choices that restrict access or entitlement to food. In short, food is used as a weapon in political struggles. The poor may not have money to buy food, even if food is available. Or governments may adopt austerity measures that reduce food subsidies. In such contexts, increases in food production—the most one would expect from better climate forecasting—might do little to alleviate hunger and starvation. The world as a whole, Broad and Agrawala note, produces more food than is consumed every year; yet famines still occur.

Broad and Agrawala acknowledge that some situations may exist in which climate forecasts may reduce famine and hunger. Their analysis suggests care, however, in interpreting events around the world. Climatic events may be used as cover for deliberate policy to create food shortages. Projects sold as merely informational may ultimately end up reconstructing the political economy of agricultural production and distribution as governments act on them. Or, vice-versa, such policies may end up distracting attention from the root causes of hunger by providing an apparently easy, but ultimately unsatisfying, technological fix. In either case, such projects could further alienate people from international institutions.

Transforming Experiences and Expectations

In point of fact, IRI application projects often involve more than information. Using climate predictions to make better decisions also frequently entails changes in how people conceptualize their lived experiences. Although climate scientists may have changed their view of the atmosphere, most people continue to think of the weather as a local, random phenomenon. Making use of climate predictions involves reshaping decision makers' understanding of the atmosphere so that they conceive of it as global in scope, predictable, and therefore subject to rational foresight and planning. From there, IRI programs train participants to rethink their own activities and decisions in the light of this new conceptual framework. The success of these training programs depends on making the local and the global interdependent—on coproducing "global information" and "local users" that fit together in stable arrangements.

An IRI agricultural workshop held in Toowoomba, Australia in February 1999 offers a useful example of the coproduction of global information and local users in IRI training programs. The course trained agricultural experts to use seasonal climate forecasts to improve agricultural decision making. For two days, IRI scientists taught their audience to see atmospheric dynamics as global and predictable, describing the Earth's climate system, El Niño, and seasonal climate forecasting. Subsequently, the workshop shifted focus, training participants to view agricultural production as a system, both on the farm and in regional and national planning. Workshop organizers presented this as a key step that would help participants find ways to insert climate predictions into the day-to-day operations of farm managers and agricultural officials. Without a systemic perspective on agriculture, additional information about the climate system had little value. To help achieve this perspective, participants were trained in the use of APSIM, Agricultural Production Systems Simulator, a computer program for integrated modeling of cropping systems, as well as other computer models of agricultural systems.[4]

In turn, experiential transformations such as these may prompt reevaluation of social and political norms, behaviors, and institutions.[5] Another

IRI project, using climate forecasts to reduce El Niño's impacts on Peruvian fisheries, illustrates the political tensions that can arise as concepts of nature and society shift. Convinced of the potential value of climate forecasts to user communities in developing countries, IRI scientists established a pilot project in Peru. El Niño's effects on Peruvian society, and especially fishing, were large and well known. Peruvian fishermen first named El Niño because of its effects on their catch. IRI scientists knew that sea-surface temperature fluctuations and ocean currents associated with the El Niño / Southern Oscillation alter the amount of food available to fish off the Peruvian coast, as well as its location, creating highly localized conditions when fish are either abnormally abundant or vanishingly scarce. By providing information about El Niño to fishermen, IRI felt it could convincingly demonstrate its utility (Broad and Pfaff 1997).

When IRI scientists arrived in Peru, however, they found a more complex setting than expected. First, the fishing industry in Peru was divided into commercial fishing operations and local fishermen who lived in coastal villages. Many of the former already guided their fleets to the likely locations of concentrated fish populations using sophisticated technologies to access climate forecasts and download satellite data on sea surface temperature. Their success had created a political morass, putting the fishing industry in conflict with village fishermen, who had no means or skills to access climatological data and so had seen their catch decline precipitously, with labor unions in fish processing facilities, and, especially, with government regulators, who saw this new information as a threat to sustainable management of the Peruvian fisheries (Agrawala, Broad, and Guston 2001).[6]

Here, I want to focus on two groups of actors, the fishing industry and fisheries managers in the Peruvian government. Based on the idea that they could forecast the onset of El Niño, both organizations altered their traditional practices. For example, faced at one point with a prediction that their catch would decline precipitously over the next several months due to climatic conditions, the fishing industry took preemptive steps:

During the 1997–98 El Niño, people responded both to the changing ocean environment and to a series of forecasts of the event's duration and magnitude. Industrial firms closed plants and canneries, moved fishing fleets south, and kept vessels idle. Illegal fishing increased, including industrial boats pursuing fish into the zone reserved for artisanal [village-based] fishing, which increased tensions between the groups. Artisanal fishermen shifted to tropical species catchable only during El Niño conditions, but their revenues were limited by drops in market prices and climate-related interruptions of transport to markets. (Pfaff, Broad, and Glantz 1999)

At another point, anticipating dramatically rising catches due to climatic conditions, the government banned anchovy fishing outright along the Peruvian coast, angering many in both fishing groups. Within these actions, one observes two important features. First, these actions point to the kinds of conflicts that may arise over efforts to profit from new kinds of climate information. Put in its simplest form, although IRI sells its products in terms of reducing the impacts of natural disasters, and thus benefiting all, its products may in actuality distribute benefits differentially, generating both winners and losers. Second, as climate predictions become generally accepted, new expectations arise both about the relationship between different groups in society and the proper role of institutions, particularly public agencies, in managing and regulating social and economic behavior. Needless to say, both of these features are intensely political and likely to involve IRI in difficult socio-political conflicts.

The Politics of Knowledge Production, Dissemination, and Use

IRI's experiences in Peru illustrate, I suggested above, that the dissemination of information can significantly affect the distribution of wealth and power. IRI has also discovered that the distributional effects are frequently magnified by differential access to information. The United States has a fairly universal system in place for distributing weather and climate forecasting. The presumption is that if weather and climate information are made available through that system, almost everyone in the country will have access to it. Also, if information is made available on the Internet, those who want to make greater use of it may do so. There is, in other words, an assumption that these methods of dissemination provide a kind of equal opportunity to access and use information. IRI has found, however, that this assumption is not necessarily true in all societies, and how information is disseminated can have enormous impacts on who is able to access and make use of it. In Peru, differential technological capacity of the fishing industry and the village fishermen led to vastly different abilities to make use of climate information.

IRI responded to its early experiences in Peru by incorporating extensive planning of dissemination strategies into its projects to ensure that each makes climate information widely available locally. In turn, they discovered that the problem is not so easily fixed. Norms of equal opportunity and access are not necessarily widely shared in all societies, suggesting that IRI must work hard to adapt its protocols not only to local communication practices and technologies but also to local norms of public information. This issue becomes even more complicated due to the nature of the information provided. Where climate information is uncertain, and thus easily misused, or forecasts indicate the likelihood of significant downturns in economic activity (as with a drought projection in an agricultural region or with a particular phase of El Niño in Peruvian fisheries), pressure may be put on IRI to restrict access to the information provided: to avoid panic, for example. Put simply, IRI and the users it works with must negotiate difficult, politically contentious decisions about who should have access to information, what kinds of information they should be able to access, and under what conditions.[7]

Moreover, access to information is not the only issue of potential concern. Social studies of science suggest that scientific models inevitably incorporate tacit assumptions and values (see, e.g., Shackley 2001; Jasanoff and Wynne 1998). Do people in developing countries whose lives might be substantially affected by decisions made on the basis of IRI's forecasts have a right to review these tacit features of climate forecasting models? Can they hold forecasters accountable for mistakes that flow from tacit assumptions that turn out not to mirror exactly conditions in their particular region of the planet? In the United States, by law, any citizen may review the scientific basis of public decisions. Regulatory agencies must publish the scientific rationales for their decisions, and judges have often overturned executive agency decisions on the grounds that they have insufficiently explained the reasons for their choices. Do IRI's customers have similar rights? What kinds of institutional arrangements might support the exercise of such rights?

IRI's current practices and organizational arrangements, just like those of other international knowledge-producing institutions, embed certain tacit norms concerning the organization of political institutions, rights, and responsibilities. These norms can carry enormous implications for the reception and use of knowledge by user communities. Questions about how to produce and disseminate policy-relevant knowledge are about more than just generating information; they are also about "what constitutes legitimate knowledge, who is entitled to speak for nature, and how much deference science should command in relation to other modes of knowing" (Jasanoff 1996). Who has access to global knowledge claims? To whom is knowledge provided? Who has the right to subject data and knowledge claims to critical review? What rights and responsibilities do public institutions hold to set standards for the production and validation of knowledge? How did they acquire those rights? How much weight should global decision makers give various forms of scientific and local knowledge? As global regulatory regimes expand, and as people begin to re-imagine these regimes as a system of global governance—as protesters at G-8, IMF, and WTO meetings clearly already have—these kinds of questions about the basic constitutional arrangements of international society seem destined to grow in importance.

Transplanting Knowledge and Expertise

When IRI seeks to relocalize climate information, IRI users currently do not engage in extensive reviews and critiques of IRI's activities, and especially the production of climate forecasts. Their absence from these discussions is rooted at least in part in IRI's institutional structure and the attitudes of its scientists. The differentiation of the institution into separate forecasting and applications divisions means that few if any forecasters work closely, on the ground, with the recipients of their information; they rely instead on informal feedback from staff in the applications division. More generally, there is a sense among IRI's climate modelers that forecasting is a scientific task to which future users have little to contribute. Consequently, they rarely seek out user feedback. The absence of a user advisory committee forecloses another path through which users might oversee or provide commentary on IRI's activities.

The problem goes deeper than just one of opportunity and institutional structure, however. It is also a problem of capacity. Few IRI users have scientists working for them who are up to speed on the latest climate modeling techniques. Perhaps more importantly, few developing countries can draw upon robust, critically engaged communities that help integrate global knowledge and local perspectives. This places scientists interested in transplanting knowledge in a doubly troubling situation. First, the biological, geophysical, social, and political contexts in which knowledge is transplanted are often quite heterogeneous, and what is a reasonable assumption in one context may be quite inappropriate in another. Second, the kinds of social actors and arrangements that have emerged in industrial democracies for subjecting policy-relevant knowledge to intense critique (the presence of a knowledgeable and active citizenry, powerful and vocal NGOs, adversarial administrative proceedings, activist judges, expert advisory committees, etc.) are often either absent or not applied to scientific claims. Hence, the kinds of voices that could help identify discrepancies between global models and local contexts are frequently not present, just when the need for them is most critical.

Finally, the absence of effective review and critique is also a problem of political accountability. As currently organized, IRI is accountable to two groups: its donor agencies, which decide how much to continue to spend on these kinds of activities, and the scientists who sit on its scientific advisory board and give guidance on IRI's scientific work. By contrast, IRI is not accountable to the users of its information. In fact, formal power relationships generally favor IRI and not its users. If recipients want access to the grants, training, and knowledge available through partnering with IRI, they must come to the project on IRI's terms.

The contrast between the production and use of policy-relevant science at IRI and in comparable domestic regulatory contexts in the United States is striking. Regulators at EPA and FDA, for example, regularly police laboratories whose work they depend on in making regulatory decisions, and they set standards for acceptable laboratory practice. Audits and inspections are commonplace. These agencies also have scientists on staff who review external studies for accuracy and reliability. They hold adversarial hearings in which opposing interests are allowed to present competing interpretations of scientific evidence. US courts, too, routinely reexamine scientific evidence used in policy decisions. Such settings have not only established important forms of accountability between knowledge producers and those whose lives are affected by that knowledge, they have also helped stimulate the emergence of critical communities who regularly police the conduct of science and its connection to policy. In adversarial regulatory contexts like the United States, critical audiences quickly become essential to the production of reliable knowledge. Expert and lay observers affiliated with many different organizations and groups in society constantly subject knowledge claims to critique and review, exposing weaknesses, tacit assumptions and values, and otherwise helping to fit general claims to local circumstances. In IRI, and most other international institutions, however, few such mechanisms of accountability, critique, and feedback exist, and this creates the potential for serious problems.

Consider, for example, IRI's growing concern with uncertainties in its forecasts. IRI's basic presumption is that any forecast that is more than 50 percent reliable offers advantages to decision makers over random guessing. However, climate forecasts are easily misinterpreted if one does not fully account for uncertainty. In a case reported by Fagan (1999), Brazilian researchers released an El Niño forecast accompanied by extensive advertising to the public encouraging them to make use of the information. These ads specifically highlighted the benefits of using reliable, scientific predictions instead of local rain prophets. Many people took actions to mitigate the impacts of the forecast climatic conditions. When the forecast turned out to be wrong, however, those actions backfired and many people lost money. Consequently, they have been less willing to trust subsequent forecasts, even though these more recent efforts have turned out to be correct. Too little initial skepticism of the forecasts has now contributed to an overly skeptical view.

This story illustrates the difficulties that can arise in getting people to have appropriate levels of trust in forecasts—neither too much nor too little. Scientists often have a good sense of the degree of uncertainty associated with particular forecasts, but such understandings can be difficult to communicate, especially in modern forms of mass communication (see, e.g., Pfaff, Broad, and Glantz 1999). Moreover, scientists argue that appropriate measures of the benefits of using climate information should not be judged on the basis of individual forecasts. An IRI tutorial puts it as follows:

One might wonder whether, and how, forecasts that have only modest skill levels can be used beneficially in decision making. The answer to these very valid inquiries, first, is that they can indeed be used beneficially, *when used very carefully.* If used inappropriately, they may not be beneficial and in fact could be detrimental, at least in the short term. The economic benefits from using the forecasts properly should be expected to accrue over an extended time frame, and to accrue somewhat irregularly, rather than to appear immediately and to occur uniformly from one year to the next. . . . Because of the forecasts' uncertainty, decisions should be made cautiously. . . .[8]

Here we see quite clearly that users need to know a great deal about uncertainty in order to properly interpret and use forecasts. Yet, in response to these complexities, instead of opening up its modeling activities to greater scrutiny, IRI has restricted access to its climate forecasts, password-locking the information on its web site and restricting access to individuals who have participated in IRI training. Far from being open and accountable to the people who might benefit from (or be harmed by) its activities, IRI has asserted its own authority over its users in an effort to discipline them to behave properly.

The problem, however, involves more than just training. Not all users are equally well situated to take advantages of benefits that "accrue somewhat irregularly." Efforts to evaluate whether or not information is beneficial have to take into account the decision context. Forecasts made with "modest skill" may work fine for farms or businesses that can survive a few bad years in the hopes of accruing the benefits of the irregular good years. However, farmers who survive on the year-to-year stability of their harvests rather than on their long-term revenue prospects may be less able to afford such risks. In such a context, model information, if it encourages farmers to believe they are reducing their risks, when in actuality they are increasing them, may give rise to backlash or mistrust in scientific knowledge.

Overall, IRI's operations reflect the view that modeling and forecasting the Earth's climate is an entirely technical task, and should therefore be accountable only to scientific accuracy. This is simply not true. Many modeling choices have clear implications for subsequent use of the information. Incorporating accountability relationships between IRI and its users could help to fit global knowledge to local circumstances and to fit global and local politics. To date, to be sure, IRI scientists have made good faith efforts to rethink and reorganize their programmatic activities in the wake of user concerns over such issues as the distributional impacts of disseminating climate forecasts, mistrust in forecasts, and uncertainty. But a willingness to make projects work cannot fully substitute for political relationships that hold IRI accountable to its users. Appropriately structured, accountability might go far to reducing the politicization of climate forecasts and strengthening IRI's legitimacy in developing countries.

In an instrumental framework, the transplant of scientific knowledge and technical assistance to developing countries is largely conceptualized as a matter of transmitting information and facts and getting policy makers to use them. Perhaps it might be better understood, however, as a matter of building the institutional, social, and political capacity to bring multi-vocal, expert critique to bear on the knowledge claims used in designing and implementing policy.[9] One of the strong points of IRI's programs, compared to many other international institutions, is its effort to tie global modeling to local decision making. This is not merely a technical task. It is an effort to connect knowledge and power in stable relationships in both global and local settings. Since global and local power-knowledge formations are often already relatively well articulated and established, these formations must be adjusted and brought into mutual accommodation through constant back-and-forth translation. In turn, this mutual adjustment demands mutual accountability. Accountability occupies a key normative juncture in the relationship between the producers and users of knowledge in the case of IRI and other international institutions. Achieving accountability will demand attention not only to the structure of international institutions—to create institutional pathways through which that accountability can be exercised—but also to the capacities of audiences in developing countries to inquire into and make demands upon the processes of producing and using knowledge.

Conclusion

Science and technology have long occupied center stage in Western notions of progress and civilization (Smith and Marx 1994). They have also long served to buttress the authority of transnational and global governing arrangements. In *Machines as the Measure of Men*, Michael Adas observes that nineteenth century Europeans often assessed a society's level of civilization by its technology (Adas 1988). Colonial governments and elites relied on science and technology to shore up their power, militarily, economically, and, crucially, also through practices of classification and surveillance (Storey 1997; Anderson 1983). After World War II, decolonization transformed imperialism's "civilizing mission" into the pursuit of development; yet the emphasis on science and technology remained (Sachs 1999; Miller 2001). Today, science and technology not only link the people of every corner of the globe through extensive systems of communication and transportation, they also serve as the basis of authority for a wide range of emergent institutions of global governance.

At the same time, the political institutions holding Western science and technology accountable to people in developing countries have largely disappeared. Despite significant increases in the domestic regulation of science and technology in Western democracies, the broad project of decolonization

dismantled the political institutions that once helped maintain accountability between science and its colonial subjects. Colonial states obviously
drew much of their authority from their relation to imperial governments.
They were also accountable, however, to imperial citizens and companies
in the colonies and, at least tenuously, to their colonial subjects (even if that
accountability was highly paternalistic and often enforced only through the
good will of the imperial governor or the threat of revolt—see Storey 1997).
Today, that accountability has all but vanished in many places that Western
expertise still operates, often even more extensively than before.

Of course, the solution is not to reinvent the office of colonial governor.[10]
Nonetheless systematic attention needs to be paid to making emerging institutions of global governance accountable to *all* of their subjects and clients,
poor as well as rich. The call to democratize the decision making of the IMF,
WTO, and other international institutions is not new. Yet such calls rarely
recognize the extent to which accountability must reach not only to the formal political bodies of these institutions, but also to their knowledge-mak-
ing divisions and even further into the networks of scientific expertise that
support them. This can be done only if we recognize that the production of
knowledge is not something that occurs outside of social and political relationships but is rather integral to them. Constraints on international institutions tend to be oriented toward minimizing their impact on national
sovereignty and hence minimizing, as much as possible, direct political relationships between the subjects of global regulation and the places where
decisions are made. Framing international institutions as expert institutions
that only provide information and advice to governments has only exacerbated this trend. As we strive to create institutions of global governance
that can secure trust and credibility from the world's citizens, we must work
to reestablish political accountability between those who make knowledge
and those whose lives are shaped by it—no matter how remote or marginal
their position on this planet.

Notes

1. On the concept of "boundary work," see Gieryn 1995.

2. Source: "IRI's Mission Statement."

3. "Improving climate forecast communications for farm management in
Zimbabwe."

4. See Yves Tourre, "Applications of Climate Forecasting to Agriculture: A Report from a Regional Training Course," February 1999.

5. Compare Jasanoff 1996, p. xiv: "Advances in the realm that is conventionally labeled 'technological' inevitably require the readjustment of existing human behaviors, institutions, and relationships. They enable new modes of conduct—and sometimes foreclose old ones—thereby calling into question notions of fundamental significance to the law, such as agency, causality, rights, responsibility, and blame."

6. Additional source: author's interviews with IRI scientists at Palisades, New York, in 1998.

7. Wynne (1990) showed that European countries exhibited very different ideas of who should have access to information about hazardous facilities, what kind of information people should have access to, and under what conditions.

8. "The Science and Practice of Seasonal Climate Forecasting at the IRI" (emphasis added).

9. The absence of such critique carries with it very dangerous possibilities. Vandana Shiva has argued that erroneous assumptions embedded in Green Revolution programs about the relationship between agrarian societies, agricultural production, wealth, and political stability helped to spark violence in the Punjab, and William Storey makes similar arguments about riots in Mauritius. See Shiva 1991; Storey 1997. Jasanoff (1994) describes how the failure to recognize similarly erroneous assumptions helped contribute to the disaster at Bhopal.

10. Although the Germans discovered that wholesale adoption of one people into the institutions of another should not necessarily be dismissed as a possibility.

References

Adas, M. 1988. *Machines as the Measure of Men: Science, Technology, and Ideologies of Western Dominance*. Cornell University Press.

Agrawala, S., K. Broad, and D. Guston. 2001. "Integrating Climate Forecasts and Societal Decision making: Challenges to an Emergent Boundary Organization." *Science, Technology & Human Values* 26, no. 4: 454–477.

Anderson, B. 1983. *Imagined Communities*. Verso.

Bowker, G., and S. L. Star. 1999. *Sorting Things Out: Classification and Its Consequences*. MIT Press.

Broad, K., and S. Agrawala. 2000. "The Ethiopia Food Crisis: Uses and Limits of Seasonal Climate Forecasts." *Science* 289: 1693–1694.

Broad, K., and A. Pfaff .1997 "Prediction, Profit-Motive, and Policy in the Peruvian Fishery." *Columbia Earth Institute Earthmatters*, May: 1–2.

Cowell, A. 1999. "Annan Fears Backlash over Global Crisis." *New York Times*, February 1.

Ezrahi, Y. 1990. *The Descent of Icarus: Science and the Transformation of Contemporary Democracy*. Harvard University Press.

Fagan, B. 1999. *Floods, Famines, and Emperors: El Niño and the Fate of Civilizations*. Basic Books.

Foucault, M. 1973. *The Birth of the Clinic*. Pantheon Books.

Gieryn, T. F. 1995. "Boundaries of Science." In *Handbook of Science and Technology Studies*, ed. S. Jasanoff et al. Sage.

Hardt, M., and A. Negri 2000. *Empire*. Harvard University Press.

International Research Institute for Climate Prediction. 1997. *Strategic Plan*.

Jasanoff, S. 1994. *Learning from Disaster: Risk Management after Bhopal*. University of Pennsylvania Press.

Jasanoff, S. 1996. *Science at the Bar: Law, Science and Technology in America*. Harvard University Press.

Keohane, R., and J. Nye. 2001. *Power and Interdependence*. Longman.

Martello, M. "Negotiating Global Nature and Local Culture: The Case of Makah Whaling." In this volume.

Miller, C. A. 2001. "Scientific Internationalism in American Foreign Policy: The Case of Meteorology (1947–1958)." In *Changing the Atmosphere*, ed. C. Miller and P. Edwards. MIT Press.

Miller, C. A. (forthcoming). "Climate Science and the Making of a Global Political Order." In *States of Knowledge*, ed. S. Jasanoff. Routledge.

Miller, C., and P. Edwards, eds. 2001. *Changing the Atmosphere: Expert Knowledge and Environmental Governance*. MIT Press.

Moura, A. D., L. Bengtsson, J. Bulzer, et al. 1992. "International Research Institute for Climate Prediction: A Proposal." Proposal submitted to the Intergovernmental Tropical Ocean—Global Atmosphere Board of the World Meteorological Organization.

National Research Council, Advisory Council for the Tropical Oceans and Global Atmosphere Panel. 1996. *Learning to Predict Climate Variations associated with El Niño and the Southern Oscillation*. National Academy Press.

Nussbaum, M. 2000. *Women and Human Development: The Capabilities Approach*. Cambridge University Press.

Pfaff, A., K. Broad, and M. Glantz. 1999. "Who Benefits from Climate Forecasts?" *Nature* 397: 645–646.

Philander, S. G. 1999. "El Niño and La Niña: Predictable Climate Fluctions." *Reports on Progress in Physics* 62, no. 2: 123–142.

Porter, T. 1995. *Trust in Numbers: The Pursuit of Objectivity in Science and Public Life*. Princeton University Press.

Sachs, W. 1999. *Planet Dialectics: Explorations in Environment and Development*. Zed Books.

Said, E. 1978. *Orientalism*. Random House.

Shackley, S. 2001. "Epistemic Lifestyles in Climate Change Modeling." In *Changing the Atmosphere*, ed. C. Miller and P. Edwards. MIT Press.

Smith, M. R., and L. Marx. 1994. *Does Technology Drive History? The Dilemma of Technological Determinism*. MIT Press.

Storey, W. K. 1997. *Science and Power in Colonial Mauritius*. University of Rochester Press.

Takacs, D. 1996. *The Idea of Biodiversity: Philosophies of Paradise*. Johns Hopkins University Press.

Watson, R. 1998. Interviewed by Phil Ponce on *The NewsHour with Jim Lehrer*, December 29.

Wynne, B. 1990. "Risk Communication for Chemical Plant Hazards in the European Community Seveso Directive." In *Corporate Disclosure of Environmental Risks*, ed. M. Baram and D. Partan. Butterworth.

4

The Local, the Global, and the Kyoto Protocol

Cathleen Fogel

The Clean Development Mechanism (CDM) of the 1997 Kyoto Protocol originated with United States resource economists and negotiators under the Clinton administration. When the protocol enters into force, the CDM is poised to channel billions of dollars to the developing world in exchange for industrialized countries acquisition of greenhouse gas emission reduction credits. A portion of CDM credits will be produced through tree planting for carbon sequestration. Some observers have pegged this policy development as a "win-win" solution, due to the low cost of the emissions credits it will produce (Levy 1999). Indigenous peoples, however, have referred to the same policies as threatening to transform them into "slaves to the carbon trade" (SIIFCC 2000). This chapter explores the origins of such wildly differing perspectives and illustrates why the Kyoto Protocol's carbon "sink" provisions provide an important location to examine how global institutions and discourses envision, constitute and are subsequently resisted by local actors.

Between 1999 and 2001 most indigenous peoples groups opposed the use of tree planting for carbon sequestration within the CDM.[1] They feared an onslaught of poorly designed projects that would undermine their efforts at self-determination and improved quality of life. Indigenous peoples saw themselves as unrepresented in the discourse of either the Intergovernmental Panel on Climate Change (IPCC) or the official Kyoto Protocol negotiations. Responding to this, they demanded that governments acknowledge their existence and contributions, the specialized knowledges that they hold, and their rights to participate in global climate change institutions that impact their sovereign territories.

Elite climate-change discourses deployed in relation to the Kyoto Protocol typically render local communities and indigenous peoples in developing countries as invisible or unimportant. They depict vast areas of the world's forests and land as underutilized and as therefore available for carbon-driven management or tree planting. They portray global emissions trading policies as technical rather than political in character and imply that they will generate few social consequences (and therefore require few social protections). This dominant framing has meant that most governmental negotiators at Framework Convention on Climate Change (FCCC) meetings lack experience in rural development or working with indigenous peoples. This has further hampered awareness of the potential negative local impacts of global inter-governmental policies.

The exclusion or marginalization of indigenous and other local actors from global institutions triggers a backlash wherein fear and resistance dominate. This resistance may be mitigated when representative local leaders are integrated into global networks of access and trust. To be useful, however, such networks must provide the possibility of iterative interactions between local actors and global policy elites and open pathways for information flows. But many local communities have experienced exploitation, a decline in well-being, or violence at the hands of processes or events that they label "global" in origin. Processes typically included in this category include poorly implemented development projects, the extraction for global markets of oil, minerals, coal, timber, or other commodities, and economic dislocation. In this case, building global networks of trust requires not only the promise of participation in global institutions, but the recognition and restoration of past harms as well.

Analyzing elite constructions of nature and the local as seen in the Kyoto Protocol's tree planting provisions sheds light on the way in which powerful global institutions contribute to destructive local-global tensions. Elite global discourses and practices around trees, forests and climate change have several common tendencies—they simplify nature, construct empty spaces, erase the local, re-enroll the local, and favor existing elites. This chapter begins by introducing the protocol's basic forest elements. It then explores five components of the elite global gaze and concludes by describing indigenous peoples' networks resistance to Kyoto policies.

The Kyoto Protocol and Forests

Deforestation has long been considered a major contributor to global climate change. As early as 1988, at the Toronto Conference on Our Changing

Atmosphere, scientists and policy analysts proposed slowing deforestation and planting trees in order to mitigate global climate change (Betsill 2000). But the framework for how governments would use forests' carbon dioxide absorption functions to reduce the accumulation of greenhouse gases in the atmosphere only became clear with the adoption of the Kyoto Protocol in 1997 (Fogel 2002). Protocol land use and forestry policies were refined further, and in 2001 governments agreed that industrialized country investors could acquire emissions credits under the Clean Development Mechanism (CDM) for tree planting but not for forest conservation.[2]

The establishment of a Clean Development Mechanism in 1997 reflected the growing popularity of market-based frameworks for environmental management with both economists and representatives of environmental non-governmental organizations (ENGOs) in the United States. It also reflected emerging discourses reifying the certification of eco-goods and services transferred from South to North (for instance, the certification of green timber, organic or fair trade coffee). US corporations favored emissions trading because of its potential to reduce or even eliminate greenhouse gas control costs (Frumhoff et al. 1998, p. 6). Developing country governments welcomed the flows of capital investments that the CDM implied.

The development of the specifics of forest and tree planting policies within the protocol between 1997 and 2001 was controversial, however, with many prominent ENGOs arguing that such provisions would reduce the ecological effectiveness of the treaty. Lobbyists with Greenpeace and the World Wide Fund for Nature (WWF) criticized forest carbon sequestration provisions as "loopholes" that would undermine the "environmental integrity" of the protocol. They argued that tree planting and forest management for carbon benefits would produce temporary atmospheric benefits at best, while allowing industrialized countries to avoid necessary changes such as the reduction of industrial greenhouse emissions at source and the development of renewable energy sources.[3]

ENGOs focused less on the design of protocol governance institutions or the potential impact of its implementation on local communities. In contrast, indigenous peoples and their supporters, such as the ENGOs Friends of the Earth, FERN, and Amazon Watch, worried that the market basis of the CDM would impose ill-conceived large-scale projects on already marginalized rural and indigenous communities in the developing world, further harming rather than benefiting them. Examining the idea of a "global gaze" constructed through elite Kyoto Protocol discourses helps illuminate why indigenous peoples and their supporters feared this outcome.

The Global Gaze

The idea of a global gaze traces back to European colonial views of nature and new world cultures in the seventeenth century. More recently, Karen Litfin described the global gaze as a fundamentally masculinist perception of the natural world as seen from a position of detachment and power (Litfin 1997). Essential to the construction of the modern global gaze are satellite technologies that produce images of Earth from space as well as computing powers allowing the production of statistical information integrating environmental data from vast regions of the world. Armed with these technologies, global managerial elites then perform five transformational discursive moves.

Simplifying Nature
As has been widely described, government bureaucrats and scientists necessarily simplify representations of natural and human objects in order to know and then govern them from afar (Scott 1998; Latour 1987). Government-designed classification systems select a few elements from localities and communities and emphasize these while downplaying real life complexities (Bowker and Star 1998). In the case of the Kyoto Protocol, climate scientists and government administrators had to simplify their representations of forests ecosystems so that they might be known and monitored solely for their carbon content. Likewise, what constituted a "forest" had to be defined, standardized and made universal.

Creating a standardized and universally acceptable definition of a forest proved difficult, however, as some 200 definitions of forests were in use in 1999 (Lund 1999). Many of these included lands with no trees. Governments variously classify forest-lands administratively, by tree crown cover, or by the basal area of commercial timber stock per unit of land, among other methods. But the 1997 protocol defined nations' carbon balances as based on net changes in forests' carbon content (in addition to industrial greenhouse gas emissions). Responding to this, governments in

1998 began negotiating a standardized definition and method of measuring a "forest." They needed a definition enabling the use of similar scales and estimation techniques across national borders as well as similar scales and estimation methods for different forest processes—deforestation, reforestation, and afforestation, for instance.

After a great deal of controversy, government negotiators in 2001 adopted a single definition of a forest for use under the Kyoto Protocol:

"Forest" is a minimum area of land of 0.5–1.0 hectare with tree crown cover (or equivalent stocking level) of more than 10–30 percent with trees with the potential to reach a minimum height of 2–5 metres at maturity *in situ*. A forest may consist either of closed forest formations where trees of various storeys and undergrowth cover a high proportion of the ground or open forest. Young natural stands and all plantations which have yet to reach a crown density of 10–30 per cent or tree height of 2–5 metres are included under forest, as are areas normally forming part of the forest area which are temporarily unstocked as a result of human intervention such as harvesting or natural causes but which are expected to revert to forest. (UNFCCC 2001, p. 58)

In addition, governments would account for "all changes in the following carbon pools: above-ground biomass, below-ground biomass, litter, dead wood, and soil organic carbon" in relevant lands. "Once land is accounted for, all anthropogenic greenhouse gas emissions by sources and removals by sinks on this land must be accounted for throughout subsequent and contiguous commitment periods" (UNFCCC 2001, p. 61). Data for 2001 suggest that some 1.7 billion hectares of forests within industrialized countries would be subject to this type of continuous carbon content scrutinization, not an insignificant task (FAO 2001).

Temporal and physical scaling problems with measuring forests' carbon values are compounded by the dual social and natural character of forests. Only "direct human-induced" conversions of forest land to non-forest land and vice-versa are to be accounted for as deforestation and reforestation under the protocol. On the other hand, "natural" reforestation, such as the unassisted regrowth of trees in abandoned farmlands, should not generate carbon credits. But defining what constitutes "direct, human-induced" as opposed to "natural" land use change and then determining the area of land falling into this category is a complicated and arbitrary process.

Having started down this path, however, new problems emerge. If "forest" and "deforestation" were to be defined and tracked, changes in forests' carbon content below these limits should also be understood. This proved difficult: if governments applied a 10 percent minimum tree cover value to define a "forest," then the disappearance of up to 90 percent of any given forest area could remain unaccounted for. Although misleading, such problems remain challenging as long as forest-based carbon accounting is central to the protocol.

The abstract definition of a "forest" adopted by governments omits and thus obscures characteristics such as forests' biological diversity, quality and history of human use, the cultural diversity of communities living in and around forests, or the capacities of local or national institutions to manage forests. In short, the Kyoto Protocol introduced a monolingual forest discourse founded solely on the idea of forests' carbon values. As such, its implementation risks propagating the very simplifications that it purports to track

Market pressures will exacerbate these scientific and bureaucratic pressures to simplify forests through protocol implementation. Some companies offer tree-based greenhouse gas emission reduction credits to industrial purchasers exclusively from projects employing ecologically or culturally high standards (Future Forests 2001). But most carbon entrepreneurs will not pursue such approaches, as doing so is not required. One US firm recommends "normal" forestry practices to sequester carbon, advising that some 300 trees per hectare be planted on unused farmlands (MCOC 2000). These or similar carbon cropping techniques will maximize land-based carbon storage in single-species plantations but minimize ecological diversity.

National politics will play their part as well. In Ireland, government officials invoked the Kyoto Protocol in order to rebuff ecologists seeking to slow the establishment of Sitka spruce plantations in the countryside (Hurley 2000). Governments and markets focused on just a few elements abstracted from highly complex local systems exert the power needed to simplify the very objects they seek to govern (Scott 1998). It is this relentlessly homogenizing aspect of the global gaze that invokes resistance among actors interested in protecting nature's diversity.

Constructing Empty Spaces

Scientific advice produced for governments by the Intergovernmental Panel on Climate Change (IPCC) contributes to pressures to simplify nature under the Kyoto Protocol. IPCC reports emphasize the physical attributes of

forests and their role in global carbon cycling, while giving short shrift to
people and communities living in and around forests and to historical and
political causes of deforestation (IPCC 1990, 1995, 2000). Climate-change
advisory scientists more broadly invoke the idea of empty and available
space. The "global knowledge" that the IPCC produces helps governments
erect and then justify their simplified constructions of people and nature,
and the institutions based on them.

The construction of land as empty and responses to deforestation as tech-
nocratic begins with the 1990 IPCC Response Strategies Working Group
report (IPCC 1990). While the report acknowledges that many social practices and groups of people cause deforestation—contributing causes from
small scale farming to highway construction and governmental subsidies
are mentioned—when proposing policy responses, IPCC authors stress
market-based solutions over others. This emphasis prefigures later Kyoto
Protocol emissions trading mechanisms. For instance, IPCC authors argue
that "the forest crisis is rooted in the agricultural sector and in people's
needs for employment and income" and that "deforestation will be stopped
only when the natural forest is economically more valuable for the people
who live in and around the forests than alternatives for the same land"
(IPCC 1990: xlii). This statement ignores the role of government policies in
causing deforestation through, for example, land titling practices or the lax
enforcement of existing laws. It also overlooks the traditions of many
indigenous and local communities who have maintained their territories as
forested for centuries. Furthering this economic global vision, however, the
1990 IPCC report goes on to recommend the widespread establishment
of plantations for climate-change mitigation, estimating that some 200
million hectares of land in developing countries might be available for this
purpose (IPCC 1990, p. 88).

The IPCC's 1995 Second Assessment Report takes this global economic
vision a step further by describing how vast areas of the world's forests and
lands might be harnessed to fight climate change. One chapter argues that
"the tropics have the potential to conserve and sequester by far the largest
quantity of C (80%), followed by the temperate zone (17%), and the boreal
zone (3% only)" (IPCC 1995, p. 784). This same chapter omits mention of
indigenous peoples and local communities almost entirely, rather portraying
forests, trees and especially plantations as attractive climate-change mitigation options because of their presumed lower costs (IPCC 1995). When

the social complications relating to large-scale plantations are mentioned, these are quickly brushed aside: "Expansion of C pools through the establishment of plantations is becoming less socially and politically desirable. . . . However, in many situations plantations are the only option. . . ." (ibid., p. 781) In this way, the 1995 IPCC report depicts the world's major forested regions as uninhabited and essentially "empty" spaces immediately available for government sponsored carbon interventions to aid the global good (ibid., p. 780). People, their histories and the complexities of specific localities are for the most part excluded. These moves sketch entire regions of the world as underutilized, while people and politics are made invisible. IPCC discourse likewise depicts market-based policies as technical and "clean;" it stresses benefits to industrial investors while downplaying social and environmental complications.

Other climate-related institutions similarly construct the notion of "empty" space for carbon management by refiguring the Earth's biota into a blank field. In 1999, US Department of Energy experts called for the "intensive management and/or manipulation of a significant fraction of the globe's biomass" (DOE 1999, p. xxii) for carbon storage. DOE officials argued that this instrumental approach was necessary in order to ensure the "continued large-scale use of fossil fuels" (ibid., pp. 1–3). Likewise, in 1998, scientists with the intergovernmental International Geosphere-Biosphere Program (IGBP) argued: ". . . eventually all terrestrial ecosystems, both managed and unmanaged, should be included [in global climate management institutions] to recognize and potentially increase all terrestrial sinks, to minimize sources, and to avoid the surprise of large unanticipated releases of carbon from unmanaged systems" (IGBP 1998).

These visions target the bio-geo-chemical functions of the natural world and allude only to the measurement and management actions that may be applied. As such, they both decontextualize and naturalize politically and socially diverse regions. As with the IPCC, such discourse misrepresents vast areas of the world as "empty" and "available;" it downplays the history and aspirations of nations and local people as factors for consideration. Perhaps most importantly, however, these discourses transform the ambitious project of the global management of nature to produce, trade and track carbon emissions into something desirable and unproblematic. The astonishing appears "natural"—as a sort of predictable evolution or a logical next step.

Erasing the Local

The 2000 IPCC Special Report on Land Use, Land Use Change and Forestry gives more attention to local concerns than does the 1990 or the 1995 report. IPCC authors discuss past problems with externally driven tree planting projects in several chapters (IPCC 2000). They identify the numerous risks to local communities from carbon tree-planting projects. These include the displacement of indigenous communities from their land, or loss of access or tenure to such lands, and reduced time for subsistence production. Financial investments may flow to only the cheapest projects, not those favored by communities. The uneven distribution of economic benefits from carbon trees within communities frequently leads to division and conflict. In addition, project areas often degrade once outside support for the project has concluded (IPCC 2000).

Unfortunately, the most politically relevant part of the IPCC's 2000 report, its Summary for Policy Makers, only acknowledges these risks in passing. This omission led indigenous peoples to conclude that they and their concerns had been overlooked entirely. This observation was strengthened by the fact that indigenous peoples experts had not been included in writing or peer reviewing the IPCC report.

Local communities and indigenous peoples, and the practices and epistemologies of such groups, are similarly disappeared in the protocol's discourse of market efficiency. Arguments emphasizing "reducing transaction costs" (Newcombe 2000) during the design and implementation of greenhouse gas emission reduction projects in the developing world end up perpetuating the misconception that "standardized" carbon units can be produced through standardized sequestration projects in standardized developing countries. Minimizing transaction costs includes minimizing the time and money spent involving local people in the design of projects that meet their priorities. Global economic discourses thus consign local actors and the complexities of their worlds to obscurity or at best to crude mitigations recommended as part of socio-cultural impact assessments. In order to economically benefit from global institutions, the "local" must accept its construction as compliant, homogeneous and safe, which is to say, as absent.

Two case studies released in 2000 offer a damning indictment of carbon development interventions based on these assumptions (Eraker 2000; Staves 2000). The Norwegian ENGO Norwatch reviewed two carbon tree-farming projects in Africa, one in Uganda and one in Tanzania. In a report on the first, researchers alleged that some 8,000 peasants faced forced eviction should a planned carbon tree project go forward. Norwatch quotes Ivar Lovhauen, the managing director of the project: "Everyone living and farming inside our area are illegal intruders. But we don't want to do the dirty job chasing them out. We have told the forest authorities quite clearly that this is their responsibility." (Eraker 2000, p. 14). The second Norwatch report suggested that rural Tanzanian farmers providing casual tree planting labor for the carbon tree project had received less than the minimum wage for their work and had not been paid in months (FERN 2000). Together these reports suggest the deeply social nature of carbon tree planting for climate mitigation in developing countries and the limitations of policy making that ignores this.

Re-Enrolling the Local

After local people, cultures, and knowledges are largely erased from view, the stage is set for their re-enrollment on different terms in the now-dominant elite global vision (Latour 1987). 1997 and 2001 Kyoto Protocol decisions treat local communities and local knowledges as of little importance; since they were not acknowledged, they were understood to be expendable. Governments agreed to only minimal stakeholder consultation requirements for carbon projects financed through the Clean Development Mechanism. Theoretical ideals of enlisting local knowledge to meet local needs were overridden by the drive for climate policies that minimize costs while maximizing North-South financial transfers.

To offer some attention to the local, however, governments did agree that carbon entrepreneurs must publicly report how they took "due account" of stakeholder views during planning exercises. Stakeholder representatives, including those representing local communities or indigenous peoples, might observe meetings of the Executive Board of the Clean Development Mechanism (at the discretion of government advisors) (UNFCCC 2001). Live video conferencing of CDM Executive Board meetings was promised.

But governments opposed the creation of an independent CDM appeals panel through which local communities might file complaints against poorly implemented projects. Governments did not require carbon project developers to demonstrate capacities to consult with local communities or indigenous peoples. Organizations conducting post-implementation assessments of CDM carbon tree-planting projects were not required to report on their social or environmental impacts. Rather, they were required to report only on the carbon values of the land and trees in question (UNFCCC 2001).[4] Developing country governments opposed the imposition of all such protections, arguing that as sovereign states they alone would design CDM national processes. Northern governments were only too happy to concede the point.

In this sense, local actors *are* to be enrolled within the Kyoto Protocol, but only on the terms decided upon for them by global elites. Once erased from representation within scientific, economic and policy discourses, local and indigenous communities can be effortlessly re-enrolled as simplified, standardized "stakeholders" with little to distinguish them and little to offer. The "local" is transformed into social anonymity or at best, in this case, into an idealized "global carbon worker." Local knowledges concerning traditional, indigenous uses of forest species are so unvalued as to never be mentioned (Shiva 1993).

Favoring Existing Elites

James C. Scott discussed the reconfigurations of power and resources that occur when elites master emergent, government-endorsed standards and policies (Scott 1998). Similarly, the Kyoto Protocol's CDM tree planting provisions will most benefit those institutions, corporations and ENGOs that already command existing global environment and development repertoires. As is common, elite groups involved in protocol negotiations helped draft the very policies they stand to benefit from.[5] This is a final characteristic of the global gaze that induces anger and resistance among local actors.

The favoritism offered to existing elites is illustrated in the first developing country terrestrial carbon sequestration project up for approval under the World Bank's Prototype Carbon Fund and the Clean Development Mechanism. The Plantar project in Minas Gerais, Brazil proposes the re-establishment of eucalyptus plantations in a region where plantation-based charcoal production was in 2000 suddenly declared "financially unviable" without an infusion of carbon funds. The primary financial beneficiary of the proposed scheme is the Brazilian conglomerate Plantar and associated pig iron smelting operations, as well as the Brazilian state. When this project was announced in November 2001, the ENGO CDM Watch denounced it on several accounts, one being the claim of financial insolvency for the plantations without the addition of carbon funds. CDM Watch fought to extend the public comment period for this project from the two weeks proposed by World Bank officials to the 30 days required under the protocol. Other ENGOs later suggested that the plantation involved a range of social and labor violations (Prototype Carbon Fund 2002; Soares dos Santos André et al. 2003).

World Bank Prototype Carbon Fund policy makers proposed the establishment of a $100 million Community Development Carbon Fund and a $100 million BioCarbon Fund in 2001 (Prototype Carbon Fund 2001). The Community Fund is intended to focus on small-scale greenhouse gas emission reduction projects, including mini-hydro, agricultural waste, windmills, and agroforestry, while the BioCarbon Fund prioritizes biodiversity conservation and sustainable land management projects. Whether and how local communities or indigenous peoples will benefit from these funds remains unclear, as they had no representatives on the boards of these funds as of 2002.

Small-scale enterprises—such as the sustainable agriculture collectives and common property forest holdings common among indigenous peoples' groups (as well as small businesses)—are difficult for government planners to "see," let alone to regulate or control (Scott 1998). They are for this reason alone less likely to benefit from ambitious, centralized programs.

In contrast, global research and development agencies are well positioned to benefit from the protocol's emerging standards and policies on tree planting and forests. Many institutions began incorporating biotic carbon sequestration discourses into their work and goals in the late 1990's. Talk about increasing the carbon value of forests and soil provides unifying metaphors and strengthens claims of institutional legitimacy. The Food and Agriculture Organization (FAO), the International Fund for Agricultural Development (IFAD), the Consultative Group on International Agricultural Research (GCIAR), the International Centre for Research in Agroforestry (ICRAF), and the Center for International Forestry Research (CIFOR) all now promote themselves in relation to the protocol's research and implementation tasks (FAO 1999; Sanchez 1999). But this does not suggest that they have adopted new routines or mechanisms through which to strengthen their relationships with local communities.

ICRAF representatives active at climate talks in Lyon, France in September 2000 debated conditioning the construction of rural schools in developing countries on the performance of successful carbon tree-planting work by local inhabitants. In November 2000, CIFOR scientists promoted protocol carbon policies even while recognizing that tree planting projects sometimes harm indigenous peoples and other rural dwellers (CIFOR 2000). But they did not appear to translate this awareness into more accountable approaches; indigenous peoples representatives were not invited to a global strategy session on carbon sequestration that CIFOR subsequently organized (Hagmann 2001).

Physical science research programs such as the Global Observation of Forest Cover program (GOFC) and the Global Terrestrial Carbon Observation Initiative (GTCOI) also help legitimize and will benefit from the Kyoto Protocol. GOFC promotional materials promise "wall-to-wall" maps of the Earth's entire land cover every five years while stating that the "ultimate goal is to understand and eventually balance the earth's carbon budget" (GOFC Design Team 1999, p. 39). The GTCOI offers to produce a global database of terrestrial vegetative sources and sinks of carbon by 2004, but the accuracy that they hope to achieve in their maps is so low as to be of little use in protocol implementation (GTCOI 2001). At present, these and similar research networks offer a tantalizing array of technological products and services in such a way as to prefigure, enliven, and benefit from climate-change policy debates as much as to respond to them.

Finally, ENGOs that have managed biological reserves in developing countries for years—such as the US group known as the Nature Conservancy—stand to benefit financially from the carbon financing policies they helped design. Such ENGOs have or can relatively easily develop the institutional capacities to access carbon funds. Translocal networks such as those representing indigenous peoples' communities do not have such capacities and are unlikely to acquire them in the near future (should they so desire). Without this, however, the "local" remains consigned to its position of cautious receptivity to global carbon policies or, as has transpired, to outright resistance. This dynamic is only partially mitigated by the propensity of large ENGOs to favor ecologically and socially enlightened carbon projects, such as those involving native forest restoration or community forestry. While laudable, such projects nevertheless perpetuate existing positions of power and access.

Resisting the Global

Most indigenous peoples' organizations attending FCCC climate negotiations in 2000 opposed CDM carbon tree-planting policies and the protocol's reliance on forests for climate abatement more generally. Indigenous groups particularly feared and objected to the promotion of plantations. Unlike other Earth Summit agreements, the FCCC and the Kyoto Protocol make no mention of indigenous peoples or traditional knowledges. Fearing the worst, indigenous peoples and supportive ENGOs organized several discussion forums at FCCC 2000 talks. Indigenous leaders representing some 60 organizations from 22 countries—North and South—participated in these, holding press conferences, lobbying government representatives and distributing position papers and letters. Despite this, indigenous peoples gained little governmental recognition.

Existence and Contributions

One of the sorest points was indigenous peoples' perception that they were invisible. In response, they demanded to be seen and heard. "These negotiations have churned out more than 5 million words of text but do not even mention Indigenous Peoples rights," said Jocelyn Therese, Vice President of the Coordinator of Indigenous Peoples of the Amazon Basin (Anonymous 2001). Therese and other indigenous representatives participating in the Third International Forum of Indigenous Peoples and Local Communities on Climate Change in Bonn, in July 2001, decried global policy making that would affect them, but from which they were excluded. They termed themselves "the big losers" and condemned carbon sinks as a "new form of colonialism and genocide" (ibid.). They demanded that governments acknowledge their existence and rights as distinct peoples.

As part of this, indigenous peoples' leaders emphasized that they had already contributed to the protection of forests around the world and, as a result, to the Earth's climate system: "Our cultures, and the territories under our stewardship, are now the last ecological mechanisms remaining in the struggle against climate devastation. All Peoples of the Earth truly owe a debt to Indigenous Peoples for the beneficial role our traditional subsistence economies play in the maintenance of planet's [*sic*] ecology." (SIIFCC 2000) Indigenous spokespersons expressed their astonishment that despite their historical and ongoing contributions to the Earth's ecological health, they could not secure financing for efforts to conserve their ancestral lands unless they threatened to deforest them. Proposals for forest conservation in the CDM permitted international financing for carbon sequestration only in order avoid deforestation that "might otherwise occur."

By denouncing governments for failing to recognize their prior and ongoing contributions to maintaining forest cover and global ecological health, indigenous peoples at the climate talks to some extent embraced the positionality of the "noble ecological savage." But they simultaneously rejected an institution that they deemed immoral. As time passed, their requests became increasingly desperate as they pleaded for "the inclusion of minimum guarantees for the physical and cultural survival of Indigenous Peoples and local communities" (Anonymous 2001). The first step towards this entailed governments' acknowledgment of their existence and contributions within the FCCC.

Knowledges—Traditional, Global, and Social
Indigenous discourses at governmental climate negotiations differed markedly in tone from the global gaze of the scientific and economic discourses previously introduced. Rather, indigenous leaders emphasized respect and gratitude for the Earth. They argued for recognizing Earth's sacredness and that nature be cared for as kin:

Earth is our Mother. Our special relationship with Earth as stewards, as holders of indigenous knowledge cannot be set aside. Our special relation with her has allowed us to develop for millennia a particular knowledge of the environment that is the foundation of our lifestyles, institutions, spirituality and worldview. Therefore, in our philosophies, the Earth is not a commodity, but a sacred space that the Creator has entrusted to use to care for her, this home where all beings live (SIIFCC 2000).

The basis of this sacred world view, according to the leaders present, could be found in the traditional epistemologies and knowledges of indigenous peoples around the world: "Our traditional knowledge on sustainable use, conservation and protection of our territories has allowed us to maintain our ecosystems in equilibrium." (SIIFCC 2000) The indigenous leaders frequently commented that governments had recognized their contributions and traditional knowledges at the 1992 Earth Summit. Why had they not within the FCCC or the Kyoto Protocol?

The best answer to this lies in the market emphasis of the Kyoto Protocol and the rapid rise to prominence within the protocol of its tree and forest provisions during 1997 negotiations. Markets seek to minimize production costs; acknowledging complexity and local knowledges threatens to raise them. The tensions created by their exclusion amplified indigenous peoples' fears:

We openly oppose the measures to mitigate climate change under discussion that are based essentially on a mercantilist and utilitarian vision of the forests, seas, territories and resources of Indigenous Peoples, which are being exclusively valued for their capacity to absorb CO_2 and produce oxygen, and which negate our traditional cultural practices and spiritual values. . . . We oppose that forests are considered solely for their carbon sequestration capacity. (TIFIPLCCC 2001)

In this sense, indigenous leaders framed the "global" as devaluing, dangerous, mechanistic and homogenizing. They placed their own cultures and knowledges in counterpoint.

Indigenous leaders then argued that "Indigenous Peoples' sciences and natural resource conservation and management techniques must be recognized and valued" within Kyoto Protocol policies and institutions (Anonymous 2001). They asked governments to "recognize . . . that [the] traditional knowledge, innovations and practices of [Indigenous Peoples] are relevant for the conservation of biological diversity and for the sustainable use of natural resources" (ibid.). This rhetoric mirrored that deployed by indigenous peoples' translocal networks in other environmental forums (Martello 2001).

But indigenous peoples' leaders didn't limit their claims of unique knowledges within the FCCC context to only the traditional. In addition, they claimed unique "global" and "social" knowledges, based on a type of networked indigenous epistemology. The most important type of global knowledge they offered related to the systematic oppression of and violence against indigenous peoples by corporations and governments around the world. The very actors standing to benefit from global carbon emissions trading systems—oil, coal, gas, hydro-electric, mineral, and timber companies, they said—frequently transgress and violate indigenous territories and rights. These companies exist mainly to provide for the world's wealthy classes:

The causes of climate change are the production and consumption patterns in industrialized countries. . . . The policies of developing countries and economies in transition that promote coal and uranium mining, logging, nuclear and large hydro electric power station and oil and gas extraction and transportation contribute to climate change and the destruction of our territories. . . . There have been regional and national advances on this matter, but unfortunately, grave and systematic human rights violations and violations of the fundamental liberties of the Indigenous Peoples persist. (SIIFCC 2000)

Based on this tacit global knowledge, indigenous leaders requested that governments place moratoriums on oil, gas, nuclear, mineral and hydro-electric developments in pristine ecosystems and promote locally appropriate, renewable and efficient energy solutions instead. They argued for legally binding agreements and funding to restore indigenous territories that have already been degraded by energy and minerals activities (ibid.).

IPCC climate-change reports between 1990 and 2000 do not discuss violence against indigenous peoples nor violations to their rights and territories from oil, coal, gas and minerals exploration and extraction. But knowledge of such violations informs judgments of trustworthiness. In highlighting the harms they have suffered, indigenous leaders emphasized reasons to distrust corporations and developing country governments rather than reasons to craft policies benefiting them. By broadening the epistemology informing and substance of global knowledge, indigenous peoples' networks emerge as indispensable to the design of effective and just global institutions.

Indigenous leaders also expressed social knowledge regarding the negative consequences of poorly designed, externally driven development projects. While IPCC scientists had to some extent acknowledged risks to local communities from carbon tree projects, as described earlier, the risks indigenous leaders described were based on personal and group experiences. Indigenous leaders were most concerned about increased violence springing from land disputes relating to carbon sequestration funds. They feared increases in prostitution and declines in traditional cultural practices if industrial-scale carbon projects were located within or near vulnerable communities. They feared the impacts of climate change should tree-based carbon policies yield only illusory gains. They feared politically motivated killings: indigenous leaders opposing mining, energy or timber projects are already assassinated—"tomorrow indigenous leaders may be killed for opposing sink projects" (Anonymous 2001). With the loss or expropriation of their land, indigenous peoples and their cultures would die: "The imposition of carbon sinks in the form of large-scale plantation projects can cause the massive expropriation of Indigenous Peoples' territories, human rights violations and social unrest. When our land is stolen, our cultures and our livelihood are destroyed, and often, as a people, we die." (ibid.) Indigenous peoples' networks present at the climate talks did not back up these claims with documentation. Nevertheless, such shared global and social knowledges are based upon many centuries of declines in indigenous peoples' knowledges and cultures, and the decimation of ancestral indigenous territories. Governments that have refused to acknowledge the social harms resulting from past policies stand poised to repeat them through new institutions. Acknowledging the relevance of indigenous peoples' diverse knowledges and taking steps to include indigenous peoples' representatives within official global knowledge-generation exercises would help governments move towards more accountable and respected institutions.

Rights to Self-Determination and Participation

As governmental policy debates continued, indigenous leaders increasingly emphasized a legal basis for their claims to self-determination and participation rights. They declared rights to "possess, control, and administer our territories." They also demanded "real, full and effective participation, [including] the right to be consulted in all matters that concern us; the right to prior and informed consent and the right to veto, and that our opinions and decisions are respected" (TIFIPLCCC 2001). Spokespersons called for several institutional reforms within the FCCC and the Kyoto Protocol: Governments should recognize the role of indigenous peoples in the conservation of the environment and the prevention of climate change. They should establish a Special Status enabling representative indigenous peoples' organizations to participate in the Conference of the Parties of the FCCC and its subsidiary bodies. They should create an ad hoc Inter-Sessional Working Group on Indigenous Peoples and climate change (ibid.). These demands came on top of earlier requests to include indigenous peoples within the Intergovernmental Panel on Climate Change, the Executive Board of the Clean Development Mechanism, on expert review teams and on the protocol's compliance committee (SIIFCC 2000). The indigenous leaders bolstered these demands by citing precedents for the participation of indigenous peoples in the Convention on Biological Diversity (CBD) and other international forums (Anonymous 2001).

As time went on, however, indigenous leaders gradually reduced the scope of their demands in order to tailor them to existing governmental negotiating texts. They asked that projects on or near indigenous peoples lands be applied only with the consent of indigenous peoples and that independent socio-cultural impact assessments be conducted (Anonymous 2001). When negotiations concluded without adoption of even these limited points, the groups concluded that "not only climate change, but now the Kyoto Protocol's climate change mitigation strategies threaten the very physical and cultural survival of indigenous peoples" (ibid.).

Conclusion

In resisting and rejecting the global as defined by economists, scientists and policy makers, indigenous leaders articulated several distinct claims: We exist as distinct peoples and make important contributions. We possess unique and valuable knowledges that are traditional—as well as global and social—in scope. Our acknowledged rights to self-determination imply participation rights within global governance bodies. We face risks, not only benefits, from the globally organized mitigation of climate change through carbon tree-planting, and these risks must be acknowledged.

This chapter argues that a mechanistic, market-oriented "global gaze" threatens nature and local actors on several accounts. As seen through the Kyoto Protocol, elite global discourses simplify and reconfigure, and then move to standardize and enroll both people and the natural world into largely inaccessible global institutions. Global discourses around the protocol have valued the instrumental and utilitarian while acknowledging few limits. They have marginalized the leaders, cultures and knowledges of local communities and downplayed the risks they face. They have simplified and obscured nature.

Kyoto Protocol carbon discourses have a dynamic and seductive power that reshapes how people think and act. Through discourse and related practices the "global" enrolls the "local," but it does so in a static and unidirectional manner; only the "local" must learn from the "global," it would seem. Participation mechanisms called for by indigenous leaders barely registered with government negotiators, nor were they agreed to. Rather, indigenous peoples and other local actors were construed as standardized "stakeholders" with little to offer and little of value. Governments conceded only last minute and reactive opportunities for local actors to participate in externally driven carbon projects. Indigenous peoples' contributions and knowledges were not acknowledged, so it was easier for governments to deny them participation in institutions at the global level, where their representation would be essential in order for them to systematically protect their rights. Indigenous peoples and local communities were also denied status with regards to project design.[6]

Although indigenous leaders worked towards their goals, they had by 2001 achieved little. Because they are recognized as distinct peoples and nations, indigenous peoples and their organizations are dissimilar to many other translocal networks of local actors (see Bulkeley and Betsill 2003). But it is precisely these distinct identities and cultures that might reasonably make indigenous peoples well-equipped to resist the homogenizing global. Their failure to do so under the Kyoto Protocol and its institutions, therefore, represents a failure for all local actors. Natural places, in this story, remained essentially voiceless.

It is possible that the concerns raised in this chapter will never be realized. But the story told here—of the global gaze that constructs, marginalizes and then induces the resistance of local actors—pertains to other institutions as well. Global policy elites must start taking local complexity seriously. They must design global institutions that systematically connect local actors with governmental policy makers. They should build global networks of trust that accommodate those harmed by globalization as well as those hoping to benefit from it. The enactment of reforms that redeem the global to the local will help create institutions that are perceived as credible and just. This is an important task for the twenty-first century.

Notes

1. Indigenous peoples' organizations from Central Brazil and Southern Mexico generally supported carbon sink policies; this support was linked to their ongoing relationships with US ENGOs such as Environmental Defense or The Nature Conservancy, which positioned them well to benefit from rather than be harmed by transnational carbon financing.

2. Most Northern governments supported emissions trading in exchange for developing countries avoiding deforestation that "might otherwise occur." However, the government of Brazil strongly opposed this policy and prevented its adoption.

3. For confirmation of the basic thrust of this argument, see Food and Agriculture Organization 2003.

4. Of 71 carbon sequestration projects reviewed in 2003, only 10 reported monitoring some environmental or social impact. Most of these utilized qualitative descriptors only (Llosa and Green 2003).

5. The largest beneficiaries of carbon tree planting policies will be the 20 private and state-owned companies—mainly coal and oil firms—that currently produce about half of the world's carbon pollution (NRDC 1999).

6. Pushed by Indonesian ENGOs, the government of Indonesia was the sole developing country government that pushed for recognition of local peoples and knowledges during 2000 negotiations. The government did this in part to make more attractive their support for carbon plantation financing. It has since become the main beneficiary of the first carbon sequestration project slated to receive multilateral funding (CDM Watch 2003).

References

Anonymous. 2001. Press releases and letters distributed by the Forum on Indigenous Peoples and Climate Change at the Sixth Conference of the Parties to the FCCC, Bonn.

Betsill, Michel. 2000. Greens in the Greenhouse: NGOs and Climate Change Policies. Ph.D. dissertation, University of Colorado, Boulder.

Bowker, G., and S. L. Star. 1998. *Sorting Things Out: Classification and Its Consequences*. MIT Press.

Bulkeley, H., and M. Betsill. 2003. *Cities and Climate Change: Urban Sustainability and Global Environmental Governance*. Routledge.

Center for International Forestry Research. 2000. Local Communities and Averted Deforestation Projects under the CDM: Enhancing Benefits and Reducing Risks.

Department of Energy (US). 1999. Carbon Sequestration: Research and Development. Office of Science, Office of Fossil Energy.

Eraker, H. 2000. CO_2lonialism—Norwegian Tree Plantations, Carbon Credits and Land Conflicts in Uganda. Oslo: Norwatch.

FERN. 2000. Sinking the Kyoto Protocol: The Links between Forests, Plantations and Carbon Sinks.

Fogel, Cathleen. 2002. Greening the Earth with Trees: Science, Storylines and the Construction of International Climate Change Institutions. Ph.D. dissertation, University of California, Santa Cruz.

Food and Agriculture Organization. 1999. Prevention of land degradation, enhancement of carbon sequestration and conservation of biodiversity through land use change and sustainable land management with a focus on Latin America and the Caribbean: Proceedings of an IFAD/FAO Expert Consultation. Rome: International Fund for Agricultural Development.

Food and Agriculture Organization. 2001. *Global Forest Resources Assessment 2000*.

Food and Agriculture Organization. 2003. *State of the World's Forests 2003*.

Frumhoff, Peter, Darren C. Goetze, and Jared J. Hardner. 1998. *Linking Solutions to Climate Change and Biodiversity Loss through the Kyoto Protocol's Clean Development Mechanism*. Union of Concerned Scientists.

Future Forests. 2001. *Planting Partners.*

Global Observation of Forest Cover Design Team. 1999. *A Strategy for the Global Observation of Forest Cover.* Michigan State University.

Global Terrestrial Carbon Observation Initiative. 2001. Global Terrestrial Carbon Observation Initiative Update. CLIM-FO No.2/2001. Food and Agriculture Organization.

Hagmann, J. E. 2001. Developing a Shared Research Agenda for LUCF and CDM: Research Needs and Opportunities after COP 6: Workshop Documentation. Bigor, Indonesia: CIFOR.

Hurley, L. 2000. Friends of the Earth Ireland. Email to author.

Intergovernmental Panel on Climate Change. 2000. *Land Use, Land Use Change and Forestry.* Cambridge University Press.

Intergovernmental Panel on Climate Change. 1995. *Climate Change 1995.* Cambridge University Press.

Intergovernmental Panel on Climate Change, World Meterological Organization, United Nations Environment Program. 1990. *Climate Change: The IPCC Response Strategies.* Earth Island.

International Geosphere-Biosphere Program Terrestrial Carbon Working Group. 1998. "The Terrestrial Carbon Cycle: Implications for the Kyoto Protocol." *Science* 280: 1393–1394.

Latour, Bruno. 1997. *Science in Action.* MIT Press.

Levy, Mark. 1999. Presentation at Belfer Center for Science and International Affairs, Harvard University, September 9.

Litfin, Karen. 1996. *Ozone Discourses: Science and Politics in Global Environmental Cooperation.* Columbia University Press.

Litfin, Karen. 1997. "The Gendered Eye in the Sky: A Feminist Perspective on Earth Observation Satellites." *Frontiers* 18, no. 2: 36–47.

Llosa, Silvia, and Jessica Green. 2003. *Results of the Carbon Sequestration Project.*World Resources Institute.

Martello, Marybeth. 2001. "A Paradox of Virtue? 'Other' Knowledges and Environment-Development Politics." *Global Environmental Politics* 1, no. 3: 114–141.

Lund, H. G. 1999. *Definitions of Forest, Deforestation, Afforestation and Reforestation.* Manassas: Forest Information Services.

Montana Carbon Offset Coalition. 2000. *Standards & Specifications.*

Natural Resources Defense Council. 1999. *Kingpins of Carbon: How Fossil Fuel Producers Contribute to Global Warming.*

Newcombe, Ken. 2000. Presentation on Clean Development Mechanism. Sixth Conference of the Parties to the FCCC, The Hague.

Prototype Carbon Fund. 2002. Brazil Plantar Public Topic Area, Archived Postings.

Sanchez, P. A. 2000. *Linking Climate Change Research with Food Security and Poverty Reduction in the Tropics*. Nairobi: International Centre for Research in Agroforestry.

Scott, James C. 1998. *Seeing Like a State: How Certain Schemes to Improve the Human Condition Have Failed*. Yale University Press.

Second International Indigenous Forum on Climate Change. 2000. *Declaration of Indigenous Peoples on Climate Change*.

Shiva, Vandana. 1993. *Monocultures of the Mind*. Zed Books.

Soares dos Santos André, Marco Antonio, Rosa Roldan, Fábio Martins Villas, Maria Diana de Oliveira, José Augusto de Castro Tosato, Winfried Overbeek, and Marcelo Calazans Soares. 2003. *Evaluation Report of V& M Florestal Ltda. and Plantar S.A. Reflorestamentos*. World Rainforest Movement.

Stave, A. J. 2000. *Carbon Upsets: Norwegian "Carbon Plantations" in Tanzania*. Oslo: Norwatch.

TIFIPLCCC (Third International Forum of Indigenous Peoples and Local Communities on Climate Change). 2001. *The Bonn Declaration*. Sixth Conference of the Parties to the FCCC.

UNFCCC. 2001 and 2001a. Report on the Conference of the Parties on Its Seventh Session, Held at Marrakesh from 29 October to 10 November 2001; Part Two (Volumes 1 and 2): Action Taken by the Conference of the Parties. Bonn: FCCC/CP/2001/13/Add.2.

5

When Global Is Local: Negotiating Safe Use of Biotechnology

Aarti Gupta

At the turn of the century, the changing nature of interactions between states and markets are endlessly debated under the catch-all concept of globalization (Appadurai 1996; Rodrik 1997; Ancarani 1995). Notwithstanding disputes about the nature of this phenomenon, there is an urgent need for governance, especially transnational governance, to anticipate and address potentially transformative technological, environmental and social changes associated with globalization.

Governance, from the Greek *kubernan*, suggests navigation or steering. The pressing governance challenge is navigating change in a globalizing world in a manner that remains legitimate across contexts. It requires mediation of local or context-specific differences on the perceived nature of governance and appropriate bases for collective action. This challenge is exacerbated by the growing need for governance under conditions of extreme scientific uncertainty and normative conflict over the very existence, nature, and hence framing of particular governance challenges.

This chapter explores international negotiations over framing a governance problem in one relatively new issue area—ensuring *biosafety* or the safe transboundary transfer and use of the products of modern biotechnology[1]. In analyzing prospects for a shared framing of biosafety, I focus here on the multilateral negotiating arena of the Cartagena Protocol on Biosafety, as a site where efforts to develop such shared framings or to "globalize" biosafety can be observed in detail.

The Cartagena Protocol on Biosafety, concluded in January 2000 under the auspices of the Convention on Biological Diversity, is the newest global treaty governing the transboundary transfer and safe use of genetically modified organisms in agriculture (CP 2000). Use of biotechnology in agriculture has increased substantially over the last three decades, particularly in certain agricultural exporting countries of the Organization for Economic Cooperation and Development (OECD) (James 2000; BIO 2000). The resulting genetically modified or "transgenic" crops are being transferred across the globe, giving rise to concerns over "biosafety" or the perceived need to govern the safe transfer and use of such modified entities.

Safety, however, can be very differently understood, as is starkly evident from contentious transnational debates over the existence and nature of potential risks (ecological, health, or socioeconomic) posed by modern agricultural biotechnology (McHughen 2000; May 1999). These debates date back to the early 1970s, when gene splicing was first undertaken in the United States (Wright 1994). Ecological concerns relating to transgenic crops or seed include potential adverse impacts on biodiversity from novel gene flow or insect resistance to toxins engineered into modified plants (Wolfenbarger and Phifer 2000; Rissler and Mellon 1993). Human health concerns include the potential for increased allergenicity or toxicity from consumption of genetically altered food (Nottingham 1998; Ho and Steinbrecher 1998; FAO 2000). In addition, a variety of socioeconomic, political, and ethical concerns center on how to democratically manage the transformative potential of this technology (Egziabher 1999; Nuffield Council on Bioethics 1999).

This chapter analyzes how, if at all, local perspectives and understandings of biosafety are mediated in the Cartagena Protocol's search for shared global understandings (i.e. for meanings of biosafety that are translocally legitimate). I focus on efforts to define biosafety-related terminology within the Cartagena Protocol's Scientific and Technical Expert Group. Local knowledge is understood in this chapter as common understandings held by a collectivity within an identifiable context (Shapin 1995). By this definition, most knowledge is "local" and the interesting question becomes whether and how particular local knowledges acquire ascendancy, spread out of their original contexts, and become globalized.

With this understanding of local knowledge, I also view multilateral negotiating arenas (and their scientific and technical expert groups) as themselves sites of local knowledge production, if certain context-specific understandings are identifiable there. At a minimum, they are sites for conflict over whose local knowledge will dominate over others. Negotiations over biosafety within the Cartagena Protocol thus offer an excellent site from which to analyze how particular local knowledges come to achieve translocal status, or fail to do so.

I focus on deliberations within the Protocol's Scientific and Technical Expert Group because, more than ever, science is seen as an important tool in attempts to globalize normatively contested concepts. Science, more than any other social resource, offers an "especially powerful discursive and institutional framework for creating globally convergent understandings about environmental [and risk] problems" (Jasanoff 1998, p. 84). Reliance on science is becoming institutionalized as a basis for cross-national risk decisions in global governance forums, particularly in the influential world trade regime (SPS Agreement 1994; WTO 1998). The call for "sound" science to mediate political conflict is increasingly heard, with soundness equated with technical precision, value neutrality, and objectivity.

Yet, as analyses of domestic and international governance have long highlighted, scientific input into decision making is not isolated from politics but instead shapes and is shaped by political conflicts (Jasanoff 1987; Sterling 1999; Sarewitz 2000). In a similar vein, this chapter critiques attempts within the Protocol's Expert Group to set science apart from politics, and to distinguish globally valid science from context-specific local knowledge. The analysis illustrates, instead, the context-specific and hence *local* nature of scientists' understandings of biosafety reached within the Protocol's Expert Group. By representing scientists' understandings reached within this global forum as local, my analysis turns on its head persisting associations of local knowledge with the non-global and the non-scientific.

In the next section I explore the theoretical implications of boundary drawing between science and politics in global governance of controversial challenges such as biosafety. I then analyze disputes over biosafety terminology within the Cartagena Protocol's Expert Group. I show that shared understandings among scientists are most likely to be reached by allowing for deliberate ambiguity and local re-interpretation of the meanings of biosafety, rather than through technical precision or value neutrality. The analysis concludes that, instead of striving to find means to isolate science from politics (and distinguish globally valid from local knowledge), the governance challenge is the opposite—it requires finding institutional mechanisms which can mediate between such categories in a cross-nationally credible manner.

Boundary Making in Governance: Separating Science from Politics

The portrayal of science as the only translocally valid language through which to mediate normative conflict is the subject of increased critical scrutiny in writings on global governance (Jasanoff 1998; Herrick and Sarewitz 2000; Gupta 2001a,b). Policy makers and scientists who envision such a mediating role for science continue to view scientific knowledge as the antithesis of local knowledge, particularly in its presumed general (or across-the-board) validity, technical precision and value neutrality. A claim to value neutrality necessarily implies, however, that science can be set apart from normative conflicts, i.e., it requires *boundary making* between science and politics.

Such boundary making has long been critiqued as a political legitimization strategy in writings on public decision making (Jasanoff 1987; Gieryn 1995). Such writings take as their starting premise that scientific inquiry is not intrinsically objective in the sense of being value neutral, since value judgments permeate all stages of risk identification and mediation. Rather, they analyze where and why (i.e., for what political, cultural or institutional purposes) the boundaries between the technical and political are drawn in particular cases of science-policy interactions.

As Gieryn suggests, "social construction of the science/policy boundary is a crucial strategy through which distinctive interests of diverse players are advanced or thwarted. . . . Boundary-work occurs as people contend for, legitimate, or challenge the cognitive authority of science" (1995, pp. 436, 405). Separating science from politics also serves the equally important function of maintaining the legitimacy of contested political decisions, especially in areas of governance where scientific uncertainty co-exists with extreme political controversy (Jasanoff 1987).

Analyses of boundary making between science and politics in international governance have also came to similar conclusions. A dominant strand within international relations has long argued that consensual technical input provided by scientific "epistemic communities" can assist in reaching politically difficult compromises, as a result of its authoritativeness and value neutrality (Haas 1992). In critiquing this perspective, Karen Litfin, writing about the role of scientists in governing the transboundary ozone depletion problem, suggests that "inasmuch as scientific discourse permeates political debates, as often as not it serves to articulate or rationalize existing interests and conflicts" (Litfin 1994, p. 197).

Nonetheless, both national and global governance regimes continue to call for reliance on "sound" science in problem framing and action (SPS 1994; WTO 1998). As US President George W. Bush has stated in the context of global climate change, "We're going to make decisions based on sound science, not some environmental fad or what may sound good" (Bush, quoted in *China Post*, 2001).

Analysts of risk regulation have pointed out, however, that such boundary-drawing can render those without the requisite technical expertise voiceless in the framing of the issue or its resolution (Dietz, Stern, and Rycroft 1989; Jasanoff 1998). Thus, attempts to clearly separate the domain of science from politics in decision making, and to designate certain issues as technical, can have the negative consequence of excluding "lay" perspectives from participatory decision making about technological change (Press 1994; Rose-Ackerman 1995). In a transnational context, such exclusions can also prevent developing countries from fully articulating their concerns in "technical" debates within global governance forums (Biermann 2002). Alternatively, it may force these countries to voice broad social concerns in the narrower language of technically assessable harm (Gupta 2001b, 2002).

In contrast, if scientific input into policy decisions is recognized as one key (albeit partial) component for resolving political conflict, the interesting question becomes how, as Jasanoff (1998, p. 70) puts it, "scientific claims gain authority under conditions of uncertainty." This requires attention because of the current paradox facing global and national anticipatory governance: the paradox that "sound science" is called for most ardently and most often under conditions of the most severe scientific and institutional uncertainty and lack of trust, where consensual or agreed technical criteria are the hardest to achieve (Wynne 1987; Beck 1992; Sarewitz 1996).

As recent analyses of scientific input into governance emphasize, it is instead in areas where normative conflicts have been resolved that consensual scientific understandings are most likely to follow (Sarewitz 2000). This turns on its head the notion that transnational epistemic communities can provide consensual science as a way to mediate normative conflict. As Jasanoff suggests, an epistemic community, where it exists, is more likely to be the end-product or outcome of processes of normative conflict resolution, rather than its cause (Jasanoff 1998, p. 86).

In a detailed analysis of how scientific input can acquire (or maintain) authority in policy processes in areas of political controversy and scientific uncertainty, Shackley and Wynne put forward the concept of "boundary-ordering devices" as "contextual discursive attempts to reconcile authority with uncertainty in science" (Shackley and Wynne 1996, p. 275). Particular concepts, such as that of "uncertainty" in the global climate change regime, for example, can function as discursive boundary-ordering devices. Their key distinguishing feature is that they allow diverse and flexible interpretations of their meaning, often through deliberate ambiguity or lack of definitional precision, and hence maintain the cognitive authority of science even as they allow policy dialogue to continue. In doing so, they permit both "cooperation *and* heterogeneity" to co-exist (Shackley and Wynne 1996, p. 293).

The implications of relying on boundary-ordering devices in global governance of diverse issue areas remain important to examine. The challenge is how to juxtapose reliance on boundary-ordering devices with the contradictory imperative in global governance of harmonizing or reducing translocal differences. Harmonization through standardization, as Theodore Porter puts it, requires "separating knowledge from its local context" (Porter 1995, p. 22). Yet in a realm of normative conflicts, standardized understandings may be neither attainable or desirable. Can standardized or harmonized meanings of biosafety mediate local difference in a manner that is translocally legitimate? Such a question motivates this analysis of the search for a shared framing of biosafety within the Cartagena Protocol.

Globalizing Biosafety through Science?

A temporary framing of biosafety—arrived at after intense negotiations[2]— is contained in the stated objectives of the Cartagena Protocol on Biosafety:

To contribute to ensuring an adequate level of protection in the field of the safe transfer, handling and use of living modified organisms resulting from modern biotechnology that may have adverse effects on the conservation and sustainable use of biological diversity, taking also into account risks to human health and specifically focusing on transboundary movements." (CP 2000, article 1)

As this indicates, the Cartagena Protocol associates "biosafety" with concern over potential "adverse effects on the conservation and sustainable use of biological diversity, taking also into account the risks to human health" that may result from transboundary movement, handling and use of "living modified organisms resulting from modern biotechnology." Furthermore, the Protocol acknowledges that adverse impacts from products of modern biotechnology can result either from their "contained use" or "intentional introduction" into a "likely potential receiving environment" (CP 2000, articles 6, 7).

How these terms get defined is critical to how the newly emerging concept of biosafety is framed within this multilateral forum. Each of these terms is explicitly socio-technical, requiring both technical and political mediation in the search for translocally valid understandings. Yet in the Cartagena Protocol negotiations the task of defining these critical concepts was given over to a group of scientific and technical experts (BSWG 1999; Ex-COP 2000). This meant that some of the thorniest biosafety issues were discussed by scientists within this group.

The Expert Group, called Contact Group-1, was established to develop definitions of biosafety-related terminology for inclusion in the Protocol (Ex-COP 2000). The group consisted of those members of government delegations who were scientists, working for science ministries or agencies in their home countries. Hence, these members participated in the Expert Group both as representatives of their countries and in their capacity as technical experts. The scientific disciplines represented included, *inter alia*, genetics, biochemistry, biotechnology and ecology[3].

In establishing the Expert Group, Protocol negotiators repeatedly emphasized that it was meant to provide "technical" input into on-going "political" decision making. Member scientists saw their task as "not to negotiate" but to come to mutual agreement in their capacity as scientists about complex technical issues and, in particular, about definitions of biosafety-related terminology. The deliberations of the Expert Group offer, then, a useful case with which to analyze the implications of boundary-drawing between science and politics in global anticipatory governance.

Scientists in the Expert Group spoke on behalf of three main negotiating alliances. These included (a) the Miami Group, a group of agricultural exporting countries; (b) the European Union, often supported by Norway, Switzerland, and other non-EU OECD members; and (c) developing countries. The Miami Group included six agricultural exporting countries (Argentina, Australia, Canada, Chile, the United States, and Uruguay) that are at the forefront of producing and testing transgenic crops[4]. This group called for a "workable protocol" with a narrow scope and "sound" scientific decision making, and was supported in this call by the Global Industry Coalition, a coalition of biotechnology industry groups (GIC 1999). As representatives of the GIC put it, "decisions under the Protocol . . . must be based on sound and objective science. To do otherwise, will severely undercut the effectiveness and integrity of the Protocol. . . ."[5]

In contrast, the European Union, from the perspective of a potential importer, sought to guarantee national discretion and flexibility in restricting entries of genetically modified organisms, particularly by emphasizing the need for precautionary decisions in the face of scientific uncertainties about adverse impacts of GMOs on human health and ecological safety (EC 2000)[6]. Developing country scientists, supported by green groups and Nordic countries, pushed for the broadest framing of biosafety in the Protocol. They emphasized, for example, the need to consider adverse socioeconomic impacts, in addition to health and ecological impacts, in national decision making about GMO imports (Asfaw and Egziabher 1997; see also Gupta 2002)[7]. These diverse perspectives on how broadly to define the biosafety problem were reflected in disputes over terminology in the Expert Group.

The key biosafety-related concepts requiring definition by the Expert Group included (a) living modified organism; (b) modern biotechnology; (c) deliberate release; (d) contained use; and (e) the receiving environment for transgenic seed or crop releases.

The next section examines disputes over each and the resolution reached, with its implications for shared framings of biosafety and global governance in this contested area. The analysis is based on first-hand author observation of the Protocol's Expert Group deliberations, primary documents by the Group, and confidential interviews with its members and others involved with the Cartagena Protocol negotiations during the period 1998–2000.

Defining a Living Modified Organism: Novelty as a Boundary-Ordering Device

Although the Cartagena Protocol on Biosafety regulates products of modern biotechnology or what are commonly called genetically modified organisms (GMOs), the Protocol refers instead to "living" modified organisms or

LMOs. This change in terminology occurred before Protocol negotiations began, at the insistence of the United States, which argued that genetic engineering did not pose unique risks and hence did not need to be singled out for global regulatory attention. When this emerged as a minority position, they pushed for the change in terminology from "genetic" to "living" modified organism, in an effort to deflect attention away from genetic engineering as the focus of global regulation (Rajan 1997; Gupta 2001a).

In the Expert Group's subsequent attempt to develop a shared definition of a "living modified organism", the scientists present agreed that LMOs were novel, i.e. distinct from non-LMOs. However, the key concept of "novelty" was differently understood by participating scientists. Conflict centered on whether a novel entity was one that was "unlikely" or "unknown" to occur in nature (CG1 1998a,b). While the distinction seems subtle, selecting one or the other interpretation would narrow or broaden the understanding of novelty, and hence the definition of what constituted an LMO. This was because modified entities that are currently unknown but are also unlikely to occur in nature are a subset of those that are simply unknown; equating novel with "unlikely" therefore reduces the scope of regulation.

In supporting the narrower "unlikely to occur in nature" definition of novelty, Miami Group scientists argued that if genetic modifications resulted in a product that was likely to occur in nature (even if previously unknown), it should not be subject to regulation, since it would not pose risks distinct from existing or likely to exist non-genetically altered organisms. Scientists from developing countries and Nordic scientists contested this claim. In supporting the broader "unknown to occur in nature" definition of novelty, their scientific rationale was that it was impossible to unequivocally state what was likely or unlikely to occur in nature, and that the only verifiable and non-hypothetical scientific claim was whether an entity was known or unknown to occur in nature at the present time.

The "unknown to occur in nature" understanding of novelty thus captured a broader set of genetically modified entities within the definition, since most products of genetic engineering are likely to be currently unknown to occur in their particular modified form. If selected, this definition would be akin to a process-based definition of an LMO, since mere use of the techniques of modern biotechnology would yield a novel organism presently unknown to occur in nature. The conflict thus had clear parallels in the longer-standing dispute between the European Union and the United States over biotechnology regulation on a process or product basis (Gottweis 1998; Jasanoff 1995).

Strikingly, and of particular relevance to the argument of this paper, the divergence in opinion about the meaning of novelty was not resolved through achieving greater technical precision or scientific consensus. Instead, agreement could only be reached within the Expert Group by deleting both contested interpretations of novelty and leaving the concept unexplained. Thus, an early draft version of the definition of an LMO stated: "LMO means any living organism that contains genetic material which has been modified by modern biotechnology and of which the resulting genotype is [unlikely] [not known] to occur in nature and can confer traits novel to the organism." (CG1 1998a, with brackets denoting continuing disagreement) By contrast, the final definition read as follows: "LMO means any living organism containing a novel combination of genetic material obtained through the use of modern biotechnology." (CG1 1998b; CP 2000, article 3.g)

The "agreement" that LMOs are entities that "contain a novel combination of genetic material" hides within it different and unreconciled interpretations of the meaning of the critically important concept of novelty. Thus, instead of reaching a technically standardized understanding of novelty, the Protocol's Expert Group agreed on a definition of "living modified organism" that will necessarily be variably interpreted. This definitional ambiguity allowed dialogue to continue, which was symbolically and substantively important because an agreed definition of an LMO was necessary for the "political" component of the Protocol negotiations to continue.

The accommodation reached by the Expert Group on the concept of novelty can be seen as an example of a "boundary ordering device" (Shackley and Wynne 1996). In their ambiguity and openness to flexible interpretation, such discursive devices maintain the cognitive authority of science (which may be challenged if too much technical precision is sought in areas of normative conflict), while they simultaneously perform the critical political function of accommodating diverse context-specific (i.e. local) interpretations of contested concepts.

Defining Modern Biotechnology: Negotiated Science

Another essential term requiring a "technical" definition was "modern biotechnology" (CP 2000, article 3). A key point of conflict here was whether the techniques of cell fusion (relied upon in some countries to pro-duce genetically modified pharmaceuticals, for example) were to be con-sidered part of modern or traditional biotechnology. The importance of this turned on the fact that, if cell fusion were included in the definition of modern biotechnology, a larger category of genetically modified products traded worldwide could be subject to the Cartagena Protocol's obligations. This was an outcome desired by many developing countries, but not by transgenic producing and exporting countries of the Miami Group, the biotechnology industry, and others (Meyer 1999; Anonymous 1999; Japan 1999b).

Scientists from the Miami Group, supported by Japan and Brazil, argued in the Expert Group that cell fusion had been used for decades and was a traditional rather than a modern technique of genetic manipulation (e.g., Japan 1999b). They also pointed to lack of scientific evidence that use of such techniques threatened biological diversity or human health. Scientists from developing countries, on the other hand, pointed out that "tradi-tional" and "modern" forms of genetic manipulation meant quite distinct things in different contexts. In arguing for inclusion of cell fusion within the definition of modern biotechnology, developing country scientists sug-gested that cell fusion could be used to cross species barriers, which in their view was one of the defining characteristics of modern biotechnology (CG-1 observations, August 1998)[8].

To move beyond the impasse, the Chair of the Expert Group suggested a compromise, which would include "fusion of cells beyond the taxonomic family" in the definition of modern biotechnology. The Chair described his suggestion as a "qualified inclusion of cell fusion, as a compromise between including it and not including it" (CG1 observations 1998). While this sug-gestion provoked much debate, the main point of interest here is the response to the Chair's suggestion that this was a "compromise." The Expert Group scientist-delegate from the United States noted that "we take issue with the suggestion that we should try to find a compromise in this technical discussion, let's go with what the science tells us." Similarly, the Brazilian scientist-delegate emphasized that "we are having a technical dis-cussion, let's hear the scientific arguments." This prompted a statement from the Chair that although they were a technical group "at some point we are negotiating and then we may no longer be on technical grounds" (CG-1 observations 1998).

Equally illuminating is the final outcome. The Miami Group scientists (who had earlier argued for reliance on science alone) signaled their acceptance of the Chair's compromise, but only on condition that a qualifying footnote be added. This footnote stated that their "acceptance of the inclusion of cell fusion" within the definition of modern biotechnology was "dependent upon resolution of the question of inclusion of contained uses and/or pharmaceuticals [within the Protocol as a whole]. If contained use and pharmaceuticals are included [i.e. regulated] within the Protocol, the cell fusion issue will have to be revisited" (CG1 1998d).

This reveals that acceptance of the Chair's compromise by Miami Group scientists was contingent less on their perception of its scientific plausibility and more on the outcome of the political debate over whether the Cartagena Protocol would regulate pharmaceuticals and contained uses of transgenic entities within its scope (or whether its focus would be only on agricultural uses of biotechnology). The negotiating parties recognized that if the Protocol excluded these categories of LMOs, such an exclusion would automatically exclude most uses of cell fusion from the Protocol's oversight, making its exclusion or inclusion within the definition of modern biotechnology less consequential (regardless of how modern biotechnology is understood by scientists outside the context of the Cartagena Protocol). This example reveals clearly the locally negotiated nature of "technical" agreements about key biosafety-related terminology within the Expert Group. It illustrates the situated and context-specific nature of scientists' agreements within this global forum.

Defining Deliberate Release: Creative Language Substitution

Another task for the Expert Group was agreeing on what constituted the "deliberate release" of transgenic products into the environment. One revealing component of this debate centered on the suggestion by Miami Group scientists that the term "deliberate release" be replaced with "intentional introduction." While these terms appear identical in meaning, the Miami Group sought with this suggestion to avoid importing into the Cartagena Protocol the institutional history and underlying norms and practices already associated with use of the term "deliberate release" elsewhere, particularly within the European Union's regional directive on deliberate release of genetically modified organisms (EU 1990; see also EU 2001).

As with other examples of creative language substitution, such as "living modified organism" for "genetically modified organism", this substitution was explicitly intended to disassociate understanding of the term "deliberate release" from its meanings in other contexts, since these other contexts could well allow for broader or more stringent regulatory norms. The example again highlights that "agreeing on the science" does not occur in a vacuum devoid of institutional history. Instead, even seemingly straightforward concepts such as "deliberate release" require interpretation within particular institutional norms and practices.

Defining Contained Use of an LMO: Deferring to Context-Based Differences

The Expert Group also sought to develop a shared understanding of what constituted "contained use" of genetically modified organisms. Containment, too, can be narrowly or broadly defined. For example, it can mean physically enclosed spaces, such as research laboratories, or it can be more broadly understood to include field test sites under controlled experimental conditions. In addition to physical measures, containment can also be achieved through biological means. For example, genetic modifications which result in sterile seeds (the much contested "terminator technology"[9]) can, by some definitions, be seen as a form of biological containment of the novel genetic material in an LMO.[10]

Disputes over how to define "containment" within the Expert Group were, again, closely tied to broader conflicts over the scope of the Cartagena Protocol, and in particular, over its central obligation to solicit the "advance informed agreement" of an importing country prior to transboundary transfers of some LMOs (CP 2000; Gupta 2000a, 2001b). If LMOs intended for contained use were excluded from the Protocol's advance informed agreement obligation, *and* if containment was broadly defined to include field tests and use of terminator technology, this could potentially exclude the most widely undertaken activities (field tests) and the most controversial techniques (terminator genes) from the Protocol's most stringent obligations.

This political reality was reflected in the Expert Group's efforts to agree on a definition of contained use. Developing country scientists argued for a narrow definition of containment, to refer only to those LMOs used in physically contained structures. They stated, for example, that the potential for containment of novel genetic material within field sites depended not just on technical criteria (such as refugia or distance of potential gene flow) but also on social measures such as monitoring and sampling, the capacity for which varied greatly between countries. Others, especially exporter countries of the Miami Group and industry, argued for a broad definition of contained use. If accepted, a broader range of transferred LMOs could be exempted from the Protocol's advance informed agreement obligation.

Ultimately, the only way to reach agreement was to define the term "contained use" in a manner that allowed for multiple interpretations to persist. An earlier more explicit but contested definition of "contained use" was "any operation involving organisms which are controlled by physical barriers or a combination of physical and/or chemical and/or biological barriers which limit their contact with, or their impacts on, the potential receiving environment, which includes humans" (BSWG 1999, p. 4). This definition did not restrict containment to physical structures. Instead, it explicitly included biological containment. Since this was unacceptable to many developing countries, a revised version defined "contained use" more generally to mean "any operation, undertaken within a facility, installation or other physical structure, which involves living modified organisms that are controlled by specific measures which effectively limit their contact with, and their impact on, the external environment" (BSWG 1999, p. 5, article 3.b). In this definition, containment is clearly linked to "operations undertaken within a physical structure" thereby potentially excluding field tests. However, whether LMOs with terminator genes are included in the definition remains ambiguous. This is because it remains unclear whether the "specific measures" that are meant to limit contact or impact of LMOs on the external environment can also include techniques of biological containment.

Given the controversial implications of the definition(s) of contained use for the scope of the Protocol and for developing country concerns over field tests and terminator genes, multilateral negotiators agreed in a last-minute compromise that, in the event of conflict over what constitutes contained use, an importing country's understanding of containment would prevail over that of the Cartagena Protocol's (CP 2000, article 6.2). This final resolution is a telling instance of the impossibility of standardizing such a contested concept within, or through, this global forum. Instead, the Protocol's resolution of the issue recognizes the need for local interpretive flexibility in key biosafety-related terminology and leaves room for it.

Defining a Receiving Environment for LMO Releases

The Expert Group also sought to agree on what constituted the "receiving environment" for release of LMOs. Scientists from Nordic states and developing countries argued for a broad understanding of this term, noting that a receiving environment should include not only a particular field into which an LMO was sown, but also its surrounding areas, since these could inadvertently become receiving environments through the spread of pollen from transgenic crops. The term "potential" was added to "receiving environment" to address this concern.

However, this formulation was seen as too broad by Miami Group scientists. As one member of the Group noted, the "whole planet could be a potential receiving environment—clearly we don't want to worry in Australia about LMOs planted in Asia" (CG1 observations 1999). These scientists proposed adding the qualifier "likely" to "potential receiving environment" as a way to reduce the scope of the existing phrase.

The result is an awkward formulation—risk assessments called for under the Protocol must now assess impacts of LMO releases into a "likely potential receiving environment" (CP 2000, article 1, Annex II). The language here leaves interpretation of this term to the discretion of local risk assessors. Nor does it specify institutional means through which the limits of interpretative freedom will be defined. Inevitably, then, such considerations will be delineated on a case-by-case basis rather than through global standards or criteria established by the Cartagena Protocol.

The Protocol's reliance on ambiguity, interpretative flexibility and deference to context-based interpretation of key concepts is inevitable, and I would argue desirable, given vastly differing political, ecological and social settings for LMO releases. By denying the possibility of standardization within this global arena, this example, and the deliberations of the Expert Group more generally, negate the image of "sound" scientific decision making as being beyond negotiation. Instead, the Expert Group's deliberations reveal necessary characteristics of what could be termed a "multi-culturally sound science" as a domain in which ambiguity, technical imprecision, and even political compromises are crucial to scientific convergence.

This is because disputes over scientific terminology in this multilateral forum serve, first and foremost, as surrogates for diverse understandings of biosafety. If so, the agreements reached here link expert assessments of biosafety to particular local contexts and leave the concept of biosafety open to varying interpretations. As Wynne (1987, p. 9) points out in an analysis of European hazardous waste regulation, another attempt at standardizing diverse national concepts of risk and safety: ". . . the viability of the regulatory process may actually depend upon the very opposite of intensification of science; it may require that some imprecision and ambiguity of formal regulatory standards and definitions be maintained, as an adaptive arena in which the contending parties can interact, negotiate, and settle and renegotiate the practical meanings as they go along." Such imprecision and ambiguity is clearly evident in the deliberations of the Cartagena Protocol's Expert Group as well. The deliberations suggest, moreover, that while scientific input remains critical to governance of technological and environmental change, it cannot be the definitive and neutral, and hence authoritative, mediator of conflict envisioned by current advocates of "sound science."

Reevaluating Science-Based Framings as Universal

This chapter has shown that the definitions of key biosafety-related terms developed by the Cartagena Protocol's Expert Group are locally contingent, i.e. a function of the particular dynamics of this negotiating forum. Although they represent, on the surface, a global agreement, the terms require re-localization to be applied to alternative contexts. Instead of precise or standardized definitions, the negotiated and deliberately ambiguous compromises arrived at within the Expert Group do indeed leave substantial scope for such relocalization.

Herein lies the most important contribution of this global governance forum. This analysis suggests that it is precisely through a process of negotiation and mediation of diverse views about risk and safety that shared understandings, which are translocally robust, are likely to emerge and become institutionalized. Global governance arenas such as the Cartagena Protocol on Biosafety remain, most importantly then, sites for the on-going search for shared norms (Gupta 2001a). This is contrary to a view of multilateral regimes as vehicles which transfer unproblematic, globally shared problem framings across diverse national and local contexts, requiring only adequate implementation structures and capacities to be effective (Jasanoff 1998). The analysis suggests, more broadly, that the "global" is itself a kind of local, with the perceived legitimacy of its outcomes crucial to subsequent implementation in diverse additional national and local contexts.

Global Norms to Bridge Local Differences?

If so, the challenge for global governance in heavily contested areas such as biosafety remains how to forge globally valid norms of governance that can take account of diversity, not just scientific but also economic, moral, and cultural. Even if some predictability in international relations is a driving motivation and legitimate goal of global governance, the route to such predictability cannot lie in a denial of deep differences. Nor can it, as the analysis here shows, lie in the effort to impose precise and objective scientific standards on enterprises that are uncertain and politically charged. Instead, legitimizing the use of science in governance requires evolution of the institutions that can confer legitimacy on scientific input into decision making, especially in areas of heightened controversy.

Institutional development is important not only because the science is contested and its interpretation context-dependent but also because, as studies of science in decision making have consistently shown, "good" science for policy making requires good politics. Most generally, if predictability in international relations derives from shared norms, such predictability is more likely to obtain from institutional mechanisms that facilitate the legitimate exercise of national discretion, based on valid differences of knowledge and outlook, rather than from attempts to reduce interpretive diversity. A common or global understanding of what constitutes *legitimate* difference—and how much flexibility ought to be retained for local perspectives—remains then the continuing challenge for global governance.

Acknowledgments

The author is a Visiting Fellow at Wageningen University in the Netherlands and is currently working on a MacArthur Foundation Research and Writing Grant on biotechnology use in developing countries. She thanks Sheila Jasanoff, Marybeth Long Martello, Daniel Sarewitz, and Frank Biermann for comments on an earlier draft of this chapter. Financial support is gratefully acknowledged from the Institute for the Study of World Politics, Harvard University's Global Environmental Assessment Project, and Yale University's Center for International and Area Studies.

Notes

1. Use of biotechnology involves, most generally, the isolation and transfer of genes from one source into another, using molecular techniques. The distinction between biotechnology and modern biotechnology is said to lie primarily in the latter's use of recombinant deoxyribonucleic acid (rDNA) techniques. Deoxyribonucleic acid is the carrier of genetic information in all organisms, except viruses. Mutagenesis within an organism may also result in genetic modification even without the use of rDNA techniques, hence the identification of modern biotechnology with rDNA techniques alone is controversial. (For a detailed discussion, see McHughen 2000.)

2. For early debates about biosafety in the CBD negotiations, see McConnell 1996 and Rajan 1997. For negotiating history of the Cartagena Protocol, see Gupta 2000b and 2001a.

3. Lawyers on government delegations participated, in a similar manner, in a Contact Group 2 which was mandated to provide legal input into the negotiations (Ex-COP 2000).

4. In 2000, a total global area of 44.2 million hectares (109.2 million acres) was devoted to transgenic crops. Of this, the United States contributed 68%, Argentina 23%, Canada 7%, China 1%, and Australia and South Africa over 100,000 hectares. Global sales from transgenic crops were estimated at $75 million in 1995, $235 million in 1996, $670 million in 1997, and $1.2–$1.5 billion in 1998. Global area devoted to transgenic crops has dramatically increased in the last decade. Specifically, in the period 1996–2000 the global area devoted to transgenic crops increased from 1.7 million hectares to 44.2 million hectares (James 1998, 2000).

5. As stated by Helma Hermans, Executive Secretary, Green Industry Biotechnology Platform, in email communication to observers to the CBD Meeting (February 10, 1999, 12:51 P.M.). For similar views, see position papers of the Global Industry Coalition (e.g., GIC 1999a,b).

6. Language on the precautionary principle was included in the Protocol at the insistence of the European Union, supported by green groups and some developing countries. Many disputes over this concept occurred throughout negotiation of the Protocol, including how its inclusion would affect member obligations under the World Trade Organization, with its own (contested) version of the precautionary principle. For an analysis of the Protocol's language on the precautionary principle and its relationship to the WTO, see Gupta 2001b.

7. Including adverse socioeconomic impacts in regulating biotechnology is not without precedent. Legislation in Norway, for example, requires consideration of "benefit to the community and a contribution to sustainable development" of

biotechnology products before their approval (Norway Gene Technology Act, 1993).

8. This position was supported by green groups, who were allowed to observe Expert Group deliberations and who could lobby delegates in the corridors during negotiations. These groups circulated numerous documents justifying their claims, often with detailed scientific arguments and data (Meyer 1999; Anonymous 1999).

9. "Terminator technologies" (the term used by its detractors) or "genetic use restriction technologies" (the term used by its advocates) include genetic modifications that can product sterile seed. This is a form of technological patent protection, since it forces farmers to buy seed anew each year. For controversy over "terminator technology" in a developing country agricultural context, see *Hindustan Times* 1999; Indian Express 1998; Science for People 1999.

10. The claim that genetic modifications which produce sterile seed can address the problem of novel gene flow is an example of a regulatory trend whereby "hazards (are sought to be) controlled by the (very) technologies that produce their possibility" (Gottweis 1998, p. 104).

References

Ancarani, Vittorio. 1995. "Globalizing the World: Science and Technology in International Relations." In *Handbook of Science and Technology Studies,* ed. S. Jasanoff et al. Sage.

Anonymous. 1999. Examples of Cell Fusions Overcoming Natural Recombination Barriers. NGO coalition position paper, Cartagena, February 14.

Appadurai, Arjun. 1996. *Modernity at Large: Cultural Dimensions of Globalization.* University of Minnesota Press.

Asfaw, Zemede, and Tewolde B. G. Egziabher. 1997. "Possible Adverse Socio-Economic Impacts of Genetically Modified Organisms." In *Transboundary Movement of Living Modified Organisms Resulting from Modern Biotechnology,* ed. K. Mulongay. International Academy of the Environment.

Beck, Ulrich. 1992. *Risk Society: Towards a New Modernity.* Sage.

Biermann, Frank. 2002. "Institutions for Scientific Advice: Global Environmental Assessments and Their Influence in Developing Countries." *Global Governance* 8, no. 2: 195–220.

Biotechnology Industry Organization (BIO). Undated [2000]. Transgenic products on the market.

BSWG [Open-ended Ad Hoc Working Group on Biosafety]. 1999. "Note by the Co-Chairs of Contact Group I: Programme of work." UNEP/CBD/BSWG/6/Inf. 8. Open-Ended Ad Hoc Working Group on Biosafety, Cartagena.

Convention on Biological Diversity (CBD). 1992. "Convention on Biological Diversity." Negotiated at Rio de Janeiro, June 5; in force December 29, 1993.

China Post (Taipei). 2001. "Environment Policy to Be Sound': Bush." April 28.

Contact Group 1 (CG1). 1998a. "Draft Definition of LMO." Montreal, August 18.

Contact Group 1. 1998b. "Working Definition of LMO." Montreal, August 22.

Contact Group 1. 1998d. "Draft Definition of 'Modern Biotechnology.'" Montreal, August.

Cartagena Protocol (CP). 2000. "Cartagena Protocol on Biosafety to the Convention on Biological Diversity: Text and Annexes." Montreal: Secretariat of the Convention on Biological Diversity.

EC [European Commission] 1990. "Council Directive of 23 April 1990 on the Deliberate Release into the Environment of Genetically Modified Organisms (90/220/EEC)." *Official Journal of the European Communities* L117: 1–27.

EC. 2000. Communication from the Commission on the Precautionary Principle (2.2.2000. COM (2000)1, final). Brussels.

EC. 2001. "Directive 2001/18/EC of the European Parliament and of the Council of 12 March 2001 on the Deliberate Release into the Environment of Genetically Modified Organisms and Repealing Council Directive 90/220/EEC." *Official Journal of the European Communities* L106, 17.04: 1–8.

Egziabher, Tewolde Berhan G. 1999. "Safety Denied." *Our Planet*, June.

Extraordinary Session of the Conference of the Parties to the Convention on Biological Diversity (Ex-COP). 2000. "Report of the Extraordinary Meeting of the Conference of the Parties to the Convention on Biological Diversity for Adoption of the Protocol on Biosafety." UN Doc. UNEP/CBD/ExCOP/1/3.

FAO. 2000. Safety Aspects of Genetically Modified Foods of Plant Origin. Report of a Joint FAO/WHO Expert Consultation on Foods Derived from Biotechnology.

Gieryn, Thomas F. 1995. "Boundaries of Science." In *Handbook of Science and Technology Studies*, ed. S. Jasanoff et al. Sage.

Global Industry Coalition (GIC). 1999a. Basic Requirements for a Successful Biosafety Protocol.

Global Industry Coalition (GIC). 1999b. "Biodiversity Jeopardized in Cartagena Biosafety Negotiations." Press release.

Gottweis, Herbert. 1998. *Governing Molecules: The Discursive Politics of Genetic Engineering in Europe and the United States*. MIT Press.

Gupta, Aarti. 2000a. "Governing Trade in Genetically Modified Organisms: The Cartagena Protocol on Biosafety." *Environment* 42, no. 4: 23–33.

Gupta, Aarti. 2000b. "Creating a Global Biosafety Regime." *International Journal of Biotechnology* 2, no. 1/2/3: 205–230.

Gupta, Aarti. 2001a. Searching for Shared Norms: Global Governance of Biosafety. Ph.D. dissertation, Yale University.

Gupta, Aarti. 2001b. "Advance Informed Agreement: A Shared Basis to Govern Trade in Genetically Modified Organisms?" *Indiana Journal of Global Legal Studies* 9, no. 1: 265–281.

Gupta, Aarti. 2002. "Ensuring 'Safe Use' of Biotechnology in India: Key Challenges." *Economic and Political Weekly*, July 6: 2762–2769.

Haas, Peter M. 1992. "Banning Chorofluorocarbons: Epistemic Community Efforts to Protect the Stratospheric Ozone." *International Organization* 46: 187–224.

Herrick, Charles, and Sarewitz, Daniel. 2000. "Ex post evaluation: A More Effective Role for Scientific Assessments in Environmental Policy." *Science, Technology and Human Values* 25, no. 3: 309–331.

Hindustan Times. 1998. "Terminator Stares India in the Face." August 21.

Ho, Mae-Wan, and Ricarda A. Steinbrecher. 1998. Fatal Flaws in Food Safety Assessment: Critique of the Joint FAO/WHO Biotechnology and Food Safety Report. Penang: Malaysia: Third World Network.

Indian Express. 1999. "Monsanto puts terminator on hold." June 10.

James, Clive. 2000. Global Status of Commercialized Transgenic Crops: 2000. Brief 21, International Service for the Acquisition of Agri-biotech Applications.

Japan. 1999. Position of the Japanese Government toward a Protocol on Biosafety." Cartagena, February.

Japan. 1999b. Comments for exclusion of "cell fusion" from the term "modern biotechnology." Cartagena, February.

Jasanoff, Sheila. 1987. "Contested Boundaries in Policy-Relevant Science." *Social Studies of Science* 17: 195–230.

Jasanoff, Sheila. 1995. "Product, Process, or Programme: Three Cultures and the Regulation of Biotechnology." In *Resistance to New Technology*, ed. M. Bauer. Cambridge University Press.

Jasanoff, Sheila. 1998. "Contingent Knowledge: Implications for Implementation and Compliance." In *Engaging Countries*, ed. E. Weiss and H. Jacobson. MIT Press.

Litfin, Karen T. 1994. *Ozone Discourses: Science and Politics in Global Environmental Cooperation.* Colombia University Press.

May, Robert. 1999. "Genetically modified foods: Facts, worries and public confidence." Report of the Chief Scientific Advisor, Office of Science and Technology, Department of Trade and Energy, United Kingdom.

McConnell, Fiona. 1996. *The Biodiversity Convention: A Negotiating History.* Kluwer Law International.

McHughen, Alan. 2000. *Pandora's Picnic Basket: The Potential and Hazards of Genetically Modified Foods.* Oxford University Press.

Meyer, Hartmut. 1999. "Definition of Modern Biotechnology: reasons for inclusion of cell fusion." Third World Network briefing paper, Forum for Environment and Development of German Non-Governmental Organizations, Cartagena.

Nottingham, Stephan. 1998. *Eat Your Genes: How Genetically Modified Food Is Entering Our Diet.* Zed Books.

Nuffield Council on Bioethics. 1999. Genetically Modified Crops: The Ethical and Social Issues.

Porter, Theodore M. 1995. *Trust in Numbers: The Pursuit of Objectivity in Science and Public Life.* Princeton University Press.

Press, Daniel. 1994. *Democratic Dilemmas in the Age of Ecology: Trees and Toxics in the American West*. Duke University Press.

Rajan, Mukund Govind. 1997. *Global Environmental Politics: India and the North-South Politics of Global Environmental Issues*. Oxford University Press.

Rissler, Jane, and Margaret Mellon. 1993. *Perils among the Promise: Ecological Risks of Transgenic Crops in a Global Market Place*. Union of Concerned Scientists.

Rodrik, Dani. 1997. *Has Globalization Gone Too Far?* Institute for International Economics.

Rose-Ackerman, Susan. 1995. *Controlling Environmental Policy: The Limits of Public Law in Germany and the United States*. Yale University Press.

Sarewitz, Daniel. 1996. *Frontiers of Illusion: Science, Technology and the Politics of Progress*. Temple University Press.

Sarewitz, Daniel. 2000. "Science and Environmental Policy: An Excess of Objectivity." In *Earth Matters*, ed. R. Frodemen. Prentice-Hall.

Science for People. 1999. *Terminator Logic: Monsanto, Genetic Engineering and the Future of Agriculture*. New Delhi: Research Foundation for Science, Technology and Ecology.

Shackley, Simon, and Brian Wynne. 1996. "Representing uncertainty in global climate change science and policy: boundary-ordering devices and authority." *Science, Technology and Human Values* 21, no. 3: 275–302.

Shapin, Steven. 1995. "Cordelia's Love: Credibility and the Social Studies of Science." *Perspectives on Science* 3: 255–275.

SPS Agreement. 1994. "Agreement on the Application of Sanitary and Phytosanitary Measures. Annex IA to the Final Act Embodying the Results of the Uruguay Round of Multilateral Trade Negotiations."

Sterling, Andrew. 1999. "On Science and Precaution in the Management of Technological Risk." ESTO [European Science and Technology Observatory] Project Report, Institute for Prospective Technological Studies, Seville.

Wolfenbarger, L. L., and P. R. Phifer. 2000. "The Ecological Risks and Benefits of Genetically Engineered Plants." *Science* 290: December 15: 2088–2093.

Wright, Susan. 1994. *Molecular Politics: Developing American and British Regulatory Policy for Genetic Engineering, 1972–1982*. University of Chicago Press.

World Trade Organization (WTO). 1998. "Report of the Appellate Body: EC Measures Concerning Meat and Meat Products (Hormones)" WT/DS26/AB/R, WT/DS48/AB/R, AB-1997-4.

Wynne, Brian. 1987. *Risk Management and Hazardous Waste: Implementation and the Dialectics of Credibility*. Springer-Verlag.

II
Globalism and National Politics

6

Transnational Locals: Brazilian Experiences of the Climate Regime

Myanna Lahsen

The Politics of Universalizing Discourses

Popular environmental discourses often evoke impressions of planetary beauty, fragility, and interdependence. They merge with other universalizing discourses that similarly offer images of globalization as liberations from present and past limitations and the promise of a unified humanity no longer divided by East and West, North and South, the rich and the poor. These discourses have broad appeal, and they may be beneficial to the extent that they create a common ground through shared cognitive and normative understandings that transcend local, parochial interests and perspectives. Global environmental indicators suggest the need for some level of convergence in the form of ecological thinking that transcends narrowly nationalistic frames of reference. However, it is important to understand what is elided by universalizing discourses. Actors, including social scientists, easily fall for the "charisma" of the global (Tsing 2000), oversimplifying globalizing processes by highlighting primarily their virtues and promises. Universalizing discourses can serve problematic political programs by hiding contradictions, ambiguities, and complexities of socio-political reality. In the environmental arena, universalizing discourses—for instance, the "life-boat ethic" (Enzenberger 1974) or "sustainability"—avoid the need to analyze concrete inequalities, such as the distribution of power, costs, profits, and responsibility.[1]

Scientific knowledge is commonly associated with universality. Science and scientists are often looked to as models and stimulators of global citizenship and ecological thinking that transcends narrow, self-serving concerns and frames of reference. The sociologist of science Robert K. Merton (1973 [1942]) formulated an early sociological framework that identified a scientific "ethos," a set of cultural values and norms governing knowledge production and knowledge sharing. Merton argued that these values and norms are internalized and transmitted by scientists, guiding their thoughts and actions regardless of where they are situated in terms of politics or culture. More recently, theorists in the field of international relations (IR) have advanced a similar understanding of the role of science and scientists in global environmental politics. For instance, Peter Haas has promoted the notion of transnational "epistemic communities" (1992), transnational networks of professionals from a variety of disciplines and backgrounds with shared ways of knowing, shared patterns of reasoning, shared concern about transboundary environmental problems, and shared environmental policy agendas. These networks of actors shape national and international environmental policies. Haas distinguishes epistemic communities from scientific communities in general by the former's adherence to a shared normative framework and an associated policy agenda. Members of an epistemic community are said to identify with those who share their normative commitments, and to succeed occasionally in efforts to persuade states to transcend rational utilitarian considerations in favor of international environmental cooperation.

Powerful critiques of the epistemic community framework have emerged from the field of science and technology studies. These analyses note that support for a shared perception of environmental problems may be the result of diverse social and political influences, for example, shared disciplinary orientations, economic interests, political ideologies or discursive framings (Jasanoff 1996; see also Miller 1998). This chapter builds on and extends these observations through an ethnographic study of Brazilian scientists and policy makers engaged with international climate science and politics. Empirical data are used to chart some of the "uncharted ideological and political minefields"[2] encountered in efforts to find common ground on a planetary scale concerning the global environment. The data suggest that members of the "climate epistemic community" in Brazil have far more complex identities, more agency, more ambivalence, and more selective allegiances to the climate "episteme" than assumed by IR scholars.

The research reported here was conducted for a total of nine months spread out over a period of three and a half years,[3] ending with the end of the Fernando Henrique Cardoso government (December 2002).[4] By contrast to the standard IR depiction of epistemic communities, this study reveals the circumscribed, internally fragmented and unstable nature of Brazilian actors' adherence to the so-called epistemic community that has formed around climate science and policy. The network studied involves professional collaboration—and, often, personal friendships—that stretch across continents, yet involve frequent interaction among some members around issues of shared interest and concern. To the extent that this social formation congeals, the "glue" holding it together is the research and policy-process related to human-induced climate change, overseen in part by the Intergovernmental Panel on Climate Change (IPCC). The IPCC is a panel of hundreds of scientists from around the world charged with assessing the state of scientific knowledge related to climate change and identifying potential remedial action. Created jointly by the World Meteorological Society and the United Nations Environmental program in 1988, the IPCC provides technical assistance to international negotiations under the Framework Convention on Climate Change (FCCC) to reduce global emissions of greenhouse gases.

While identifying important transnational cultural and political dimensions of Brazilian scientists' and policy makers' lifeworlds, this chapter challenges identifications of this "community" with cognitive and normative homogeneity. The identities of Brazilian actors participating in IPCC-related arenas are complex and hybrid, with important consequences for their interpretations of international science, the global environment, and their own agency. Some of their frameworks of understanding reflect the transnational nature of their professional networks. Other levels of understanding reflect the continued impact of history, geography and socio-economic realities. Among other things, Brazilian climate scientists and policy makers are keenly aware of structures of difference within international and transnational climate-related forums in which they participate, including conditions of inequality, reflecting the dominance of actors from richer countries ("the North").

Temptation to gloss over these persistent differences and unresolved tensions is considerable, not the least in the environmental arena where various actors—whether politicians, environmental activists, and academic scholars studying international regimes—seek to consolidate support for their visions of social reality and social change. Giving in to those temptations, however, may undermine rather than strengthen efforts to create a more just, sustainable world; universalizing discourses of science and the environment risk aggravating North-South relations around global environmental problems.[5] Institutions related to global environmental governance need to integrate more sophisticated understandings of the role of science in world affairs, including how power can operate through scientific processes. The interview data presented here may serve to nurture these more multidimensional and complex understandings.

Transnational Normative Convergence

The international community of climate scientists and policy makers exhibits some of the shared norms and beliefs identified by Haas as a key component of epistemic communities. Interviews with Brazilian scientists and policy makers produced expressions of concern about human-induced climate change, supporting the notion of cognitive convergence at the transnational level within the climate epistemic community. Brazilian climate-related affairs have been directed by a few key persons affiliated with the Brazilian Ministry of Science and Technology (MCT) and the Brazilian Ministry of External Relations ("Itamaraty"). I will refer to this group as the "MCT group," which has centrally shaped Brazil's official position on climate change in international negotiations.

In his first conversation with me, one of the two longest-standing and most central actors in the MCT group stated that he is "very concerned with climate change."[6] In numerous subsequent interviews he expressed frustration with national politicians' reluctance to engage with the issue and include it among more traditional policy issues.

A second, equally central and long-standing actor in the MCT group also accepted the idea that humans are altering the global climate and endorsed the policy framework under the FCCC. He strongly identified with the IPCC and its conclusions. For instance, he characterized as "insulting" (to himself and the IPCC as a whole) the fact that President George W. Bush chose to look to the US National Academy of Sciences (NAS) rather than the IPCC in assessing the threat of human-induced climate change, and even asked the NAS to reassess the conclusions and objectivity of the IPCC. This Brazilian found consolation in the fact that most of the scientists on the NAS panel evaluating the IPCC themselves are IPCC participants, implying that privileging US scientists over the IPCC failed to take into account the interpenetration of the two communities. Himself a distinguished scientist and IPCC participant, as well as a politically appointed overseer of climate research programs and policy making in Brazil, this actor epitomizes the difficulty of establishing any neat separation between "scientists" and "policy makers."

In interviews, Brazilian scientists involved with climate science and policy expressed concern about human-induced climate change. Arguing for ecological interdependence and the need to transcend narrowly nationalistic concerns, these actors expressed frustration with Brazilian politicians. Some described the latter as stuck in mindsets characterized by zero-sum thinking and national economic interests. "All the talk is about economics: 'What can we get out of this?' As if getting money out of it was the priority," one of them said about Brazilian political meetings convened to discuss climate change. Another regretted the fact that national politicians often "have the attitude that the developed countries got rich by polluting and therefore conclude 'So why can't we?!'" The Brazilian members of the climate epistemic community also wished that the Brazilian public as a whole would get more informed about the issue. One suggested that science courses in primary education do not sufficiently include environmental issues.[7]

In this way, these Brazilian actors appear to share a set of concerns and a policy agenda with their Northern counterparts (Lahsen 1998a,b; see also Boehmer-Christiansen 1994a,b). Part of the reason for convergence is sociocultural; Brazilian scientists' life worlds are intimately interlinked with those of scientists abroad, especially Europeans and Americans. During my interviews with Brazilian scientists, I sometimes found it difficult to steer the discussion away from US scientists and politicians and toward the Brazilian context. Many of these interviews conveyed a level of knowledge of central personalities in US science and politics surpassing that of many mid- and lower-level US scientists. The discussions thus reveal the globalizing trend whereby segments of societies—and especially "symbolic analysts" (Reich 1992) involved in problem solving, problem identifying, and other knowledge-brokering activities—increasingly are connected to their counterparts throughout the world. Through face-to-face interaction as they travel, and through communications networks, Brazilian climate scientists come to collaborate and interact more with fellow scientists abroad than with most of their domestic colleagues and fellow citizens.[8]

As posited by the epistemic community framework, Brazilian scientists have been important in pushing Brazilian political leaders to focus on the issue of climate change. Brazil's diplomatic position in international discussions about the global environment reflects a partial and on-going transformation from resistance to international environmental regimes to more openness and interest in the development of environmental science. Brazil led the opposition of less-developed countries (LDCs) to the first international environmental initiative, the 1972 United Nations Conference on the Human Environment in Stockholm, which helped to identify the biosphere as a legitimate object of national and international policy (Caldwell 1996, pp. 68, 101). An important subset of Brazil's political leaders changed course in the 1980s and the 1990s, gradually becoming more receptive to international negotiations about global environmental problems. This change in receptivity was both reflected in and reinforced by the country's hosting the first Earth Summit in 1992, the meeting that gave rise to the Framework Convention on Climate Change. Scientists I interviewed claimed to have stimulated this shift.[9] They initially alerted the Brazilian government to the importance of human-induced climate change and "pushed hard" for government attention to the issue and for the appointment of technically competent persons within the government to deal with the issue.

Brazilian Cohesion and International Fragmentation along the North-South Axis

Despite some level of cognitive and normative convergence within the transnational network of climate scientists and policy makers, profound differences also persist. This reality was belatedly impressed upon a US administrator of global change science. A key promoter of the focus on global environmental change in the United States and abroad, he was also an important force behind the creation of the Inter-American Institute (IAI). Based in Brazil, and so far funded predominantly by Northern institutions (especially the US National Science Foundation),[10] the IAI funds global change science projects involving Latin American scientists. In an interview, this science administrator (a Ph.D. environmental scientist) described how his assumption of mutual understanding and transnational fraternity was exposed as an illusion after years of collaboration with Latin American colleagues:

Ever since 1989, we have been building an Inter-American Institute. President Bush called for it at a meeting in 1990. There are now eighteen or so countries of the Americas that are members of the Inter-American Institute. And its purpose is global change research. The other day I heard something really interesting [*slight laugh*]. I do not even remember what precipitated it but somehow something came along and a person from one of the countries of the Americas—from Chile—after nine years of [being involved with] this, said "There it is! There is the US motive for IAI. I knew they were up to something, I knew there was a larger political motive. It took eight years, but now it has been revealed." It was actually a group of people from several countries, joined by Chile, who said that IAI was an American rip-off. Now, I was there from the word "go." I know the motives, I know every iota of thinking behind it. There is no conspiracy. There is no hidden purpose. There is no political agenda. [*Laughs*] It is basically altruistic as hell. But it was never ever perceived that way by the other players. These are friends of mine, people I have known for years, and I suddenly realized: oh my God, they have been sitting there in their respective countries, these pals of mine, wondering what devious thing I was up to.

This science administrator calls for greater attention to the "gulf" that exists among scientists from the North and the South, a gulf involving suspicions he described as "really startling—especially to scientists."

Cognitive differences among climate scientists and policy makers at the international level are rooted in national and political identities, cultural memories, and other aspects of personal experience. For Brazilian climate scientists and policy makers, experiences of colonialism and perceptions of continuities between the colonial past and present conditions in international science constitute one line of division. Brazilian scientists and politicians share certain framings of the climate problem and its attendant science and policy frameworks, and they are attuned to attempts to promote alternative framings of responsibility. Following other members of "the South" (Agarwal and Narain 1990; Mwandosya 2000), they typically frame the issue of responsibility in terms of historic contributions to the problem, and they prefer to discuss responsibility in terms of per capita emissions rather than national totals that penalize population size. Interviews with Brazilian scientists and environmental activists alike revealed resounding support for the Brazilian government's position, indicating strong national cohesion around this issue.

Nationalist sentiment is an important element in Brazilian positions on issues of responsibility related to climate change. Brazil has been identified by some as "Latin America's most nationalist country," even during "sell-out periods" (Adler 1987, p. 201). It is "one of those countries which, in spite of its liberal rhetoric and its rhetoric in favor of foreign capital, has systematically used its bargaining power, i.e. the bargaining power of its dominant classes, of its government technocracy, and of its national entrepreneurs, to resist. . . . Even if the national technocrats consider themselves transatlantic, consider themselves liberals, in practice they have increased State intervention, have increased the strength of State enterprises augmenting Brazil's political control" (Maria da Conceicao Taveres, in Adler 1987, p. 201).

As Brazilian scientists move around international and national arenas, they shift back and forth between different realities. As Brazilians and "Southerners" in the international climate regime, they tend to be suspicious not only of Northern-created science institutions such as the IAI but also of the science that those institutions support. A nationalist ethos, memories of colonialism, and awareness of continued inequity—in the world, generally, and in science more specifically—limit the extent to which Brazilian scientists and policy makers involved in the climate regime accept at least some Northern scientific interpretations of the global environment, along with the associated policy implications. These Brazilian actors portray international science—science legitimized by transnational expert networks—as biased by Northern framings and interests, and therefore not to be accepted at face value. They have witnessed how important framings associated with the Framework Convention were put in place by primarily Northern actors with little, if any, input from developing countries, yet with important unfavorable consequences for the latter. These framings and their implications for notions of responsibility in less developed nations have been widely discussed (see for instance Agarwal and Narain 1990; Biermann 2000; Jasanoff and Wynne 1998; Kandlikar and Sagar 1999; Miller 1998; Yearley 1996).[11]

Factors Reducing (Overt) Dissent

As evident in the US science administrator's comments on the IAI, mistrust can persist despite apparent agreement on scientific and normative matters. Material and socio-cognitive factors can contribute to this state of affairs that can, erroneously, be interpreted as an intersubjective consensus:

Scarcity of Resources

Scarce resources—of funding, time and expertise—limit the ability of poorer nations to contest points they may disagree with in international climate science and policy. One policy maker noted that he and his colleagues in Brazil "have no time" to contest issues in these forums ("if we direct too much time in that direction then we can't do our business in Brazil. We are very few. So we have to forget about this").

Poorer nations such as Brazil also have difficulty producing authoritative knowledge in the realm of climate modeling. Financial limitations translate into technical limitations, which in turn translate into limited ability to contest dominant constructions in science and policy. Up to the present, Brazil has been neither able nor inclined—given more pressing domestic problems and priorities—to invest the capital necessary to produce its own projections of future global climate changes and their socio-environmental impacts. The resources required to run the most complex computer-based numerical models that simulate the interactions between the atmosphere, oceans, and land-masses are so expensive that only relatively few countries and institutions can afford them. To the extent that poor nations and other actors resort to simpler models, they are disadvantaged by a value hierarchy within the climate sciences that privileges as more reliable output produced by complex models—a hierarchy some scholars have identified as possibly arbitrary and culturally biased (Lahsen 1998a; Shackley et al. 1998). The MCT group encountered this bias when presenting a policy proposal under the FCCC on the basis of what they acknowledged as a "rather radical simplification" of a model US scientists already considered too simple to qualify as a reliable policy tool.[12]

Interviews with Brazilian scientists repeatedly revealed a vague sense that, given sufficient resources, they and other LDC scientists might possibly develop knowledge of a different kind that could serve as a critical alternative to what is now known as "international science."[13]

Financial Interests and Needs

The political economy of climate science in Brazil may also serve to muffle dissent. Brazilian climate scientists depend on foreign institutions for an important part of the funding for their science. Moreover, they may fear foregoing invitations to participate in forums such as the IPCC if they become known as troublemakers. Participation in the IPCC confers prestige at the national levels and visibility at the international levels that can result in lucrative consulting assignments with both national and international governmental and non-governmental entities (e.g., the national oil company Petrobras, the World Bank, the US Pew Foundation, the US National Environmental Trust, and United Nations, among many others). Some Brazilian institutions allow funds from consulting services to be paid as supplements to university scientists' personal salaries, a particular attraction given the national freeze on civil servants' salaries since 1995 and the present weakness of the national currency.

Intimidation, Perceptions of Prejudice, and Lack of Voice

A third reason for superficial appearances of agreement is that LDC scientists do not always feel free to voice their differences with the preferred social order. In interviews, Brazilian scientists expressed perceptions of prejudice, which they sometimes related to cultural experiences of colonialism in Brazil. In the words of a policy maker associated with the MCT group:

When the Portuguese came to Brazil, in the 1500s, they gave mirrors to the Indians. They obliged them to cut the trees and took the wood back to sell in Portugal. And they gave mirrors in payment for cutting down the trees. They worked for the whole year cutting trees and then the Portuguese loaded up all the timber and gave them a few mirrors and that was it! And some metal axes to cut the trees that were more efficient. It is something like that [with the IPCC]! They always look to the third world like that. We are Indians, we don't know how to talk, we are not. . . . We don't know what we are doing. "Poor guys, forget about them." That's how people look at us.

This same policy maker repeatedly returned to difficulties rooted in language and to associated experiences of feeling intimidated or judged. He also contrasted my credibility with his own as follows: "[Y]ou are from the developed countries. So in this sense you have more credibility than the Indians. If I talk, I have no credibility!" To be sure, this policy maker was tall, and though his hair was dark and his skin olive in tone, he looked more like a "white" Southern European than an indigenous "Indian." Nevertheless, his remarks suggest the ways in which he experiences the role of race, ethnicity, and differential levels of national development in international science. He thus points to the existence of credibility economies (Shapin 1995) in which factors other than scientific merit are at play, affecting whose voices are heard and respected in international science.

In interviews and personal conversations with me, a number of Brazilian climate scientists expressed similar feelings of tokenism, prejudice, and bias in international science:

I think that there is a very big North American bias. I think these international programs are extremely elitist, you know, English-speaking scientists getting together.

But now, there is this awareness that you have to include the developing world. You can't make a global network of observations if you don't have Brazil chipping in money, Africa chipping in money, or whatever; you have to have these countries participate. But I feel that the participation is at a minimum. You're a token scientist. If you speak English, great, but. . . .

This speaker said that she often has the impression that her input as a participant in international forums is not taken seriously, making her feel like a token rather than a true participant. She also commented about international scientific projects with which she had been involved: "You might have science talk, but it is totally political." Such statements contrast with Merton's (1972, p. 270) account, according to which only knowledge that is international, impersonal, and "virtually anonymous" is sanctioned as true.

Science as Situated Knowledge: Distrust along a North-South Axis

Interviews revealed that Brazilian actors participating in the climate regime do not, as a rule, presume Northern science to be universal and disinterested. Policy makers largely responsible for formulating the official Brazilian position on climate change in international negotiations appeared particularly opposed to such a universalizing and depoliticized understanding of science. They suspect "foreign science" of advancing foreign interests. The existence of geopolitically structured suspicions suggests that norms and values are shared only to a limited extent. Intersubjectivity is strongly circumscribed, at best, in a context marked by such suspicions.

The discourses of Brazilian climate scientists reflect some distrust of international scientific institutions such as the IPCC, which they describe as dominated by Northern framings of the problems and therefore biased against the interpretations and interests of the South. The distrust is greater among politicians, but scientists without official political roles in the domestic context express similar views. For instance, a leading Brazilian climate scientist, who received his Ph.D. from a top US university, argued that scientific arguments benefiting only poor nations probably would not be influential within the United States nor, by extension, within the IPCC, which is dominated by US scientists. "Say, if it could be proven that only tropical forests remove atmospheric carbon dioxide while Boreal forests are a source of $CO2$, then I think the US would cut funding for carbon cycle studies of that source," he said.

At the time of my first round of field work in Brazil (April 1999), the IPCC was working on a report on the environmental impact of aviation and possible policy responses. A policy maker and two university-based scientists independently brought up this example as reflecting a Northern bias that they portrayed as prevalent within the IPCC. They themselves did not see aviation as a national problem, partly because of other more pressing socio-economic and environmental needs, partly because the average Brazilian flies little compared to the average Northern citizen. To the extent that aviation ought to be subjected to additional environmental regulation, they therefore supported more stringent measures than those adopted by the IPCC. Several interviewees suggested that the IPCC's weak response reflected Northerners' unwillingness to sacrifice the luxury of frequent flying.

After attending another Northern-designed and Northern-dominated international science meeting in May 2002,[14] one of these Brazilian scientists criticized what he perceived as an over-emphasis on sources of "black carbon." Black carbon is soot generated from outdoor fires and household burning of coal and biomass fuels, as well as polluting industrial activities and traffic. Black carbon emissions are particularly large in developing countries where wood, field residue, cow dung and coal are widely used for cooking and heating. At the meeting, the Brazilian scientist observed a large number of overheads used by Northern scientists to demonstrate the inefficiency of cooking stoves used in China and India. He wryly commented to me that "the same scientists go back to the US and drives a SUV just to transport himself" [*sic*], referring to the recent trend in the US towards highly inefficient fossil-fuel Sports Utility Vehicles for personal transport. In this way, this scientist evoked a normative framework that distinguishes between "luxury emissions" and "survival emissions" (Agarwal and Narain 1990).

In short, in many instances, Brazilian scientists and policy makers alike question the impartiality of "international" science and associated framings of responsibility. This distrust extends to international peer review processes as a whole. A policy maker in the MCT group who has participated in the FCCC negotiations, and also in the review of IPCC reports as an energy expert, expressed his preference for the FCCC on the grounds that it, unlike the IPCC, does not cover its politics behind a veil of pretended objectivity:

policy maker: I don't like the IPCC. I think it is too biased. Now, I would like to have a lot of new discussion about responsibility and attribution. As it is, all this game is dirty. The science is biased; it reflects their point of view [*voice turns heated*]. In all the working groups, if you have 90 percent of the people coming from the developed countries, it is bound to reflect their perspective. I am not saying that they have prior bad intentions. Both the IPCC and the FCCC are biased by governments. . . . It is very clear when it comes to the Convention. There are no misunderstandings there, no trying to convince people through the wrong methods, no trying to give certainty to several points of view that are completely biased. The IPCC, they make believe that their point of view is objective.

Lahsen: So you perceive them as using science disguised as being objective when it is really not?

policy maker: As a basis for political discussion at the Convention, yes. And using this to help arguments supporting their point of view. That is why we present our proposals directly to the Convention. Because it cannot go through the literature; they will not allow us. If we go through peer review, the peer reviewers will be part of IPCC and they all reject our proposal saying that we are doing junky literature, and so on. They will not approve our work. They will not allow our papers to get published in any scientific magazine. Because you have to go through a peer review process and they will say that this is junky science, that what we are doing is junky science because we are Indians and we do not know what we are talking about. That kind of thing.[15]

Perceptions of bias were also evident in interviews with other persons associated with the MCT group, including the Minister of Science and Technology under Fernando Henrique Cardoso. This group of policy makers within the Ministry of Science and Technology repeatedly cited a 1995 article in *Scientific American* (Gibbs 1995) in interviews with me. The article's discussion of inequities and prejudices in international science supports their perceptions of widespread Northern prejudice in international peer review processes. Among other things, the article documents how imperfect ability to communicate in English, combined with the fact of having a mailing address in a developing country, tend to undermine third world scientists in peer review processes.[16]

National Divisions

Brazilian climate scientists and policy makers may be united in their tendency to bring an interpretive framework shaped by experiences of bias and shared memories of colonialism to bear on climate science and politics. On other issues, however, they are themselves divided.

Particularly divisive among Brazilian scientists, policy makers and even environmental groups is the issue of deforestation. Brazil's deforestation trend has brought intense criticism on the Brazilian government abroad and at home. Much of the criticism has come from environmental NGOs and scientists. Recently, a coalition of over 25 NGOs in Brazil launched the Climate Observatory, a coalition designed to push the issue of deforestation to the center of climate discussions in Brazil. These groups have looked to climate change as an opportunity to strengthen forest conservation efforts, as deforestation accounts for two thirds of Brazil's national emissions of greenhouse gases.

By contrast, the Brazilian government, including (and sometimes represented by) the MCT group, has sought to minimize attention to deforestation. The Amazon has historically been viewed in Brazil as a resource in the nation's project to modernize and become a superpower and the region is invested with nationalist sentiments, as reflected in the often-evoked slogan by former Brazilian President José Sarney: "The Amazon is ours" (Barbosa 1993, p. 119; Kuehls 1996, p. ix; Rohter 2002). Important parts of the Brazilian government and many in the general population suspect foreigners of wanting to lay claim to the Amazon. Strongly opposed to foreign involvement around this issue, factions in the Brazilian government and population frame foreign concern about the deforestation of the Amazon in terms of national sovereignty, and conspiracy theories circulate widely in Brazilian society. Such theories—circulating as fact—posit that Americans students are taught to think of the Amazon region as an "international reserve" administered by the United Nations and that US Army forces are training to seize control of the region (see Rohter 2002).

In interviews, members of the MCT group dismissed such "black helicopter" conspiracy theories. However, the MCT group is keenly aware of the play of geopolitics in science. Given the role of both foreign and domestic scientists in pressuring the government on the issue of forest conservation, the MCT group has been circumspect in their use of scientists' estimates concerning carbon emissions resulting from land-use changes in Brazil. They portray national scientists as variously naïve about how international science perpetuates Northern interests and as strategically playing along with foreign interests in order to obtain research funds and to pressure the Brazilian government. As one person in the MCT group related to me, "Normally [both foreign and Brazilian] scientists are very biased in terms of policy; they use [science] to blame Brazil for misusing the Amazon forest."

To meet its commitment under the FCCC in the form of national inventories of its levels and sources of greenhouse gases, those within the MCT responsible for the effort sought to produce their own independent estimates of Brazilian emissions from deforestation. They resisted using estimates circulating in international science and assessment processes, referring to the latter as extrapolations made by scientists on the basis of limited, available data. They believe that both foreign and national scientists exaggerate the estimates of carbon emissions from deforestation.

The MCT group thus avoided use of estimates emanating from both the IPCC and the Large-Scale Biosphere Atmosphere (LBA) experiment, an international science project seeking to understand how the Amazon functions with respect to natural cycles of water, energy, carbon, trace-gases and nutrients, and how these processes may change due to future land-use and climate changes. In interviews, the MCT representative responsible for coordinating the inventories dismissed estimates emanating from the LBA as unreliable. The same person referred disapprovingly to the IPCC special report on land-use change, pointing to a subset of IPCC lead authors and contributing authors whose estimates of greenhouse gases he considered unreliable. This MCT interviewee considered Brazilian scientists who partook in that report similarly "political," since they had apparently accepted the foreign scientists' views—and in some cases even co-authored articles on the subject with some of these scientists.

Such lack of confidence in national scientists was also reflected in the fact that the Brazilian government under the Cardoso administration did not commonly ask non-MCT Brazilian scientists and IPCC participants—leading scientific experts on the issues—to partake in its review and critique of IPCC reports and summaries for policy makers. By contrast, other countries (e.g., the United States) include a broad base of national—and IPCC participating—scientists in the review process. It appears that the MCT suspects the national scientists in question to be too closely connected to the IPCC, and to international science generally, to perform "independent" review of the IPCC reports.

Faced with this attitude on the part of the MCT, the excluded Brazilian scientists criticize the MCT group for failing to recognize that they (the scientists) can be part of international science teams while remaining "critically independent," as one scientist put it. Some point out that they have influenced foreign and national scientists to lower their estimates of deforestation and to accept the MCT group's estimates of deforestation rates. As we see below, however, several Brazilians did recognize that participating in international science likely shapes their world views.

Personal Divisions—Self-Doubts

With Emanuel Adler, Haas has claimed to "regard learning as a process that has to do more with politics than with science, turning the study of politics process into a question about who learns what, when, to whose benefit, and why" (Adler and Haas 1992, p. 370). This rare and brief acknowledgment aside, however, Adler and Haas do not sufficiently recognize the influence of power and identity formation in shaping an epistemic community's shared normative and cognitive frameworks. Several Brazilian scientists revealed perceptions of such a knowledge/politics/power nexus, even to the point of revealing doubts about the validity and independence of their own scientific and normative assumptions. A Brazilian scientist's foreign education and continued professional connections even led him to question his own ability to represent the national interest:

You know, you can't escape the international invasion of science. . . . Its definition of future research agendas is bound to trickle down. And if you want to do state-of-the-art-stuff, you want to get involved with that—but it changes things. I am a biased subject because my education has been only in the US. So no matter how nationalist I am, I don't know. . . . Do you understand what I mean? There are a lot of interests that I try to defend in Brazil. But maybe my education doesn't allow me to see that [i.e., the Brazilian] side as well as I should.

It is significant that he retains such a critical perspective despite his US training and strong transnational personal and professional networks. When I asked the above scientist whether he really believes what he asserts, he responded with an emphatic "Yes," noting that national reactions to a new president of Brazil's central bank had prompted him to think about it. That president was educated in an Ivy League school and had worked for many years for the international investor George Soros. This scientist had heard some fellow Brazilians say that Brazil had thereby "given them over to the International Monetary Fund, that they just put this guy there who caters to the Americans." This led him to reflect:

. . . I was thinking about that—that we, scientists, are the same. We [Brazilian scientists educated in the US] get a vision of science in the US and we don't know how to do it any differently. Maybe my criteria are just American and I try to apply them to a Brazilian reality; there are these things, like the-way-you-do science paradigm and what you choose to focus on.

He then conjectured that maybe if I interviewed Brazilian scientists who were educated in Brazil, I would find them to have "a different view of how things should be conducted, or about global warming or the IPCC." After some thought, he concluded that Brazilian scientists who have not been educated abroad and who are not part of international science tend to study problems that are more local in nature.

The central member of the MCT group quoted repeatedly above was himself described by a different scientist and political appointee in the Brazilian government as shaped by Northern efforts to influence Brazilian affairs:

Governments work on bureaucracies. If you don't have some bureaucrats in place, it just doesn't work; they create a momentum. The United States, they are bad but not dumb. They gave money for the national inventories. So [the persons in the Brazilian government responsible for producing these reports], who didn't have much money from the Brazilian government, got one or two million dollars from the US government to do an inventory of emissions. [The person in charge of it] was delighted, you know. It's a career for him, you know!

In a globalizing world, complex subjectivities and the role of contexts in forming them render essentialism difficult; nationality cannot necessarily be equated with ability to represent a national point of view.

Conclusion

Much like the geopolitical constructs of "North" and "South," the epistemic community concept is useful. However, like the former, it must be used with care, with sustained attention to the important divisions they fail to capture and threaten to obscure. Rather than a single, cohesive, transnational "community" united by a shared professional ethos and by scientific and policy-related concerns, this study reveals a complex domain characterized by transnational networks and cognitive convergence, but also important differences. Persistent lines of division exist—sometimes under surface appearances of shared frameworks of understanding and policy action—testimony to the precarious and unstable nature of any apparent consensus on global environmental problems and the associated knowledge (Brosius 1999; Escobar 1999). Divisions continually replicate themselves as one looks from the transnational to the national and even the individual level. On second glance, not only does the transnational epistemic community appear internally fractured along geopolitical lines; important fractures also reveal themselves at the national level and even within the subjectivities of individual scientists, at the most intimate level of personal commitments and understandings of self and the world.

Even so, patterns appear in the fractures, conditioned by history and socio-economic realities. The scientists identify as Brazilians, as citizens of "the South" and of a formerly colonized country. They are transnational locals. They are more local than transnational, perhaps, in that their discourses consistently evoke the "North-South divide," even as they know themselves to have been intimately shaped by their foreign (overwhelmingly US) educations, work experiences, and associated personal relationships. The recurrence of the North-South construct in Brazilian scientists' discourses bears testimony to the reality glossed over by epistemic community theorists, namely, the extent to which climate science and geopolitical conditions co-produce each other. Privy to this insight, and less advantaged by the associated politics, Brazilian scientists and policy makers see the shadow side of universalizing discourses about science. Matters such as race, ethnicity, and level of development shape their understandings and experiences of international science, and they perceive prevailing international climate-related knowledge as typically reflecting developed ("Northern") countries' assumptions, agendas, and interests. Such perceptions, and the differences they reveal, add complexity to the dominant, purified images of science, representations that overlook important questions about the intersection of science, culture, power, and politics.

Notes

1. See, e.g., Agarwal and Narain 1990; Escobar 1995a; Goldman, this volume; Gupta 1998; Jasanoff 1996a; Jasanoff and Wynne 1998; Sachs 1993; Tsing 2000; Yearley 1996.

2. See the introduction to this volume.

3. About 70 interviews were conducted with scientists, science administrators, and policy makers in institutions in São Paulo, Rio de Janeiro, and Brasília. A first round of interviews took place in April 1999. The same persons—along with an additional set of new actors—were interviewed in 2002 over a period of eight months. The interviews were complemented by many informal discussions and participant observation when possible. The group of Brazilian policy makers and scientists discussed

in this paper is quite small. Anonymity has been preserved to the extent possible, and sources are generally not cited. The gender of interviewees has occasionally been altered, to conceal the identify of Brazilian female climate scientists, of whom there are just a few.

4. At the time of writing, Luiz Inácio Lula da Silva of the Workers' Party has been president for 7 months. Though the Lula government may provoke changes in the governmental structures and policies with a bearing on Brazil's position on climate change, no significant changes have happened at those levels yet.

5. See below. See also Yearley 1996 (especially p. 103) and Lahsen 2001.

6. I had in fact only expressed scholarly interest in understanding Brazilian engagements and concerns related to climate change.

7. This scientist did say that this is changing, however, that younger Brazilians do learn about climate change and ozone depletion and such things now in their text books, beginning in the fifth grade or so (that is, around the age of 11). So she attaches hope to the younger generations.

8. My field work identified members of the latter group who were not similarly transnationally connected nor regular participants in international science forums. They complained about not being able to break into these arenas and associated networks due to protective measures on the part of their Brazilian colleagues serving to retain the network and associated benefits to themselves, to be shared only with a select few students and colleagues.

9. Environmental groups are also widely credited with effecting this change (Torres 1997).

10. The plan is to gradually obtain an increasing level of financial support from developing countries themselves.

11. For instance, the IPCC's decision to include land-use driven changes in carbon stored in above-ground biomass as an anthropogenic source but to exclude similar changes in below ground biomass (soil carbon) as natural source was made without input from LDCs and unfavorable to them. The same was the case with the decision to include methane from rice agriculture and cattle and not from deer and other ruminants which exist in the North (the rationale being that the latter are "wildlife," despite the fact that they are managed populations) and with the lack of distinction between subsistence and luxury emissions and the prevalent method of calculating emissions in terms of national emissions rather than per capita emissions (Miller 1998).

12. I base this statement on years of fieldwork among US climate modelers during which I came to know this simple US model and the associated criticisms.

13. This applies to scientists partaking in Working Groups II and III of the IPCC (involved with impact assessment and mitigation and adaptation measures) rather than in Working Group I, the group devoted to the natural science.

14. The meeting was headed by US scientists and involved five key IPCC members, one of whom was an advisor to President George W. Bush. The meeting involved roughly 80 scientists, roughly 70 of them from "the North."

15. All this is expressed with raised voice, indicating frustration and strong feelings on the subject.

16. Particularly revealing of the kind of bias was the comment by an editor for *Science*. When asked about his editorial practices, this editor noted that articles with imperfect English submitted for publication weren't likely to be published: if they make mistakes in English one would suspect that they are similarly sloppy in their science, he said.

References

Adler, Emanuel. 1987.*The Power of Ideology: The Quest for Technological Autonomy in Argentina and Brazil*. University of California Press.

Agarwal, A., and S. Narain. 1990. *Global Warming in an Unequal World: A Case of Environmental Colonialism*. Centre for Science and Development, New Delhi.

Barbosa, Luiz C. 1993. "The 'Greening' of the Ecopolitics of the World-System: Amazonia and Changes in the Ecopolitics of Brazil." *Journal of Political and Military Sociology* 21, no. 1 (): 107–334.

Biermann, Frank. 2000. Science as Power in International Environmental Negotiations: Global Environmental Assessments Between North and South. Discussion paper, Environment and Natural Resources Program, Belfer Center for Science and International Affairs, John F. Kennedy School of Government, Harvard University.

Boehmer-Christiansen, Sonja. 1994a. "Global Climate Protection Policy." *Global Environmental Change* 4, no. 2: 140–159.

Boehmer-Christiansen, Sonja. 1994b. Global Climate Protection Policy. *Global Environmental Change* 4, no. 3: 185–200.

Brosius, J. Peter. 1999. "Analyses and interventions: Anthropological Engagements with Environmentalism." *Current Anthropology* 40, no. 3, June: 277–309.

Caldwell, Lynton Keith. 1996. *International Environmental Policy: From the Twentieth to the Twenty-First Century*. Duke University Press.

Enzenberger, Hans-Magnus. 1974. "A Critique of Political Ecology." *New Left Review* 84: 3–31.

Escobar, Arturo. 1995. *Encountering Development: The Making and Unmaking of the Third World*. Princeton University Press.

Escobar, Arturo. 1999. "Comments." *Current Anthropology* 40, no. 3: 291–293.

Fearnside, Philip M. 2001. "Saving Tropical Forests as a Global Warming Countermeasure: An Issue that Divides the Environmental Movement." *Ecological Economics* 39, no. 2, November: 167–184.

Gibbs, W. Wayt. 1995. "Lost Science in the Third World." *Scientific American*, August: 92–99.

Gieryn, Thomas. 1983. "Boundary-Work and the Demarcation of Science from Non-Science: Strains and Interests in Professional Ideologies of Scientists." *American Sociology Review* 48: 781–795.

Gieryn, Thomas. 1995. "Boundaries of Science." In *Handbook of Science and Technology Studies*, ed. S. Jasanoff et al. Sage.

Gupta, Akhil. 1998. *Postcolonial Developments: Agriculture in the Making of Modern India*. Duke University Press.

Guston, David H. 1999. "Stabilizing the Boundary between US Politics and Science: The Role of the Office of Technology Transfer as a Boundary Organization." *Social Studies of Science* 29, no. 1: 1–25.

Haas, Peter M. 1992. "Introduction: Epistemic Communities and International Policy Coordination." *International Organization* 46, no. 1: 1–35.

Jasanoff, Sheila. 1987. "Contested Boundaries in Policy-Relevant Science." *Social Studies of Science* 17: 195–230.

Jasanoff, Sheila. 1992. "Review of Ezrahi." *American Political Science Review* 86: 233–234.

Jasanoff, Sheila. 1996. "Science and Norms in Global Environmental Regimes." In *Earthly Goods*, ed. F. Hampson and J. Reppy. Cornell University Press.

Jasanoff, Sheila, and Brian Wynne. 1998. "Science and Decisionmaking." In *Human Choice and Climate Change Volume One*, ed. S. Rayner and E. Malone. Batelle.

Kandlikar, Milind, and Ambuj Sagar. 1999. "Climate Change Research and Analysis in India: An Integrated Assessment of a South-North Divide." *Global Environmental Change* 9: 119–138.

Lahsen, Myanna. 1998a. "The Detection and Attribution of Conspiracies: The Controversy over Chapter 8." In *Paranoia within Reason*, ed. G. Marcus. University of Chicago Press.

Lahsen, Myanna. 1998b. Climate Rhetoric: Constructions of Climate Science in the Age of Environmentalism. Ph.D. thesis, Rice University.

Lahsen, Myanna. 2001. Brazilian Epistemers' Multiple Epistemes: An Exploration of Shared Meaning, Diverse Identities, and Geopolitics, in Global Change Science. Discussion paper, Environment and Natural Resources Program, Belfer Center for Science and International Affairs, John F. Kennedy School of Government, Harvard University.

Merton, Robert K. 1973 (1942). "The Normative Structure of Science." In *The Sociology of Sciences*, ed. N. Storer. University of Chicago Press.

Miller, Clark. 1998. Extending Assessment Communities to Developing Countries. Discussion paper, Environment and Natural Resources Program, Belfer Center for Science and International Affairs, John F. Kennedy School of Government, Harvard University.

Mwandosya, Mark J. 2000. *Survival Emissions: A Perspective from the South on Global Climate Change Negotiations*. Dar es Salaam, Tanzania: DUP (1996) LIMITED and The Center for Energy, Environment, Science and Technology (CEEST-2000).

Reich, Robert B. 1992. *The Work of Nations*. Vintage Books.

Sachs, Wolfgang, ed. 1993. *Global Ecology: A New Arena of Political Conflict*. Zed Books.

Schoijet, Mauricio, and Richard Worthington. 1993. "Globalization of Science and Repression of Scientists in Mexico." *Science, Technology, and Human Values* 18, no. 2: 209–230.

Shackley, Simon, Peter Young, Stuart Parkinson, and Brian Wynne. 1998. "Uncertainty, Complexity and Concepts of Good Science in Climate Change Modelling: Are GCMs the Best Tools?" *Climatic Change* 38: 159–205.

Shapin, Stephen. 1995. "Cordelia's Love: Credibility and the Social Studies of Science." *Perspectives on Science* 3: 255–275.

Torres, Blanca. 1997. "Transnational Environmental NGOs: Linkages and Impact on Policy," in *Latin American Environmental Policy in International Perspective*, ed. G. MacDonald et al. Westview.

Tsing, Anna. 2000. "The Global Situation." *Cultural Anthropology* 15, no. 3: 327–360.

Yearley, Steven. 1996. *Sociology, Environmentalism, Globalization.* Sage.

7

Localizing Global Change in Germany

Silke Beck

German environmental politics has historically been a politics of the local. It derives its power from local resistance against the destruction of particular landscapes and threats to particular livelihoods. The German response to climate change, however, took place in an era of growing awareness of the borderless nature of environmental problems and the transnational dimension of environmental science and politics. New emerging international organizations such as the Intergovernmental Panel on Climate Change (IPCC) and the Conferences of Parties under the Framework Convention on Climate Change (FCCC) promote cross-national convergence and uniformity, since they expand the base of common knowledge about global change and make limited standard setting efforts. Yet the German adjustment to global change indicates that the "same," allegedly universal scientific knowledge can lead to divergent regulatory decisions, even in economically and politically very similar countries (Brickman et al. 1985).

This chapter demonstrates the "localness" of the national response to global change, and argues that the tensions inside the "local" can be explained in relation to the national political culture.

Germany used the distinctive mechanism of two parliamentary Enquete Commissions to translate climate change into a national policy issue. It may seem strange to describe national assessments as constituting a kind of "locality" just when German science and politics were trying to establish themselves as "forerunners" (that is, proactive shapers) of international science and politics. However, this approach usefully contrasts with conventional framings of "localness" as primitive, unscientific and the product of "underdevelopment." While reframing global concerns to fit within national circumstances, both commissions were forced to anticipate political controversies and arrive at closure.

The first Enquete Commission (ECI), on "Preventive Measures to Protect the Earth's Atmosphere" (Vorsorge zum Schutz der Erdatmosphäre), was asked to assess the state of research on global changes to the earth's atmosphere, define the nature and extent of the CO_2 problem, and propose possible action. The second commission (ECII), on "Protection of the Earth's Atmosphere," was asked to develop strategies and measures for implementing the conclusions of the first. At first glance, the two commissions appear to stand for contradictory philosophies of the global and the local, with ECI apparently favoring the push of globalization and ECII succumbing to the pull of localization. I show in this chapter, however, that both commissions responded to local political contingencies, ruling out any simplistic distinction between the transformative role of ECI and the reactionary response of ECII.

The "localness" of the German assessments had much to do with their relation to the national political culture. The commissions interpreted global concerns in light of local perspectives, and thereby echoed and reinforced fundamental features of German political culture even when they appeared to transcend them.

Studying the assessments and regulatory activities on climate change in light of German political culture helps not only to illustrate its "localness" but also to highlight some of the problems and limitations of globalizing environmental science and policy. Some of the problems that surfaced during the IPCC assessment processes and the FCCC negotiations are symptomatic of tensions that are bound to arise as pressures for global harmonization collide with deep-seated differences about the proper roles of experts and the proper forms of state intervention in environmental policy making.

Localizing Climate Change in National Assessments

In Germany, two parliamentary Enquete Commissions became the nationally recognized sources of expertise and formed the national response to climate change, especially in the early years of policy making. Charged with translating international assessments to the national context, the commissions faced the challenge of regionalizing impacts, defining local "vulnerability," and developing national response strategies to global climate change. By comparing the German assessments with international ones, we observe distinct national features that illustrate their "localness."

An "Impending Climate Catastrophe"

As in other countries, scientists were the first to raise the issue of climate change in Germany. Two distinct features characterize this period. First, German scientists paid little attention to climate change for quite a while, and trailed behind developments in the US. International activities and events—especially the first World Climate Conference—alarmed German scientific and political communities. The leading research organizations, such as the Max Planck Gesellschaft (MPG) and the Deutsche Forschungsgemeinschaft (DFG), as well as the German government reacted by designing R&D-support schemes and by initiating a national climate research program to bring German science up to date with international developments (Borchers et al. 1997). Second, right from the start German scientists emphasized the political relevance of their findings.

In 1986, interest in climate change increased dramatically. German scientists had by then caught up with the international debate. They also played a prominent role in raising the profile of this issue. A subgroup of the Deutsche Physikalische Gesellschaft, the Study Group on Energy, published a paper titled "Warning of an Impending Climate Catastrophe" which presents a particular interpretation of global climate change (Weingart et al. 2000). First, in contrast to international assessments, the Study Group focused only on negative impacts of climate change leading to extremely severe damage. Second, it strongly promoted proactive policies to protect the climate. This was a change from earlier practice. Whereas in the early stage, German scientists had followed the same pattern as in the United States, and defined the issue as a matter of scientific observation, now they turned it into a political problem that had to be made the subject of regulatory policy. Unlike US climate skeptics, they used scientific uncertainty not to justify a wait-and-see approach and to call for sound science, but to legitimize immediate action. Third, the Study Group not only dramatized the "CO_2 problem" as the "climate catastrophe," but also linked it to the question of future energy policy. The group tried to take advantage of the continuing scientific debate on climate change by using it to promote nuclear energy as a clean, CO_2-free source of energy. This approach had deep impacts on the issue's political dynamics, since climate change then became coupled to one of the most polarized controversies in Germany.

The dramatization of the issue by famous scientists raised public and political concern about climate change and set the stage for a particular perception of global warming. The warning received immediate attention from the media. The text was published in the *Frankfurter Rundschau* (no. 217, September 19, 1986). The weekly news magazine *Der Spiegel* put the picture of a half-submerged Cologne cathedral on its cover, creating one of the symbols of climate change in Germany. The drowning cathedral made visible the national vulnerability to climate change. It represented extreme events such as floods in several German river basins, especially the Rhine basin, as impacts of climate change, and it claimed that the frequency of these events had dramatically increased, and, as a result, mankind had already arrived in the greenhouse world.

As an immediate response to the growing attention given to climate change, in November 1987 the German parliament (Bundestag) established, with the general consent of all of the political parties represented, an Enquete Commission on "Preventive Measures to Protect the Earth's Atmosphere." The first Enquete Commission (ECI) was given the task of assessing the state of research on global changes of the Earth's atmosphere, and of preparing national and international *precautionary* measures to protect the environment. In 1991, a second Enquete Commission, on "Protection of the Earth's Atmosphere," succeeded the first one. The second Enquete Commission (ECII) was to continue ECI's analysis, provide recommendations for its implementation, and prepare the national proposal for the 1992 Rio Conference on Environment and Development.

The Institutional Structure of Enquete Commissions

Since 1969, the German parliament has had the right to establish an Enquete Commission on any issue deemed urgent and as requiring expert advice. Like other advisory bodies, the Enquete Commissions are charged with translating complex scientific information into a knowledge base that policy makers could use as a basis for decision making (Ismayr 1998). In contrast to intergovernmental bodies such as the IPCC, however, the Enquete Commissions can play an additional role: their task is not only to assess and interpret state-of-the-art knowledge but also to provide policy recommendations. The commissions may function not only as generators and interpreters of scientific expertise, but also as a "mini-legislature" anticipating parliamentary decisions. In the German political system, the task of legitimating regulatory policy is often delegated to the Enquete Commissions. As hybrid science-policy bodies, like the IPCC, the Enquete Commissions face the challenge of reconciling democratic values with the need for expert decision making (Roqueplo 1995). As a result, the Enquete Commissions have to cope with the challenges of simultaneously gaining scientific credibility and political acceptability. The Enquete Commissions ensure their political acceptability and efficacy by meeting criteria of *breadth* and *inclusiveness* in their assessment processes. They often include experts with broader and less specialized competence. Experts can be representatives of industrial federations (Verbände), or of the NGOs, which came to play an important role in giving advice on technical matters and in setting standards. An Enquete Commission's expertise is expected to be binding, because the group as a whole is capable of speaking for the wider community it represents. The Enquete Commissions are thus thought to reflect in microcosm a cross-section of the society which will be affected by its policy advice. Participation also enhances the political efficacy of policy recommendations. In order to avoid conflicts with industry, for example, representatives of major companies are brought on board right from the start.

The Enquete Commissions play a particular role in German parliamentary process. Experts who have not been elected democratically are given an equal voice with parliamentarians in approving assessment reports. At the same time, their policy recommendations are not legally binding for parliament. Yet it is important for the commissions to promote consensual statements in order to play an influential role in policy making. As a result, they also have to manage and resolve both technical and political conflicts latent in scientific controversies. Claiming neutrality and independence from sectarian interests, expert advisory bodies are also thought to provide a forum where people from different perspectives and world views can be brought together and can set aside their differences in favor of a common, rationalistic approach to problem solving. Problems of uncertainty and expert conflict, however, tend to reduce the power of science as a "harmonizing force." Under these conditions, one of the main challenges for the Enquete Commissions is to orchestrate a policy-relevant, scientific consensus that secures their status as the single most authoritative source of information.

Protecting the Global Atmosphere and Protecting National Interests

It is usually thought that the role of expert advisory bodies is to achieve technical consensus in order to facilitate policy development. The two Enquete Commissions, however, did much more: they reframed global concerns to fit within national circumstances. Moreover, although both succeeded in closing scientific controversy, their policy recommendations were strikingly different. To understand these features, I will look more closely at each commission's practices.

The first Enquete Commission was able to bring about the closure of the scientific debate in a field which had become controversial in many ways. It developed different approaches toward keeping controversies between experts within bounds and toward managing the latent political conflicts. First, ECI tried to coordinate national and international assessment efforts and to integrate different bodies of research. Second, ECI initiated a research program. In relation to previous commissions, the scientific input was extraordinary in terms of its extent and comprehensiveness. ECI succeeded not only in integrating a large number of German research institutes (including the skeptical ones) into the assessment process, but also in forcing mainstream German science to provide a consensual assessment of the state of knowledge, and to broaden consensus within the scientific community. Third, ECI and ECII adopted a step-by-step approach. In the first step, they prepared assessment reports on the "facts" (Sachteil) laying out the state of research on the causes and impacts of changes in the atmosphere. In the second step, they approved policy recommendations. The purpose was to separate "diagnosis" from "prescription." This approach proved to be very valuable for both, developing a consensual knowledge base and resolving conflicts on what kind of scientific evidence is acceptable to justify political measures. ECI reached an agreement that climate science had provided enough knowledge to initiate abatement measures. In this way, it was able to set the stage for the shift from risk-benefit standards of environmental protection to the precautionary principle.[1]

Both Enquete Commissions noted that scientific uncertainty could become a resource in politics, and could be distorted in opposite directions by different interest groups. They used the step-by-step-approach to prevent political opponents of climate regulation from transferring political conflicts into the scientific arena by deconstructing scientific claims and mobilizing divergent interpretations of the evidence. In this way, the Enquete Commissions successfully averted a controversy on the "science of climate change." Thus, they were able to partly prevent climate skeptics from transforming the politics of climate change into a battle over truth and focusing on the epistemology of modeling, just as in the US. As a result, opponents of immediate action could not use scientific uncertainties as a rationale for shunting funds and attention back to "basic" research, or for denying the validity of climate change projections in Germany. Last, but not least, this approach was crucial, especially for ECI, in securing the confidence in "sound" climate science, and in warranting its status as the primary resource for addressing ecological challenges and legitimating regulatory decisions.

When it came to translating the diagnosis into a policy recommendation, however, both Enquete Commissions had to deal with issues (such as energy and transport), which had become strongly politicized in German politics since the 1970s. In addition, the work of ECII led to particular problems. While ECI determined the definition of the problem, as well as the general direction of action, ECII had to develop specific strategies and concrete measures for implementing ECI's framework.

As regards the recommendations in detail, there are remarkable differences between the two Enquete Commissions. ECI in general upheld the frame of climate change as a global environmental risk (Miller and Edwards 2001). Analogous to international bodies, like the IPCC, it highlighted the Earth's fragility and ecological interconnectedness, as well as a concern for preserving the biosphere's limited resources. ECI endorsed the understanding of the Earth as "one world," thus reinforcing the idea that, when it comes to the ecological crisis, "we are all in the same boat," and called for global solutions. It also declared the urgent need to act immediately. In the line with this framing of climate change, ECI proclaimed a target of reducing Germany's CO_2 emissions no less than 30 percent. It defined climate change as part of what is called ecological modernization (Hajer 1996). According to this paradigm, policies for mitigating climate change must reach into a broad range of economic and social activities, from agriculture and forestry to the most central sectors of industrial production and private consumption, such as transport and energy. It also suggested that traditional muddling through is insufficient to reach such ambitious targets and called for fundamental changes, embracing not only the restructuring of central economic sectors, but also individual behavior.

ECII, however, reframed the issue of climate change—in effect by converting it from a "global" to a "local" concern. The conservative coalition, which had the majority in parliament, used its power to select experts to ensure its dominance over ECII. Moreover, the coalition began to recruit experts from industry and interest groups. The new chairman, Klaus Lippold (CDU), was active in an industrial federation, and maintained close ties to the chemical industry. Parliament also nominated a lobbyist for the automobile concern Mercedes-Benz and appointed a further expert affiliated with the nuclear industry (Bals 1994; Ganseforth 1996). In contrast to ECI, representatives of the Green Party and NGOs did not participate in ECII. By nominating stakeholders, the conservative coalition offered them opportunities not only to lobby from the "outside," but also to gain access to ECII and to influence it from the "inside," thus opening the door for the culture of neocorporatist conflict.[2] Stakeholders recognized ECI's important role as a virtual "mini-legislature," and had great interest in participating in a body which they perceived as anticipating political decisions immediately.

The alliance between the conservative coalition and industrial stakeholders and lobby groups was built to undermine ECI's far-reaching policy targets and to block environmental reformism. Thus, ECII began to redefine global climate change from a field of international solidarity to one of national competition and to place concerns about Standort Deutschland (the competitive position of German economy) and the nation's survival in a globalizing world at the forefront of the political discussion. In this way, it succeeded in restoring the primacy of national interest politics, which continues to determine the German response to climate change. The alliance also changed the acceptable justification of policy measures from scientific evidence to economic criteria, demanding that policy would have to be justified in terms of its "cost neutrality." This strategy offered the starting point for undermining central elements of the paradigm of ecological modernization by polarizing ecological and economic goals and by presenting the former one as a "job killer" and as a "cost factor." Finally, it performed the shift from fundamental institutional and individual change to "business as usual."

The Political Function of the Enquete Commissions

Each commission decided to resolve controversial questions in ways that reflected the majority view of the political function of the assessment. ECI was committed to providing not only far-reaching, but also consensual rec-ommendations in order to play a constructive role in politics and decision making. Consistent with its willingness to make comprehensive recom-mendations, ECI was dedicated to open and dynamic communication processes. ECII, however, sought to delay extensive regulatory action by undermining its justification through common expert statements. Thus, ECII shifted from communication to confrontation and competition and used the commission as a forum for political bargaining.

The controversy on energy illustrates these different views of the polit-ical function of assessment. The two Enquete Commissions were at odds regarding the role to be played by nuclear energy in climate policy. The research program initiated by ECI revealed the contrary positions in pre-vious debates on nuclear energy. While other advisory committees focused on the controversial question of nuclear energy (and failed), ECI decided to postpone these potential conflicts in favor of arriving at a consensus for a clear and far-reaching emission reduction target. The alliance between the conservative coalition and stakeholders dominating ECII, however, tried to transfer political controversies into the assessment process. It used the commission as a forum for emphasizing differences and promoting contradicting policy targets, resulting in a deadlock on energy policy. In sum: the two Enquete Commissions played different roles in policy mak-ing. While ECI proved able to absorb the new issue and to virtually act as a "mini-legislature," ECII seems mainly to have served as a forum for displaying political controversies predetermined by particular political interests.

By making policy recommendations, both Enquete Commissions had to moderate deep-seated differences between political parties. Both had to cope with controversies that reflected deeper political cleavages among political parties about the boundaries of state intervention. While the Conservatives leaned toward deregulation and the self-controlling forces of the market, the Red-Green wing opted for an active role for the state and preferred political intervention. The policy statements of the Enquete Commissions represent the extremes of political choice, swaying between ECI's ambitious national target on the one hand and ECII's preference for the incremental implementation of this target on the other. The need to anticipate controversies and arrive at closure made both Enquete Commissions vulnerable to political pressure and led to ambivalent and interpretively flexible conclusions. ECI, for example, tried to promote a strong and clear-cut reduction target. At the same time, it was reluctant to translate the scientific knowledge base into a concrete policy scenario. It remained very vague on the human dimensions of global change; it was careful about attributing the causes of manmade change to nations and economic sectors; and it did not explicitly assign responsibilities to particular social actors and groups. ECII's policy proposals are generally more vague, have many more caveats than ECI's statements and are written in noncommittal language.

Assessments: Sites of Transformation, or Restoration?

What role did the Enquete Commissions play in relation to German political culture? Did they interpret global concerns so as to transform national politics, or did they simply restore local perspectives in assessing the global problem?

The first Enquete Commission contributed to maintaining a cycle of symbiotic, reciprocal interplay between science and politics. In German political culture, science and politics are traditionally seen as relatively autonomous, distinct systems operating according to their own criteria of rationality. Continuing to regard *science as autonomous*, climate research programs were structured by scientific self-organization and academic disciplines. German scientists were also relatively reluctant to get involved in national and international assessment bodies. ECI came to play an important role in bridging the gap between scientists and politicians by initiating communication between them. ECI was also instrumental in broadening commitment to its knowledge claims within the scientific community.

ECI was not only instrumental in forcing scientific and political closure, but also in accelerating decision making by intensively communicating with Parliament and the ministries, especially the Ministry of Environment led by Klaus Töpfer. ECI's findings were translated into parliamentary decision making and set the stage for a short phase of lively political activity in the early 1990s. Moreover, even before ECI published its own policy recommendations, including the national reduction target, in June 1990, the German government adopted the precautionary principle for the national response to climate change and finalized the target of a national 25 percent reduction of CO_2 emissions (Kords 1996).

ECI also played an important role in raising and stabilizing the issue in public discourses. Indeed, ECI contributed to setting the stage for national consensus on the "climate catastrophe" (a peculiarly German framing of the issue; see Weingart et al. 2000). As a result, the overwhelming majority of Germans did not doubt the existence of global warming and its dangerous impacts, and were willing to accept the ambitious national reduction target.

The pattern of interactions between ECII and political parties as well as other social actors changed radically during the second assessment process. As within the commission, the pattern of political communication also shifted from cooperation to competition and bargaining. At first, Parliament, empowered by ECI, gained a degree of influence on policy making that was rare in its history. When the government realized the independent role Parliament was beginning to play, it changed its tactics from cooperative to competitive strategies. It tried to take the lead in the regulatory process by transferring advisory and decision-making powers from the Parliament to the executive. It sought to keep the knowledge base for regulation under its own control in order to prevent specific regulatory issues from gaining high political priority. The strategy of insulating the regulatory process undermined the role and authority of ECII in particular and of parliament in general.

A simple comparison between ECI and ECII might prompt us to draw a sharp contrast between ECI as a site of transformation and ECII as a site of restoration of traditional German political culture. This, however, would be misleading. To avoid simple conclusions, we should take the political climate, the constellation of power, and the broader context of the state-society relationship into account.

ECI appeared to transcend the traditional politics of expertise in Germany in several ways: through its framing of climate change as a global environmental risk; through its advocacy of ecological modernization; through its openness to a wide range of political actors; and through its open and dynamic pattern of interaction inside and outside the commission. Yet the political and public resonance of ECI's assessments can be traced to historical patterns of environmental politics in Germany. In the early 1980s, Waldsterben (forest death) and acid rain enjoyed high priority on public agendas. After the Chernobyl accident in 1986, the German public was particularly sensitive to environmental dangers and felt directly vulnerable to them (Betroffenheit). French observers, for example, are inclined to say that environmental problems, especially "le Waldsterben," originated in Germany (Roqueplo 1995). ECI's work reflects the political climate of the second half of the 1980s, which proved to be a "golden age" of environmental politics. Since the oil crises of 1973–74 and 1978–79, the idea of conserving energy and using alternative energy sources, such as solar and wind power, had grown in popularity. In the 1980s, the paradigm of ecological modernization dominated political discussion. The widespread demand for comprehensive policy action can partly be attributed to the role the state traditionally plays in German political culture. It is generally accepted as the addressee for the rational solution of problems, as well as for the integration of centrifugal social forces. In keeping with this expectation, the government's approach to decision making is, as a rule, primarily proactive (Richardson et al. 1982). These historically entrenched patterns partially account for the relatively uncontested acceptance of ECI's recommendations.

ECI sought a broad scientific and political consensus, and, through perseverance, was able to arrive at results which were accepted by a wide spectrum of political and social actors. Influential scientific organizations, the parliament, the government, the administration, and even industry all tried to speak with "one voice." This political convergence can be read as a symptom of Germany's strongly consensus-oriented political culture. Open resistance to climate protection would immediately have led to a loss of credibility. This feature of German political culture is partly grounded in the legal tradition of "The Rule of Law" (Rechtsstaat), which requires unambiguous and unequivocal statements (Eindeutigkeit). In addition, the demand for consensual solutions can be traced to the structure of the political system. After World War II, the West German parliamentary system was organized according to the principles of coalition government and cooperative federalism, which also reinforced the preference for consensual solutions.

The second assessment process, by contrast, took place during an era of historically contingent, singular transformations, such as German reunification. From that time, "traditional" social issues and economic concerns began to dominate the agenda, and environmental issues increasingly lost their political prominence (Huber 1997, p. 65; Kords 1996, p. 209). Furthermore, a backlash set in, directed particularly against one of the symbols of German environmental policy, Waldsterben. Climate change became, at best, a marginal issue in German politics. In addition, the influence of the Green party declined rapidly in German politics. In 1990, in the first election after reunification, the Green party lost a large number of seats in the Bundestag. The West German Greens failed to gain the 5 percent of votes needed to enter the parliament, and only the Eastern German party Bündnis 90 acquired the status of a minority group in parliament. These transformations partly explain why ECII came to play only a marginal role in German politics.

The transfer of the regulatory process from parliament to the executive was also significant. Politically insulated governmental officials sought to work with informal procedures and flexible control strategies. They were able to make the necessary deals and compromises without being subjected to parliamentary control or required to present reasoned justification in public. The executive in this respect simply regained the relative independence as a decision maker that it historically has enjoyed in the German political system. In Germany, Parliament regularly confirms the broad outlines of policy through legislation and places the details of implementation at the executive's discretion. Since parliaments have neither the means nor incentives for exercising effective post-legislative control, such as in the US, the German executive enjoys considerable independence in implementing policies recommended by the parliament (Brickman et al. 1985, p. 305).

The government's strategy of insulating the regulation process not only marginalized the ECII politically but restored one of the most typical features of German political culture. Free to organize access with relatively few statutory constraints, German regulators decided in favor of a confidential process of consultation with stakeholders. They granted representatives of industry—the Association of the German Power Stations (VDEW) and two economic research institutes—special access to the regulatory process on climate change. These interest groups typically sought to influence policy by cultivating a good relationship to bureaucracy.

The ambivalence of the commissions' recommendations can also be traced to general features of the German regulatory process. At first glance, the German government seems to have enacted a broad legislative framework for promoting CO_2 reduction. Yet this framework cannot be characterized as legislation in the strict sense of the term, because the national target was implemented neither by law and regulatory standards nor by economic instruments. Instead of threatening legal enforcement, the government communicated with industry and tried to convince companies to prepare for reduction as soon as possible. The government passed a declaration of intent, to which the Federation of German industry (BDI) responded by announcing voluntary obligations to reduce CO_2 emissions. Stakeholders also succeeded in transferring implementation from the government to industry. This result partly reflects conscious attempts on the part of industry to influence the political "rules of the game" to their own advantage. Compliance was achieved in the neocorporatist mode by bargaining and behind-the-scenes negotiation between corporations and government. The pattern of stakeholder participation in the second assessment process parallels the interactions between ECII and the political and social actors in the broader context of state-society relationships. These processes of neocorporatist bargaining (and the decentralized federal system) reinforced political inertia and thereby widened the gap between the targets and the efforts for their implementation (Huber 1997).

The Global and the Local

We have seen that German conceptions of the role of experts in politics and of the role of the state played a major part in national climate assessment and policy making. They also matter in international assessments and negotiations.

The Ambivalence of the "Forerunner" Strategy

The relationship of German scientists to the IPCC reflected deep-seated national views of the proper role of scientists in policy making. In keeping with science's self-conception as being autonomous, scientists seldom participated in hybrid science-policy panels such as the IPCC. During the formation of the IPCC from 1986–1988, for example, the German climate community did not visibly contribute to these activities. Only two German scientists (Hermann Flohn and Hartmut Grassl) attended the first meetings of the IPCC. Furthermore, at first, German scientists and politicians were occupied with catching up to international research instead of shaping it; the integration of the climate issue into national science and politics nevertheless was conceived with the aim of positioning Germany as a "forerunner" in international negotiations. German government officials, for example, preferred to establish their own scientific facilities and advisory bodies in order to improve the state's own capabilities and increase its independence from transnational institutions.

ECI provided some of the incentives for German scientists to participate in the IPCC. As we have seen, ECI played an important role in bridging the gap between scientists and politicians by initiating communication and by broadening consensus within the scientific community. By translating scientific findings into a knowledge base for policy making, both commissions helped to demonstrate the political relevance of scientific findings and partially protected scientists doing basic research from political pressure and demands. ECI, in particular, treated the problem of scientific uncertainty and its translation into the political arena carefully in order to minimize the risk of politicization and to restore the view of science as "univocal."

During the negotiation phase in preparation for the Rio Summit, the IPCC faced considerable pressure from many oil-exporting countries and special interest groups such as the US fossil-fuel lobby. German scientists, however, were seldom subjected to such critical scrutiny, partly because both commissions acted as "filters." The EC's approaches served to close controversies on the reliability and validity of scientific claims. In effect, the debate on climate change could be not used as a forum in which scientific skeptics challenged the mainstream view, and critical voices doubting the scientific hypothesis were virtually excluded. As a result, resistance against the global warming hypothesis was much stronger in the US than in Germany (Weingart et al. 2000). ECI also upheld the confidence of politicians and the public in science's ability to produce "sound" results, and thus protected science's image as a "neutral" and "rational" decision-making tool. The commissions' practices conformed to a national tradition of decision making that disapproves of open polarization of expert opinion. Following this line of argument, one can see the US climate backlash and the controversies surrounding the IPCC as further reasons for German scientists' relatively marginal involvement in that institution.

In their 1986 warning, scientists linked the climate change issue to the question of nuclear energy and the commissions were thus forced to anticipate policy making on long-standing political controversies. Both ECs reflected the problems of coming to an agreement on polarized issues, reached contradictory results, and presented fragile accommodations between the extremes of comprehensive regulation and postponing its implementation.

The tensions between the "push" of globalization, and the "pull" of localization characterize not only the national assessment and regulatory activities but also the German "forerunner" strategy. This was driven in part by a desire to catch up with internationalization, but in part also by a desire to internationalize the German perspectives so as to maintain the competitiveness of German industry. As seen above, the German executive was in a position to shape the regulatory process, including formulating the national position for the international negotiations on the FCCC. According to Klaus Töpfer, then Minister of Environment, the ambitious national reduction target of 25 percent CO_2 reduction was addressed to both the national and the international level. German representatives in international bodies also had to cope with these tensions between different forms of state intervention, which partly explains the ambivalence of the German position in international negotiation. On the one hand, German government set up the "forerunner" strategy to further the political process on climate change and to demonstrate its responsiveness and competence. On the other hand, the strategy was motivated less by a desire to protect the climate than to gain the initiative, and to improve the national bargaining position instead of being forced to act against national interests. The primary goal was to prevent imposing regulatory burdens that would impair the competitiveness of German industries and their attractiveness for foreign investors or set up trade barriers. The official strategy was to involve as many countries as possible in developing congruent policies, which would lessen the likelihood of competition-distorting regulatory action and bring about comparable legal standards and economic conditions worldwide. At the same time, German government decided to postpone comprehensive, legally binding national regulation until agreement was reached on the European and international levels. This strategy helped to win time before immediate action had to be undertaken. Governmental officials realized that participation in transnational negotiations would encourage the tendency to seek lowest common denominator-solutions. This strategy reflects the politics of ECII and, last but not least, the logic of neocorporatist regulation.

Sites of Local Resistance?

The neocorporatist closure of the German climate assessment and regulatory process was achieved at the cost of eliminating some voices and their needs. This particular closure led to asymmetries of power with respect to the opinions presented in the public debate, as well as access to the scientific resources necessary to express those views. This holds especially true for NGOs, which promote the "push" of globalization.

The late twentieth century is often seen as a period of an apparent loss of trust among experts, politicians and the public (Beck et al. 1994). Surveys show striking parallels in Western countries—for example in changes from materialist to post-materialist values, new forms of social mobilization, and increased interaction between state and non-state actors (von Beyme 1987). In the 1970s, in particular, German environmental politics had already been adopted as part of the executive repertoire and had received its bureaucratic "stamp." The German public often complained about "over-bureaucratization," and this can be seen as one reason for the rise of citizens' and non-governmental groups "outside" established political institutions (Ulbert 1997). The controversy over nuclear energy is another indicator of this trend. The prominence of nuclear power made it a natural target for critical attention, and scientific controversies on energy policy often became a symptom of deeper social and political conflicts and cleavages. The mobilization of experts was accompanied by challenges to the authority of scientific and political institutions, and of the policy paradigm based on the values of growth, prosperity, and distribution of wealth (Offe 1985). One can, in such circumstances, expect resistance from peripheral groups, such as NGOs, which were unable to reach their objectives through consultation. The case of climate change, however, does not comfortably support these expectations.

At the outset, stakeholders in German industry (Siemens and AEG) and the conservative government used the scientists' warning to defend nuclear power. The "capture" of the issue by these stakeholders confronted NGOs with a dilemma. On the one hand, influential NGOs, such as the BUND (Bund für Umwelt und Naturschutz Deutschland), had long been aware of the greenhouse effect, and organized internal meetings to discuss the issue. They recognized the urgency of initiating policies to protect the climate. On the other hand, they hesitated to endorse the issue through their fear of building an alliance with the nuclear energy lobby. The integration of an alternative scientific perspective (Öko-Institut Freiburg) into the first assessment turned out to be an important step towards marginalizing potential opposition and contributed to the acceptance of ECI by NGOs.

In the 1990s, NGOs could derive legitimacy from ECI to highlight the fundamental danger of climate change as well as the urgent need for far-reaching measures. They were also supported by alternative scientific assessments, which argued that preventing climate change was no longer necessarily dependent on nuclear energy, and advocated renewable resources, such as wind and solar energy as well as energy conservation, as alternatives. Based on these scientific findings, NGOs felt themselves well prepared to go public, but decided to follow their own climate agenda (Bals 1994). First, NGOs still faced particular problems in reconciling the global, systemic perspective of scientists with the political dimensions of climate change and practical needs of local politics. Their mobilization tends to focus on a particular place, a concrete polluter or a company like Shell in the Brent Spar affair, to which environmental damage can be attributed and protest be addressed. Responding to these needs, different research institutes and advisory bodies have recently begun to assess regional impacts of climate change.

At the same time, NGOs (with the exception of Greenpeace) resist technocrats and "faceless bureaucrats" who care little about the needs of local communities. Their critique reasserts local knowledge claims and local identities against the simplifying and universalizing forces of global science, technology, and capital. Thus, NGOs called for an alternative framing of climate change, not restricted to scientific aspects but also including political problems. They challenged scientific approaches to counting emissions for not explicitly addressing value choices, including responsibility for past emissions and responsibility for ensuring future equity, which are crucial dimensions of the problem. Robust solutions to global warming, they argued, can be found much more readily by addressing the moral and political issues at stake than by producing more intricate and detailed science.

Second, the neocorporatist pattern of closure was accompanied by a lack of political transparency and accountability. NGOs were virtually excluded from assessment and decision-making processes, which, in turn, facilitated orchestrating the closure of the scientific and political debates (Ulbert 1997). German advisory bodies tend to be informal and restrictive in terms of full public access to assessment and decision-making processes (Brickman et al. 1985, p. 23 and p. 315). They include those voices, which they pre-defined as "legitimate"; at the same time, they keep the processes confidential. In effect, they offer only limited opportunities for scrutinizing assessment processes from the outside. The IPCC, by contrast, adopted extended and open review procedures, subjecting assessments to wide-ranging scrutiny by governments and the scientific community, and played a major role in establishing the credibility of expert knowledge for policy purposes (Miller and Edwards 2001). NGOs were also reluctant to call for access to assessment and regulatory processes for fear of being "coopted" by the stakeholders participating in ECII and regulatory circles.

A more promising line of argument might challenge the globalizing discourse of science altogether. Indeed, this seems to be happening in German environmental politics today. As the institutional arrangements of global environmental politics are no longer seen as the "zenith" of all political developments, new, more regional approaches seem the way of the future. If the globalization of environmental discourse was just a station along the way, it has now become obvious that it was a mistake to ignore cultural differences and different forms of knowledge. The next phase in environmental politics may therefore be about the repositioning of environmental issues in a broader cultural context. Environmental politics, then, is not about the implementation of a single, universal scientific solution but about a self-conscious political development of society, taking cultural differences and local concerns into account.

"Think globally, act locally" has become the flag for environmental politics in Germany and points to the continued importance of local knowledge and place-based identity formation in designing and implementing environmental policies. First, different national research programs (Sozial-ökologische Forschung) and political bodies, such as the Council on Sustainability (Nachhaltigkeitsrat), have recognized the need to expand the range of knowledge sources and to integrate additional knowledge about local weather conditions and adaptation to extreme weather events into environmental assessments and politics. Second, the term "governance" was introduced to cover new forms of politics as complements to traditional electoral politics and administrative procedures. Finally, regions were discovered as sites for revitalizing political acceptance and legitimacy, which transnational and national institutions had lost over recent years. (See the chapter by VanDeveer in this volume.)

Conclusion

The German assessments of climate change can only be understood in the light of the surrounding political culture. We have observed the relatively unchallenged emergence of consensual science, enforced and maintained by the Enquete Commissions. These bodies reinforced the traditional image of science as consensual and autonomous, consistent with the structure of a political system which implies and requires "univocal" expert statements. When it came to political issues, however, both commissions had to resolve controversies that reflected deeper political cleavages about the boundaries of state intervention. This led to ambivalence in framing global change and in endorsing policy recommendations about the national response to global climate change. Tensions between the "push" of globalization and the "pull" of localization characterized not only national assessments and regulatory activities, but also the German "forerunner" strategy in the international arena.

It seems at first reading as if the Enquete Commissions represent the extremes between the opening and closing of German political culture. While ECI tended to incorporate global views to bring about a transformation in German policy and politics, ECII stands for a return to the (traditional) status quo of German political culture. However, I have suggested that this is a misleadingly simple reading. First, the work of both commissions reflected specific aspects of national political culture: especially the drive for consensus, the ability to marginalize dissident views, the desire to keep conflict out of science, and the creation of a mini-politics to anticipate and legitimize both legislative and policy action. Second, differences between the two commissions can be explained in part as a result of historical contingencies, that is, at first the "capture" of climate by nuclear interests, and then reunification, with changes in party representation and the reassertion of executive independence. Backed by the structure of the political system, the alliance of industrial stakeholders and conservative politicians succeeded in dominating the assessment and regulatory processes, thereby capturing the "pull" of localization and infusing it with the logic of neocorporatist regulation.

Notes

1. The translation of the first commission's title, "Vorsorge zum Schutz der Erdatmosphäre," as "Preventive Measures to Protect the Atmosphere" is misleading. The German word "Vorsorge" is equivalent to the English "precaution." "Precaution" seems to express more than mere prevention. It means heightened caution in the face of uncertainty. In comparison with a risk-based approach, the precautionary principle seems to display greater sensitivity to human ignorance and uncertainty. It implies a greater need for uncalculated judgment and, where necessary, restraint.

2. Neocorporatism can be defined as a form of governance in which influential groups with different interests draw mutual advantage by acting in concert and by developing forms of cooperation for common goals. This pattern of ordered state-society relationships characterizes a broad range of policy processes in Western Europe. Major social interests are organized in large representative hierarchies by the state, and are drawn into a close relationship to public decision makers (Brickman et al. 1985, p. 24).

References

Bals, Christoph. 1994. "Mercedes Benz, die Klima-Enquete-Kommission und der Treibhauseffekt." In *Käufliche Wissenschaft. Experten im Dienst von Industrie und Politik*, ed. A. Bultmann and F. Schmithals. Droemer Knaur.

Beck, Ulrich, Anthony Giddens and Scott Lash. 1994. *Reflexive Modernization.* Polity Press.

Beyme, Klaus von. 1987. "Politische Kultur." In *Politikwissenschaft. Eine Grundlegung.* Band II, ed. K. von Beyme et al. Kohlhammer.

Borchers, Jutta, Leen Dresen, Aant Elzinga, Carsten Krück, Chunglin Kwa, Jan Nolin, Simon Shackley, Peter Weingart, and Brian Wynne. 1997. Climate Change Research and Its Integration into Environmental Policy: Conditions for the Establishment of a European Political Climate Region (CIRCITER). IWT Paper 18, Bielefeld University.

Brickman, Ronald, Sheila Jasanoff and Thomas Ilgen. 1985. *Controlling Chemicals: The Politics of Regulation in Europe and the United States.* Cornell University Press.

Dyson, K. 1982. "West Germany: The search for rationalist consensus." In *Policy Styles in Western Europe*, ed. J. Richardson. Allen & Unwin.

Ganseforth, Monika. 1996. "Politische Umsetzung der Empfehlungen der beiden Klima-Enquete-Kommisssionen (1987–1994)—eine Bewertung." In *Klimapolitik*, ed. H. Brauch. Springer.

Hajer, Marten. 1996. "Ecological Modernisation as Cultural Politics." In *Risk, Environment and Modernity*, ed. S. Lash et al. Routledge.

Huber, Michael. 1997. "Leadership and unification: Climate change policies in Germany." In *Cases in Climate Change Policy*, ed. U. Collier and R. Löfstedt. Earthscan.

Ismayr, Wolfgang. 1996. "Enquete-Kommissionen des Deutsches Bundestages." *Aus Politik und Zeitgeschichte* 46: 29–41.

Jasanoff, Sheila. 1986. *Risk Management and Political Culture*. Russell Sage Foundation.

Kords, Udo. 1996. "Tätigkeit und Handlungsempfehlungen der beiden Klima-Enquete-Kommissionen des Deutschen Bundestages (1987–1994)." In *Klimapolitik*, ed. H. Brauch. Springer.

Miller, Clark A., and Paul Edwards, eds. 2001. *Changing the Atmosphere: Science and the Politics of Global Warming*. MIT Press.

Offe, Claus. 1985. "New Social Movements: Challenging the Boundaries of Institutional Politics." *Social Research* 52: 817–868.

Richardson, Jeremy, Gunnel Gustafsson, and Grant Jordan. 1982. "The Concept of Policy Styles." In *Policy Styles in Western Europe*, ed. J. Richardson. Allen and Unwin.

Roqueplo, Philippe. 1995. "Scientific expertise among political powers, administrations and public opinion." *Science and Public Policy* 22: 175–182.

Ulbert, Cornelia. 1997. *Die Konstruktion von Umwelt*. Nomos.

Weingart, Peter, Anita Engels, and Petra Pansegrau. 2000. "Risks of communication: discourses on climate change in science, politics, and the mass media." *Public Understanding of Science* 9: 261–283.

8

Social Movements and Environmental Democratization in Thailand

Tim Forsyth

Much recent environmental debate has suggested that social movements perform a crucial role in communicating "local" environmental knowledge to policy processes. Arturo Escobar (1996, p. 65), for example, remarked: "We need new narratives of life and cultures. . . . They will arise from the mediations that local culture are able to effect. . . . This is a collective task that perhaps only social movements are in a position to advance." Building on this, Peet and Watts (1996) have described a new approach to environmental politics called "Liberation Ecologies" in which social movements may democratize environmental discourse towards more locally determined concerns.

This chapter takes a more critical view. In contrast to these statements, the chapter argues that there is no necessary and logical connection between social movements, the elevation of local knowledge and concerns, and environmental democratization. Instead, there is a need to understand how the ideology of environmental globalism may shape the perception of what is considered to be "local," and how apparently "local" social movements may adopt "global" discourses. Indeed, political activism through social movements may not result in environmental democratization, but in a reinforcement of pre-existing political hegemonies.

The chapter illustrates these points by discussing two examples of social movements in Thailand: opposition to the filming of the Hollywood movie *The Beach* and political activism concerning community forestry. As one rapidly industrializing country, Thailand is an appropriate example of where social movements have voiced concern against apparently global forces of environmental degradation. Yet these disputes contain further social divisions and contestations about environmental policy that draw into question common uses of the terms "local" and "global." Such political construction of these concepts needs to be acknowledged before social movements or knowledge can be claimed to be "local."

Social Movements and Environmental Democratization

There is now little doubt that social movements are a key component of a full and inclusive civil society. Indeed, Cohen and Arato (1992, p. 492) noted, "social movements constitute the dynamic element in processes that might realize the positive potentials of modern civil societies." Social movements have also been largely responsible for establishing environmental concern as a significant topic of national and international politics. Indeed, some have argued that the combination of a successful civil society and environmental social movements may be called "environmental democratization": "Environmental democratization is defined as a participatory and ecologically rational form of collective decision making: it prioritizes judgments based on long-term generalizable interests, facilitated by communicative political procedures and a radicalization of existing liberal rights." (Mason 1999, p. 1)

But can the process of "environmental democratization" be defined simply in these terms? While Mason is clearly correct to point out the need to privilege the existence of rights under democratization, he overlooks the diversity of perceptions of the environment, or how social movements themselves may shape, rather than act upon, notions of environmental concern. For example, Mason does not discuss how, and for whom, collective decision-making may be "ecologically rational" or with "long-term generalizable interests." We will see in this section how social movements may be associated with different and competing visions of ecological rationality, and why these differences are important for environmental democratization.

Environmentalism has been described as one of the classic "new" social movements that developed in Europe and North America during the 1960s, resulting from resistance to the perceived instrumentality of modern industrial life (see Tourraine 1981). As such, new social movements are claimed to be different from "old" social movements based on historic class divisions because they concern topics such as environmentalism, gender, or racial rights, which (allegedly) cannot be expressed in terms of class alone. Yet, significantly, new social movements have often been composed of relatively more powerful middle classes who have sought to achieve reform for the sake of all classes. Giddens (1973), for example, claimed that new social movements are "class-aware" but not "class-conscious." Offe (1985, p. 833) wrote: "New middle class politics, in contrast to most working class politics, as well as old middle class politics, is typically a politics *of a* class but not *on behalf of* a class." And Beck (1992, p. 39), writing about the "risk society," proclaimed: "With the globalization of risks a social dynamic is set in motion, which can no longer be composed of and understood in class categories."

These claims that class does not influence environmental concerns associated with social movements are questionable. US environmental historians, for example, have highlighted how perceptions of wilderness as fragile or beautiful was limited to the emergence of urban middle classes. (See Nash 1982.) Giddens (1994), again, has linked the desire to conserve nature to the anxieties about then perceived "loss of tradition" in late modernity, rather than to real environmental threats. Marxist theorists have also claimed that environmentalism, and wilderness-based approaches to conservation fail to acknowledge the kinds of environmental risks that affect less powerful workers. Enzensberger (1974, p. 10) famously commented: "The social neutrality to which the ecological debate lays claim having recourse as it does so to strategies derived from the evidence of the natural science, is a fiction. . . . In so far as it can be considered a source of ideology, ecology is a matter that concerns the middle class."

Environmentalism associated specifically with middle classes not only places high value on threatened wilderness, but may influence the use and interpretation of scientific knowledge. In particular, the overt focus upon the preservation of wilderness has prompted links between the environmentalism of the new social movements with so-called "balance of nature," or equilibrium-based, notions of ecological fragility. (See Botkin 1990 and Zimmerer 2000.) These approaches are generally associated with beliefs that ecosystems illustrate principles of entropy, balance, and progression to pre-defined points of stasis, such as the original model of vegetational succession (Clements 1916). Increasingly, however, these approaches have been questioned by so-called "non-equilibrium" or "new" ecologies reflecting insights from chaos theory. Non-equilibrium ecology urges more attention to the influence of disturbance as a creative and influential force in ecology and landscape. In valuing wilderness as "pristine" or fragile activists also appear to favor ecological stability over ecological change (Adams 1997). Yet such notions of stability and fragility may sometimes be used to legitimize policies—such as resettling villages, or forbidding some agricultural practices—that might otherwise attract criticism for their impacts on forest settlers or shifting cultivators (Leach and Mearns 1996; Zimmerer 2000).

The environmentalism of new social movements and equilibrium-based approaches to ecology illustrates one key point. Social movements represent no uniform and universally agreed form of environmentalism. Indeed, middle-class environmentalism may not always acknowledge diverse alternative framings from different classes, or other social divisions such as gender, caste, or age. Consequently, environmental social movements, *per se*, may not necessarily lead to a universally agreed form of "environmental democratization." Reflecting such concerns, Guha and Martinez-Alier (1997) have urged recognition of "varieties of environmentalism," based on class differences, and have called for an "environmentalism of the poor," which focuses less on landscape conservation, and more on sustainable local livelihoods and environmental protection for poor people. But there are also wider reasons to worry that international environmental social movements may represent, or impose, environmental agendas of poor people.

There has been a trend in recent years to highlight the beneficial role of international alliances or advocacy coalitions in assisting grassroots or livelihood struggles in developing countries. Bryant and Bailey (1997, p. 190), for example, argued that environmental grassroots activists and non-governmental organizations (NGOs) represent a "natural alliance" against states and transnational corporations. Keck and Sikkink (1999, p. 215) claimed that international advocacy coalitions among environmental NGOs and campaigners in different countries allow "ecological values to be placed above narrow definitions of national interest." (While NGOs, or grassroots organizations, of course, are not social movements *per se*, they often represent the political expression of movements, and can help institutionalize the activism associated with social movements.)

Critics have suggested that these views overlook how more powerful agendas may be imposed on less powerful local activists. The concept of expanding "ecological values" via epistemic communities,[1] for example, has been criticized for overlooking divisions within such "communities" and the social or political factors necessary for networks to be extended. (See Jasanoff 1996; Lahsen, this volume.) Some critics have also suggested that "green globalism" represents innate tendencies for control within Western cultures (Lohmann 1993). More pragmatically, the act of alliance itself may also weaken less powerful voices. Covey (1995), for instance, demonstrated that alliances between middle-class NGOs and grassroots organizations in the Philippines became dominated by the NGO concerns, and consequently led to an avoidance of poverty-related aspects of environmental policy.

Yet it is still unclear how far it is possible to represent such weaker, "local" voices. Vandana Shiva, writing about the apparent misappropriation of local livelihood struggles by global environmentalism, wrote:

In recent years, the two decades of the green movement are being erased. The "local" has disappeared from environmental concern. Suddenly, it seems only "global" environmental problems exist, and it is taken for granted that their solution can only be "global": "The 'global' in the dominant discourse is the political space in which a particular local seeks global control, and frees itself of local, national and international restraints. The global does not represent the universal human interest, it represents a particular local and parochial interest which has been globalized through the scope of its reach." (Shiva 1993, p. 149).

Yet Shiva herself was later criticized for allegedly falsely representing subaltern voices either through her own statements or by allowing other critics to use her voice (Jackson 1995, p. 139).

Similar concerns have also surfaced around scientific principles underlying environmental management. Studies of scientific discourses in developing countries have often revealed that many popularly established notions of environmental degradation such as deforestation or desertification may not be simply blamed on local land uses or increasing populations as commonly suggested (see Thompson et al. 1986; Leach and Mearns 1996). Many locally based studies of land management in supposedly fragile environments have revealed that common assumptions about the universal applicability of concepts of environmental degradation may neither be considered degrading by local inhabitants, nor necessarily caused by their activities (see Forsyth 2003).

Indeed, in relation to the Machakos region of Kenya, for example, Tiffen and Mortimore (1994) famously found that "more people" may mean "less erosion" because of the importance of local land-management practices. Similarly, in Guinea, West Africa, Fairhead and Leach (1996) also found that villagers had contributed to the growth of forest "islands" in the savanna–forest convergence zone, rather than causing deforestation as commonly assumed by generations of expert scientists and policy makers. In such cases, the "local knowledge" of land management and conservation had been overlooked by the universalistic and globalizing discourses of many conservationists. Consequently, social movements adopting global discourses may not succeed in environmental democratization because they may instead re-impose such unrepresentative explanations in locations where they are not warranted (see Agrawal 1995).

So, how can the "local" be represented—especially if it lacks sufficient power to achieve its own voice, or if engaging in social movements risks sacrificing that voice? The example of Vandana Shiva above illustrates an important paradox in the harnessing of "local" versus "global" knowledge in environmentalism. In order to gain legitimacy, environmentalism has called upon global science and universal ecological principles to highlight environmental fragility and the need for conservation. Yet at times it has also called upon "local" knowledge or the local adoption of its principles to legitimize these claims politically. The criticisms of sociologists and researchers of environmental science have indicated that universalizing ecological principles overlook insights from local or unrepresented social groups. But perhaps the most important question to ask first is how to achieve local representation when the very definitions of "local" and "global" are so insufficiently understood, and so open to manipulation.

Social Movements and Ecological Discourse in Thailand

Thailand is a rapidly developing country in which struggles over natural resources occur, and policy is affected by a variety of global scientific discourses and local activism. Yet, perhaps less visibly, Thailand is also a site of environmental conflict that represents in many ways the tensions between local resistance and global invasion. Now a major tourism destination, Thailand epitomizes many projections about beautiful paradise and complex oriental cultures. Many activists see Thailand as an innovative site of local resistance against the material impacts of globalism (such as industrialization), as well as more discursive effects of imposing Western visions of nature and culture upon distant people. As the only Southeast Asian country never to have been officially colonized by Western powers, Thailand has a history of asserting independence. These factors are influential in the case studies of Thai social movements and environmental activism discussed in this section.

Many commentators trace the emergence of environmentalism as a politically potent social movement in Thailand to the years 1988–1989. In 1988, a long-term campaign finally succeeded in persuading the government to postpone the construction of the proposed Nam Choan dam in a rain forest in western Thailand. Later in the year, a related campaign to ban all forms of logging within Thailand also finally succeeded in enacting a logging ban effective in 1990. Before these successes, overtly "environmental" concern in Thailand was almost totally restricted to the activities of urban, educated citizens, such as the Association for Wildlife Conservation of Thailand, or specific locations such as the mountain of Doi Suthep in Chiang Mai where residents proposed a cable car.

The activism in 1988 coincided with the election of Thailand's first long-term democratic government. Some analysts have argued that environmentalism has always been linked with democratization, by demonstrating the importance of natural resources to small communities, or by providing a means of political expression during periods when more overt activism would have been suppressed by military governments (e.g. Hirsch 1997). Campaigns after 1988 also opposed the state in various ways: rejecting corruption (or illegal logging by officials); exposing inefficiencies (such as the inability of the centralized Royal Forestry Department to protect resources); protesting the use of public resources by private companies; or resisting enforced reforestation and resettlement of villages on land officially owned by the state.

Concern about deforestation, in particular, reflects a variety of deep-rooted political and ecological uncertainties (Hirsch 1997 1998). The common and overriding concern is that Thailand, having lost some 50 percent of its forests within the last 40 years, has been deeply degraded by rapid industrialization and agricultural extension, with subsequent loss of wilderness, and biodiversity. Rapid social change and perceived "loss of tradition" have also arguably increased the perception of a loss of heritage (Stott 1991).

These framings have influenced environmental discourse, and the selection of "local" knowledge as both a target and source of environmental policy. Deforestation in the northern mountains, for example, has been blamed for water shortages in the central plains and cities, but such an explanation may overlook both the increased demand for water, or the ability of upland farmers to protect resources (e.g. Alford 1992; Forsyth 1996).

Similarly, some Thai scholars and social activists have deliberately sought to promote the concept of so-called "community (or "local") culture" (*wattanatham chumchon*) on the basis that "village culture" is older, better, and worthier than state-led development. Yet other critics have suggested this is both romantic and counter-productive to development (Rigg 1991).

The following example reveals two markedly different discourses of "local" wisdom concerning watershed degradation in the far northern hills of Thailand. The first is from an environmental magazine that described the types of environmental problems experienced by poor farmers in Thailand:

When I was a boy, our village was surrounded by dense forest. There were tigers and lots of big trees, some two meters in diameter. When I was about 30, I saw the forest beginning to disappear, but then there was still water in the streams. Fifteen years later, the stream had disappeared too. Now we only have artesian wells which are so inadequate that people fight over them. (*Watershed* 1, 1990, no. 1, p. 5).

Although this statement is represented as being from one "local" inhabitant, and a victim of environmental degradation, it may also be seen to reflect a variety of classically middle class concerns. These include the loss of wildlife; a sense of lost equilibrium or harmony in the countryside; and encroaching conflict and strife as a result. This quotation, however, stands in stark contrast to the views of another "local" inhabitant collected during my own in-depth research in the hills. A highland farmer (Iu Mien, or Yao) who historically practiced shifting cultivation including the occasional burning of forest, and who traditionally lived high up in the hills rather on the plains beneath them, spoke as follows:

It has been a saying in our people for many, many years that in order to get a regular, year-round long-term supply of water you need to cut down the largest trees around the village. I have seen it myself. It is only since we arrived in Thailand that we have heard people claim that this is not the case, and it is the Thai extension workers who tell us this. (Forsyth 1996)

These statements represent radically different evaluations of environmental change based on contrasting experiences of hydrology and water supply. (Indeed, water shortages are a major problem for middle classes and peasantry alike). Rather than assessing why each statement may be considered accurate by each speaker, it is important to note that government policy and middle-class actors in Thailand generally consider the first to be the more accurate and urgent. Water shortages are among the most common and politically potent social problems in Thailand. Yet debate focuses more on presumed causes of declining water supply in the uplands than on increased uses of water in the lowlands from practices such as irrigation of fruit crops and rice fields, industrial estates, and cities.

Government policy has generally been to restore lost forests through plantation reforestation, and to restrict upland agriculture where it is seen to be threatening to forests or watersheds. Yet these policies may also be justified for many potentially more controversial reasons, such as the middle-class concern at lost forests and wilderness; the historic government desire to gain control over land lived in by mountain minorities; or the need to somehow maintain a supply of wood from forest plantations for construction and industry. "Scientific" (or "global") ecological principles are likely to be used to legitimize such policies. Below, we consider two more detailed case studies exemplifying different uses of "local" and "global" concepts of environmental knowledge and social activism.

Enforcing the Balance of Nature: Resisting *The Beach*

The first case concerns the dispute associated with the filming of the Hollywood movie *The Beach* in 1998–99. (See also Forsyth 2002.) In this case a campaign dominated by middle class activists adopted both "global" principles of ecological balance and fragility, and an emphasis on "locality" to enhance its objectives.

Protests against the film centered on the decision of the Royal Forestry Department (RFD) to allow a foreign company access to a national park in the Phi Phi Islands, in Krabi province, south of Phuket in 1998. During the 1970s, a distinctive limestone cave in neighboring Phangnga Province became known as "James Bond Island" after *The Man with the Golden Gun* was filmed there, and has remained a tourist attraction since. It was hoped that *The Beach*, starring the Hollywood idol Leonardo Di Caprio and featuring a story about backpackers, drugs and self-exploration, would also generate a flow of tourism and publicity for Thailand.

Unfortunately, however, the film crew wanted to change the physical properties of the selected beach in Maya Bay, Phi Phi Leh Island. Bulldozers were used to widen the area covered by sand in order to shoot a soccer game, and 60 coconut palms were imported and planted on the beach in order to make it conform to the desired image of a tropical paradise. This was in clear contravention of the 1961 National Park Act of Thailand that made it illegal to damage or change any aspect of landscape in parks. The decision by the RFD therefore appeared to be a case of the government both bending national laws for international investors, and failing to protect natural resources.

Throughout the dispute, campaigners sought to represent the actions of the RFD as an assault on a unique and fragile ecosystem. A woman campaigner, who had been active for years as a freelance journalist and environmentalist, was quoted as follows: "If they were just shooting the film, that would be fine, but they're going to take out the indigenous plants and keep them in pots in a nursery. The place is beautiful but it's not Hollywood's idea of a tropical island. For them a tropical island needs coconut trees so they're going to plant 100 coconut trees. This is a major ecological disaster." (*Bangkok Post*, October 18, 1998) A particularly graphic editorial in the October 17, 1998 issue of *The Nation*, an English-language national daily newspaper, stated: "Imagine filming an ambitious Hollywood blockbuster on Phi Phi Island, one of the most beautiful islands in the Pacific. All the elaborate and crushing equipment and ravaging crew laying waste to most of what they touch. This is what is about to descend on Phi Phi if Twentieth Century Fox gets the final go ahead from the Thai Government to shoot *The Beach*."

Much concern focused on the disturbance to the plants, sand and coral in the bay. Newspaper reports and information on web pages mentioned exotically named local plants such as Giant Milkweed, Sea Pandanus, Spider Lily, and other beach grasses. Some journalists also suggested that introducing coconut palms to the island might be damaging because they might not be indigenous. A university biologist also expressed concern at the company's restoration efforts: "From years of experience and numerous experiments around the world, there's never been a case where the altered environment can be completely restored." (Surachet Chetmas, Dean of Faculty of Forestry, Kasetsart University, quoted in *Bangkok Post*, December 19, 1998)

Meanwhile, the campaign also maintained pressure on the RFD and its high-profile head, Plodprasob Suraswadi, for alleged corruption in overturning national legislation, and also for accepting a payment of some $200,000 from the company to assist with cleaning up the site. Fishing communities and villagers on neighboring islands and the mainland also joined the protest, although newspapers reported that many villagers supported the filming. Although middle-class activists dominated the campaign, the national labor organization, the Assembly of the Poor, sent representatives to show support. Indeed, several organizations supported a lawsuit against the RFD in Thailand, and some 20 civic and environmental groups filed a petition to the US Department of Justice alleging that Fox had acted corruptly by offering the RFD a bribe.

The campaign effectively ended when the filming stopped and when the film was eventually released to poor reviews. Although the campaigners had failed to stop the filming, or successfully initiate a lawsuit, they did succeed in drawing attention to the apparently undemocratic and highhanded actions of the RFD. A discourse of ecological fragility was used to generate public concern, even when statements were exaggerated. Under "new ecological" thinking, for example, it is not surprising that "there has never been a case where the altered environment can be completely restored" (as stated by the biologist above) because such environments are constantly changing. Coastal beach environments are well known to be dynamic and changeable over short time scales. Erosion on beaches is common and not always problematic. Suggesting that coconut trees might damage the ecosystem because they are not indigenous ignores the fact that such palms are found throughout the region, and that the various influences (other than filming) act upon the Maya Bay landscape (*Bangkok Post*, February 18, 1999). Indeed, the film company claimed to have removed some two tons of garbage left on the beach by tourists, and which the RFD had not removed.

In fighting the RFD, the campaigners therefore relied mainly upon the construction of the beach itself as a fragile and exotic locality. Such "locality" was further reinforced by the emphasis on endemic (and exotically named) species. The filming was also said to offend national sensibilities by superimposing foreign conceptualizations of landscape upon the beach, and transcending national laws for the sake of foreigners. The campaign permitted activists from various social backgrounds to resist undemocratic behavior from the state. But it adopted and reaffirmed a dominant ecological discourse in order to empower their action in one locality, rather than seek to define a new and more locally determined discourse.

Challenging the Balance of Nature: Community Forests

The second case centers on the debate about community forests in Thailand and reflects both the adoption of "global" ecological principles of fragility and balance and "local" campaigns to reverse such thinking in favor of more locally determined and locally governed resource use.

The term "community forestry" refers to the governance and management of forest resources by local people, such as villagers. "Community forests," however, suggest an alternative conceptualization of forests from that usually associated with the scientific discourses of "forestry." Indeed, "community forests" are often governed by lay people, rather than through consultation with or control by external experts in forestry science.[7] According to one internationally respected Thai scholar of forestry (Somsak Sukwong, Director of Regional Community Forestry Training, Center, Bangkok, quoted in *Watershed* 6, 2001, no. 2, p. 12), the key difference between so-called "community" and "scientific" forestry is in the villagers' rejection of plantations as a sustainable and usable form of forest: "The village people look at forests as the whole of nature rather than just as a monoculture. This is a different view from that of a forester. . . . Forestry education follows the curriculum and style of Western forestry education. . . . It ignores the local knowledge as it not scientific."[8]

Proponents of community forestry—such as many villagers, academics and social development NGOs—claim that it allows greater access to forests by different stakeholders, with the intention of safeguarding local livelihoods, plus better management and protection than possible from a centralized body such as the Royal Forestry Department (RFD). Opponents—such as conservationist NGOs, and the RFD—have generally claimed that increasing access to forests will only increase deforestation. It is worth noting, however, that many different concepts of community forestry exist, and the debate mainly focuses on defining where, and by whom, forests may be communally governed. The debate has gone on for years in Thailand, and since 1996, the government and activists have proposed and rewritten several drafts of a proposed community forestry bill, intended to become law in the early 2000s. (See Johnson and Forsyth 2002.)

The debate about community forests illustrates social divisions between activists seeking to protect forests by restricting public access and campaigners seeking to increase public participation in resource management. Yet the underlying themes are complex. The RFD has generally opposed liberal approaches to community forestry because it challenges the central management role performed by the department since its establishment in the late nineteenth century. This position is shared by many conservationists (often middle class) who oppose community forestry because they fear it will never allow sufficient protection of biodiversity, or will be abused to allow more commercialized forms of logging and mining concessions.

Against this position, many pro-development activists support community forestry because it may offer a model for devolved governance. Indeed, the 1997 Constitution of Thailand was considered the most democratic to date because it allowed public participation in decisions about resource use and infrastructure. The debate also concerns the long-standing problem of addressing the issue of upland minorities (so-called "hill tribes") in northern Thailand, who are commonly blamed for causing deforestation and water shortages, and for whom the RFD has traditionally proposed enforced plantation reforestation and resettlement as a means of land management. Indeed, one representative of such a "hill tribe," the Karen, commented:

Community forestry's main concern is the livelihoods of local people and local communities. . . . Scientific foresters [such as the RFD] assume that humans only make problems in a protected area, but our work is to let outsiders understand how local people conserve the forest. . . . Community forestry is about decentralized management by communities, but conventional scientific forestry is about centralized management. (Saw Frankie, Coordinator of Karen Education Information Center in Bangkok, quoted in *Watershed* 6, 2001, no. 2, p. 22)

Much initial debate about community forestry in the 1990s focused on the attempts of the state to reforest and forcibly resettle villages on state-owned land in northeastern Thailand, particularly around the locality of Pa Kham in Buri Ram province. Such action by the (then military) state was considered insensitive to local development, and helped enforce a new discourse of poverty and environment. One campaigning journalist later expressed it as follows: "We must . . . stick together, work together, and we just couldn't kick the poor out of the scene just to save the trees." (Santisuda Ekichai, *Bangkok Post*, interview with author, March 19, 1999) Indeed, sentiment like this was not restricted to community forestry, but was also important in public protest against the construction of dams in rural areas involving the destruction of agricultural land and fisheries.[2]

Protests like these sought to represent previously unrepresented "local" people in the policy process concerning natural resources management. There have also been attempts to highlight the role of "communities" in protecting forest or watershed resources, in apparent contradiction to orthodox scientific beliefs about ecological fragility. For example, a variety of Thai and foreign researchers have argued that upland agriculture by ethnic minorities may not be as damaging to forests and soils as commonly thought, and that lowland activities such as irrigated rice and fruit trees may also share responsibility for apparent water shortages (e.g. Hirsch 1997). Activists have hoped that highlighting these additional concerns might indicate that state-controlled plantation reforestation and resettlement of villages in the uplands may not be necessary, and that more locally governed forest management may be achievable by working with, rather than against, village practices.

Clearly, however, these campaigns also use "local" knowledge to further their non-political interests or to counter the opposition's claims. For example, many observers have criticized research on local forest management for commoditizing and romanticizing village wisdom at a time when the pressures on forests and so-called traditional rural lifestyles have never been higher (Walker 2001). Some critics have also suggested that the attention to colorful minorities (or "hill tribes"), with distinctive costumes and historic involvement in opium production, may reflect an interest in the exotic that overlooks both their environmental impacts and also the rights of lowland Thai groups who are comparatively less researched. For example, one recent colorful coffee table book about the Akha ethnic minority used the title, *Akha: Guardians of the Forest* (Goodman 1998) because the Akha have a reputation for protecting forest zones close to villages for spiritual purposes. Research on Akha shifting cultivation, however, has suggested that agricultural land tended by Akha is less biodiverse than land tended by other groups such as the Karen and Lawa (Schmidt-Vogt 1999).

Opposition to the community forestry campaign has reflected a continued adoption of the discourse of the balance of nature. The RFD director, Plodprasob Suraswadi, has on various occasions stated that "man [sic] and nature cannot coexist" in order to use scientific discourse to weaken any proposal for community forestry. Similarly, in discussions and interviews, Plodprasob also refers to the purpose of upland land management purely in terms of generating water supply for the lowlands; national security (in excluding migrants); or protection of wilderness and biodiversity. Such clinical descriptions of the problem restrict the debate to the perspectives of the state and lowlanders.

Conservationists have also used "local" knowledge for their own purposes. In 1991 an Australian television documentary about forest disputes in northern Thailand used the title *The Monk, the Princess and the Forest* (van Beld 1991) in order to focus on one particularly notorious conflict at Chom Thong, where lowland villagers, with the support of a local monk and royal benefactor, were working to exclude highland farmers from the forest. The documentary inaccurately described the local forest as "rainforest" and claimed the dispute was a good example of grassroots resistance against environmental degradation. Later analysts have criticized this group as racist and inflammatory for their actions, and particularly for erecting a new barbed-wire fence with posts painted in Thai national colors around land used by upland farmers (Pinkaew 1997; Lohmann 1999). Indeed, the use of Thai colors in this context again highlights nationalism as another means to define locality, or the boundary around which certain actors will allow debate to take place. Nationalist discourse again surfaced at a conference in Chiang Mai in 2001, when members of this conservationist group sought to delegitimize scientific statements from foreign academics on the grounds that they were "foreigners" who wanted to "steal Thai nature from Thai people." (personal observation at International Symposium on Watershed Management, Chiang Mai University, March 23–26, 2001) Some activists have resisted the ratification of the international Convention on Biological Diversity because it may allow foreign companies to "steal" Thai biodiversity. In these cases, the national territory itself is being used as a form of dominant locality, a device to include or exclude participants in debate.

Some of the barriers to community forestry are more direct. In May 1999, for example, some 5,000 upland and lowland farmers demonstrated outside the provincial hall of Chiang Mai with a variety of demands including better access to Thai citizenship and an end to unwanted reforestation. The protest was forcibly broken up by RFD and police. When Thai academics called for a more informed approach to forest rights and citizenship, the governor of Chiang Mai denounced them as "traitors." In 2001, a coalition of pro-democracy groups also called on Plodprasob to resign because of his use of force to resist calls for community forestry, and his tendency to declare agricultural or settled land as "sanctuary forest" in order to legitimize resettlement (*Bangkok Post*, July 30, 2001).

Such conflicts have had varied impacts on environmental discourse. While public concern at the plight of different "communities" seems variable, there still seems little general rethinking of scientific discourses about ecological fragility or deforestation. When poor farmers protested the government reforestation of land in Dong Lan in Khon Kaen province in the northeast in 1999, newspapers generally reported the event as lawlessness and trespassing by the villagers. The land was described as "degraded," and reforestation (generally of eucalyptus plantations) was seen to be progressive.

Yet, while such descriptions generally increase criticism of the concept of community forests, there also seems to be a simultaneous transition to construct other local groups as protectors of forest. The Karen are Thailand's largest "hill tribe" group, and live, generally, in the northwest of Thailand on the Thai-Burmese border among the teak forests of the Salween and Ping basins, and unlike more recent migrants to Thailand such as the Hmong or Akha, they have lived in Thailand for some 200 or more years. The Karen, stereotypically, have adopted a "rotational" form of shifting cultivation that allows the cultivation of regular units of land over a cycle of some years, and therefore allows the recovery of forest land, and permits villages to remain semi-permanent for some years at the same site. (Other forms of shifting cultivation may use land continuously until it is exhausted, and hence imply that villages have to relocate every 10–20 years; see Grandstaff 1980.) Such rotational shifting cultivation is now increasingly referred to with the words, "local knowledge." While represented in the 1970s as another form of "hill tribe" with potential security threats, Karen people are now increasingly held up as examples of *phumibanyaa chaobaan* (local wisdom) because of their willingness to protect forestland despite shifting cultivation, and their extensive knowledge of plants and trees. Indeed, arguments *against* community forests have increasingly cited the potential risks of lead mining or deforestation to Karen as forest dwellers and potential victims of development. This new representation of the Karen as both a defined "community" and as protective of forest may indicate how one "local" ethnic group has been used by both proponents and opponents of community forestry to support their respective campaign (Walker 2001).

Different actors in community forestry in Thailand, therefore, have adopted concepts of "local knowledge" in order to empower their own campaigns and to define who is to be included in or excluded from the debate. Proponents of community forestry have sought to represent "local" people and environmental knowledge to create alternative framings of environmental problems to those of so-called scientific (or plantation) forestry, and the problems faced by marginalized social groups. Opponents of community forestry, however, have sought to discuss "locality" in terms of demonstrating the fragility of specific forest ecosystems; the nationalistic unity of Thailand; and the small-scale, and unusual, and hence allegedly illegitimate, practices performed by minorities.

Conclusion

How far can social movements democratize environmental discourse by allowing the communication of "local" as opposed to "global" knowledge to science and policy debates? This chapter's main conclusion, based on the analysis of the discourse of ecological fragility and exclusion of people from forests in Thailand, is that social movements have not succeeded in such democratization, and indeed may strengthen pre-existing discourses. In particular, social movements may powerfully reproduce and reinforce equilibrium, or "balance of nature," conceptualizations of ecology that may overlook underlying ecological complexity, and may lead to repressive land-use policies despite evidence that suggests such policies may be unnecessary.

Indeed, the case studies support a need for wider work on the potentially repressive impacts of "balance of nature" approaches to ecology, and on conservation strategies based on globalized scientific statements of causality rather than looking to see how local experience may contradict such statements. As Zimmerer noted (2000, p. 357): "Many abuses that have stemmed from conservation policies are rooted in the belief, held by policy makers, politicians, scientists, and administrators, of a balance or equilibrium-tending stability of nature."

Thus, instead of seeking to extend "ecological values" across national boundaries and enhance so-called epistemic communities of ecological rationality, as some have proposed (see e.g. Keck and Sikkink 1998), a more effective and socially just form of environmental democratization is to allow greater participation in the formation of such concepts of ecology in the first place. Such participation may be achieved both by seeking to represent "local" (or in some way previously socially marginalized) knowledge, but also through an appreciation of the temporal and cultural specificity of such statements of supposed ecological rationality.

The examples relating to protests against *The Beach* and the campaign for community forestry show that activists have used the concept of "local knowledge" in a variety of ways both to strengthen their campaigns, and to recruit or exclude other actors. Activists arguing in favor of ecological fragility have used the word "local," particularly about places, to indicate uniqueness, nationalism, and the need to protect against unwanted outsiders. Indeed, the perceived threat of global culture, as symbolized by Hollywood, and its apparently unlawful alliance with part of the Thai State, may be seen as particularly hostile by concerned activists who have seen Thailand transformed radically in the space of some decades, with loss of historical and cultural identities.

On the other hand, activists seeking to challenge ecological fragility and promote devolved governance have applied the term "local" more specifically to people and their alternative perspectives on ecological processes and land management. At times, such perspectives may have led to the construction of "hill tribes," and the Karen in particular, as discrete social units exemplifying alternate forms of sustainable development. In both cases, environmental activism has reflected these wider social framings, rather than just the short-term details of each specific case.

These findings, then, stand as a pessimistic response to the optimism of much writing on social movements as instruments of environmental democratization, such as Peet and Watts's (1996) discussion of "Liberation Ecologies." It is sometimes more important to analyze what forms of environmentalism are being communicated by social movements, and who wins and loses from environmental discourses, rather than simply to assume that environmentalism or "ecological values" are necessarily progressive. Yet rather than abandon hope of democratizing environmental discourses on behalf of "local" or unrepresented groups, it may be more productive to change the focus of debate from the avoidance of particular perspectives to the reform of the debate itself. Instead of assuming the benefits of what we may think is "local" before joining the debate, perhaps the best route to environmental democratization is an analysis of how different actors use the term "local." A politically powerful "localization" of environmental discourse may depend in the end on granting identity and meaning to disadvantaged groups and neglected locations.

Acknowledgments

This work was written with assistance from the Economic and Social Research Council of the United Kingdom, award number 22 2245 ("The

Local and the Global: Social Movements and Environmental Knowledge in Thailand"), and the Global Environmental Assessment Research Program of the Kennedy School of Government, Harvard University.

Notes

1. Haas (1992, p. 3) defined an epistemic community as follows: "An epistemic community is a network of professional with recognized experience and competence in a particular domain and an authoritative claim to policy-relevant knowledge within that domain or issue area. . . . What bonds members of an epistemic community is their shared belief or faith in the verity and the applicability of particular forms of knowledge or specific truths."

2. Several dams have been proposed and opposed on these grounds. The most famous is the Pak Mul dam in Ubon Ratchatani province, in eastern Thailand, which has been claimed to destroy local fishing livelihoods without adequate creation of electricity generating capacity.

References

Adams, W. 1997. "Rationalization and Conservation: Ecology and the Management of Nature in the United Kingdom," *Transactions of the Institute of British Geographers* NS 22: 277–291.

Agrawal, A. 1995. "Dismantling the Divide Between Indigenous and Scientific Knowledge." *Development and Change* 26, no. 3: 413–439.

Alford, D. 1992. "Streamflow and Sediment Transport from Mountain Watersheds of the Chao Phraya Basin, Northern Thailand: A Reconnaissance Study." *Mountain Research and Development* 12, no. 3: 257–268.

Beck, U. 1992. *Risk Society*. Polity.

Botkin, D. 1990. *Discordant Harmonies: A New Ecology for the Twenty-First Century*. Oxford University Press.

Bryant, R., and Bailey, S. 1997. *Third-World Political Ecology*, Routledge.

Clements, F. 1916. *Plant Succession: An Analysis of the Development of Vegetation*. Carnegie Institution.

Cohen, J., and Arato, A. 1992. *Civil Society and Political Theory*. MIT Press.

Covey, J. 1995. "Accountability and Effectiveness in NGO Policy Alliances." In *Non-Governmental Organizations*, ed. M. Edwards and D. Hulme. Earthscan.

Enzensberger, H. 1974. "A Critique of Political Ecology." *New Left Review* 84: 3–31.

Escobar, A. 1996. "Constructing Nature: Elements for a Poststructural Political Ecology." In *Liberation Ecologies*, ed. R. Peet and M. Watts. Routledge.

Forsyth, T. 1996. "Science, Myth and Knowledge: Testing Himalayan Environmental Degradation in Thailand." *Geoforum* 27, no. 3: 375–392.

Forsyth, T. 1999. "Environmental Activism and the Construction of Risk: Implications for NGO Alliances." *Journal of International Development* 11, no. 5: 687–700.

Forsyth, T. 2000. "Environmental Social Movements in Thailand: How Important is Class?" *Asian Journal of Social* Sciences 29, no. 1: 35–51.

Forsyth, T. 2002. "What Happened on the Beach? Social Movements and Governance of Tourism in Thailand." *International Journal of Sustainable Development* 5, no. 1: 325–336.

Forsyth, T. 2003. *Critical Political Ecology: The Politics of Environmental Science.* Routledge.

Giddens, A. 1973. *The Class Structure of the Advanced Societies.* Hutchinson University Library and Harper and Row.

Giddens, A. 1994. *Beyond Left and Right: The Future of Radical Politics.* Polity.

Goodman, J. 1998. *The Akha: Guardians of the Forest.* Bangkok: Teak House.

Guha, R., and Martinez-Alier, J. 1997. *Varieties of Environmentalism: Essays North and South.* Earthscan.

Haas, P. 1992. "Introduction: Epistemic communities and international policy coordination," *International Organization* 46, no. 1: 1–35.

Hamilton, L. 1988. "Forestry and Watershed Management." In *Deforestation*, ed. J. Ives and D. Pitt. Routledge.

Hirsch, P. 1997. *Seeing Forests for the Trees: Environmentalism in Thailand.* Chiang Mai: Silkworm.

Hirsch, P. 1998. "The Politics of Environment: Opposition and Legitimacy." In *Political Change in Thailand*, ed. K. Hewison. Routledge.

Jackson, C. 1995. "Radical Environmental Myths: A Gender Perspective," *New Left Review* 210: 124–140.

Jasanoff, S. 1990. *The Fifth Branch: Science Advisers as Policy makers.* Cambridge University Press.

Jasanoff, S. 1996. "Science and Norms in Global Environmental Regimes." In *Earthly Goods*, ed. F. Hampson and J. Reppy. Cornell University Press.

Johnson, C., and Forsyth, T. 2002. "In the Eyes of the State: Negotiating a 'Rights-Based Approach' to Forest Conservation in Thailand," *World Development* 30, no. 9: 1591–1605.

Keck, M., and Sikkink, K. 1998. *Activists Beyond Borders: Advocacy Networks in International Politics.* Cornell University Press.

Leach, M., and Mearns, R. eds. 1996. *The Lie of the Land: Challenging Received Wisdom on the African Environment.* James Currey.

Lohmann, L. 1993. "Resisting Green Globalism." In *Global Ecology*, ed. W. Sachs. Zed and Fernwood.

Lohmann, L. 1999. Forest Cleansing: Racial Oppression in Scientific Nature Conservation. Briefing 13, Corner House, Sturminster Newton, UK.

Nash, F. 1982. *Wilderness and the American Mind*, third edition, revised. Yale University Press.

Offe, C. 1985. "New Social Movements: Challenging the Boundaries of Institutional Politics." *Social Research* 52, no. 4: 817–868.

Peet, R., and Watts, M., eds. 1996. *Liberation Ecologies: Environment, Development and Social Movements*. Routledge.

Pinkaew Luangaramsi. 1997. "Reconstructing Nature: The Community Forest Movement and Its Challenges to Forest Management in Thailand." In *Community Forestry at a Crossroads*, ed. M. Victor et al. Report 16, Regional Community Forestry Training Center, Bangkok.

Princen, T., Finger, M., et al. 1994. *Environmental NGOs in World Politics: Linking the Local and the Global*. Routledge.

Rigg, J. 1991. "Grass-Roots Development in Thailand: A Lost Cause?" *World Development* 19, no. 2/3: 199–211.

Schmidt-Vogt, D. 1999. *Swidden Farming and Fallow Vegetation in Northern Thailand*, Geoecological Research, vol.8. Stuttgart: Franz Steiner Verlag.

Shiva, V. 1993. "The Greening of the Global Reach." In *Global Ecology*, ed. W. Sachs. Zed and Fernwood.

Stott, P. 1991. "Mu'ang and Pa: Elite Views of Nature in a Changing Thailand." In *Thai Constructions of Knowledge*, ed. M. Chitakasem and A. Turton. School of Oriental and African Studies, London.

Thompson, M., Warburton, M., and Hatley, T. 1986. *Uncertainty on a Himalayan Scale*. Milton Ash.

Tiffen, M., Mortimore, M., and Gichuki, F. 1994. *More People, Less Erosion? Environmental Recovery in Kenya*. Wiley.

Tourraine, A. 1981. *The Voice and the Eye*. Cambridge University Press.

Van Beld, J. 1991. *The Princess, the Monk, and the Rainforest*. Video for television,

Walker, A. 2001. "The 'Karen Consensus,' Ethnic Politics and Resource-Use Legitimacy in Northern Thailand." *Asian Ethnicity* 2, no. 2: 145–162.

Zimmerer, K. 2000. "The Reworking of Conservation-Geographies: Non-equilibrium Landscapes and Nature-Society Hybrids." *Annals of Association of American Geographers* 90, no. 2: 356–369.

9

Merchants of Diversity: Scientists as Traffickers of Plants and Institutions

Astrid Scholz

The production of scientific knowledge takes place in a diverse array of settings. In addition to much studied laboratories (see, for example, Latour 1987), scientists inhabit a variety of geographical, political, and cultural sites and frequently travel between these. Indeed, as I argue in this chapter, scientists are among today's vanguard agents of globalization and localization. As wanderers between local and global realms circumscribed by scientific explorations of biological diversity for drug discovery, they are central to emerging institutions for the governance of nature in the twenty-first century.

Natural products chemistry is the systematic study of secondary metabolites—chemical compounds produced by plants and other organisms as defenses against predators, in skin and hair color and for other functions. Its practitioners rely on expeditions to collect the organic raw material for their scientific inquiries, both retracing geopolitically charged botanical expeditions of past centuries and charting new relationships. Botanical expeditions of the eighteenth and nineteenth centuries extracted local knowledges and resources, and strategically relocated them to serve the interests of the British Empire and the nascent United States. The practices of modern-day natural products chemistry, however, constitute a more complicated set of relationships that is characterized by a hybrid localization-globalization dynamic. Scientists, as I will argue in this chapter, have become central to the global management of genetic resources as they transport biological samples, knowledges, technology and institutions between different knowledge production sites, localities, and cultures. Through these practices, they are simultaneously at risk of reinforcing colonial hierarchies and uniquely positioned to overcome these hierarchies.

"Bioprospecting" illustrates the new roles that scientists play as knowledge and institution brokers, mediating between diverse geographical localities and concomitant knowledges through expedition-based science. This echoes the argument that, in creating classification schemes and parsing the natural world in particular ways, scientific practices also create political structures and order (e.g., Bowker and Star 1999). Classification schemes such as taxonomy—accompanied, in the case of "bioprospecting," by records of useful knowledge associated with particular species—are designed to be global and universal. Shared nomenclature and protocols for relating biological samples to the body of botanical knowledge, as well as the common language of chemical structures are key to enabling traffic in genetic resources, producing knowledge about them, and creating institutions for their governance. Scientists performing these classifications, sifting through their own and others' knowledges and determining what is a valuable, genetically encoded chemical compound and what is not, are indispensable to the management of biological diversity.

In this chapter, I consider the role of past and present botanical explorations. Historically, transfers of botanical knowledge were typically one-way, and advanced imperial needs for standardized knowledge and commodities. They also established institutional structures whose very design still shapes modern botanical expeditions, which may thus inadvertently perpetuate older hierarchies of knowledge and power. Many present-day botanical expeditions take place in the service of natural products chemistry. Natural product chemistry, in turn, plays a central role in modern pharmaceutical research, where it is located at a critical juncture of competing drug discovery paradigms. Its practitioners entered the limelight of international environmental politics in the late 1980s, when "bioprospecting" raised the triple promise of plant-based cures, sustainable development, and scientific laurels.

I also consider how natural products chemists and their colleagues negotiate the historical echoes and contemporary exigencies of their practice in the context of a novel institutional form of environmental governance: bioprospecting agreements. The International Cooperative Biodiversity Group (ICBG) projects serve as a case study. Contrasting one of these—based in Panama and run by principal investigators (PIs) from the United States—with the rest of the ICBG projects, I argue that local-global knowledge and power relationships are being worked out by scientists, and indeed that the emerging international framework for governing biological diversity relies on scientists to do this work.

From Botanical Expeditions to Bioprospecting Agreements

The German naturalist and explorer Alexander von Humboldt wrote of his research in *Ideen zu einer Geographie der Pflanzen* (Ideas for a Geography of Plants):

> It entails contemplating the influence of nutrition on the formation of character, as well as considering the long sea voyages and wars through which distant nations have sought to gather and disseminate plant products. In this manner, plants affect the moral and political history of man. (Humboldt 1807, p. 61, quoted in Flitner 1995, p. 10; my translation)

In thus promoting the study of natural history, Humboldt pointed to the intimate links between plant collections and geopolitics, which characterized his times and that persist today.

Science in the National Interest

Botanists accompanied the voyages of Captain Cook and other naval expeditions from the 1770s onward. Botanists of that time have been called the "global agents" of Adam Smith (Schaffer 1996, p. 339), creating some of the conduits through which Britain could establish and exercise her economic power. In his 1776 book *The Wealth of Nations*, Adam Smith promoted governmental regulation of a nation's economy for the purpose of augmenting state power at the expense of rival nations' powers, notably through the pursuit of a positive balance of trade. Key to this mercantilist agenda was the development and protection of new trading opportunities. A pivotal figure among the botanizing gentleman explorers of this time was Sir Joseph Banks, who not only conducted extraordinarily extensive collections on a number of voyages, but also created an international network of collectors. These supplied both his private collection and Kew Gardens, which had been created under George III in 1772 by the joining of two royal estates (Miller 1996; Drayton 2000).

Under Banks, Kew Gardens became the hub of an extensive network in which knowledge of the natural world *became* the source of new economic and imperial opportunities (Miller and Reill 1996; Drayton 2000). Kew Gardens served as an obligatory passage point (in the sense used by Latour

1987, pp. 244–245) for accumulating, organizing, and disseminating materials from voyages undertaken by Banks and others. Central to these botanical expeditions was the procurement of plants with existing or potential practical uses.

By the eighteenth century, the East India Company employed botanists to find "drugs and dying materials fit for the European market" (Mackay 1996, p. 50, quoting from a letter written by Sir Joseph Banks), instructing them to find and collect local knowledges and resources and bring them back to Britain and Kew Gardens. Over 100 collectors—trained horticulturists and botanists as well as Navy personnel and employees of the colonial administration—traveled the globe on behalf of Banks (Mackay 1996). Equipped with veritable shopping lists of desirable species, they scoured every continent except Antarctica for plants such as tea from China, the cultivation of which Banks was exploring in India in collaboration with the East India Company (Mackay 1996).

Typically, transfer of botanical knowledge was one-way and collectors were furnished explicit instructions to observe local methods of cultivation and manufacture. Kew Gardens provided the space and facilities "where the possibilities of acclimatizing plants from one part of the globe to another might be tested and from which material for the experimental work in any climate would always be available" (Cameron 1952, quoted in Frost 1996, p. 75). For example, breadfruit trees were transplanted to the British West Indies to provide a cheap staple food for the slaves there (Fowler and Mooney 1990; Frost 1996).

Initially, the American colonies were one of the botanical experimenting grounds of the British empire. As early as 1699, a farm was established in South Carolina to test the adaptability of mulberry trees, indigo, tobacco, hemp, flax, and cotton to the local climate (Klose 1950, p. 10). Rice was introduced in 1688, and sugar cane in the early eighteenth century. Shortly after the United States gained independence, botanical collections became important for achieving the country's self-sufficiency.

In *First the Seed*, Jack Kloppenburg traces the early US quest for foreign germplasm to the interests of the propertied elites: "George Washington, like many large landowners, imported large quantities of seed from Britain and other European countries. His papers record orders of a wider variety of species from an English supplier and, in 1794, 39 kinds of tropical plants, including the breadfruit tree then popular in the West Indies as a food for slaves." (Kloppenburg 1988, p. 52) Thomas Jefferson, another large landowner, used his personal wealth and connections to obtain rice and other germplasm from as far away as China. Jefferson was furthermore active in disseminating rice and other seeds among his friends and members of agricultural societies. Prompted by Jefferson's and other private, unsystematic and largely unremunerated efforts to obtain plants and seeds from abroad, Secretary of the Treasury William L. Crawford issued a directive calling for the assistance of naval and consular personnel in 1819. Echoing Jefferson's sentiment that "the greatest service which can be rendered to any country is to add a useful plant to its culture" (quoted in Mackay 1996, p. 49), Crawford argued for state-support of botanical collections: "The introduction of such [agricultural] inventions, the results of the labor and science of other nations, is still more important, especially to the United States, whose institutions secure to the importer no exclusive advantage from their introduction." (quoted in Klose 1950, p. 26)

In other words, agricultural self-sufficiency was a matter of national importance that could not be achieved by individual efforts, especially since these were then not rewarded financially.

This early focus on incentives helped establish the US Patent and Trademark Office as a central institution for the transfer of botanical knowledge. Interpreting the Patent Office's charge to encourage innovation broadly, Henry Ellsworth (Commissioner of Patents between 1836 and 1849) considered the provision of novel plant varieties to be just as much worth protecting as mechanical inventions. He pursued, and in 1839 obtained, Congressional funding for the collection and distribution of seeds, plants, and agricultural statistics. The ensuing collections by naval and consular personnel all over the world were preserved in botanical collections or propagated in greenhouses and gardens, much as in Britain. From there, however, useful plants were distributed by the Patent Office, which sent out a steadily increasing stream of seed packages to farmers. By 1855, over a million packages had been distributed (Kloppenburg 1988), illustrating the success of the government's efforts to foster the economic utilization of exotic plants.

Significantly, this division of labor put botanic gardens in the role of supplying the raw material for state-sponsored private entrepreneurial activity. Initially this role was limited to the propagation of seeds that were shipped out to farmers by the Patent Office. This institutional arrangement, however, also came to facilitate the growth of the pharmaceutical industry.

Following the example of British gardens, US institutions such as the New York Botanical Garden (NYBG) had been collecting medicinal plants as part of their scientific research programs.

Botanical expeditions to South America for the Parke Davis company, for example, also produced samples that by 1882 had been marketed as 46 new preparations (mostly fluid extracts) for a variety of ailments (Liebenau 1987). And by the 1930s, NYBG curator Boris A. Krukoff had begun a profitable collaboration with Merck Sharpe and Dohme (now Merck), collecting and working on curare and quinine (Landrum 1986).[1] NYBG's collaborations with Merck and other pharmaceutical companies continue to the present, placing it and other US botanic gardens firmly in an international network of "bioprospecting," natural products chemistry and drug discovery.

The institutional structures established for colonial botanical knowledge transfers may by their very design perpetuate older hierarchies of knowledge or power, or are at least perceived to do so. As one scientist at Kew whose lab screens and analyzes plant samples from all over the world remarked: "We should not go in with [what] we would now term imperial views of things. But we are caught up within our own history, aren't we? We can't change what happened. We can change what we do now to make it reflect the situation of the world."[2]

The colonial echoes pervading botanical expeditions put considerable responsibility on individual scientists in how they conduct the negotiations for the central tool governing the exchange and transfer of botanical knowledge today, bioprospecting agreements.

The word "bioprospecting" was coined by the Cornell University chemist Thomas Eisner to describe the systematic search for secondary metabolites with potentially therapeutic properties as a strategy for creating economic incentives for conserving biological diversity (Eisner 1989; 1991). "Bioprospecting" connotatively likens the search for natural products to surveying and mining of other natural resources, and is contested because of its associations with the colonial, one-sided transfer of botanical knowledge in the pursuit of economic power and commodities.[3] Before considering the Panamanian case of scientists brokering bioprospecting agreements, we turn to the science of natural products chemistry. In this field, knowledge generation is intrinsically tied to the development of new institutions and power relationships.

Natural Products Chemistry and Drug Design

Natural products chemistry is the systematic study of secondary metabolites—chemical compounds produced by plants and other organisms as defenses against predators, in skin and hair color and for other functions. From its inception in the early twentieth century, the pharmaceutical industry has relied on botanical collections and natural products chemistry. It is commonplace to note that modern medicine has roots in plant-based folk medicine,[4] a tradition that has gradually been displaced by modern technology and biochemistry. Far from being a linear progression, however, the development of the pharmaceutical industry exhibits a cyclical pattern around two distinguishable, but interwoven approaches to drug design that carry with them very different understandings of knowledges and the (local and global) practices central to them.

The first, "random" or empirical screening, originated in biology and the plant-based traditions of medicine. The isolation, purification, and manufacture of plant-derived medicines extended the study of drugs such as opium, hemlock, and belladonna, which were well known and systematically studied as far back as ancient Greece. In modern times, H. E. Merck—the founder of the eponymous company—had been manufacturing purified plant extracts, notably alkaloids, on a large scale since 1827. A host of other companies such as GlaxoSmithKline, Bristol-Myers Squibb, and Pfizer likewise trace their origins to the traditional apothecary, and natural products continue to be investigated in these companies. This empirical or random approach to drug discovery relies on the localized efficacy of natural products, typically as recorded in folklore, anthropological reports, or past expeditions, which it then seeks to refine and bring to bear on universal disease categories.

By contrast, the "rational" approach to drug design is premised on the knowledge about disease mechanisms and attempts to design the perfect molecule to intervene in particular biochemical pathways "from scratch" (Aylward 1995). This approach grew out of the chemical-manufacturing roots of the second major branch of the pharmaceutical industry. Initially motivated by war-time shortages of drugs, the Swiss dyestuff manufacturer Sandoz (later Novartis) turned to pharmaceutical research. Sandoz also founded one of the first dedicated industrial research departments in 1917, following a trend set by the founders of Burroughs, Wellcome and Company (later GlaxoSmithKline) in the 1880s.

Over the course of the twentieth century, these two approaches—the random/biological and rational/chemical—have been in constant tension, both within companies and drug discovery generally. In the early stages of the pharmaceutical industry, scientific research turned to increasingly sophisticated experiments to study diseases and their biochemical mechanisms. Alexander Fleming famously observed the bacteria-inhibiting activity of penicillin in 1929, leading other scientists to investigate the compounds produced by the soil microbe *Streptomyces* in the hope of finding further antibiotic activity. Similarly, using a combination of laboratory tests and subsequent methodical screening of great numbers of chemical agents (in this case microorganisms) that still characterizes modern drug discovery practices, the anti-tuberculosis agent streptomycin was discovered (Albers-Schönberg 1995).

Marking the beginning of the "rational" approach to drug discovery was the increasing knowledge about the biochemical functioning of vitamins and steroid hormones. Scientists isolated and synthesized these compounds in order to study the metabolic processes they were part of. These newly identified compounds were viewed as potential templates for drugs that could intervene in metabolic processes, for example to correct a malfunction. The steroid hormone cortisone eventually became the first therapy for arthritis and inflammatory disease (Albers-Schönberg 1995).

By the middle of the twentieth century, empirical and rational approaches co-existed and were increasingly integrated within companies, foreshadowing modern practices of identifying molecules and turning them into medicines through alternating biological testing and chemical modification. Combining the strengths of both approaches, the increasing capacity to synthesize new compounds from scratch was coupled with "blueprints" for new classes of compounds derived from plants. Increasing systematization of screening efforts and the demand for new sources of interesting compounds like alkaloids led firms to undertake massive collection efforts. Based on the historical success of plant and microbial compounds, they turned to natural products to feed the research pipelines. Drugs like the *Rauwolfia* alkaloid reserpine (used in the treatment of high blood pressure) or the cancer drugs vinblastine and vincristine derived from the rosy periwinkle (*Catharanthus roseus*) form part of the canon of success stories about the healing capacity of plants and other organisms that, in turn, is central to the bioprospecting story promoted by conservation biologists in the 1980s.

Many of these discoveries were made without the permission, contractual involvement, or remuneration of local knowledge holders or national governments. Pharmaceutical firms either collaborated with botanical gardens to obtain plants for extraction—thus using the historical arrangements and conduits for botanical knowledge transfers—or established programs to facilitate foreign collections by their own employees. This latter practice resulted, for example, in the transfer of a soil sample from Norway that eventually yielded the best-selling immune suppressant drug cyclosporin A (Svarstad and Dhillion 2000).

With the advent of biotechnology in the 1970s, natural products and the empirical approach to screening fell out of favor. Techniques such as combinatorial chemistry and polymerase chain reaction put the rational dream of creating therapeutic compounds from scratch within apparent reach, and companies invested heavily in the new technologies. The early success of human growth hormone, protease inhibitors and other biotech drugs notwithstanding, by the 1990s it was apparent that biotechnology would not deliver on its promise. As firms shifted their drug discovery direction again, biotechnology techniques and equipment, however, remained the gold standard for drug discovery.

Rather than generating new drugs, the greater importance of biotechnology, therefore, may lie in defining how drug discovery is done. Both the techniques and the institutional structures engendered by the biotechnology business model have contributed to the renaissance of natural products. By the end of the twentieth century, natural products chemists not only utilized biotechnology techniques, but became embedded in a set of practices and premises about how scientific research is done. Part and parcel of the biotech business model are contractual collaborations between specialized "R&D service providers" (including academic research laboratories) and large pharmaceutical companies, with the early identification of patentable knowledge and innovations as their goal.

This business model has come to dominate the practices of natural products chemists, including the domain of publicly funded research. For example, the Developmental Therapeutics Program of the National Cancer Institute (NCI) is premised on the promotion of research for the benefit of the public, which it facilitates via an extensive licensing process to private industry (Mays et al. 1997). The NCI acts as a clearing house for many industry-academic collaborations, and in particular serves as a repository for biological samples collected all over the world. Researchers at the NCI conduct the initial research on compounds derived from these samples, which—if promising—are licensed to industry for further development.

A prominent example is the anti-cancer drug Taxol, which was derived from an extract of the bark of the Yew tree (*Taxus brevifolia*), and licensed to Bristol-Myers Squibb (Goodman and Walsh 2001). Significantly, after having failed the whole-mouse screens used in the 1960s, the sample that eventually led to the discovery of Taxol lay dormant in the NCI's storage facility until scientists re-screened all natural product samples in the 1980s using the new molecular assays developed in the biotech era. Taxol entered the market in the early 1990s, just as bioprospecting emerged as a new model for biological knowledge transfers.

Since natural products chemists not only prepare, extract, and analyze botanical and other organic samples, but also collect them, they have become central to the negotiation of bioprospecting agreements. Dealing with economic and legal issues has become part of their practices. Indeed, by virtue of the NCI's funding structure, which requires principal investigators to be associated with universities, many academic scientists serve as coordinators of multilateral bioprospecting collaborations. To these collaborations they frequently bring years, sometimes decades, of familiarity and rapport with host countries, often in the global South. One natural products chemists said his lab group was being allowed into Palau "basically on a handshake and a gentleman's agreement in exchange for providing some educational opportunities."[5] In return for local samples and knowledge, scientists also transport the biotech techniques and even the business model to other countries, notably when they negotiate bioprospecting collaborations between developing countries and pharmaceutical companies.

At its core natural products chemistry is the transformation and harnessing of nature through chemistry, processes that bring biological material and associated knowledge into the realm of Western science and industry. As a field central to drug design, however, it has also been reconfigured over the course of the twentieth century. While the random/biological approach relies on local knowledge about diseases and agents effective against them, it has had difficulties generalizing locally effective chemical compounds to larger disease categories. By the same token, the rational/chemical approach has not delivered on its promise to design molecular keys that unlock entire diseases. Its biotechnological extension, meanwhile, has produced many new techniques and organizational innovations that have come to define contemporary drug discovery practice.

Natural products chemistry experienced a renaissance in the 1990s, at the intersection of these competing drug discovery philosophies, when hybrid possibilities opened up at the intersection of biotechnological innovations and the conservation agenda of Western biologists, promoting "bioprospecting" as a vehicle for sustainable development. Natural products chemistry is currently embedded in the biotechnological business model. In this model, scientific practices are embedded in extensive transnational, contractually mediated, networks, and scientists relocalize biological diversity in the nodes of this network as brokers of samples, knowledges, and institutions for bioprospecting.

Scientists in Action: Making Biodiversity Politics in the ICBG Projects

The scientific work of natural products chemists and other collectors of botanical samples takes place across large geographical distances and cultural divides. The resulting traffic in knowledge, biological materials and money is central to global efforts to manage biological diversity. To paraphrase Bruno Latour (1999), it is not just the references to the natural world that circulate as they are multiply transformed and translated over the course of scientific work; the scientists making the transformations themselves circulate across a number of political, cultural, and epistemological boundaries.

A case in point is the Panamanian ICBG project, one of five projects of the International Collaborative Biodiversity Groups (ICBG) program. The ICBG program is jointly sponsored by the National Institutes of Health (NIH), the National Science Foundation (NSF) and the US Agency for International Development (USAID). The ICBG seeks to explore potential relationships between drug development, biological diversity and economic growth (Rosenthal 1997). Among international bioprospecting agreements, the ICBG projects are considered among the "best practices" examples for relating to local communities and host countries, collecting biological specimens, and benefit sharing.

Common to all ICBG projects is the use of multilateral contractual mechanisms for regulating access to and sharing benefits from genetic resources.

Since the signing of the Convention on Biological Diversity (CBD) in 1992, the modalities of individual bioprospecting agreements and the people who negotiate them have come under scrutiny both globally and locally. For example, in 2000 the ICBG projects were among the recipients of the "Captain Hook" awards for biopiracy given out by an international alliance of NGOs opposing the trade and transfer of genetic resources from countries of the South to laboratories and companies in the North. Scientists are typically centrally involved in crafting bioprospecting agreements, and in the process negotiate not only the ways in which local knowledges and resources are relocated. They also mediate between the historical trajectories of past botanical expeditions and the economic expediencies of contemporary drug discovery practices.

Science and Scientists at the Panama ICBG

The Panamanian ICBG project is based on a particular, ecologically motivated rationale for screening tropical plants. For years, the American scientists heading the project and their graduate students have been coming to Panama to conduct research on the chemical defense mechanisms of young plants, which have been shown to produce different and more concentrated metabolites in the early life stages than older plants. Like conservation biologists since the 1970s (Takacs 1996), these scientists eventually turned their interest into funding proposals to combine their research with conservation strategies. The results have been published and promoted as a "new paradigm for drug discovery in tropical rainforests" (Capson et al. 1996; Coley and Kursar 1996; Kursar et al. 1999).

The project is spread across labs at the Smithsonian Tropical Research Institute (STRI), facilities at the University of Panama, and a local medical research institute. Benefiting from the compact geography of Panama, the project's resident, locally trained botanists collect new leaves from plants on a list of currently 600 species cleared for collection by the Panamanian authorities. These samples are processed at STRI and the other labs, and extracts are shipped to a number of collaborating industry labs in the United States. This transfer of samples is governed by a contract negotiated by the three principal investigators (PIs), and reflects their unique collecting rationale.

Firstly, by collecting young leaves and processing them fresh and locally, the Panamanian project deviates from standard practices. Historically, botanists and natural products chemists typically collected samples in one place, dried or otherwise preserved them before shipping, and then extracted and analyzed them in laboratories located in another country. As one PI pointed out, however, drying plants is like leaving drugs out in the sunshine and then being surprised that they lose their efficacy.[6] This divergence from the prevailing practices of natural products chemists and botanists (including the other ICBG projects) is not accidental. By appealing to the "better science" of their particular, ecological, approach, the PIs were able to attract the funding of the ICBG program and subsequently to engage in the most extensive and complex research project of their careers.

Secondly, processing samples locally keeps a lot of the analytical work local. Researchers in the Panama ICBG project have developed biomedical assays for use at STRI and the collaborating institutions in Panama. One US PI is a biochemist whose background in enzyme chemistry was helpful in adapting some of the assays used in drug discovery for local conditions. He credits his local colleagues with considerable creativity in setting up a malaria assay using fluorimeter technology, which identifies active compounds by the light-emitting chemical tag they activate. By contrast, the standard assay used in American and European labs uses radioactive isotopes, an unusable technique in Panama because of the lack of nuclear waste disposal facilities.

The analytical chemistry being done at STRI and the other project institutions is a source of pride to both the team and the broader local community. The project labs employ about a dozen Panamanian chemistry and biology students who eagerly embraced the opportunity to present their work during a site visit by NIH and NCI officials. Also, several project activities have garnered considerable media attention, with national newspapers reporting on the fluorimeter, and on the recognition that the project will bring to Panama's biodiversity. The PIs repeatedly pointed to this external validation as an important by-product of their bioprospecting goals. They hope that pride in Panamanian science and the country's natural resources, bolstered by the positive media coverage, will increase environmental awareness in Panama.

The Economics of Bioprospecting in Panama

The PIs for the Panama project negotiated the agreement governing the transfer of samples, technology and benefits with the help of an intellectual property lawyer. The three PIs initially felt overwhelmed at the sheer volume of legal theory and examples they had to absorb before drafting their own agreement. Precedents set by numerous bioprospecting agreements, particularly those in the mold of the bilateral agreement struck between the Costa Rican National Institute for Biodiversity (INBio) and the pharmaceutical giant Merck in 1991 (see the examples in ten Kate and Laird 1999), served as templates. It is not surprising, therefore, that the Panamanian agreement contains structural elements similar to those in other collaborations: upfront payments, milestone payments and royalties, and a scheme for dividing these monies.

With regard to the latter, the PIs in the Panama ICBG project designed a "club model" that is notable for its unusually favorable treatment of the host country, local knowledges and the conservation agenda. All incoming monies are split three ways: 30 percent go to a trust fund set up by a Panamanian environmental organization, Fundacion Natura, for its environmental micro-grant program; 20 percent to the Panamanian national parks authority; and 50 percent to the club of collaborators, who get equal shares. This club includes STRI, the University of Panama and a Panamanian medical institute. In the future, if for example indigenous groups chose to participate, they would simply join this club and "the pie would be shared equally so that there's no haggling over whose contribution counts for how much and how important it is."[7] In this model the various host country institutions get the lion's share of any financial benefits, which are earmarked for conservation projects. Equal weight is given to knowledge produced in a variety of localities, including (in principle) indigenous knowledge about plants.

By contrast, multilateral agreements set up by other ICBG projects are biased toward the "inventors" of any discoveries and toward the later-stage royalty benefits from an eventual discovery. For example, an ICBG project involving researchers at the University of Illinois at Chicago (UIC) uses a fairly common trust fund model. In this model, 40 percent of any monies received go to a UIC trust fund and another 40 percent to the inventors at UIC.[8] 20 percent are split between various host organizations involved in the ICBG project in two countries (75 percent total, weighted according to their contribution to the royalty-generating project) and the lab group at UIC (25 percent). The trust fund is intended for projects in collaborating countries, but whether these will include conservation measures is left to the discretion of the fund administrators.

Clearly, the UIC model presumes that the more significant part of the scientific work governed by a bioprospecting agreement is done at the US academic institution involved. A simple numerical accounting of a hypothetical royalties payment of $1 million from a drug discovery illustrates this. In the Panamanian club model, three-quarters ($750,000) of that amount would accrue to source country institutions, with half allocated to conservation purposes. By contrast, host country collaborators in the UIC model could only expect $150,000. Where scientists see the center of their knowledge production—both geographically and philosophically—thus has significant implications for institutional mechanisms of biodiversity management.

With more of the analytical work being done in-country, technology transfer also takes on a different dimension. In many bioprospecting agreements, the technology transferred is limited to trucks and other tools needed for collecting, and occasionally includes used lab equipment for teaching purposes. Even much-touted *quid pro quo* schemes that trade samples and medicinal knowledge for infrastructure projects have apparently fallen far short of expectations on the part of the local communities involved (Svarstad 2000). The PIs of the Panamanian ICBG, however, have made technical capacity-building a priority. As part of the project—and in addition to the usual trucks, GIS equipment and lab instruments—they financed the purchase of a Nuclear Magnetic Resonance (NMR) machine, housed at STRI. This instrument has allowed the PIs to attract international postdocs, and made possible a sufficiently sophisticated level of chemical analysis of the biological samples.[9]

This strategy institutionalizes natural product research to levels comparable to those typically found in laboratories in industrialized countries. It is an example of building capacity in a source country beyond what would be required for just supplying the drug pipeline with raw materials. Not coincidentally, the NMR purchase benefits STRI, which used to be a prime US-funded tropical disease research facility. Its role diminished when the United States pulled out of Panama in 1999. The PIs may well succeed in "translating" (Latour 1999) their goals of finding drugs, protecting biodiversity, and capacity building into a future for STRI as a "center of excellence" for natural products research on a par with the leading labs in the United States.

The use of the NMR machine as a key technology for doing scientific work illustrates the capacity of "technology packages"—that is, techniques and tools born of and embedded in particular institutional and scientific practices that prescribe how a particular technology is used and deployed (Fujimura 1996)—to affect the distribution of power in biodiversity management. Proponents of bioprospecting frequently point to the lack of sophisticated scientific infrastructure and personnel as a reason for considering samples from source countries little more than raw materials. The main work of finding the pharmacological value of such samples is done with the help of expensive and sophisticated technology, typically at university or industry labs in wealthier "user" countries. Many standardized biotechnology packages require an auxiliary infrastructure, for example to deal with radioactive waste from assay technologies, that does not exist in "source" countries. In other words, the lack of key technologies is both caused by and perpetuates the perceived backwardness of a country. It is by countering these dynamics that the actors involved in crafting multilateral agreements such as the Panamanian ICBG can have real impact on framing the global management of biodiversity.

Rainforest Politics

The Panamanian ICBG project resonates with political issues at the international level. It is directly tied to on-going negotiations over the Convention on Biological Diversity (CBD). At the 5th Conference of the Parties in Nairobi in May 2000, rumors circulated among indigenous observers that the Panamanian project was about to fold because of its reportedly worst record of all ICBG projects in terms of involving local communities. One observer, repeating the common political rhetoric, attributed this failure to the quasi-colonial relationship between Panama and the United States and said that "the Smithsonian" (i.e., STRI) was very top-down and paternalistic.[10] His characterization illustrates how even well-intentioned and seemingly well-executed bioprospecting projects can be associated, albeit rhetorically, with the exploitative history of past botanic expeditions.

The ICBG projects have been cited by opponents of bioprospecting as examples of biopiracy, but the one most often singled out by international NGOs is one located in the politically charged Mexican province of Chiapas, where the PIs became embroiled in negotiations over access that eventually led to the project's termination in early 2002 (*Nature* 2001). The ICBG program director characterized the Chiapas experience as being ambushed by a "stochastic NGO," i.e., one that just happens to be where the ICBG program is considering a new project and proceeds to intervene in the negotiations with local communities.[11] The case of the Chiapas ICBG underscores the effectiveness of the narrative of "biopiracy," and local NGOs' ability to tap into global networks that have formed around this narrative. This shared narrative connects them with the global environmental movement and reinforces their local political power (Gille 2000).

The PIs in Panama also had to learn how to negotiate with indigenous communities and to develop both a language and mechanisms for equitable agreements. For example, the Naso, an indigenous community with whom the project team collaborates on an inventory of medicinal plants, are not interested in participating directly in drug discovery activities. The Naso, however, have asked the project to expand its shamans' apprentice program, which provides communities in remote parts of their territory with health care. The program pairs the remaining practicing shamans in the tribal area with students from the communities who learn the medicinal uses of plants, as well as how to collect, cultivate and catalog them.[12]

The Naso have opted not to participate in the academic-corporate research aspect of the project, but reserve the right to do so at a later date. The group's primary concern is with preserving its own local knowledge, aided by the ICBG PIs and funds set aside for that purpose in the Panama project. Thus, the same channels are used both to globalize local knowledge and to re-localize this knowledge and keep it relevant on Panamanian terms. A presentation by one of the PIs at the 2000 annual meeting of all ICBG projects underscored the spirit of epistemological equity with which the Panamanian project PIs approach their indigenous and local collaborators. In her exposition, she included the shamans in the scientific team while talking about the project personnel. By contrast, all the other ICBG project reports included similar work in a category "outreach to indigenous communities." One talk underscored the implicit "naturalness" of indigenous knowledge and culture by interspersing slides of bare-chested tribal women in traditional head-dress with images of rainforest flora and fauna.

Different practices and experiences within the group of ICBG projects demonstrate that a lot hinges on the sensitivity and sophistication of individual scientists, especially those in positions to negotiate access to and benefits from biological resources. Bioprospecting agreements govern the transfer of local knowledges and resources to other localities and their transformation into natural products chemistry and drugs. Being able to conduct these contractual negotiations, however gracefully and reflexively, has become part of the "scientist" job description, at least in the case of natural products chemists, ecologists, taxonomists and other experts who rely on the collection of biological samples.

The PIs for the Panama ICBG—like many conservation scientists working in other countries—are also making national biodiversity policy while negotiating bioprospecting agreements. In Panama they were directly involved in articulating the country's policy on handling and trading biological diversity, showing that in the case of bioprospecting, the "drift" of scientific practices into political outcomes persists across geographical as well as temporal distance (Latour 1999b). In the Panamanian case, the PIs were able to translate their interests (conducting cutting edge research and contributing to biodiversity conservation) into STRI's institutional interest in becoming a center of excellence again, as well as into Panamanian national pride (at the individual, university and state levels). In the process, they prepared for the transfer of local knowledges and resources on terms that are more fair and sensitive to history than the other ICBG projects.

Conclusion

International biodiversity collection programs, I have argued, play a role in constructing, traversing, and translating between realms of local and global knowledges and resources. The Panamanian ICBG continues the mold of historical botanical expeditions in some respects: Northern scientists spend part of the year in a foreign country collecting specimens, using formerly colonial institutions and conduits of materials and knowledge, and relying on local knowledge holders in a variety of ways. Yet while these sorts of expeditions have a long history, they have also been reconfigured since the 1990s with the renewed importance of natural products for drug discovery.

Contemporary expeditions—or rather the modern production of scientific knowledge across a network of contractually linked places around the globe and the movement of people, plants and resources between them—illustrate the importance of scientific practices in shaping the power relationships of environmental governance. The Panamanian ICBG project shows that the practices of individual or groups of scientists are significant in shaping the institutional framework for bioprospecting and biodiversity management. These practices do not necessarily have to follow the historical example of one-sided extractions and delocalizations of biodiversity and local knowledge that continues to characterize many modern botanical expeditions. Rather, there is an element of reciprocity in the exchange of knowledge about plants' medicinal properties and of material benefits accruing from this knowledge.

The PIs of the Panama ICBG project have created a contractual form that is more even-handed and fair than those employed by other ICBG projects. They did this by engaging in both globalizing and localizing practices that successfully produce natural products for the world. The pharmaceutical industry gains samples for its drug discovery departments in the context of the biotech business model, but resources, knowledges, and technologies (such as the NMR) are also given back to the localities from which the products are derived, and local knowledge is preserved and strengthened *in situ*. This is not to suggest that the Panamanian institutional arrangement is exemplary; rather, it illustrates that scientists play a potentially important and beneficial role in respecting local perspectives in the governance of global environmental resources.

Notes

1. And author's interview with a present-day botanist at NYBG, November 1997.

2. Author's interview with lab director, Kew Botanical Gardens, March 1999.

3. Critics coined the word "biopiracy" to reflect the perspective of people whose knowledges and resources have been appropriated by past and present botanists (Kloppenburg and Rodriguez 1992; Shiva 1997).

4. The association with a folk, primitive, or otherwise "lesser" scientific knowledge is of course one way in which indigenous knowledge cultures are both localized and naturalized in the biodiversity discourse, while modern Western knowledge has become universalized.

5. Author's interview with John Faulkner, Scripps Institution for Oceanography, La Jolla, November 1999.

6. Author's interview with Tom Kursar, Smithsonian Tropical Research Institute, Panama, June 2000.

7. Ibid.

8. An additional provision allows for the possibility that the discovery is made in the labs of the industrial collaborator, in which case the ICBG institutions get 40% and the UIC lab group only 20%. In either case, the patent and the remaining 98%

of royalties go to the pharmaceutical company. The fact that most benefit sharing agreements are negotiations over a rather small share (royalties typically range from 1% to 5% of net sales) has prompted some commentators to dismiss this concept altogether (GRAIN 2000).

9. Author's interviews with Todd Capson, Smithsonian Tropical Research Institute, Panama, June 2000, and Lissy Coley, University of Utah, May 2003.

10. Author's interview with Alejandro Argumedo, Nairobi, May 2000.

11. Author's interview with Joshua Rosenthal, Bethesda, Maryland, November 15, 1999.

12. As part of this program, voucher samples are sent to the National Herbarium of Panama. These, however, contain no information on the traditional and medicinal uses associated with these plants, which is kept, in coded form, for exclusive use by the trainee shamans within their community.

References

Bowker, G. C., and S. L. Star. 1999. *Sorting Things Out: Classification and Its Consequences*. MIT Press.

Cameron, H. C. 1952. *Sir Joseph Banks*. Angus and Robertson.

Capson, T. L., P. D. Coley, and T. A. Kursar. 1996. "A New Paradigm for Drug Discovery in Tropical Rainforests." *Nature Biotechnology* 14: 1200–1201.

Coley, P. D., and T. A. Kursar. 1996. "Anti-Herbivore Defenses of Young Tropical Leaves: Physiological Constraints and Ecological Trade-Offs." In *Tropical Forest Plant Ecophysiology*, ed. S. Mulkey et al. Chapman and Hall.

Drayton, R. 2000. *Nature's Government: Science, Imperial Britain, and the "Improvement" of the World*. Yale University Press.

Eisner, T. 1989. "Prospecting for Nature's Chemical Riches." *Issues in Science and Technology* 6, no. 2: 31–34.

Eisner, T. 1991. "Chemical Prospecting: A Proposal for Action." In *Ecology, Economics, and Ethics*, ed. F. Bormann and R. Kellert. Yale University Press.

Flitner, M. 1995. *Sammler, Räuber und Gelehrte: Die Politischen Interessen an Pflanzengenetischen Ressources 1895–1995*. Campus Verlag.

Fowler, C., and P. Mooney. 1990. *Shattering: Food, Politics and the Loss of Genetic Diversity*. University of Arizona Press.

Frost, A. 1996. "The Antipodean Exchange." In *Visions of Empire*, ed. D. Miller and P. Reill. Cambridge University Press.

Fujimura, J. 1996. *A Sociohistory of the Quest for the Genetics of Cancer*. Harvard University Press.

Gille, Z. 2000. "Cognitive Cartography in a European Wasteland: Multinational Capital and Greens Vie for Village Allegiance." In *Global Ethnography*, ed. M. Burawoy et al. University of California Press.

Goodman, J., and V. Walsh. 2001. *The Story of Taxol: Nature and Politics in the Pursuit of an Anti-Cancer Drug.* Cambridge University Press.

GRAIN. 2000. *Biodiversity for Sale: Dismantling the Hype about Benefit Sharing.* Barcelona: Genetic Resources Action International (GRAIN).

Humboldt, A. v. 807. *Ideen zu einer Geographie der Pflanzen nebst einem Naturgemälde der Tropenländer.* Tübingen.

Kloppenburg, J. R. 1988. *First the Seed: The Political Economy of Plant Biotechnology.* Cambridge University Press.

Kloppenburg, J., and S. Rodriguez. 1992. "Conservationists or Corsairs?" *Seedling,* June-July: 12–17.

Klose, N. 1950. *America's Crop Heritage: The History of Foreign Plant Introduction by the Federal Government.* Iowa State College Press.

Kursar, T. A., Capson, T. L., Coley, P. D., Corley, D. G., Gupta, M. B., Harrison, L. A., Ortega-Barria, E., and Windsor, Donald M. 1999. "Ecologically Guided Bioprospecting in Panama." *Pharmaceutical Biology* 37, supplement: 114–126.

Landrum, L. R. 1986. *The Life and Botanical Accomplishments of Boris Alexander Krukoff.* New York Botanical Garden and Missouri Botanical Garden.

Latour, B. 1987. *Science in Action: How to Follow Scientists and Engineers through Society.* Harvard University Press.

Latour, B. 1999. *Pandora's Hope.* Harvard University Press.

Liebenau, J. 1987. *Medical Science and Medical Industry: The Formation of the American Pharmaceutical Industry.* Johns Hopkins University Press.

Mackay, D. 1996. "Agents of Empire: The Banksian Collectors and Evaluation of New Lands." *In Visions of Empire,* ed. D. Miller and P. Reill. Cambridge University Press.

Mays, T. D., K. Duffy Mazan, G. Cragg, and M. Boyd. 1997. "Triangular Privity—A Working Paradigm for the Equitable Sharing of Benefits from Biodiversity Research and Development." In *Global Genetic Resources,* ed. K. Hoagland and A. Rossman. Association of Systematics Collections.

Miller, D. P. 1996. "Joseph Banks, Empire, and 'Centers of Calculation' in Late Hannoverian London." In *Visions of Empire,* ed. D. Miller and P. Reill. Cambridge University Press.

Miller, D. P., and P. H. Reill, eds. 1996. *Visions of Empire: Voyages, Botany, and Representations of Nature.* Cambridge University Press.

Nature. 2001. "The Curtain Falls." *Nature* 414: 685.

Rosenthal, J. 1997. "Integrating Drug Discovery, Biodiversity Conservation, and Economic Development: Early Lessons for the International Cooperative Biodiversity Groups." In *Biodiversity and Human Health,* ed. F. Grifo and J. Rosenthal. Island.

Schaffer, S. 1996. "Visions of Empire: Afterword." *In Visions of Empire,* ed. D. Miller and P. Reill. Cambridge University Press.

Shiva, V. 1997. *Biopiracy: The Plunder of Nature and Knowledge.* South End.

Svarstad, H. 2000. "Local Interests and Foreign Interventions: Shaman Pharmaceuticals in Tanzania." In *Bioprospecting*, ed. H. Svarstad and S. Dhillion. Spartacus.

Svarstad, H., and S. S. Dhillion, eds. 2000. *Bioprospecting: From Biodiversity in the South to Medicines in the North*. Spartacus.

Takacs, D. 1996. *The Idea of Biodiversity: Philosophies of Paradise*. Johns Hopkins University Press.

ten Kate, K., and S. A. Laird. 1999. *The Commercial Use of Biodiversity: Access to Genetic Resources and Benefit Sharing*. Earthscan.

III

Knowledge Communities

10

Knowing the Urban Wasteland: Ecological Expertise as Local Process

Jens Lachmund

The last two or three decades have witnessed the growing importance of nature conservation in the city. Whereas traditional nature conservation tended to concentrate on the protection of rare species and pristine landscapes, the protection and promotion of natural habitats is now widely considered indispensable for environmentally friendly or "sustainable" urban development. As with many other environmental problems, the global and the local have become closely connected in this field. Issues such as biodiversity or habitat protection figure prominently on the agenda of global environmental problems (Yearley 1996; Hannigan 1995). They are framed according to universalizing discourses (Yearley 1996) of science as well as transnational policies and agreements. For example, the interdisciplinary field of urban ecology includes scholars and institutions from all over the world. Likewise, the notion of sustainability and its recent career in urban policy is linked to global initiatives such as the Agenda 21 and related scientific and political discourses. Given its geographical scope and its relation to these discourses, the rise of urban nature conservation can be seen as an almost global phenomenon. Moreover, Roger Keil (1995) has argued that the emergence of environmental issues in urban politics is in fact the result of other, mostly economic, processes of globalization which are centered particularly on large world-cities and which have made them hotspots of global environmental degradation. However, the globalization of environmental issues in general, as well as of those which are specific to the urban environment, should not lead us to underestimate the extent to which the constitution of environmental agendas remains embedded in and shaped through the particularities of local settings. Although increasingly backed by global discourses and policies, ecological planning has only been successfully implemented in a limited number of cities. Moreover, the way in which it has been articulated and implemented in local policies differs significantly from country to country and from city to city.

This chapter is a case study of the construction of a nature park in the German capital of Berlin. The park is now widely recognized as a pioneering project of urban ecology. By choosing a place-based approach, I want to shed light on the role of local settings in the construction of scientific environmental knowledge and related policies of nature conservation. Conceptually, the analysis draws upon the notion of science as local practice as it has been developed in various strands of recent science and technology studies. In particular, the scientific research laboratory has received much attention from this angle, although other "places of knowledge" (Shapin and Ophir 1991) have been considered in a similar way (see Smith 1998). As various studies have shown, such places are not merely passive sites in which knowledge is produced; rather they participate actively and constructively in shaping the content of scientific knowledge (cf. Knorr-Cetina 1981).

In focusing on a particular site, however, I do not mean to ignore the importance of space relations on a much larger scale, such as, for example, nation-wide debates on nature conservation and urban planning or the global processes mentioned above. As social geographer Doreen Massey (1993) has argued, places should not be regarded as enclosed spatial territories which have stable essential identities. Rather, in the globalized space of contemporary societies, places are to be seen as dynamic and open entities whose meanings and identities are constituted within a cross-cutting network of often global social relations and understanding. Likewise, studies of the local practices of science have emphasized the extent to which particular places of knowledge are implicated in translocal relationships. Accordingly, scientists routinely draw upon discursive and material resources which have been translocally accepted as standards of good science. At the same time, it is only by means of the standardization of objects, procedures and situations in different places that locally constituted phenomena are transformed into more or less universalized facts (Latour 1987). Rather than being an intrinsic property of scientific knowledge per se, universality is thus seen as the outcome of contingent processes of spatial extension which are full of internal ambivalences between, on the one hand, the deep-rootedness of science and technology in particular places and, on the other, the homogeneity of its trans-locally applied practices (Timmermans and Berg 1997; Singleton and Michael 1993).

Drawing upon the above considerations I consider the nature park not just as a preexisting object on which ecology projected its newly invented notions of nature in the city, nor just a passive container of ecological field-work practices. Berlin and the park were locales which interacted in multiple mutually constitutive ways with the epistemic and political practices that were situated within them. First, they acted as an intermediary space in which new forms of ecological expertise and urban policy were coproduced. A clear-cut boundary between science and other forms of knowing and acting on behalf of the sites never existed during this process. On the one hand, ecological knowledge formed part of the very definition of the park as a form of "nature" in the city and it materialized in new forms of ordering this space. On the other hand, it was also a local setting in which issues of urban politics and nature conservation were translated into research practices and in which new kinds of knowledge of the city's flora and the fauna were produced which in turn informed the discourse and practices of governing these spaces. Berlin and the site of the park can also be regarded as open or extraverted places. In terms of material-ecology, cities as much as railway-stations function as nodes within a world-wide traffic system which is always associated with a highly intensive, albeit unintended, exchange of organisms and seeds. Thus plants and animals from all over the world used to be brought to these places. At the same time, the project of turning the site into a park was also connected to the trans-local, and to some extent even global, discourses of science and conservation policy. Its protagonists not only drew upon concepts and practices which are widely shared among ecologists and conservationists in different places around the world; they also helped to create new insights which, to some extend, entered the wider culture of ecological expertise.

I will start my analysis with a brief overview of the local development of urban ecology in Berlin and the political process that led to the creation of the nature park. I will then examine the mutual interaction of ecological knowledge, governance, and place through three different phases of the trajectories of the wasteland: the process of ecological claims making, the design of the parks, and the development of park maintenance schemes. As I will argue, in all of these respects, ecological knowledge was locally appropriated, adapted and partly recreated by the participants. In this way

workable alignments were created between trans-locally established ecological knowledge traditions and the social, political and material contexts
provided by the site.

Urban Ecology in Berlin

Since the 1970s, environmental scientists of different backgrounds have
joined with local policy makers, citizens groups, and other institutions in
calling for ecological planning and landscape promotion in cities. This campaign not only fitted well with broadening concerns about environmental
issues in Germany, but also linked up with some international activities, such
as the UNESCO's Man and the Biosphere Program (since 1971) or Agenda
21 (since 1992) (Sukopp 1990, 1994). A basic tenet of this newly emerging
discourse was that cities were not devoid of nature. In contrast, they were
considered specific habitats or "biotopes" which hosted various species,
often even more than some rural landscapes. On the other hand, these ecologists argued that nature in the city was endangered by intensifying urban
development, and therefore that, measures should be taken to integrate
nature promotion systematically into the planning process. They maintained
that nature in the city should not only be preserved for its own sake, but also
for creating better conditions of life for urban citizens (Auhagen and Sukopp
1983). Regular contact with natural environments was considered a pre-
rogative of city-dwellers. Ecologists also considered nature conservation in
the city as a means of strengthening other components of the urban ecosystem, such as the quality of air, soil or water supply.

The former West Berlin was one of the foremost centers of this turn
toward urban nature conservation and planning. Whereas previous forms
of urban ecology had focused primarily on the relationship between
humans and the city, the Berlin ecologists based their view of the city on the
exploration of the plants and animals which spontaneously settled within
its confines. From this angle, they expanded their research interests to
include other factors such as the city's soil and climate and, furthermore, the
effect of human interventions on the interplay of these environmental factors. In many ways the emerging interest in studying the local ecosystems
of the city was a reflection of the local situation of the divided city. The lack
of accessible countryside around the western part of Berlin had long been
a pragmatic reason for biologists and ecological scientists to choose inner-

urban areas as research sites for field work. In particular, the large fields of rubble which had been left in the city from bombardment during World War II attracted the interest of botanists and other ecological field-scientists. From the 1970s, most of this research became centralized at the Institute for Ecology of the Technical University.

The Südgelände Project

Berlin is also a city in which ecological concepts were successfully translated into urban planning schemes, and, as a consequence, inscribed into the material order of the urban landscape. The seamless interconnectedness of these two aspects of urban ecology is exemplified by the city's most prominent nature conservation project, the nature park Schöneberger Südgelände.[1] The Südgelände is a former shunting station in the district of Schöneberg, the southern part of the former West Berlin. Because of the decline of traffic, large parts of the station fell out of use after the end of WWII. The site formed part of the railway system which was maintained by the East German Reichsbahn and was, therefore, inaccessible from surrounding neighborhoods. In the 1970s, officials of the West Berlin Senate were engaged in negotiations with the Reichsbahn in order to reach an agreement about the future use of the Südgelände and other parts of the railway system in the western part of the city. In 1974 an agreement was reached that a new freight station should be built at the site at the expense of the West Berlin Senate. However, as these plans became public around 1978, they met opposition from adjacent allotment tenants and other neighborhood activists who feared detrimental effects, such as traffic and noise.[2] Moreover, biologists and conservation activists were impressed by the dense vegetation which meanwhile had settled on the site. This was the starting point of a long campaign for preserving the Südgelände as a nature park.

Although this campaign faced strong resistance from government officials and the railway company, plans for a nature park were included in Berlin's land-use scheme (Flächennutzungsplan) and landscape program, both issued in 1988 (Senator für Stadtentwicklung und Umweltschutz Berlin 1988). One year later, a revision of the agreement between the Senate and the East German Reichsbahn paved the way for the realization of the nature park. However, it was only in 1995, five years after unification, that the site was given to the Senate, and its official legal status as a railway area was changed to that of part nature reserve and part a so-called landscape reserve (Landschaftsschutzgebiet). In this way, the railway company met the legal requirement of providing compensation for the environmental encroachments caused by its huge construction projects underway in the center of Berlin. Under the jurisdiction of Grün Berlin, a quasi-governmental agency, the area was widely reshaped in the following years until it was opened to the public in 2000.

With the Südgelände, a new form of nature entered the world of Berlin's open spaces. Hitherto, parks and urban greenery had been artfully designed, either according to geometric forms derived from classical renaissance garden aesthetics, or—as with the majority of Berlin's green space—as landscape parks simulating some kind of non-urban natural environment. In line with the concept of the Volkspark (people's park), which had been promoted by social reformers since the late nineteenth century, many parks also included facilities for sports and amusement. As with the landscape parks, the project also aimed at creating space for nature in the city. However, the park was not meant to put on stage some kind of imagined rural landscape. Rather, it aimed at protecting the flora and fauna that had developed spontaneously, and whose characteristics mirrored the influence of the urban environment. Nature was no longer seen as an attribute of the non-urban flora and fauna. The category of nature itself became urbanized. Based on his field work at the Südgelande as well as an adjacent closed-down railway triangle (Gleisdreieck), the Berlin ecologist Ingo Kowarik (1991) argued that the flora and fauna of urban wastelands represented a new form of nature ("fourth nature"), that should be highly esteemed and protected.

Although Berlin acted as a local center for the rise of urban ecology, the significance of these developments was far from confined merely to this city. Ecologists have always maintained close relationships with researchers and urban planning experts from other cities.[3] Besides publications and presentations at conferences, excursions in which ecologists showed their visiting colleagues around the most spectacular sites of their own city have been one of the most effective means of exchanging knowledge and fostering a common agenda of interest. In this context, the Südgelände became a kind of model system for urban ecologists and planners. Booklets, official documents and web sites of activist groups as well administrative agencies promoted the nature park as a successful example of nature promotion in the city. In 1998, even the report of the German government on the implementation of the Rio agreement on biodiversity mentioned the Südgelände as an attempt to foster biodiversity in a conurbation (Bundesumweltministerium 1998, p. 44). Two years later, the newly designed nature park was one of the local demonstration projects of sustainable development that Berlin contributed to Expo 2000, the world's fair that took place in Hanover. As a consequence of these activities, the name of the Südgelände and the knowledge and experiences derived from there were mobilized and circulated far beyond their place of origin. However, as I will show in the remainder of this chapter, the actual development of the site, and thus also the form of urban nature it represented, emerged through a local process. It was inextricably embedded in the knowledge culture of Berlin and the setting around the Südgelände itself.

Ecological Expertise and Claims-Making

The first way in which scientific knowledge was involved in the project was the process of ecological claims-making. Although the success of the project was highly dependent on legal regulations and various political contingencies, it was based on the claim that such sites were ecologically valuable habitats. Ecological experts were thus important spokespeople in the process of agenda setting and political negotiation around the site. These experts drew upon their local experiences as well as on a range of translocal resources such as national traditions of vegetation science (Nicolson 1989; Schulte-Fischediek and Shinn 1993), or the "idea of biodiversity," which, since the 1970s, has become the normative focus of a globalizing conservation biology (Takacs 1996).

When making claims for nature conservation, ecologists not only acted as expert advisors in planning affairs; they were themselves stakeholders who had their own interests in land-use decisions. As already noted, the rubble areas that had existed in the city since WWII had always been important sites of field work for these ecologists. Whereas these wastelands disappeared in West German cities during the 1960s, different factors hampered their total reconstruction in Berlin. They were of interest to biologists since they allowed, in an experiment-like constellation, the observation of successive settlement of plant societies. Moreover, the composition of plant species in these areas displayed many features which set them apart from the vegetation known from more conventional sites of observation, most importantly the abundance of plants considered "alien, or " so-called neophytes. It is just the specific local history of this place which has made Berlin enormously productive in ecological knowledge and, hence, literally the center of an emerging trans-local network of urban ecology discourse. However, when rebuilding also intensified in Berlin, during the 1970s and the 1980s, urban ecology ran the risk of losing its most promising research resource. Thus ecologists called for permanent preservation of outstanding wasteland areas in order to enable them to observe their further development (Kunick 1974, p. 46).

These local claims-making activities resonated with trans-local debates on nature conservation and species protection. At the same time, however, they were articulated in a way which reflected the local constellation and the specific problems ecologists were faced with in Berlin's urban environment. When in 1983 the ecologists Auhagen and Sukopp (1983) put together a list of arguments in favor of the protection of species diversity in Berlin, they distinguished between the arguments for species diversity in global and national contexts and those that they considered relevant for the city. They considered urban biodiversity as highly relevant for ecosystem stability as well as the landscape experience of citizens. In contrast, the potential technical value of genetic resources was considered an argument that applied at the global level but was of no relevance for urban nature conservation. Furthermore, the claims were based as much on the provision of ecological evidence about flora and fauna as on furnishing a local sense of place and related identities for these sites. Thus, the construction and stabilization of conservation claims hinged upon a constant interplay of global scientific and political discourse with the local peculiarities of the site and the policy arena which evolved around it.

Ecologists' claims also drew upon their experience from field work in the city. Previous studies of rubble areas and other urban wastelands had already provided ample evidence of the richness of the flora and fauna of these spaces (Kunick 1974, 1979; Kohler and Sukopp 1964; Sukopp 1971). The surveys of the Südgelände (Asmus 1981; ÖkoCon 1991; Kowarik 1986) also concluded that species diversity was extraordinarily rich. The value of the place was also underlined by the range of species which were considered endangered and which, from 1982, were filed in a comprehensive "red-list of endangered species" for Berlin (Sukopp 1982; Auhagen

1991). According to a survey conducted in 1980, the area contained about 334 species of fern and blossom plants, about one third of Berlin's total (Asmus 1981). Among these species were various plants of foreign origin, which had presumably been brought into the area by previous railway traffic. Among the animals of the Südgelände were, for example, foxes, falcons, and a rare species of spider which is usually only found in caverns in Southern France, and which might have been transported to Berlin by freight trains during the war (Asmus 1981). In 1981, three hitherto unknown species of beetle were discovered in the area. These findings were soon reported in the city's daily press, and for the critics of the freight-station project they provided a most valuable argumentative resource.

Traditional nature conservation had tended to focus on what were deemed to be "native" species as objects of conservation concern. Likewise, recent debates consider the "invasion" of plants and animals as a potential threat to global and regional species diversity (cf. Drake et. al. 1989). It is one of the peculiarities of the Südgelände project, and Berlin urban ecology in general, that they were based on a rather positive evaluation of alien species, that is, species, mostly plants, which had been introduced to the region from outside, often from foreign countries or even continents. Rather than seeking to preserve some kind of pristine nature, the ecologists believed that nature conservation in cities should attune its concepts to these specificities and therefore accept alien plants as an enrichment of the local flora. This reflected the local experiences of ecologists at the Südgelände and other urban wastelands, where non-native plants abounded and figured as the most interesting objects of field work. In this respect, Berlin ecology not only "discovered" that there was natural diversity worthy of protection on the wastelands; it also reshuffled the criteria of accounting for and judging nature in its continuous intercourse with the particularities of theses sites.

Claims-making for the two nature parks was also claims-making for the preservation of specific vegetation structures and habitat types. In phyto-sociology—an approach of vegetation science which has been particularly popular in continental Europe (Nicolson 1989)—a complex taxonomy was developed which allowed for the classification of vegetation by territorial units. The Südgelände provided a patchwork of rather small and distinct forms of vegetation, including various kinds of woods, scrubs and meadows. Ecologists considered precisely this diversity of plant-communities a further reason for calling for preservation.

The term "fourth nature," which was coined during these claims-making activities encapsulated many of the site's features (Kowarik 1991). The term contrasted urban wastelands such as the Südgelände or the nearby Gleisdreieck with the other three types of "nature" in the city: the remnants of the prehistoric landscape, the remains of landscape used for agriculture, and the artificially shaped urban greeneries. Kowarik argued that in contrast to these other types of nature, the "fourth nature" of urban wastelands had evolved by the spontaneous adaptation of vegetation to the urban environment and that it, therefore, constituted the most characteristic form of nature in the city. Kowarik argued that "fourth nature" should be valued as equally important as the other types of nature in the city and that, therefore, it should be actively promoted in urban planning politics. Moreover, the term emphasized that urban wastelands had to be evaluated according to different standards than less anthropogenically influenced environments. As already mentioned with respect to alien plants, the flora and fauna were not to be evaluated according to the norm of a pristine state of nature. Thus, the way in which the urban environment had left its imprint on features of the flora and fauna was not considered a degradation of its natural qualities. In contrast, it was deemed to be just what nature was about in a city, and it was meant to be preserved precisely because of these peculiar features.

Scientific experts and other proponents of the park project also emphasized the value of the place for city residents, particularly within the adjacent neighborhoods. The site was articulated as a locus of rich visual, historical, and even mythological meaning. Protagonists succeeded in furnishing a vernacular sense of place which hinged upon the visual quality of the site as well as its significance for urban memory. These views were closely connected to their ecological features as they were emphasized in the surveys. Ecological knowledge claims thus became packaged with other issues, forming a much more comprehensive definition of the place.

Discursive practices of argumentation, in this context, went hand in hand with practices of visual display such as guided excursions, an exhibition, and the circulation of photographs. Activists described the visual scenario presented by the Südgelände as a form of wilderness that had grown in the midst of the city, although hidden from the inhabitants' view for a long time (Bürgerinitiative Schöneberger Südgelände 1985). Again, however, this was seen as a wilderness in which human history had left its traces. The juxtaposition of nature and the remnants from former railway traffic became a visual motif which articulated a new sense of place. The images of trees growing in the middle of former railway tracks or the silhouette of a wild grove which was dominated by the water tower of the former freight station became the emblematic representation of the place. This visual scenario evoked imaginations of nature which had reconquered human artifice. As such, the Südgelände became a place of urban memory as well as a place of visual pleasure.

Ecology and Design

A second way in which ecological knowledge was involved in the construction of the park was its design as a space of—mostly visual—consumption of nature.[4] Basically, the notion of a nature park can be seen as a compromise between two traditional concepts: first, a nature reserve which primarily aims at protecting a valuable piece of flora and fauna, and, second a public park. Initially, the plasticity and comprehensiveness of this concept served to create alliances between groups of actors who tended to prioritize one or other of these two aspects. However, during the process of planning and designing the park, the tensions inherent in this concept became evident through various conflicts.[5] Ecological considerations thus had to be carefully balanced with aesthetic aspirations.

First design proposals had already been elaborated under the care of a citizen activist group in the 1980s. From 1991 on, the design process was organized by Grün Berlin. Design plans were elaborated by two landscape planning offices, one of them led by Kowarik. Both offices maintained close relationships, personally as well as intellectually, to scientific urban ecology (ÖkoCon 1991; Grün Berlin 1995). Other conservation experts, such as the office of the Nature Conservation Advisor, gave further support for ecological considerations in park design. They called for a relatively restrictive policy with respect to public access, as well as strong reservations towards artful design. As the landscape planners argued, nature as it already existed at the two wastelands should be made perceptible for the visitors. The creation of artificially enhanced sceneries which would have turned the site into a kind of "eco-Disneyland" should be avoided (ÖkoCon 1991).

However, when the landscape planners presented their first conception in 1992, it met harsh resistance from Grün Berlin as well as from the local activist group at the Südgelände. The Allianz Umweltstiftung, which provided financial support for the project, also became a strong opponent of strict regulations. These issues were debated by a consulting panel in which all of these groups were represented. Although the participants agreed that the existing features of the flora and fauna should be protected and made the major theme of the park, design plans show a constant move from a relatively rigid conservation scheme toward a park which was more accessible to the public and, at least in part, artistically designed.

According to the original plan, the meadows in the center of the area were to be turned into a nature reserve and fenced off to the public. Only a small viewing platform at the fringe of the site would have allowed visitors visual access to the area. A revised plan presented in 1995 included a wooden foot bridge for visitors in the nature reserve (Grün Berlin 1995). The trail which was eventually constructed, however, moved the design a considerable step toward landscape art. A group of metal sculpture artists who had their workshop in an old railway shed on the fringe of the Südgelände proposed an alternative design for the pathway. This "walkable sculpture" (begehbare Skulptur), was made of rusty steel and consisted of a narrow path which rested on low metal rolls. At some points, further sculptures also made out of rusty steel were added along the track. The rusty material and the wheel-like shape of the rolls were an explicit allusion to the history of the site as a railway station. The track allowed people to walk into the center of the nature reserve without having any physical contact with the soil and vegetation even though they remained as close as possible to the ground and not restricted by a railing. More than being just a pathway system, this sculpture turned the Südgelände into an artsy place. Nature and art became closely connected to each other, one providing the background for the other.

As these debates show, ecological considerations and the attempt to design the park aesthetically existed in a relatively uneasy relationship with each other. However, aesthetic design was not intrinsically at odds with ecology. Rather the often discordant processes of negotiation between ecologists and conservationists, on the one hand, and designers, on the other, resulted in mutual alignments between these perspectives that most of the participants were willing to accept. As with environmental claims-making, these were processes in which ecological knowledge took part in the local process of space-making and vice versa. Ecological concepts and definitions of the site were incorporated into the design schemes and thus became part of the visual scenario the designers aimed to put on stage.

Managing the State of Nature

The operation of management schemes was a third way in which ecological knowledge was involved in the local trajectory of the site. Protecting nature at the Südgelände was conceived of as a form of active maintenance, directing the development of the flora and the fauna toward their optimal states.[6] This was by no means peculiar to this site. However, as an urban ecosystem this park was scarcely comparable with conventional nature reserves, and, therefore, existing management schemes could not easily be translated to these sites. Rather than reconstituting some allegedly more pristine state of nature, management aimed at promoting the flora and fauna which had actually developed on the site. According to the concept of "fourth nature," settlement and other human influences which had shaped the site were to be accepted as its peculiar features. Thus, knowledge about the pre-settlement vegetation of the region could not serve as criteria for evaluating their present state or for defining maintenance goals. At the same time, however, not everything that happened to the flora and fauna of the place was deemed optimal. It was through fixing and negotiating maintenance schemes that new boundaries between what was to be deemed as "natural" and "unnatural" states of the wasteland were locally produced.

In the early 1990s, a survey (ÖkoCon 1991) concluded that since 1980 woody vegetation had increased dramatically. The authors estimated that it would not have taken much time for the entire wasteland to be covered with dense woods. They considered this to be a serious form of deterioration. First, many of the rare species which populated the site depended on the existence of meadows. If left alone, succession, that is the trajectory of different stages of vegetation development, would have reduced the species diversity of the area. Second, the meadows themselves consisted of plant-societies which were deemed worthy of conservation. A third argument emphasized the visual quality of the landscape. As the survey authors maintained, the juxtaposition of woody and open sites was one of the Südgelände's most appealing visual features.

It was on these three grounds that active maintenance became seen as inevitable if the quality of the area was to be preserved. Trees which had spread into the meadows were cut in order to prevent the expansion of the woodland. Earlier forms of vegetation succession in the meadows were also countered. Workers mowed parts of the meadows meant to remain in the state of very early succession. Further, individual plants, which tended to abound in the meadows and which were likely to make them more homogeneous were taken out. These interventions aimed at maintaining or even increasing the existing diversity of plant societies, including those at a very early stage of succession.

The need for maintenance activities was far from self-evident. Some participants deemed the very idea of fighting succession an illegitimate intervention in what they considered a natural process. What impressed so many people at the Südgelände was the alleged wilderness of the vegetation and the related imagery of nature having "reconquered" this place in the city. Members of the citizens group, the representative of the Allianz Stiftung, or the artists who constructed the track, were hostile to these maintenance measures. As one of the artists put it in an interview, making decisions on which plants to accept and which to extinguish was "a kind of fascism." Although the ecologists succeeded in convincing most skeptics that a complete dominance of wood in the area should be avoided, more fine-tuned interventions in the meadows, such as mowing, still received harsh criticism. Park visitors also articulated indirect opposition to maintenance measures. In contrast to traditional nature reserves, the Südgelände formed part of a city and maintenance work in the was therefore always done under the critical gaze of the urban public. Gardeners who cut trees or mowed meadows in what was known to be a valuable biotope aroused the suspicion of many visitors, who asked the workers for an explanation.

Ecological scientists took a rather ambivalent stance with respect to maintenance. On the one hand, they were expert advisers for park maintenance and in that position they had initially promoted the idea of maintenance. On the other hand, the course of the succession on the site was their research object. Therefore, they had an interest in keeping the site free from intervention. The conflict was partly resolved by a division of the park into two areas in which both policies now coexist. In the black-locust wood which contributed to the image of wilderness and on which the research interest of ecologists has focused, succession has been allowed to proceed spontaneously. In the open meadows, however, a quite rigid conservation scheme applies.

The definition of maintenance schemes was further complicated by the diversity of goals that coexisted within the maintenance agenda. What some conservation experts deemed to be an intervention on behalf of flora and vegetation types was often criticized by others for its effects on specific plants or animals. An important point related to these issues was the role of alien plants. As already noted, in other nature conservation reserves these plants usually would have been one of the main targets of extinction. This was also the policy of the Berlin nature conservation administration in reserves in the fens and woods at the margins of the city. Given the urban character of the Südgelände, however, alien plants were seen as a typical feature of "fourth nature" and thus often actively promoted by maintenance measures.

Conclusion

The Südgelände project was a local exercise in creating and reconfiguring ecological knowledge. Transforming a wasteland into a park went hand-in-hand with the emergence of new ways of knowing and acting. This was a local process because it was inextricably linked to the history of Berlin, and the local culture of ecological expertise that had evolved here. More specifically, the nature park was the result of a very particular constellation of research and policy which crystallized around that site. During the process of claims-making, ecological concepts such as species or vegetation diversity were discursively related to the ecological particularities of the Berlin environment, as well as to the site itself. Further, ecological claims were based on argumentative packages which were also related to local history and place identity. Ecological knowledge claims were locally negotiated in the process of designing the park and thereby flexibly adapted to the design issues at stake. As we have seen, designers were not mere passive recipients of ecological concepts and practices; rather they drew upon their own experiences and evaluations when incorporating ecological considerations into their design proposals. Finally, knowledge about maintenance emerged from a local circle of intervention and observation, which interacted with the materiality of the site and whose components were continuously negotiated among the various participants of the management scheme. It was because of these local knowledges and policies that the Südgelände became the hallmark of urban nature conservation in Berlin.

Although other cities have developed similar projects, it is by no means self-evident that ecological planning or species protection in cities entails the same kinds of policies. In contrast, ecologists in favor of "dense cities" have argued for building-up urban brownfields in order to avoid the destruction of nature due to urban sprawl. Moreover, other projects of greening the city have often taken a quite different tack. Vienna's Wildgärten, London's William Curtis Park, Toronto's renewed waterfront, or the ecologically shaped environments of the French science city Sophia Antiopolis all represent recent attempts to ecologize the city. (See Rotenberg 1995; Graham 1997; Wakeman 2000.) However, they differ in what is considered as "nature" in these projects, and they reflect quite different local political constellations and knowledge cultures. For example, at London's William Curtis Park, as in the two Berlin cases, there was also an attempt to re-naturalize an inner-urban wasteland, and it was also based on a conception of promoting urban wildlife. However this ecological park had been created on an area almost totally denuded of vegetation and, in striking contrast to the Berlin concept of promoting "fourth nature," it was planted with a diverse mixture of native plants.

This does not mean that, the discourse and practice of urban nature conservation in Berlin was isolated from what was going on elsewhere in the world.

First, we can view the project as an example of an approach to urban ecology that has become quite characteristic for Germany in general. Indeed, the Berlin ecologists have been very influential in shaping the agenda of landscape planning in other cities in Western Germany, and, after 1990, also in the previous GDR. For example, similar ideas of nature conservation became very important in the reshaping of industrial wastelands in the economically declining Ruhr region.[7] Probably, nowhere else in the world were issues of ecology and sustainability so much identified with species protection and the conservation of the spontaneous nature of urban wastelands.

Second, the Berlin project can also be seen as a local and national variety of a now almost globalized effort towards ecological planning in cities. We can indeed only speak of Berlin as a local center of urban ecology to the extent that it has been successfully linked up with scientific and political discourses in other places around the world. On the one hand, we have seen that in the course of their local activities around the site ecologists drew upon knowledge resources from globalizing ecological and conservationist discourses. On the other hand, particularities of Berlin and notably, the Südgelände as a research field, allowed them to generate knowledge which could not have been as easily produced in other places, but which nevertheless was of potential relevance for researchers and planners elsewhere in the world. Rather than isolating Berlin's ecologists from the rest of the world, the particularity of their city was an asset for creating the global significance of their field work and their knowledge products.[8] The case might thus be read as an example of what can be observed in many areas of environmental and developmental policy (see Lahsen, this volume). Global issues that have become the foci of international policy regimes—such as species and habitat protection or the call for sustainable cities—are, at the same time, very local constructions which are shaped by the conditions of their vernacular contexts.

Third, the presence of non-native species which have been seen as a most peculiar feature for the place can also be seen as the result of a long-term process of globalization (Clark 1999). Since the colonization of North America and other parts of the world, plant and animal migration has always been closely connected to the increasing human interaction and economic exchange between distant places. Likewise, more recent intensification of economic, social and cultural connections throughout the world have also opened-up new ways for species to migrate. For example, the speeding-up of world-wide ship traffic and the use of high amounts of ballast water has caused a dramatic increase in the presence of tropical species in European coast waters and rivers. The (potentially negative) impact of such world-wide plant and animal migrations on global biodiversity is now widely discussed among conservation biologist. What Berlin's ecologist discovered at the city's wastelands and what they admired as a "fourth nature" was also to a large extent a product of such global flows. The nature park and the new sense of place on which it was based, can thus also be seen as an alternative way of locally framing such global process.

As the final two points make clear, contemporary natural environments have to be seen as both constructions of the global as well as constructions of the local. Rather than reducing one aspect to the other, we are to understand their complex relationships and the way in which they interact with each other. This is not only an important consequence to be drawn for any sociological theorizing about nature in the age of globalization. It might also be of relevance for policy makers with a commitment to an environmental agenda. If there is any way of "thinking globally and acting locally," this should be based on an awareness of the full productivity of the local, that is not only as a site in which global schemes are to be implemented by local people, but as site from which new political visions and knowledges emerge which in turn, might refigure our notions of the global.

Acknowledgments

I would like to thank the ecologists and planning officials who donated their time and provided material that is analyzed in this chapter. My thanks are also due to the participants of the workshop "Localizing and Globalizing" in Cambridge, Massachusetts, April 6–7, 2001, the two editors of this volume, Sheila Jasanoff and Marybeth Long Martello, and my former colleagues at the Max Planck Institute for the History of Science, Berlin, for their comments on earlier versions of this chapter.

Notes

1. On the exemplary character of the park and its history, see Häkli 1996 and Mohrmann 2002.

2. Allotment gardeners were organized in a so-called Interessengemeinschaft Südgelände. In late 1980, conservation activists and residents founded the Bürgerinitiative Südgelände, which in the following years became the main local pressure group against the freight station and for the creation of a nature park in that area.

3. For example, Sukopp and his institute have always maintained close relationships to researchers in Czechoslovakia, Poland, Finland, Britain, and Japan. Berlin and its ecology were also among the topics discussed at international conferences, notably the Second European Ecological Symposium in 1980. For this conference an excursion guide was published which later became extended to a monograph on urban ecology (Sukopp 1990). Berlin ecologists also published various articles on the spontaneous development of the vegetation of urban wastelands, among them articles which drew upon experiences made on the Südgelände (Kowarik 1986).

4. On nature as an object of visual consumption, see Macnaghten and Urry 1998.

5. What follows is partly based on author's interviews with Senatsverwaltung für Stadtentwicklung und Umweltschutz, Abt. Naturschutz, 1/29/2001; Planland, 1/23/2001; Ingo Kowarik, January 19, 2001; Rita Mohrmann, 1/11/2001;. Klaus Hartmann 2001; Lutz Spandau 1/7/2001; Grün Berlin, 1/8/2001.

6. Proposals for maintenance schemes were laid down in the design plans (ÖkoCon 1991) and maintenance protocols (Planland 2000).

7. This was the case with the Emscher Park Project.

8. According to Robert Kohler (2000), the epistemic exploitation of local particularity distinguishes field sciences, such as ecology, from the experimental sciences. Whereas the latter created laboratory environments that erased the particularity of place, the latter capitalized on what is do-able only in particular places that then often acquire the status of universally acknowledged model systems.

References

Asmus, Ulrich. 1981. *Vegetationskundliches Gutachten über das Südgelände des Schöneberger Güterbahnhofs*. Berlin: Senator für Bau- und Wohnungswesen/VIIdA.

Auhagen, Axel, and Herbert Sukopp. 1983. "Ziel, Begründungen und Methoden des Naturschutzes der Stadtentwicklungspolitik von Berlin." *Natur und Landschaft* 58, no. 1: 9–15.

Bürgerinitiative "Schöneberger Südgelände," ed. 1985. *Das Verborgene Grün Von Schöneberg—Naturpark Südgelände*. Berlin: Freihold.

Bundesumweltministerium. 1998. *Bericht der Bundesregierung nach dem Übereinkommen über die biologische Vielfalt*. Bonn.

Clark, William C. 1999. "Environmental Globalization." In *Governance in a Globalizing World,* ed. J. Nye and J. Donahue. Brookings.

Drake, James A., ed. 1989. *Biological Invasions: A Global Perspective*. Wiley.

Grün Berlin. 1995. *Natur-Park Südgelände*. Berlin.

Häkli, Jouni. 1996. "Culture and Politics of Nature in the City: The Case of Berlin's 'Green Wedge.'" *Capitalism, Nature, Socialism* 7, no. 2: 125–138.

Hannigan, John A. 1995. *Environmental Sociology*. Routledge.

Keil, Roger, and John Graham. 1998. "Reasserting Nature: Constructing Urban Environments after Fordism." In *Remaking Nature*, ed. B. Braun and N. Castree. Routledge.

Keil, Roger. 1995. "The Environmental Problematic in World Cities." In *World Cities in a World System*, ed. P. Knox and P. Taylor. Cambridge University Press.

Knorr-Cetina, Karin. 1981. *The Manufacture of Knowledge*. Pergamon.

Kohler, A., and H. Sukopp. 1964. "Über die Gehölzentwicklung auf Berliner Trümmerstandorten." *Berichte der Deutschen Botanischen Gesellschaft* 76: 389–406.

Kohler, Robert E. 2000. "The Particularity of Biology in the Field." University of Pennsylvania.

Kowarik, Ingo. 1991. "Unkraut oder Urwald? Natur der vierten Art auf dem Gleisdreick." In *Gleisdreick Morgen. Sechs Ideen für einen Park*. Bundesgartenschau Berlin.

Kowarik, Ingo. 1986. "Vegetationsentwicklung auf innerstädtischen Brachflächen. Beipiele aus Berlin (West)." *Tuexenia* 6, no. 75-98, 75-99: 57–99.

Kunick, Wolfram. 1974. "Veränderungen von Flora und Vegetation einer Großstadt, dargestellt am Beispiel von Berlin (West)." Technische Universität Berlin.

Kunick, Wolfram. 1979. *Stadtbiotopkartierung Berlin*. Berlin: Institut für Ökologie, Ökosystemforschung und Vegetationskunde der TU Berlin.

Lachmund, Jens. 2003. "Exploring the City of Rubble." In *Science and the City,* ed. S. Dierig et al. (*Osiris,* issue 18).

Latour, Bruno. 1986. *Science in Action*. Harvard University Press.

Macnaghten, Phil and John Urry. 1998. *Contested Natures*. Sage.

Massey, Doreen.1993. "Power-Geometry and a Progressive Sense of Place." In *Mapping the Future*, ed. Jon Bird, Barry Curtis, Tim Putnam, George Robertson and Lisa Tickner. Routledge.

Mohrmann, Rita. 2002. "Beitrag der Landschaftsplanung zur städtischen Freiraumplanung: Beispiel Natur-Park Schöneberger Südgelände in Berlin." In *Landschaftsplanung in der Praxis*, ed. A. Auhagen et al. Verlag Eugen Ulmer.

Nicolson, Malcolm. 1989. "National Styles, Divergent Classifications: A Comparative Case Study from the History of French and American Plant Ecology." *Knowledge and Society* 8: 139–186.

ÖkoCon. 1991. Ökologisch-Landschaftsplanerisches Gutachten Natur-Park Südgelände, 1. Zwischenbericht. Bundesgartenschau Berlin 1995 GmbH.

ÖkoCon. 1995. *Ökologisch-Landschaftsplanerisches Gutachten Natur-Park Südgelände, 1. Zwischenbericht*. Bundesgartenschau Berlin.

ÖkoCon and Planland. 1998. *Natur-Park Südgelände—Bio-Monitoring. Zielsetzung, Konzept, Aufnahmeflächen—Lage Und Erstaufnahme*. Berlin: Grün Berlin and Garten GmbH.

Planland, unter Mitarbeit von Prof. Dr. Ingo Kowarik. 2000. *Schöneberger Südgelände. Pflege- und Entwicklungsplan*. Berlin: Senatsverwaltung für Stadtentwicklung.

Robertson, Roland. "Globalisation or Glocalisation?" *Journal of International Communication* 1, no. 1: 33–52.

Rotenberg, Robert. 1995. *Landscape and Power in Vienna*. Johns Hopkins University Press.

Saure, C. 1992. *Zur Stechimmenfauna des Südgeländes in Berlin-Schöneberg*. Berlin: Berliner Landesarbeitsgemeinschaft Naturschutz.

Saure, Christoph. 1992. *Faunistisch-Ökologisches Gutachten zur Stechimmenfauna des ehemaligen Flugplatzes Johannisthal in Berlin-Treptow (Insecta: Hymenoptera Aculeata)*. Berliner Landesarbeitsgemeinschaft Naturschutz.

Schulte-Fischedick, Kaat, and Terry Shinn. 1993. "International Phytogeographical Excursions, 1911–1923: Intellectual Convergence in Vegetation Science." In *Denationalizing Science*, ed. E. Crawford and T. Shinn. Kluwer.

Shapin, Steven, and Adi Ophir, eds. 1991. *The Place of Knowledge. Science in Context* 4, no. 1.

Singleton, Vicky, and Mike Michael. 1993. "Actor-Networks and Ambivalence: General Practicioners in the UK Cervical Screening Programm." *Social Studies of Science* 23: 227–264.

Smith, Crosbie, and Jon Agar. 1998. *Making Space for Science: Territorial Themes in the Shaping of Knowledge*. Macmillan.

Sukopp, Herbert. 1971. "Beiträge zur Ökologie von Chenopodium Botrys L. I. Verbreitung und Vergesellschaftung." *Verhandlungen des Botanischen Vereins der Provinz Brandenburg* 108: 3–74.

Sukopp, Herbert. 1990. "Ökologische Grundlagen für die Stadtplanung und Stadterneuerung." In *Ergebnisse Der 10. Sitzung Der Arbeitsgruppe "Biotopkartierung im besiedlten Bereich,"* ed. H. Condert. Frankfurt: Courier Forschungs-Institut Senckenberg.

Sukopp, Herbert. 1994. "Stadtökologie in nationaler und internationaler Perspektive." In *Biotopkartierung im Besiedelten Bereich. 15. Jahrestagung der Arbeitsgruppe der Landesanstalten und -Ämter und des Bundesamtes für Naturschutz 15.–17. September 1994 in Erfurt*. Landeshauptstadt Erfurt.

Sukopp, Herbert, and H. Elvers. 1982. *Rote Listen der gefährdeten Pflanzen und Tiere in Berlin (West), Landschaftsentwicklung und Umweltforschung 11*. Berlin: Technische Universität.

Sukopp, Herbert, and Rüdiger Wittig, eds. 1996. *Stadtökologie*. Fischer.

Takacs, David. 1996. *The Idea of Biodiversity: Philosophies of the Paradies*. Johns Hopkins University Press.

Timmermanns, Stefan, and Marc Berg.1997. "Standardization in Action: Achieving Local Universality through Medical Protocols." *Social Studies of Science* 27: 273–305.

Yearley, Steven. 1994. "The Environmental Challenge to Science Studies." In *Handbook of Science and Technology Studies*, ed. S. Jasanoff et al. Sage.

11

Negotiating Global Nature and Local Culture: The Case of Makah Whaling

Marybeth Long Martello

Globalization, according to scholarly accounts discussed in the introduction to this volume, is something that happens *to* people as a process or processes that shape the contexts in which they live. Increasing interconnectedness and worldwide flows generally overwhelm individuals, except when individuals or groups effectively oppose them as forces to be dealt with or embrace them as opportunities to be taken. A person can resist some forms of globalization, for example, by refraining from purchasing a cell phone or by buying local produce. Alternatively, someone may take advantage of globalization by investing in a multinational corporation or by using travel and communication networks to build a non-governmental organization. In many respects, however, globalization seems like climate change, almost a natural phenomenon, though with anthropogenic sources. It arises from the discrete choices and actions of people all over the world, but it is bigger than any single individual or nation. In response to the level of climate change (and globalization) already set in motion, humans have only a few choices: to go about their business as usual, resist within limits or adapt.

Contradicting this singular vision, the ecology, institutions, cultures, and communication methods at play in the Makah whaling controversy reflect multiple narratives of globalization. The Makah, like other aboriginal tribes in Canada and Alaska, maintain that whaling is necessary for preserving their identity and cultural heritage. However, the Makah face strong resistance from those claiming that Makah whaling does not qualify as subsistence whaling, violates animal rights, and threatens to pave the way for commercial whaling worldwide. The Makah story centers upon ecological interdependencies associated with a whale population that has progressively been globalized. Policies for managing this population at a global scale are negotiated in the transnational forum of the International Whaling Commission and focus largely on questions concerning the viability of whale stocks in relation to international trade and commerce. The indigenous peoples and animal rights organizations engaging in the debate are globally networked. Many of the channels and platforms through which state and non-state actors interact are similarly global in reach and include the Internet, television, and the press. And the history and dynamics of the story replay some classic themes of globalization such as colonization, the intermingling of Native American ideals and ways of life with "outside" materiality and practices, and new cultural amalgamations that have arisen from interactions among previously separated groups.

So, on its surface, the Makah story is both a product and manifestation of globalization. But a closer look reveals a need for new ways of thinking about globalization. First, current approaches to globalization tend to overlook questions about what kinds of things come to be counted as global or local, how this happens, and in what ways resources considered local and global get used. As the Makah case illustrates, globalization is not simply about transcendent phenomena and flows emanating from aggregate transformations in world order, science, environmental change, and financial and communication networks. As we see throughout this volume the very categories of global and local, along with processes of globalization and localization serve as important political resources and strategies for individuals and groups. They can offer novel and constructive opportunities for people to understand and relate to one another. Or, as in the case of the Makah and the animal rights activists, they can establish and perpetuate impasses between opposing viewpoints. Second, the case illustrates that the global does not by any means always overtake the local. Debates about the fate of a worldwide whale population have been as much about asserting, constructing, and contesting local norms, as about forging transnational agreements and conducting universal scientific assessments of ecological interdependencies. Third, claims-making based on the resources of globalism or localism in a given debate may depend significantly on the type of institutional setting in which the debate takes place. Decision makers in the modernist policy forums concerned with Makah whaling practices have continually deferred to the translocal resources of science and law as found in whale biology, cetology, and treaty obligations. In contrast, exchanges between the Makah and their opponents (primarily animal rights activists) as played out via the web, press media, and public demonstrations, have focused on constructing and deconstructing claims about nature and culture—the localness of the former and the authenticity of the latter.

In what follows, I first present the Makah controversy within the framework of globalization as a transcendent phenomenon. This story plays out in transnational and national forums and the debate turns largely on scientific claims, legal decisions, and the dynamics of international cooperation. I then examine the Makah case as one in which globalization and localization throw seemingly stable categories open to debate and serve as political strategies for pro-whaling Makah tribespeople and anti-whaling activists. Through media networks, the Makah attempt to localize nature and culture. The activists, on the other hand, appeal to ethics and universal human/animal kinship while globalizing Makah culture in efforts to portray it as inauthentic.

Makah Whaling in the Discourse of Globalization

The Makah have lived in the Pacific Northwest for centuries, most recently on a reservation located approximately 150 miles west of Seattle, Washington. A 1992 census estimated the tribal population at 1869 with 1709 living on the reservation (Renker 1997). Despite the tribe's small size and relatively isolated location, its recent history has been profoundly affected by US and world politics.

In 1855 members of the Makah tribe signed the Treaty of Neah Bay with a territorial governor, Isaac Stevens. With this treaty, the Makah "gave up" territory and took up residence in the Makah Reservation while retaining specific rights to continue their 2,200 year-old practice of eating whale meat, and their 1,500 year-old practice of hunting whales (Renker 1997). Oral histories and an archaeological dig conducted in the mid 1970s indicate that whaling was the backbone of Makah society. Makah hunted primarily humpback and gray whales, and whaling roles and responsibilities of tribal members reflected their hereditary status in the social stratification system and guided decisions about marriage, leadership, and day-to-day activities (Renker 1997).

Between the middle years of the nineteenth century and the early years of the twentieth century, the influence of "outside" societies caused both Makah and whale populations to decline to a point that made whaling impossible. Contact with white people led to smallpox and measles epidemics that reduced the tribe's population from between 2,000 and 4,000 before contact, to as few as 360 in 1910 (Dunagan 1998; Tizon 1998a). The whale population similarly declined under the stress of worldwide commercial whaling. A gray whale population estimated around 18,000 to 20,000 prior to commercial whaling dropped to less than 5,000 by 1920 (Watters and Dugger 1997).

The collapse of the whaling industry helped to transform whales into a threatened and shared global resource and the focus of international regulation. International action took the form of the Convention on the Regulation of Whaling in 1931. This agreement put an end to unlimited exploitation, prohibited the killing of specific species, and constituted some first steps toward conservation. A series of amendments during the 1930s and the 1940s culminated in 1945 with a protocol capping the total number of kills per year. And in 1946, the United States signed a treaty to manage sustainable stocks and create the International Whaling Commission (IWC, the Commission), which that same year named the gray whale a protected species and imposed limits on how many could be taken per year (Watters and Dugger 1997). The IWC allows for two types of exemptions from the regulations: one for scientific research and one for subsistence whaling. To invoke the latter exemption a member nation must petition the IWC requesting that a native group be permitted to hunt a particular species (ibid.). The IWC stipulates that any whale taken under a subsistence exemption must be used for local consumption only. In recent decades the IWC has relied on several legal instruments to protect gray whales; two are particularly important for this story. First, in 1973, the gray whale was listed as an endangered species under the Endangered Species Act. Second, the IWC has supported a non-binding moratorium on commercial whaling since 1986.

In the early 1990s, the Makah began a series of initiatives to engage with national and global forums on whaling with the aim of regaining their right to whale. First, the Makah, along with 14 commercial whaling groups and 19 tribes, petitioned for and succeeded in bringing about the de-listing of the gray whale as an endangered species. The tribe also approached the National Oceanic and Atmospheric Administration (NOAA) with their plans to resume a gray whale hunt. NOAA is a federal agency within the Department of Commerce. Its mission is "to describe and predict changes in the Earth's environment, and conserve and wisely manage the Nation's coastal and marine resources." NOAA agreed to work with the tribe in presenting their case to the IWC and in 1996, the agency informed the Commission that it intended to submit a subsistence whaling request at the upcoming IWC meeting in July of that year (Watters and Dugger 1997).

The US plan to support the Makah drew strong reactions internationally. US delegation leader D. James Baker defended the Makah's activities on the grounds that they were non-commercial (Associated Press 1996). Baker framed the issue as one concerning the rights of indigenous people. The Global Guardian Trust, a group associated with the Japanese whaling industry submitted a statement supporting the 1996 US attempts to reintroduce small-scale whaling for the Makah. However, groups within and outside government protested the delegation's plans. The Makah proposal was particularly controversial because the US has long been a leader in supporting the commercial whaling moratorium and marine mammal conservation efforts more generally. Anti-whaling nations and NGOs expressed concern that US backing for the Makah request would damage the IWC's credibility and efficacy. On June 26, 1996, a resolution of the US Congress spearheaded by Representative Jack Metcalf of Washington denounced the delegation's intention to request an IWC exemption on behalf of the Makah. The resolution also noted the recent de-listing of the gray whale and cited a group of Makah elders who fear the tribe's whaling will turn commercial. The resolution further warned that thirteen Canadian groups had suggested that they too would pursue whaling if the Makah did. Environmentalists and animal rights groups similarly voiced opposition to Makah whaling when over 300 of these organizations signed an open letter calling on the tribe to reconsider its plan. When anti-whaling organizations attended the 1996 IWC meeting they brought along two Makah elders who opposed whaling. When these elders spoke out against their tribe during an IWC assembly and when IWC member countries expressed strong opposition to the Makah plan, the US temporarily withdrew its request (Watters and Dugger 1997).

In 1997, the US government followed through in petitioning the IWC to authorize an aboriginal subsistence exemption to allow the Makah to hunt five gray whales per year (Watters and Dugger 1997). At the request of NOAA, the Makah prepared a Statement of Need which described the tribe's whaling history, the cultural significance of tribal whaling, the role of the whale for food and ceremonial purposes, and the means of whale harvest and distribution (Watters and Dugger 1997; see Renker 1997). The Needs Statement also pointed out that the Makah believe that health problems afflicting their population such as diabetes, obesity, lactose intolerance, and digestive illnesses arise from the disappearance of seafood and whale meat from their diets (Renker 1997). With the Needs Statement in hand the US government prepared a formal proposal to the IWC. US delegation members remarked that the Makah request met IWC "requirements" (Reuters 1997) and maintained that a small subsistence hunt would not affect the gray whale population (Hardy and Hudgens 2000). The ensuing debate did not focus on the cultural aspects of the Statement. They instead hinged on the projected effects on whale stocks, the meaning of subsistence, the existence of nutritional need, and potential weakening of the global moratorium. Exemption opponents said that Makah whaling was not for subsistence purposes. Countries like Australia and New Zealand rejected the economic and nutritional arguments on the grounds that there was no clear proof of need. Other challengers warned that a Makah whaling quota would broaden the definition of subsistence, open the door for Japanese subsistence whaling exemptions, and lead to commercial exploitation of whales.

Ultimately, the IWC decision turned on a deal between the US and Russian governments. At the IWC meeting in Monaco in 1997, the US traded 20 whales from its Alaskan bowhead quota to the Russian delegation. In turn, Russia included the US in a gray whale quota request on behalf of the Chukotka people. The Chukotka live in northern Russia and hunt gray whales under an aboriginal subsistence exemption. This trade was agreeable to both the Alaskan Eskimos and the Chukotka because neither group was planning to kill its allotted quota (Schmidt 1999). On October 22, 1997 the IWC did not specifically recognize the right of the Makah to hunt, but did vote to allow the Makah to share in the subsistence hunting quota granted to Russian whalers in Siberia (Hardy and Hudgens 2000). The IWC granted the Makah permission to kill a total of 20 gray whales between 1998 and 2002, with no more than five whales in a given year. The Commission prohibited the tribe from selling whale meat (Dornin and Associated Press 1998). When faced with conflicting views of members, the IWC sidestepped the debate by portraying its actions as based purely on scientific information about the whale population. According to IWC officials, the organization "did not pass judgment on the Makahs' claim, neither recognizing it, nor rejecting it." As noted by IWC Chairman Peter Bridgewater, "Our main concern remains the responsibility and viability of the (whale) stocks" (Reuters 1997). This focus on whale counts enabled the Commission to avoid discussing difficult questions of culture, tradition, and what counts as subsistence need. The IWC decision in conjunction with a 1997 environmental assessment by the National Marine Fisheries Service cleared the way for Makah whaling, but limited hunting to the late Fall and to migratory whales only (NMFS 1997; Shukovsky and Barber 2001).

Decisions of the IWC and NMFS, however, met with opposition from American lawmakers and the courts. Deliberations in these arenas similarly focused not on culture, but on technical issues of economics, environmental science, and agency protocols concerning the timing of environmental assessments. When Jack Metcalf and environmental groups brought a court case challenging the government-supported quota in September 1998, a federal judge upheld the Makah's whaling plans, dismissing arguments from tour boat operators, environmentalists, and others that Makah whaling would be both economically and environmentally detrimental (Associated Press and Reuters 1998). With a green light from the court, the Makah, after several failed attempts, succeeded in killing a whale in May 1999.[1] However, in June 2000 a federal appeals court overturned the lower court's ruling. According to Judges Trott and Silverman of the Ninth Circuit Court of Appeals, the federal government improperly signed a contract to help the Makah get authorization from IWC before preparing an assessment of potential environmental consequences. The court concluded that it was highly likely that the environmental assessment conducted in 1997 "was slanted in favor of finding that the Makah whaling proposal would not significantly affect the environment" (Hardy and Hudgens 2000, citing court decision). This ruling, in effect, put an end to Makah whaling until a new environmental assessment could be carried out. A second assessment published in July 2001 cited biological arguments for lessening the restrictions on Makah whaling. But the most recent decision by the US Ninth Circuit Court of Appeals in December 2002 prohibits the gray whale hunt on the grounds that the federal Marine Mammal Protection Act overrides the Treaty of Neah Bay (Bernton 2002).

Countering Globalization: Discourses of Locality

When we turn from international negotiations, administrative agencies, and US courts to the web pages, newspaper reports, and even placards of pro and anti-whaling factions, we see a debate focused less on whale stocks and environmental assessments and more on clashing world views, identities, and community expectations as articulated by the Makah tribe and animal rights advocates.

Pro-whaling Makah tribespeople and anti-whaling activists in the whaling controversy have made a number of moves to take advantage of the dynamics of localizing and globalizing. The Makah have lobbied for the right to interpret and relate to nature in ways that express their local culture, with the whale represented as an integral part of their physical, social, and spiritual life. The tribe claims a special connection to gray whales based on knowledge and a sense of oneness derived from observing, hunting, and consuming these animals. Whaling advocates within the tribe maintain that whaling will re-awaken their culture which was lost to the US government's assimilationist practices and the effects of commercial whaling in the late nineteenth and early twentieth centuries. They claim that whaling will enhance community spirit on the reservation, lessen problems of alcohol abuse, and infuse youth with "discipline and pride." The Makah's opponents such as animal rights activists, US politicians, and members of the general public, by contrast, assert more general moral claims to nature as embodied in the whale, and challenge Makah arguments about culture. Like the Makah, anti-whaling groups represent the whale as possessing human-like traits and as socially connected to humans. Whaling opponents also contend that tribal whaling violates the rights of whales as majestic, intelligent, and social beings (Walker 1999) and opens the door to commercial whaling and huge decreases in whale numbers. Many of their arguments, however, contest the "purity" (in many respects the "localness") of Makah culture and the authenticity of the Makah's cultural claims.[2]

Localizing and Globalizing Nature

The Makah portray the whale as integral to their way of life. The tribe's symbol, for example, is a thunderbird grasping a whale in its claws. According to Makah legend, the eagle-like creature would lift whales from the ocean and carry them into the mountains to be devoured. When the thunderbird died it passed the privilege of whale-hunting to the Makah (Russell 1999) and the tribe integrated the whale and the whale hunt into nearly every facet of its social system. Whaling was central to the Makah's diet, technology, social hierarchy, social relations, and spiritual life (Renker 1997). Many Makah note the special kinship they have with whales and other mammals of the land and sea after living among them for over 2000 years. This interaction, they explain, has imparted to the Makah a special understanding of whales. Tribal leader Keith Johnson contrasts this understanding against what he sees as a romantic and misleading construction of the whale promoted by animal rights activists. According to Johnson, the tendency of these groups to ascribe almost human characteristics to whales and to celebrate their near-human intelligence is "nonsense" (Johnson 1998).

Animal rights groups also have their methods of acculturating nature as embodied in the gray whale. They do so, however, using universalist claims of a human-whale kinship based on biology and morality. Activists argue that because whales share certain biological and social traits with humans they should be afforded the right to live. One of the most active and vocal of the anti-whaling groups is the Sea Shepherd Conservation Society (SSCS) led by Paul Watson, an original co-founder of Greenpeace. Based in Venice, California, SSCS has 40,000 members, a fleet of vessels, and an annual budget on the order of $1 million (Tizon 1998c). This group prides itself on being one of a few organizations to "actively enforce" the IWC's whaling moratorium. One activist noted: "The Makah are the cowboys here . . . and we're the Indians. We're protecting nature with very few resources; the Makah are hunting with high-caliber weapons, and with the Coast Guard and the US government behind them." (Schmidt 1999) But what are these organizations protecting? For an answer we need only turn to their descriptions of the whale and what they see as its place in the world. Oftentimes these groups point to the whale's inherent biological vulnerabilities and values as deserving of respect and study.[3] The long gestation periods of whales and the late age at which females reproduce make whales particularly susceptible to extinction. Furthermore, their complex social behavior has given whales a special place in the mythology, literature, and art of nearly all cultures that have come in contact with them (Scheiber 1998).

Just as the Makah argue that they should be permitted to hunt because the whale is an integral part of their culture, whaling opponents contend that the place of the whale in American culture and its connection to humanity writ large make whaling morally offensive. Jack Metcalf, the Washington congressman who prompted the anti-Makah congressional resolution, spoke of the American people's "special relationship with whales" (quoted in Sullivan 1998). According to Metcalf (quoted in Verhovek 1999a): "These majestic, highly intelligent creatures deserve better than to be brutally slaughtered as pawns in a political game orchestrated by Japanese and Norwegian whaling interests and supported by the Clinton-Gore administration."[4] Animal rights groups build on these conceptions of the whale with vivid personifications. Ascribing human characteristics and even human names to whales blurs conventional human/animal boundaries and implies strong connections across them. While protesting the Makah hunt, activist Erin Abbott was accidentally run over and injured by a Coast Guard boat. Abbott's comments suggest a sort of kinship she feels with the whales: "I just wanted to be a voice for the animals. Nothing gives us the right to take their lives just because they can't communicate in words like you and I do. . . . Whales are defenseless creatures. They bleed just like you and I do." (Sanders 2000)

Personification is an especially popular way of describing a whale who is threatened or harmed. The following whale descriptions were taken from the web pages and articles of animal rights groups.

We see whales desperately trying to avoid the sonar and merciless exploding harpoons, the eyes of innocent seal pups reflecting the descending club, and the panic of dolphins drowning in the lethal bondage of plastic nets. (www.seashepherd.com)

As the young female moved toward the Makah canoe (possibly seeking friendly human contact, as they are known to do in Baja California's lagoons), she suddenly found a harpoon in her back. She was Finished-off [sic] with a 50-caliber rifle. (Berman 2000)

She was an unarmed young female whale who had been ambushed by a gang of men armed with harpoons and high-powered rifles. (Humane Society 1999)

These excerpts portray whalers as violent and cruel and whales as fearful and in pain. In the last excerpt, references to "unarmed young female," and "gang of men" suggest a rape. In keeping with these sorts of portrayals, animal rights groups accused the Makah whaling crew of betraying the whale they killed in May 1999. According to the activists, this whale was part of a group en route from the Arctic to Mexico that regularly interacted with tourist boats and whale-watchers (Humane Society 1999).

So both the Makah and anti-whaling constituencies assert special connections with whales. The Makah localize the whale by portraying it as integral to their culture and by emphasizing a mutual understanding between the tribe and the animal. Whaling opponents draw upon universalist resources of science, morals and rights to support their own version of human-animal kinship. For the activists the whale is connected, not to a single tribe, but to all people. These activists argue for whale protection by noting biological and behavioral similarities between whales and humans and by representing the whale as a personified victim of gratuitous violence.

Localizing Culture

Just as the Makah portray the whale as part of their social and cultural systems, they present whaling as part of their unique, innate, even instinctual abilities. In arguing for the right to whale, Makah also claim that hunting is natural and necessary for nutritional purposes and that their culture is vulnerable to extinction and must be kept alive. Whaling opponents, on the other hand, challenge the Makah on the grounds that their practices are not as pure and authentic as the Makah suggest.

The Makah point to an archaeological dig at the Makah village of Ozette in 1970 as proof that whaling has been a part of the tribe's heritage for hundreds of years. The dig's thousands of well-preserved artifacts led scientists to confirm the Makah's strong whaling tradition of 1500 years and its average annual yield of five or more whales (Watters and Dugger 1997). The Makah emphasize this tradition in defending their whaling practices. Theron Parker, the Makah who threw the first harpoon during the successful hunt in 1999 remarked: "This is not about money. . . . This is about a great tradition. It's about calling out to our ancestors. It's all about who we are as a people" (Verhovek 1999b). Other tribal members suggest that whaling is, in fact, a genetically imparted skill and allows the application of the Makah's innate whaling knowledge. On the day of the successful hunt, Jim Cook of the tribe exclaimed: "Getting this whale today proved that it is in our blood. A lot of people were saying we were inexperienced, we don't know how to do it. . . . Today proved it's in our blood." (Murphy 1999)

But hunting techniques were not the only thing whaling supporters described as natural. Some of the Makah also portrayed the hunt itself as a natural and necessary act. As Keith Johnson (1998) noted, "we are all part of the natural world and predation is also part of life on this planet." Similarly, a whaling advocate attending the public hearing for a draft of the second environmental assessment for the Makah hunt carried a sign reading "To hunt is natural." Many Makah maintain that hunting is not only natural, but also necessary for improving the tribe's nutrition and the health problems they believe stem from the loss of seafood and sea mammals from their diet. Native Americans have the highest diabetes rates in the world and some health professionals suggest that the introduction of "Western" foods like refined sugar and flour, beef, and lard are in large part to blame for the prevalence of diabetes. Research into links between genetics and nutrition-related illnesses suggests that whale oil could help remedy problems such as lactose intolerance, digestive illnesses, and attention deficit disorder (Renker 1997). The National Institutes of Health along with other American health organizations conducted a 30-year study of the Pima Indians in Arizona. The findings suggest that particular populations may develop a genetic code especially suited for a specific environment and its food resources so that disruptions to a diet dependent on these resources could result in health problems (Renker 1997; NIH 1996). Based on these sorts of studies, many Makah contend that a return to whaling will restore the Makah's natural, nutritional balance.

Just as whaling opponents fear that far-reaching repercussions of Makah whaling will ultimately endanger gray whale populations, the Makah believe that prohibitions against whaling will endanger their traditions, identity, and community. In this respect, Makah culture is portrayed as a species in danger of extinction and the Makah's efforts aim literally at keeping this culture alive. "The Makah," one observer noted, "are as much at risk as the whale here." (Erickson 1999, p. 6) The Makah maintain that the whale hunt formed the center of their worldview and social life. Whaling, they claim, is essential for preserving their identity and tradition and will revive a sense of "community, self-worth, and spirituality" (Watters and Dugger 1997, pp. 324–325). Hunting, for example, requires the building of canoes and equipment, physical training, spiritual preparations, and knowledge of the ocean and marine life (Erickson 1999). The Makah believe that by reviving these practices, the tribe will save its culture from extinction and will keep it alive, not as a dead culture encased behind museum glass, but as a living and breathing culture that resides in a community of people. They also believe that these activities can restore discipline and a sense of purpose to tribal members. The tribal police chief expressed hope that the intense physical and mental discipline of the whale hunt and the attendant interest in traditional values would reduce crime (Watters and Dugger 1997).

Makah tribal members claim that whale hunting is helping to remind the Makah who they are. Greig Arnold, tribal chairman, described the successful hunt as "a moment-of-life change, something very deep. We are connecting with our past, and that is hugely important." Other tribal members have noted increased enrollment in Makah language classes, two high school graduation speeches spoken in Makah in the last two years, and new interest in courses such as ethnobotany which teach about plant use by Makah ancestors (Shukovsky and Barber 2001).

As these claims and tactics suggest, the Makah's campaign for cultural preservation is an attempt to reclaim and reenact cultural practices because they are uniquely Makah and stand to benefit ways of life on the reservation. Yet the Makah's assertions of localness drew on and exploited global resources. Print media, television and the Internet have proven important (albeit not always welcomed) venues for publicizing the Makah and the whaling controversy. A local television station broadcast the successful whale hunt live in May 1999. And as Robert Sullivan describes in *A Whale Hunt*, an account of his two-year stay among the Makah, the media "blew into town like a great howling Aeloian force, armed with walkie-talkies and expense accounts and cellular phones" (2000, p. 104). In the words of another journalist: "The Makahs did not invite us to their hunt. We came, dozens of us from all over the globe, because it promised to be a sexy story. We have, by our collective presence placed enormous pressure on the tribe. We've put the Makahs on the free-throw line and focused the eyes of the world on them." (Tizon 1998d)

As journalists "camped out" in and around Neah Bay, tribal leaders attempted to teach reporters about Makah culture and whaling traditions by inviting these visitors for press conferences and for tours around the reservation. Some Makah responded to the media attention as an opportunity to share their views and ways of life with the world. Other tribal members resented having to explain and defend their ways of life to a global audience. As Denise Dailey remarked, "This should be a Makah event, not a world event." (Mapes 1998)

The tribe's interests in cultural revival and preservation also link up with important trends in global environment-development politics where asserting the importance of the "local" is itself becoming a "global" preoccupation. After all, the challenge at the heart of *Our Common Future*—to meet the needs of present generations without compromising those of future generations—aligns closely with the seventh generation principle by which Native Americans consider how their decisions and interactions with their surroundings are likely to affect the safety and well-being of their progeny as far as seven generations into the future. And international environmental institutions are increasingly looking to local, traditional, and indigenous knowledges and ways of life as models and resources for promoting sustainability (Martello 2001; UNEP 2001).

Globalizing Culture

In challenging the Makah, anti-whaling activists have focused largely on what they see as the global dimensions of whaling, Makah culture, and citizenship. In particular, whaling opponents attack potential links between whaling and commercial interests, the modernization of whaling practices, and a lack of consensus on whaling within the tribe. These challenges aim at weakening the tribe's representations of its culture as natural, true, and encompassing an innate set of needs and abilities on the part of tribal members.

According to some activists, Makah cultural claims are a front for economic motives that call these claims into question. Even though the Makah historically traded in whale-derived materials, anti-whaling groups contend that culture and commerce should not mix. They believe that aspirations to participate in global capitalism cause the tribe to forfeit its right to cultural preservation. Some skeptics contend that the Makah's interest in cultural preservation emerged only after it became clear that whaling for commercial purposes was out of the question given IWC regulations and general public attitudes (Hogan 1996). But even if the Makah do not profit from whaling, activists maintain that the Makah's privileges will set whaling on a slippery slope that will eventually enable other indigenous peoples and countries to whale for financial gain (Dornin and the Associated Press 1998). SSCS further suggests that Japan attempted to "purchase allies" against the ban on non-subsistence whaling by originally encouraging the Makah to pursue commercial whaling. Critics have maintained that Japan would like to latch onto the indigenous rights movement, align itself with first nations, and loosen IWC restrictions on commercial whaling. Alleged Japanese assistance to the Makah tribe has taken the form of money, boats and lessons on whale hunting. SSCS claims that Iceland, Norway, and Japan want to obtain their own cultural exemptions for whaling (Associated Press and Reuters 1998). SSCS also claims that Japan and Norway are working through the World Council of Whalers (WCW) to restart commercial whaling through aboriginal whaling communities and that groups from the Makah and from other Nuu-Chah-Nulth tribes have taken part in WCW meetings despite US government warnings to the Makah to stay clear of commercial interests.

Whaling opponents also take issue with the Makah's reliance on modern technologies. Originally, Makah used canoes and speared the whale with cedar harpoons and mussel-shell barbs and points. The Makah tracked the whales with air-filled sealskin bladders attached to harpoons. After a harpoon struck the whale, the bladder floated in the water allowing the Makah to trace and follow the whale's path and "drive it to exhaustion." While Makah who once hunted whales are no longer alive, the present generations have learned about the tradition through songs and stories. A group of hunters also met with Eskimo whalers from Alaska and from the Russian far east to learn the procedure. Nowadays the Makah conduct their hunt from two 36-foot cedar canoes each carved from a single log and able to hold eight or nine men.[5] These canoes are accompanied by two motorized "chase boats" (Anderson and Associated Press 1998). The Makah use a stainless steel harpoon mounted on a wooden shaft, but only to make their first strike. Departing from tradition, they employ a specially designed .50 caliber rifle to kill the whale (Anderson and Associated Press 1998)[6] and motorized boats to tow it home (Associated Press and Reuters 1998). To learn how to best use the rifle, the Makah consulted with Dr. Allen Ingling, a veterinarian at the University of Maryland who, with colleagues at the National Marine Fisheries Service and the National Marine Mammal Laboratory, tested the rifle. The rifle causes immediate unconsciousness and death when fired at a target area near the base of the whale's skull. According to the Makah, "It is the most humane method that can be employed." During the whale hunt in May 1999, divers entered the water to lash shut the whale's jaws to prevent the animal from sinking and attached lines to allow boats to tow the whale to shore. They beached the whale at one of the Makah's traditional beaches and whaling family representatives carved the blubber and meat and distributed it in accordance with traditional Makah practice.[7]

Many of the more modern elements of the hunt came under strong fire from anti-whaling factions who denounced the use of the power boat and the rifle as untraditional and belying the sincerity of the Makah's cultural reasons for whaling. Paul Watson summed up the sentiments of many anti-whaling activists when he remarked on Makah hunting practices by noting "we don't see any tradition in this" (Erickson 1999). In many cases animal rights advocates present themselves as authorities on what counts as Makah culture and what does not. They generally portray older whaling techniques and practices as those the Makah should adopt if they are truly serious about reviving their culture. Paul Watson took issue with the attitude of the hunters, saying they were not sufficiently serious about the task at hand: "One of the most obscene parts of this situation is that the elders are reporting that the younger members are dancing and singing with glee in reaction to the news. Traditionally, the death of whale would have been greeted with great sadness. . . . What we have here is a group of redneck hunters having a good time." (Murphy 1999) Alberta Thompson, a tribal elder who opposed the hunt, also questioned its authenticity and its value: "They are not hungry. And tradition? I don't see any tradition in towing a canoe with a motorboat. That's not the whaling I heard my elders talk about. They said it would get kids off drugs and booze, but this town hasn't changed; it's like any other town." (Bernton and Mapes 2000) Other criticisms focused on the inability of the crew to successfully sew the whale's mouth before the animal filled with water and sank to the ocean floor. Protesters challenged the use of a large fishing boat to refloat the whale and tow it to shore (Verhovek 1999a).

But attacks against Makah culture reached beyond the whaling expedition itself. The Progressive Animal Welfare Society, for example, took issue with the existence of lighted tennis courts, Pepsi, and Fedex on the reservation (Johnson 1998). These arguments suggest that local culture or interest therein cannot exist among people who engage with and adopt aspects of the "outside," globalized world. According to whaling opponents, imbibing soft drinks and sending overnight packages indicate that the tribe either has no culture to preserve, is insincere about reviving the one they lost, or else is too implicated already in global culture to make a credible claim for opting out of the whaling moratorium.

Dissension among tribal members has also drawn attacks from anti-whaling groups who equate authentic cultural claims with unanimous, rather than overwhelming, tribal support. In a tribal referendum on the issue in 1995, 85 percent of those voting favored whaling. In a recent tribal election for a seat on the five-member council, one of the most aggressive whaling opponents ran for office, but received only 35 out of 360 votes. Yet some of the staunchest whaling challengers also happen to be elders and some of the most outspoken and activist tribal members. Animal rights groups have devoted considerable effort and resources to publicizing these intra-tribal divisions. In 1994 seven tribal elders signed a petition against resuming the whale hunt (Humane Society 1999). In 1996, nine animal rights organizations sponsored a newspaper ad by Makah elders denouncing plans to carry out whale hunts. That same year, these organizations flew some of the elders to the IWC meeting where they helped to postpone the Makah's whaling request.

Many anti-whaling groups believe that the Makah belong to a world community and should adapt their values and priorities accordingly. As we have seen, they fault the Makah for buying into aspects of Western culture and failing to maintain an insulated and homogeneous community. And they urge the Makah to be good global citizens. An open letter to the Makah noted:

The resumption of the slaughter of these benign and trusting beings would bring to your nation swift and ongoing *world-wide condemnation*. We submit that important spiritual traditions must be observed in the *context of a planet* whose wildlife are being destroyed by habitat reduction, human overpopulation and exploitation, competition for food, and the proliferation of toxic chemicals. As *global neighbors* also committed to healing our spiritual connection to the natural world, we appeal to you to work with us to pursue creative alternatives to your planned whaling, avoiding a conflict that will have no winners. (emphasis added)

Activists plead with the Makah to recognize that they are players in the global politics of whaling (Walker 1999), and therefore to adhere to some sort of global standards and assume membership in a world community. In the words of Roger Caras, President of the American Society for the Prevention of Cruelty to Animals, "You can't live in the 15th or 16th or 17th centuries. They're gone. You have to live in the here and now." (Tizon 1998b) Whaling opponents warned the Makah that the tribe will face global denunciation if they try to resurrect traditional cultural practices and fail to sufficiently engage with the global community.

Reflections on Globalization and Cultural Preservation as a Goal of Environment-Development Politics

In many ways, the Makah controversy reflects conventional notions of globalization. Ecological interdependencies and the effects of a worldwide whaling industry, the framing of whales as a global resource, global whale counts, and the encroachment of "other" ways of life into Makah villages ultimately led to transnational debates over the tribe's right to assert its identity by hunting whales. But the Makah story also reveals that globalization is not simply a transcendent, aggregate phenomenon that happens to us, without our volition. Globalization can be a powerful political strategy, and it can be as much about constructing and questioning the meaning of the local as it is about crafting and negotiating the global. The policy forums and courts in this story played it safe by relying on "universal" resources of science and law. Debates happening outside of formal policy forums ventured into seemingly more "local" territory by raising questions of cultural preservation. Yet here too globalism's discourses underpinned the positions of various parties.

Lessons from the Makah case could benefit environment-development policy institutions that are not following in the footsteps of the IWC and US courts, but are instead making cultural preservation the focus of some of their programs. Attempts by international institutions to foster the preservation of traditional ways of life, in part through the systemization and dissemination of local and traditional knowledge and practices, provide just a few examples (see Martello 2001; UNEP 2001). The Makah story highlights additional questions that these initiatives are likely to face upon implementation. In particular, what is culture in a globalizing world? How do we determine and mediate the needs of "local" culture and "global" nature? And who decides?

The Makah controversy is one, seemingly insignificant case that has opened up these questions to a global audience. As various voices weighed in, the impasse they created had a lot to do with the incongruous localizing and globalizing strategies the two sides employed. Proof of local culture, however, has been the thorniest issue for the Makah. While claiming a local culture, the Makah have had to engage in globalization strategies that their opponents hold against them. The Makah aim to revive some aspects of their traditional ways of life long threatened by globalization in the form of

European visitors, the American government, and commercial fisheries. Yet, in the eyes of some tribal members, globalization also necessitates that they recognize the environment as a global resource, pay heed to international agreements aimed at its protection, and represent and explain their culture to a worldwide audience. Global networks and strategies are necessary for attaining legal permission to whale; yet these networks and strategies threaten to further erode local culture, while opening it up to global scrutiny. Interactions with the news media for example, have played into divisions within the tribe. Yet good relations with the media and a positive portrayal of their reservation were important for gaining public support for pro-whaling tribal members. Similar contradictions are apparent in the arguments of activists. Anti-whaling groups challenge the Makah's cultural authenticity because of their Fedex, lighted tennis courts, and modern technology, while at the same time calling upon the tribe to be global citizens. Globalization appears at once to be a defining element of local cultures, a threat to these cultures, and a set of obligations for traditional and indigenous peoples.

By examining the localizing and globalizing strategies of the Makah and activists, we can see that, before embarking on cultural preservation programs, environment-development institutions would do well to ask themselves what it means to preserve local knowledge and traditional ways of life in a globalizing (and localizing) world, and to explore means for reconciling the sorts of tensions between traditional and modern and traditional and commercial that we see in the Makah story. At the very least, it appears useful to revise conventional ways of thinking about the meaning of tradition in environment-development debates. While tradition is generally associated with historic, local, static ways of life, an approach to understanding traditional lifestyles as ever-changing and as creatively interacting with and accommodating the global and modern,[8] could clear away some of the confusion that has plagued the Makah controversy.

Notes

1. Funding for the hunts come in part from a Commerce Department grant of $310,000 approved by the Clinton administration.

2. The varied notions of indigenous culture and identity that are contested in this debate have no doubt been shaped, in part, through anthropology, history, museums

and the like (e.g., Erikson 1999; Clifford 1997). The particularities of such influences, however, are beyond the scope of this chapter.

3. See, for example, the web site of the West Coast Anti-Whaling Society.

4. Whaling opponents have suggested that financial and other enticements from Norway and Japan are behind the Makah's renewed interest in whaling.

5. "Makah Whaling: Questions and Answers."

6. See also "Makah Whaling: Questions and Answers."

7. "Makah Whaling: Questions and Answers."

8. On "modernized tradition" in the context of Inuit hunting communities in West Greenland, see Dahl 2000.

References

Anderson, Peggy, and Associated Press. 1998. "Indian Tribe Moves to Resume Whaling Tradition." October 1.

Associated Press. 1996. "American Indian Whaling Plan Faces Opposition." June 24.

Associated Press and Reuters. 1998. "Makah, Protesters Stay Ashore on First Day of Whale Hunting Season." October 2.

Berman, Mark. 2000. "Gray Whales Still at Risk." *Earth Island Journal* 15, no. 3: 8.

Bernton, Hal. 2002. "Court Bars Makah Whale Hunt." *Seattle Times*, December 21.

Bernton, Hal, and Lynda V. Mapes. 2000. "Court Voids Approval of Makah Whale Hunt." *Seattle Times*, June 10.

Clifford, James. 1997. *Routes: Travel and Translation in the Late Twentieth Century*. Harvard University Press.

Dahl, Jens. 2000. *Saqqaq: An Inuit Hunting Community in the Modern World*. University of Toronto Press.

Dornin, Rusty, and Associated Press. 1998. "Anti-Whaling Activists Clash with Indians." November 2.

Dunagan, Christopher. 1998. "Whale Watch: To Sight the Mighty Gray." *Sun* (Bremerton, Washington), October 6.

Erikson, Patricia Pierce. 1999. "A Whaling We Will Go: Encounters of Knowledge and Memory at the Makah Cultural and Research Center." *Cultural Anthropology* 14, no. 4: 556–583.

Hardy, Dian, and Susan Hudgens. 2000. "Washington Whalers Try Again." *The Animals' Agenda* 20, no. 4: 14–15.

Hogan, Linda. 1996. "Silencing Tribal Grandmothers—Traditions, Old Values at Heart of Makah's Clash over Whaling." *Seattle Times*, December 15.

Humane Society. 1999. "Slaughter at Sea: The Makah Celebrate Becoming Whalers." *HSUS Today's News*, May 21.

Johnson, Keith. 1998. "The Makah Manifesto." *Seattle Times*, August 23.

Mapes, Lynda V. 1998. "Feds Have Whale of a Conflict—Makah Hunt Puts Some Government Agencies in a Dilemma." *Seattle Times*, October 15.

Martello, Marybeth. 2001. "A Paradox of Virtue?: 'Other' Knowledges and Environment-Development Politics." *Global Environmental Politics* 1, no. 3: 114–141.

Murphy, Kim. 1999. "Indians Finally Get Their Whale." *Los Angeles Times*. May 18.

National Institutes of Health. 1996. *The Pima Indians: Pathfinders for Health*. NIH publication 95-3821. Government Printing Office.

National Marine Fisheries Service. 1997. Environmental Assessment of the Makah Tribe's Harvest of up to Five Gray Whales per Year for Aboriginal Subsistence Use.

National Marine Fisheries Service. 2001. Environmental Assessment on Issuing a Quota to the Makah Indian Tribe for a Subsistence Hunt on Gray Whales for the Years 2001 and 2002. July 12.

Renker, Ann. 1997. "Whale Hunting and the Makah Tribe: A Needs Statement." In Environmental Assessment of the Makah Tribe's Harvest of up to Five Gray Whales per Year for Aboriginal Subsistence Use (National Marine Fisheries Service).

Reuters. 1997. "Indian Tribe Gets OK to Resume Whaling." October 23.

Russell, Dick. 1999. "Tribal Traditions and the Spirit of Trust." *Amicus Journal* 21, no. 1: 29–32.

Sanders, Eli. 2000. "Whale-Hunt Protester Hurt in Coast Guard Collision Has No Regrets, Activist Could Face Fine, 6 Years in Prison." *Seattle Times*, April 21.

Scheiber, Harry N. 1998. "Historical Memory, Cultural Claims, and Environmental Ethics in the Jurisprudence of Whaling Regulation." *Ocean and Coastal Management* 38, no. 5: 5–40.

Schmidt, Sarah. 1999. "The One That Got Away." *Saturday Night* 114, no. 2: 78–84.

Sea Shepherd Conservation Society. 1999. "Indigenous Whale Hunting: Made in Japan."

Shukovsky, Paul, and Mike Barber. 2001. "'Resident' Gray Whales Now Fair Game for Makah." *Seattle Post-Intelligencer*, July 14.

Sullivan, Robert. 1998. "Permission Granted to Kill a Whale. Now What?" *New York Times*, August 9.

Sullivan, Robert. 2000. *A Whale Hunt*. Scribner.

Tizon, Alex 1998a. "The Whale Hunt." *Seattle Times*, September 20.

Tizon, Alex. 1998b. "Which Animals Are Pettable, and Which Are Edible?" *Seattle Times*, October 8.

Tizon, Alex. 1998c. "My Job Is to Rock the Boat—Unflappable Marine Activist Often Unbearable." *Seattle Times*, November 1.

Tizon, Alex. 1998d. "Deadliest Part of Whale Hunt Is the Long Wait." *Seattle Times*, December 1.

Treaty of Neah Bay. 1855.

United Nations Environment Programme. 2001. Globalization Threat to World's Culture, Linguistic, and Biological Diversity.

Verhovek, Sam Howe. 1999a. "Reviving Tradition, Tribe Kills a Whale." *New York Times*, May 18.

Verhovek, Sam Howe. 1999b. "After the Hunt, Bitter Protest and Salty Blubber." *New York Times*, May 19.

Walker, Peter. 1999. "The Makah Whale Hunt: Politics Meets Tradition." *HSUS Today's News*, June 2.

Watters, Lawrence, and Connie Dugger. 1997. "The Hunt for Gray Whales: The Dilemma of Native American Treaty Rights and the International Moratorium on Whaling." *Columbia Journal of Environmental Law* 22: 319–352.

12

Patching Local and Global Knowledge Together: Citizens Inside the US Chemical Industry

Alastair Iles

In the past 20 years, the dominant role of technical experts in environmental regulation has been widely questioned. Many citizens distrust industry and government experts because of crises that revealed their advice to be flawed and undemocratic (Fischer 2000; Irwin and Wynne 1996). In response, some environmental groups and lay citizens concerned about industrial pollution have fought to become technical experts in their own right, alongside industry and government. Instead of litigating, lobbying, or campaigning to shape regulation, they have expanded the notion of expertise to encompass alternative forms of knowledge situated in their local experiences of pollution. Countering these challenges, industry maintains that production choices must be standardized everywhere to be efficient and economical. Globally standardized processes promise predictable control over outputs and entrenches corporate power over other categories of expert participants (Bowker and Star 2000).

Struggles between local citizens and the global industry are especially visible in the United States, where pollution prevention has emerged since the early 1980s as a voluntary alternative to direct regulation. Prevention is an ensemble of practices and ideas that aim to stop pollution before it is produced in the first place. The American Chemistry Council states in its Pollution Prevention Code that source reduction is "[a] practice that reduces the amount of any release or waste generated at the source, including closed loop recycle and reuse before exit from a process" (CMA 1991). Instead of regulators instructing industry on what to do, and industry complying, prevention occurs through the site-specific problem-solving activities of employees and, occasionally, citizens (Iles 2000). One key development has been the growing effort of citizen groups, not just regulators, to enter plants to observe whether prevention is being put into practice and, slowly, to begin participating in the process of deciding how to reduce pollution. These groups include residents who are concerned about their neighboring plant's environmental impacts and who are determined to decrease them. In the United States, such groups are often, but not always, part of a loose network of people who share experiences and strategies across state and federal borders.

The chemical industry is heavily globalized, with technical knowledge, equipment, and business practices assumed to be capable of being used irrespective of context. Expertise is understood to pertain to chemistry, process and chemical engineering, process control, plant operation, and financial management. In demanding greater access to plants, some citizen groups have argued that the knowledge used in preventing pollution is not simply technical, but also involves, for example, "local" knowledge such as community priorities in choosing which chemicals to reduce. People living and working in the neighborhoods that surround chemical facilities are using local knowledge both to gain entrance to decision making inside plants and to challenge the industry's hegemony over defining what counts as expert knowledge. They have contended that citizens can acquire and understand technical knowledge alongside conventional experts, making industry practices more responsive to real-world conditions of each individual facility.

These groups also have begun to show that they can combine their knowledge of community health and project evaluation politics with the industry's scientific and technical resources to yield a hybrid knowledge that mixes global and local dimensions. Thus, they can gain credibility in the eyes of managers and employees when making environmental claims. As a result, the meanings of expertise can potentially change away from specialized skills and knowledge to a more general criterion of being prepared to participate in decision making inside and outside plants on *both* local and global scales. Nonetheless, corporate power continues to inhibit the use of local knowledge through drawing strong divisions between employees and outside actors, and controlling access to plants and process information. Standardized prevention methodologies squeeze out the potential for local action. Most important, by adopting technical discourses, citizens may succumb to the ability of companies to frame pollution prevention on their own terms.

Arthur Mol (2001) and other scholars who write on ecological modernization (a theory of how environmental values and goals are incorporated into governance practices) have emphasized the changing relations between environmental movements and the chemical industry as a key driver. These scholars provide insights into the green strategies that industry has embraced, and highlight how some adversarial groups have changed their stance to cooperate with corporations in improving environmental management. Ecological modernization, however, tells only part of the story. In particular, it does not address how citizens can change industry's technical assumptions through their own knowledge and resources. Nor does this framework explain how such actors shape what occurs on the ground inside companies rather than in corporate boardrooms.

In this chapter, I investigate some re-workings of expertise to include local perspectives in the case of pollution prevention in the US chemical industry. First, I sketch the chemical industry's views of knowledge, highlighting its standardization of expertise worldwide. Then I outline a theory of knowledge making that shows how citizens, as emerging political actors, can adapt the technical, economic, and managerial knowledge used by companies to their needs and conditions. Using source reduction projects at Dow Chemical's plant at Midland, Michigan and Lyondell's facility at Channelview, Texas, I explore three examples of the reworkings of expertise at century's end:

- enforcing prevention (or assuring from the outside that plants actually carry out preventive measures to reduce pollution)
- visualizing pollution (such as carrying out process audits to identify where pollution is generated, or producing emission numbers in analyzing plant performance)
- considering economic, as against health and environmental, criteria in making preventive decisions.

These examples demonstrate how global and local knowledges are constituting each other in new ways that are nonetheless constrained by corporate power.

The Chemical Industry's Global Knowledge

Historically, the US chemical industry has portrayed itself as a global, science-based enterprise. Chemical manufacturing is the design, development, and operation of reactions taking place within engineered systems of vessels, pipes, tanks, and energy supplies to yield chemicals, or products as diverse as clothes, cars, and kitchenware. In the 1920s, the Bakeland Corporation described plastics as "the material of a thousand uses," implying that science would create and transform consumer societies around the world (Meikle 1995). In the 1950s, DuPont used the slogan "better living through chemistry," linking its production with scientific progress.

Firms have worked to standardize the knowledge of chemistry, engineering, business, finance, and marketing. Engineers sought universally applicable principles ("unit operations") to design diverse processes. Plant managers tried to optimize processes to maximize production yields, relying on heuristics and principles that could be used across processes. More recently, computer technology was melded with chemical processes, thus strengthening the industry's ability to regulate reactions and improve production yields. In principle, the programming and oversight of machinery worldwide could be done from a single location. The industry worked to make technology usable by trained experts; it came to take for granted the universality and transportability of technical knowledge within its own boundaries (Jasanoff 1994).

In 1997, Craig Doolittle, the waste reduction manager at Dow Chemical's Midland plant, summed up these industry views:

We can apply the same state-of-art technology for manufacturing polystyrene, whether in Joliet, Illinois, or Map-Ta-Phut, Thailand. A network of global technology centers ensures that our sites utilize the latest innovations to maximize productivity and limit waste. We are also working to standardize our operating practices, to ensure that each pound of polystyrene is made with the same attention to quality, environmental protection, safety, and health, no matter where it's made. (EPA 1997, p. 78)

By the 1960s, chemicals were associated with the very fabric of modern society; their use in diverse products signaled progress. As a result, the early experimental uncertainties and problems of translating ideas into products faded (Meikle 1995). Chemical manufacturing has been stabilized. Its technologies and manufacturing pathways seem part of a natural order and this order has been enormously lucrative and successful worldwide.

One concomitant of industry's global self-image is the tendency to draw sharp boundaries between lay citizens outside, and expert personnel inside, chemical plants. In 1984, Monte Throdal, a Monsanto vice-president, argued that the interests relevant to environmental protection could be divided into three groups: technical, popular, and political. Of the first two, he wrote:

The first group is "technical" but the title "industry" or "scientific" might also be used. This group sees itself as dealing in objective reality. It relies on quantitative calculation, technical accuracy, and a concern for economic consequences. The second group, called "popular," might also be labeled "public interest." It sees itself as holding personal values paramount and taking a humanistic approach. It uses qualitative assessments, anecdotal evidence, analogy, and metaphor—all applied to a broad societal framework—to make moral or ethical judgments and thus arrive at "the truth." (Throdal 1984)

Throdal presumed that knowledge could be split into technical and popular realms. In each domain, different methods, criteria of proof, arguments, and conclusions would be expected to prevail. The technical group would predictably reject experience-based arguments as immaterial, whereas the popular group would be skeptical of objective risk assessment grounded in numbers. The technical group would *determine* the truth, whereas the popular group would *postulate* "the truth," with the former superior to the latter. This echoed the views widely held in industry and government of the broader relationship between science and policy (Jasanoff and Wynne 1998). That is, policy making should be a process in which political actors make decisions on the basis of scientific and technical information supplied by experts. In short, it was believed that who the experts were and what expertise was could be known in advance of making policy decisions. These were not recognized as constructed categories, but were naturalized as part of the modernist epistemology that underwrote the chemical industry's existence.

In this context, pollution prevention might be expected to mark a shift in the creation and use of knowledge. Nonetheless, the early development of prevention as a new norm of environmental protection during the 1980s continued earlier modernist tenets. Neither industry nor regulators conceived of a role for citizens or environmental groups. The US Environmental Protection Agency, the Congressional Office for Technology Assessment, and the National Research Council released key reports calling for waste reduction between 1985 and 1987. These reports did not conceive of any role for citizens to play in practicing or enforcing prevention.

Similarly, chemical companies supposed that citizens were not equipped to deal with the technology and science of chemical engineering, toxicology, pollution releases, and plant operations. As a method aimed at increasing production efficiency, prevention was defined as principally within the expertise of employees. The design and operation of processes for better yields and less wastage were said to be "a variation of traditional chemical process design as practiced for decades by chemical engineers" and to "require all the traditional skills required of chemical engineers and some additional degree of specialization" (Allen 1992). One important change in corporate practice during the 1980s was to expand the categories of employees who could be entrusted with the details of processes, and with the risks of changing these processes. These were not only process operators, but also financial managers, marketers, chemists, and raw material purchasers. Nonetheless, only those who worked inside plants could decide on preventive measures. The American Institute of Chemical Engineers recently published a leading prevention textbook that lists the employees who ought to be involved but does not include citizens or regulators as possible participants (Mulholland and Dyer 1999).

Making Local Knowledge

Alongside the chemical industry's dominant technological knowledge, local knowledge has emerged as an alternative mode of understanding the technical and scientific aspects of manufacturing. I define local knowledge as the bundle of knowledge that pertains to the locally variable, contingent conditions under which environmental protection occurs. This knowledge is commonly, but not always, held by the people who live or work in a geographical area (like a community surrounding a plant) or socio-technical situation (such as inside a manufacturing plant). The knowledge may be place-related, covering a place's social, biological, climatic, cultural, and ecological conditions. But it may also be society-based, extending beyond the locality. Local actors may accumulate knowledge through their experiences, interactions, observations, and conversations with each other. These actors include plant employees, physicians, regulators, environmentalists, and school teachers.

A defining feature of local knowledge is that its nature and content grow out of each setting, who or what is engaged in the setting, and the ways in which actors shape the setting through their activities and choices. In chemical manufacturing, this knowledge can concern matters such as detecting the health and ecological impacts of contamination (Irwin and Wynne 1996), the fear of illness by residents (Kroll-Smith and Floyd 1998), and the watercourses by which factory pollution may enter the ecosystem

(Mazur 1996). Actors may have views situated in their experience about who is politically important, how to mobilize resources inside plants (Szasz 1994), and how to articulate risk assessments in terms that residents can understand and are willing to accept (O'Brien 2000).

In turn, people can make knowledge local through their interpretations and activities. Knowledge can be given multiple layers of geographical, social, political, scientific, engineering, and cultural referents. No single actor is likely to hold all the knowledge relating to a given issue, as these referents are distributed across the locality. Knowledge can be local in being difficult to discern and communicate beyond the particular setting where it is generated and held (Geertz 1983). It may be embodied in people, take the form of social and cultural practices, rely on institutions and relationships that cannot be easily replicated elsewhere, or grow out of shared histories of people living together. Precisely because these conditions or histories are contingent, they are less available to be observed beyond the locality. If more remote actors such as corporate headquarters, governments, or national environmental groups are to control, or understand, developments in a particular setting, they need actors "on the ground" who can act as guides (Scott 1998).

Conversely, locally generated knowledge need not be self-contained, or separate from knowledge made in other places or thought to apply universally. Based on experience, observations, relationships between people, and interpretive conventions, local knowledge seems to resist ready translation into standardized practices, databases, tools, numbers, and other objects that can be used anywhere by anyone on the globe (Latour 1987). Local actors may, however, have the capacity to borrow, adapt, and use scientific and technical knowledge to advance their political activism. They can create new dynamics of knowledge through their experiments—mixing, for example, quantitative risk analysis with community health problems documented through photographs, geographical information systems, and surveys. They can choose to use nationwide pollutant inventory databases but develop their own technical tools to make the data more meaningful at their own scale.

Instead of people simply mobilizing their "local" knowledge more visibly against "global" knowledge promoters such as companies, this chapter argues, these actors can synthesize new forms of expert knowledge. The case of pollution prevention shows how companies and citizens alike can mix scientific and local knowledge in highly distinctive ways. In doing so, they can challenge the division that Throdal draws between technical and popular knowers. Simultaneously, companies can force citizens to adopt their technical discourses, just as citizens can pressure companies to seek better health outcomes. Local and global modes of knowledge may come to depend on each other through being negotiated together. It becomes crucial to examine what hybrids of knowledge are emerging from combining local and global modes of knowing, and what factors shape the making of these hybrids. In practice, the politics of local and global actors intersect; corporate power and standardization interact with resident power and site-specific activism. This leads to the patchwork of knowledge that we observe not just in pollution prevention, but in environmental protection generally.

Citizens Entering Plants

In the 1980s and the early 1990s, the chemical industry and environmentalists gave increasing priority to local knowledge in their efforts to accomplish prevention. They began to define expertise, and to draw lay-expert boundaries differently, according to what they perceived as the knowledge needed to deal with the locally variable, contingent features of prevention. In the early 1990s, however, national environmental groups reinforced the chemical industry's assumptions about differences between lay and expert actors. For example, in 1990, INFORM, a technical consulting firm based in Manhattan, advised citizens:

When you start to gather information about a plant in your community, you will realize that, as a plant outsider, you probably will never become familiar enough with the details of each production process to identify the most appropriate source reduction opportunities yourself. What you can do is promote the atmosphere and procedures within the company that will enable it to develop an effective source reduction program. (Wise and Kenworthy 1990)

This argument recurs in the early manuals written by national groups such as Greenpeace. These manuals advised activists to recruit their own technical experts to review chemical processes, and to focus on the politics of pressuring firms instead of trying to get inside plants to shape production decisions directly. In this way, the guidelines maintained a line between the technical and political aspects of prevention, and allocated pre-determined roles to agents, emulating Throdal's classification of technical and popular actors. Such attitudes prevail among companies, regulators, and many environmentalists.

Still, some citizen groups, such as the Good Neighbor Agreement Movement, Texans United (based in Houston), and Communities for Better Environments (located in the Bay Area), have questioned the lay-expert boundaries that industry, regulators, and even national environmental groups have created or accepted. Through their contacts with chemical plants in the course of campaigns, particularly those motivated by the advent of the Toxics Release Inventory (TRI) in 1988, they perceived that changes were underway inside plants that could make it more feasible for them to adapt scientific and technical knowledge to their situations. Moreover, because prevention is not mandated in the United States, and no recourse to litigation is available, the groups further concluded that they needed to develop alternative ways of enforcing prevention where regulators seemed unwilling to do so. Sanford Lewis, a leading activist lawyer, commented: "What citizens can see for themselves through direct inspections with their own expert consultants can be far more reliable and extensive than what a government inspector may report to them." (Lewis 1993)

As a result, the groups began to experiment with using different institutional pathways to demand a role in plant decision making (Iles 2000). They adopted new strategies not just for securing access to technical expertise and information , but to demand entry into plants, invoking their local knowledge. At first, the groups relied on being residents potentially at risk from pollution and accidental releases, and therefore interested in prevention activities inside plants. Subsequently, they claimed expertise not only in community health and politics, but in evaluating company actions and prevention data, and in developing tools to enable laypeople to understand prevention.

Citizens Acting as Experts

In the late 1990s, a small number of citizen groups across America tested another approach to redefining expertise. They contended that they should be regarded as participants in their own right, sharing decision making power inside plants, without always needing the aid of more technically qualified professionals. Facility managers should view citizen concerns as having a weight equal to those of company actors. To be regarded as knowledge possessors, however, the citizen groups needed to demonstrate that they could not only provide valuable input about community health risks and politics, but also bring fresh perspectives to improve the production system. By learning something about the technicalities of chemical manufacturing, and even making their own technical tools to prioritize chemicals for reduction, citizens converted their local knowledge into terms that employees and companies could understand and value more easily. These citizen groups further blurred the boundaries between lay and expert actors, but only to a point, with the formidable inertia of industry's standardized practices discouraging site-specific innovation. Speaking in technical terms can be empowering if citizens can change these terms to encompass their needs and experiences, but can also trap citizens within the industry's status quo position of doing nothing to fundamentally change its production.

Two examples offer insights into how expertise is constituted in such plant-citizen relationships: the Michigan Source Reduction Project, in which local activists and the Natural Resources Defense Council conducted a study of preventive options at Dow Chemical's plant in Midland, Michigan between 1996 and 1999; and the Lyondell/Equistar Project, in which community members evaluated Lyondell's petrochemical operations at Channelview, Texas, from 1997 to 2000. Like earlier attempts by citizens to enter plants, these cases can be seen as experimental ventures, with the meanings of expertise not settled in advance but worked out through site-specific negotiations between employees and citizens.

In the Midland Source Reduction Project, company staff collaborated with several local activists and the NRDC to identify preventive options at Dow's vast Midland, Michigan plant. The project set out to reduce 26 priority chemicals, chosen in negotiation between activists and company staff, by at least 35 percent over two years. It was initiated by staff at the NRDC office in Washington DC, following their earlier attempt to establish a joint prevention project at the company's plant in La Porte, Texas. Dow had failed to implement the preventive measures that this study identified, claiming that these would not yield significant economic gains (Greer and Sels 1998).

Linda Greer, a toxicology expert at the NRDC, theorized that enlisting local activists as lead participants (not as observers outside the plant, as at La Porte) might fundamentally change the dynamics of industry-environmentalist cooperation. She insisted that Diane Herbert and Mary Sinclair, activists living in Midland, along with three regional groups (Citizens for Alternatives to Chemical Contamination, the Lone Tree Council, and the Ecology Center of Ann Arbor), should be included with the engineers, managers, and process operators who surveyed processes (Greer 2000). Greer's mix of technical and advocacy expertise, along with personal contacts with Dow managers, helped catalyze a project that otherwise would not have occurred because of the company's distrust of the local activists as a result of previous disputes.

Greer was able to convince Dow to pay for two technical consultants with vast experience in prevention. One, Bill Bilkovich, acted as an external adviser to the company (but helping advise the activists), while the other, Steven Anderson, worked with the activists, teaching them about prevention, and independently doing audits of the company. Bilkovich and Anderson were not locally based, but came from Florida and New Jersey respectively. While relying on these experts, the activists insisted on being part of the preventive decision-making process, contributing their knowledge of community health concerns and priorities to guide the use of technical expertise. They asked for the same data that employees used. They demanded a voice in choosing the chemical emissions to be cut and the methods to be used, knowing how this might benefit the surrounding community. They brought their pre-existing knowledge of the plant's behavior to bear in negotiations with company personnel, acting as locally trustworthy monitors of what Dow was doing. Instead of simply claiming the right to enter the plant as concerned residents, the activists argued that they could combine scientific and technical knowledge with their own knowledge to drive the project. In this way, the Midland project differed from earlier prevention ventures.

In contrast, the Lyondell Source Reduction Project grew out of the efforts of residents on the company's Community Advisory Panel for Lyondell and Equistar (CAPLE) to transcend their assigned roles. Led by LaNell Anderson, and supported by Diane Sheridan, both community activists, the CAPLE members worked with employees at the two adjacent Lyondell and Equistar olefin plants in Channelview, Texas to try to understand the processes at the plant and to recommend areas for action (CAPLE 2000). Lyondell had proposed massive plant expansions after buying a neighboring plant from Equistar. Concerned about the health risks posed by plant emissions, notably of benzene, the residents demanded source reduction. They issued a set of six "citizen demands" asking Lyondell to implement measures that they had personally identified after studying the plant and holding 32 meetings with employees. It was only afterwards that Dr. Neil Carman of the Sierra Club in nearby Houston was invited to help review the company's responses to the demands for their technical adequacy.

Both projects were motivated by exceptional citizen group interest in developing methods independent from government intervention to enforce prevention against firms, and to perform surveillance of plant activities that were almost impossible to track through litigation or the Toxics Release Inventory. Neither project materialized fortuitously, but evolved from the local histories of environmental protest over the prior decade. Residents had repeatedly sued Dow and Lyondell for accidental releases, while the EPA imposed penalties on both firms for exceeding permitted pollution levels in the late 1990s. Citizen groups already possessed substantial knowledge and resources built up over time, which they could apply to source reduction projects. Regulators were already engaged in scrutinizing each plant, thus predisposing the plant managers to cooperate more with their local communities. Such circumstances may not exist elsewhere.

Yet both projects reveal that citizen groups can translate scientific and technical expert resources into their local conditions with regard to at least three issues: enforcing prevention; visualizing pollution inside and outside plants; and considering economic, as against health and environmental, criteria in making preventive decisions. By doing so, these groups show that speaking with technical terms and expertise does not necessarily have to lead to citizen co-option by industry.

Citizens as Enforcers Inside Plants

The Midland and Channelview projects show that citizens are framing relevant expertise not simply as technical knowledge, as the industry has defined it, but as knowledge covering diverse topics such as familiarity with local politics, awareness of community health issues, the use of quantitative analysis, and advocacy skills. While the citizens in these cases have gained, or shown that they can gain, access to conventional forms of expertise, they have introduced local knowledge into enforcing prevention in two ways: providing information about locally variable conditions that affect production choices inside the facility; and critiquing the company's technical explanations for its choices.

First, citizens argued that the company needs their local knowledge (regarding place, history, society, and politics) if it is to make preventive decisions that are accepted as legitimate outside the plant, or that take authentic account of community dynamics. They argued that summoning an outside technical expert alone would not provide adequate input into company decision making. By knowing about matters such as the prior history of plant-community relations, the personalities of the employees involved, geographical and climate conditions around the plant, and suspected health effects in the neighborhood, citizens can help guide company staff. Dow and Lyondell had presumed that technical and economic criteria would not only satisfy their prevention priorities, but also convince the neighboring residents of their commitment. Conversely, the activists told the plants that any reported prevention would lack credibility unless local political issues, such as deep distrust held by some people in the community, were taken into account.

Second, citizens in these cases tried to learn more about the technical sides of chemical manufacturing and to better position themselves to interrogate employees about preventive possibilities. Though technical consultants can provide a fresh, external perspective to employee deliberations, citizens can also bring this viewpoint and add urgency through their concern for environmental and human health. At Midland, with their local knowledge of Dow's environmental practices and community relations, the activists could aim their intervention more effectively in the monthly meetings with company staff. Importantly, Dow told its production managers and line operators to present their ideas and analysis directly to the activists, and to seek their approval for prevention measures.

Linda Greer (2000) commented: "We were sort of articulate critics of the status quo [and] created the atmosphere where Dow felt like it had to go and review its processes in a new way." When managers claimed that prevention was not feasible, Diane Herbert and Mary Sinclair would ask questions such as "Have you considered a substitute for this solvent?" or "Can you perform this chemical reaction at a lower temperature?" (NRDC 1999). They monitored the company's response to determine whether preventive options were being considered seriously. Sometimes, with the aid of Bilkovich and Anderson, the citizens proposed measures that Dow could evaluate.

Such questions reflect what employees might ask at any facility. Nonetheless, the history of prevention is full of cases where employees on their own did not discover promising prevention opportunities. In 1992, EPA obliged DuPont to survey waste reduction options at its Chambers plant in Delaware. Much to the company's surprise, many solutions were identified, and a plant engineer noted, "The most sensible answers are right under your nose and you do not see them unless you look for them" (ENDS 226 1993). Similarly, Dow found that some simple measures had been overlooked at Midland, such as recycling a solvent that it had considered too degraded for reuse. Employees often assume that chemical technology cannot be changed, because they are accustomed to its everyday operation. But citizens can pressure employees to reconsider their interpretation of the limits of technological feasibility.

Similarly, CAPLE members demanded answers in their meetings with the firm. In contrast to the Midland venture, these citizens viewed themselves as voluntary advisors to Lyondell, but they came to acquire some knowledge about the technologies and practices inside the plants. The citizens studied technical books on petrochemical processes, took lengthy tours of the plants, and reviewed prevention options. They developed sufficient technical expertise to identify the areas needing attention by Lyondell. CAPLE insisted that Lyondell explain how past emission reductions were achieved through source reduction, if at all. LaNell Anderson asked employees: "Why are you flaring so much? What are the causes of the flaring? What can you do about this?" (CAPLE 2000). The activists asked employees to explain why reaction upsets occurred at a perceived high rate, and therefore imposed greater accountability on the employees for their actions.

Though the activists wanted technical advice, they were concerned about compromised expertise (i.e., experts identifying with each other, rather than with the laypeople they are supposed to serve), and therefore deferred the choice of experts until the point when they felt that they understood clearly what additional knowledge was needed. The activists were willing to trust the company's experts once they had evaluated the company's process of looking for and choosing prevention projects. After establishing their bona fides as participants, and issuing their demands to Lyondell, they could hire an independent technical expert. Still, as LaNell Anderson said, "We made specific requests, set specific goals, and they responded to these" (Houston Chronicle 2001). Eventually, the CAPLE issued six "citizen demands" to the firm, including the creation of a fugitive emission monitoring program, reduced flaring, a new maintenance program, and reductions of butadiene emissions through process changes. In response, the company set up teams of employees to put most demands into practice.

Visualizing Pollution and Prevention through Numbers

Rather than relying on regulators to monitor and enforce environmental protection, citizen groups can carry out these functions themselves. To do so, however, they need ways to see and monitor what is occurring inside chemical facilities. One of the major developments in prevention since the 1980s has been the invention of means to visualize pollution and prevention inside plants (Iles 2000). These means have been predominantly quantitative, ranging from pollutant inventory numbers, to materials accounting figures. According to industry's normal understanding of expertise, different kinds of numbers are meant to cover discrete realms for particular audiences. Inventory numbers, for instance, are intended to be used by anyone anywhere in America. Conversely, process mapping (such as waste audits) is intended to be only for employees. In developing and using numerical methods to visualize pollution, citizen groups have blurred these boundaries considerably, combining supposedly universal numerical measures with their more situated knowledge of how to use these.

Since 1988, environmental groups have used TRI numbers in campaigns to pressure the chemical industry to reduce emissions (e.g., Gottlieb 1995). They have accomplished this by translating emission figures into terms of individual plants or local pollution loads, and by insisting that companies should be identified as sources of emissions. Originally, EPA had provided TRI data only in aggregated form at the state and national level, without identifying particular facilities. But in 1990, EPA succumbed to immense political pressure from environmentalists, such as the Right to Know Network (with 1,500 NGO members across America), and allowed citizens to search the database by zip codes or plant names that enabled pollution to be linked to specific neighborhoods and plants. This stimulated an even greater expansion of local campaigns.

However, the citizens at Midland and Channelview further adapted these TRI numbers, and effectively used additional sets of numbers, notably process level data and waste stream analyses that firms do not usually make publicly available to citizens and regulators. Activists, it is assumed, will not understand or will misuse process data, which are depicted as highly confidential and valuable to competitors. Yet citizens at both Lyondell and Midland were able to demand access to quantitative data. They relied on quantitative analyses to set targets, choose chemicals to be reduced, assess company proposals, follow employee activities, and communicate progress—just as industry experts had in previous prevention efforts. It transpired that the citizens could preserve the confidentiality of the data without needing to sign agreements with the firms.

The Channelview case is particularly interesting. As their first step in studying the Channelview petrochemical plant, CAPLE members studied the TRI numbers for the plant, the country, the state, and the nation as a whole for the period 1994–1998. They wanted to determine which emissions were most troublesome. It emerged that their zip code was rated first in the nation for butadiene releases in 1996. CAPLE developed several innovative methods to facilitate quantitative analysis of emissions and processes. Citizen members, who were ostensibly not technically expert, were able to create a matrix to help select the chemicals to target for reduction, based on the quantified volume of emissions and known health risks. The group invented two charts to measure the emission for each pound of product in site-specific facility conditions, with the goal of distributing these tools to activists elsewhere to avoid duplication of effort.

In turn, project meetings constituted a micro-institution where employees and citizens could pool their knowledge in the process of adapting scientific and technical knowledge to specific situations. Contrary to industry suppositions about the interest and capacity of citizens to demand and understand technical information, the citizen members of CAPLE asked for quantitative analyses and performed their own tests of the data provided by the firm. In studying leaks of styrene from storage tanks, a major source of pollution at other petrochemical plants, the activists not only visually inspected the tanks, but also reviewed, with employee assistance, the methods used by the company to estimate such "fugitive" releases for regulatory purposes. During the meetings, the company reported highly esoteric evaluations to CAPLE regarding potential process changes to a benzene drying column. Through these meetings, CAPLE set out to generate new information about emissions at the plant and therefore made it easier for both employees and citizens to visualize pollution. Similar developments occurred at Midland, with the regular monthly meetings serving as a key institution where participants could negotiate the mixing of standardized and site-specific knowledge.

The Lyondell project also stimulated novel ways of seeing what "the local" means in terms of the distribution of health risks. The citizen participants sought to assign a new moral dimension to the quantitative analyses that Lyondell employees used. Instead of reductionist risk assessments defined in terms of what each plant actually emits, the citizens argued that health risks should be evaluated for the region as a whole. The Midland activists had adapted plant-specific TRI numbers to justify their participation inside the plant. In contrast, the Lyondell activists invoked TRI numbers not just for the plant, but also for the county and the region, both of which were the highest in Texas. They contended that it made little sense in public health terms to demarcate between plants and the surrounding region. Even if Lyondell could not be proved to be a causal agent in environmental disease in Channelview, which was likely, the plant could be made politically liable for helping create the polluted regional atmosphere.

Finally, the activists at Midland and Channelview, along with their employee partners, used numbers to measure and communicate the results of the projects. Their reports used quantitative data to demonstrate the efficacy of their demands. At Channelview, CAPLE could point to statistics showing declines in releases of butadiene (by 41 percent) and benzene (40 percent). Lyondell reduced its volatile organic compounds by 15,600 pounds. Similarly, the Midland project accomplished a reduction of 43 percent in emissions of the 26 selected chemicals. A table of emission reductions, investment costs, and economic benefits was generated for each of the 17 measures undertaken. In other words, the citizens converted the standardized quantitative discourse previously used by the chemical industry into terms of site-specific preventive measures taken inside plants, thus enabling citizen groups to enforce prevention.

Choosing Priority Chemicals: Health vs. Economic Criteria

Since the 1980s, the chemical industry has focused on developing standardized technical and economic criteria to assess prevention opportunities across plants. A textbook published by the American Institute of Chemical Engineers lists the criteria that companies should use in screening the hundreds of candidate preventive measures that are typically found after a detailed pollution audit. It recommends that potential measures should be prioritized against a checklist, with productivity, economics, regulatory exposure, and waste stream size among the most important categories, and with environmental health among the least important (Mulholland and Dyer 1999). Such screening marginalizes the health and environmental outcomes that are most important to citizen groups. This is ironic because the norm of prevention presumes that prevention can both increase profitability *and* protect health and the environment.

At Midland and Channelview, citizens and employees engaged in protracted debates over whether chemical emissions posed significant health risks to the surrounding community. These controversies are still unresolved, even after years of project implementation. Lyondell refused to accept that its pollutants posed a health risk: it bracketed this issue as a dispute not to be resolved during the project. In the resulting report, the firm pointedly withheld acceptance of the citizen analysis of health risks. Likewise, Dow has steadfastly rejected decade-long claims that its production at Midland generates large quantities of dioxins. Nonetheless, company managers at both plants reluctantly decided to reduce the emissions that activists had specifically targeted for health reasons, to demonstrate that they were making progress and to improve relations with residents.

In both places, the citizens used scientific and technical resources extensively, and achieved much greater influence than they might otherwise have. This knowledge included toxicology, risk assessment, medical information, and public health records. Activists had access to toxicology books, Material Safety Data Sheets, and toxic chemicals databases created by EPA and the Occupational Health and Safety Administration. In contrast to INFORM's position that activists could never participate equally with employees, the citizens were able to demand participation because they combined standardized, technical expertise with local knowledge, making the companies more receptive.

Both projects involved efforts to enlist employees as allies in demanding prevention locally. Facilities are not monolithic entities, since employees and managers may have widely varying views of the value of prevention and including citizens in decision making. Midland and Channelview featured a great spread of interest, competence, and degree of engagement among employees. During both ventures, managers and process operators met regularly with the activists to discuss process level data, choose specific options to pursue based on health, technical, and economic considerations, and review progress towards emission reduction goals. Activists, especially at Midland, pressured managers to abandon their standardized technical and economic decision making, and to embrace more flexible, health-oriented criteria (Johnson 1999).

At Midland, the production managers lacked interest in the toxicity of emissions. Diane Hebert remembered: "I was ready to bite my tongue in half listening to some of the presentations. They really just didn't understand why we were concerned" (NRDC 1999). Mary Sinclair and Diane Hebert had a 20-year history of campaigning against Dow's dioxin emissions. They pointed out to company staff that their children all drank the same polluted water. The activists relied on the same quantitative data that Dow created, but drew on their own health concerns to stress reducing the chemicals that they were most worried about. Dow managers regarded the activists as much more credible and salient because they lived locally, rather than visiting from distant organizations headquartered in Washington.

At Channelview, CAPLE members emphasized their knowledge of community exposures to toxics. While they used TRI numbers, they also assembled evidence of unusually high cancer rates especially for lung cancer reported by local health authorities for Harris County. The Texas Department of Health did not provide an explanation, but the activists suspected that butadiene emissions from the Channelview plant might interact with other pollutants to increase cancer risks. They also invoked stories about neighbors who had contracted cancer to personalize the health effects associated with the plant. During meetings, citizens "voiced frustration that emergency flaring is used to get rid of off-spec product and described the health effects they attribute to flaring" (CAPLE 2000). The six citizen demands emphasized the health benefits of prevention. Lyondell executives, like Dow's, acknowledged that they were more impressed by such arguments if made by neighboring residents.

Conclusions

In the past two decades, a few citizen groups in the United States have questioned the chemical industry's global knowledge by demanding that their local knowledge be used in environmental decision making. The industry has historically sought to abstract and standardize knowledge for use in chemical manufacturing anywhere in the world. In contrast, some activists have insisted that their knowledge of the locally variable, contingent conditions under which pollution can be prevented is needed for not just effective, but credible and legitimate, industry action. In doing so, citizen groups have begun to weaken entrenched divisions between expert and lay actors. The nature and extent of expertise is coming to be negotiated, and re-negotiated, by citizens, companies, and regulators at each site over time (Iles 2000).

Instead of accepting the chemical industry's perceived distinction between "technical" and "popular" actors—suggesting concomitant epistemological differences in methods, knowledge, and goals—citizen groups are demonstrating that they, too, can make use of knowledge believed to be in the province of engineers, chemists, and business managers. Concurrently, citizens are reminding technical employees that they, too, are citizens and residents, whose health may be affected by plant emissions. As the Channelview and Midland cases show, activists can sometimes succeed in combining site-specific and standardized knowledge into a hybrid form that not only gains them entry to plants, but also wins them a greater role in corporate decision making.

The industry, however, continues to oppose attempts by citizen groups to participate inside plants and to reshape the meanings of expertise. This is illustrated by the few examples of successful citizen intervention in prevention, revealing the patchwork of global and local knowledge taking shape. In November 2002, it was reported that Dow Chemical had allowed its Midland project to lapse, following the death of the technical consultant Bill Bilkovich (Feder 2002). The NRDC approached 30 firms to adopt projects based on citizen-company collaboration, but all refused to try. The industry controls access to plants and technical information, and excludes the vast majority of local citizen groups from plants because they do not fit the template of experts who can work anywhere with standardized tools and knowledge. Even when citizens enter plants successfully, they face an ongoing struggle to win influence over company employees, and can be co-opted through being forced to depend on technical expertise.

However, the cases do suggest that local and global knowledge increasingly depend on each other for existence, and that finding ways to build and use their intersections can help advance pollution prevention, along with environmental protection more generally.

First, local actors such as citizen groups can strengthen considerably their ability to participate in corporate decision making by combining scientific and technical resources with their situated knowledge. For many activists, linking local knowledge with technical capability is a means of equalizing power relations. Having access to experts not only strengthens the claims of activists for entry into plants, but allows them to negotiate who is expert, what experts should speak on, and when they should be accompanied by conventionally trained experts. More important, local actors can be empowered through new ways to visualize pollution, to enforce prevention measures, and to incorporate health concerns into the economic and technical design of prevention.

Second, the creation or expansion of institutions that cross previously constructed boundaries can lead to greater pressures on industry to join citizens in combining local and global dimensions of knowledge. After working at more than 200 plants in his career, Bilkovich declared: "I can tell you that nothing drives pollution prevention like the exposure of people in the manufacturing business to environmental activists." (Johnson 1999) Citizen groups can help create new social, political, and cognitive institutions in the form of joint employee-activist teams, or of "citizen inspectors" standing in for regulators. Changes in practices and beliefs about what is "local" and "global" are likely to follow. Instead of accepting commercial confidentiality and plants being off limits, laypeople can move between communities and plants without jeopardizing the plant's operations and competitiveness.

Pollution prevention in the US chemical industry is a site where "the local" has been imagined afresh, in that people both inside and outside the plant have increasingly come to think of environmental issues, such as health effects or community rights, as crossing plant-community boundaries. The local is not confined to employees and managers inside a plant, nor are citizens merely trying to enter and inspect plants. Instead, plants and communities are places where people engage in redefining their societies and environments. Citizens and employees may translate global goals of environmental protection into their particular settings, making tools and ideas that they can use locally, while others, notably governments and companies, continue to insist on worldwide criteria of standardized expertise. Making local knowledge, then, is an ongoing struggle with global knowledge systems. But determined citizens can help change the production system in the long term.

References

Allen, David. 1992. "Prepared Discussion Response: Industrial Pollution Prevention." *Journal of Air and Waste Management Association* 42, no. 9: 1159.

Bowker, Geoffrey, and Susan Leigh Star. 1999. *Sorting Things Out: Classification and Its Consequences*. MIT Press.

CAPLE (Community Advisory Panel for Lyondell and Equistar). 2000. Source Reduction Report: Phase 1, November 14.

Chemical Manufacturers Association. 1991. Pollution Prevention: Code of Management Practices.

Feder, Barnaby. 2002. "Dialogue on Pollution Is Allowed to Trail Off." *New York Times*, November 23.

Fischer, Frank. 2000. *Citizens, Experts and the Environment*. Duke University Press.

Geertz, Clifford. 1983. *Local Knowledge: Further Essays in Interpretive Anthropology*. Basic Books.

Geiser, Kenneth. 2001. *Materials Matter: Towards a Sustainable Materials Policy*. MIT Press.

Gottlieb, Robert. 1995. *Reducing Toxics: A New Approach to Policy and Industrial Decision-Making*. Island.

Greer, Linda, and Christopher Van Loben Sels. 1997. "When Pollution Prevention Meets the Bottom Line." *Environmental Science and Technology*. 31: 9. 246A.

Iles, Alastair. 2000. Learning to Prevent Pollution: The Chemical Industry in Britain and the United States. Ph.D dissertation, Harvard University.

Irwin Alan, and Wynne, Brian. 1996. *Misunderstanding Science? The Public Reconstruction of Science and Technology*. Cambridge University Press.

Jasanoff, Sheila. 1990. *The Fifth Branch: Science Advisers as Policy-Makers*. Harvard University Press.

Jasanoff, Sheila, ed. 1994. *Learning from Disaster: Risk Management after Bhopal*. University of Pennsylvania Press.

Johnson, Jeff. 1998. "Opposites Attract at Dow Chemical." *Chemical & Engineering News*, August 17: 33.

Latour, Bruno. 1987. *Science in Action*. Harvard University Press.

Lewis, Sanford. 1993. The Good Neighbor Handbook: A Community-Based Strategy for Sustainable Industry. Good Neighbor Project, Waverley, Massachusetts.

Lewis, Sanford, and Diane Henkels. 2000. "Good Neighbor Agreements: A Tool for Environmental and Social Justice." *Social Justice*, vol. 23, no. 4.

Mazur, Allan. 1998. *A Hazardous Inquiry: The Rashomon Effect at Love Canal.* Harvard University Press.

Meikle, Jeffrey. 1995. *American Plastic: A Cultural History.* Rutgers University Press.

Mol, Arthur P. J. 2001. *Globalization and Environmental Reform: The Ecological Modernization of the Global Economy.* MIT Press.

Mulholland, Kenneth, and James Dyer. 1999. *Pollution Prevention: Methodology, Technologies and Practices.* American Institute of Chemical Engineers.

Natural Resources Defense Council. 1999. Preventing Industrial Pollution at Its Source: The Final Report of the Michigan Source Reduction Initiative. Meridian Institute.

O'Brien, Mary. 2000. *Making Better Environmental Decisions.* MIT Press.

Reisch, Marc. 1992. "Responsible Care." *Chemical & Engineering News*, October 5: 13.

Right-to-Know Network. February 1990. "Goodrich Facility." *Working Notes on Community Right-to-Know.* 3.

Right-to-Know Network. January/February 1993. "New Approaches Show Promise." *Working Notes on Community Right-to-Know.* 1.

Right-to-Know Network. November/December 1994. "Project Spurs Good Neighbor Involvement." In *Working Notes on Community Right-to-Know.*

Szasz, Andrew. 1994. *Eco-Populism: Toxic Waste and the Movement for Environmental Justice.* University of Minnesota Press.

Throdal, Maurice. 1984. Editorial. *Hazardous Materials and Hazardous Wastes* 1, no. 2: v.

Wise, Marian, and Lauren Kenworthy. 1990. *Preventing Industrial Toxic Hazards: A Guide for Communities.* INFORM.

US Environmental Protection Agency. 1997. *Second National Pollution Prevention Review.*

13

Ordering Environments: Regions in European International Environmental Cooperation

Stacy D. VanDeveer

In international environmental institutions, "science" often holds a privileged position. Scientific and technical information, particularly as associated with organized environmental assessment processes, has become increasingly institutionalized in international environmental politics (GEA 1997). Accordingly, many international relations scholars and practitioners claim that international environmental cooperation generally remains difficult to coordinate and formalize in the absence of accepted scientific and technical consensus regarding problem definition and some appropriate means to address it. International relations scholarship treats scientific and technical advice as a kind of "input" to international policy-making processes—as a vehicle for bringing state actors to consensus positions or as an important influence on agenda setting processes, for example. Theories of international relations tend to ignore social processes involved in the production of the scientific and technical knowledge, assuming that knowledge production occurs outside the processes of international conflict and cooperation that are placed at the center of analysis.

Whereas traditional IR theory tends to treat the production of scientific knowledge and artifacts as separate from politics, another school of thought sees the former as contingent on social institutions—from small groups of scientific and technical specialists to larger professional communities of integrated assessment practitioners, state environmental policy makers, and international diplomats (see, e.g. Miller and Edwards 2001). This literature reveals a close intertwining of environmental science and environmental politics where knowledge and policy are "coproduced" (Jasanoff and Wynne 1998).

Following Jasanoff (forthcoming), I use the concept of coproduction in this chapter to refer to the mutual construction and legitimation of the natural and social worlds. Ideas about the natural world (and/or the human environment) and "the organization and practices of institutions that enable people to act in that world" can be said to be co-produced (Miller 2001, p. 285). Coproduction calls attention to the mutual construction and reinforcement of scientific and technical ideas and the organization of international scientific and technical assessment processes and collaborative research programs.

This chapter treats "regionality" as a particular form of locality and examines the roles of scientific assessment and policy maker practices in the construction of regions. If actors and institutions are influenced by their own discourses (and their constituent artifacts) (Hajer 1995), then the pervasive character of "regionalizing" discourses within many international environmental protection regimes is worthy of detailed investigation. This chapter argues that two regional environmental protection regimes[1]—those associated with the Baltic Sea and Long Range Transboundary Air Pollution in Europe—construct and stabilize three types of "order" through the interaction of scientific and technical assessment processes, environmental activists and state environmental policy makers.

First, the interaction of assessment participants and policy makers provides order and discipline for complex, highly variable and often chaotic information about the natural world. Within international environmental cooperation regimes, scientific and technical experts organize knowledge for use in policy making and for use in attempts of advance their collective research agendas. They have developed institutions and practices for regional standardization and calibration of data from environmental monitoring systems across Europe and from a host of scientific and technical disciplines. In addition, the regimes provide an organizational (bureaucratic) structure to administer the collection and analysis of relevant information.

Second, by ordering information about the natural world for policy maker and public consumption, participants within these assessment processes construct and stabilize particular notions of the "region." Of particular interest are maps and other visual images used by regime participants to illustrate regional environmental functions, connections, problems, and solutions.

Third, the interaction of scientific, technical, and policy-making actors produces a set of explicit, and collectively sanctioned, policy "options" and/or "recommendations." In other words, while ordering information about the natural world and helping to stabilize collective notions of transnational regions, science/policy interaction helps to order policy making by narrowing policy options and (as described below) offering mutually legitimized tools to compare these options.

Imagining Regions

Interest in regions has a long tradition among social scientists (see e.g. Mumford 1938). Questions about how to define regions in theory and in practice—and about what makes some regions salient in political, cultural and/or economic terms—have plagued the study of regions. What then are regions? How should we define regions? Scholars in political science, IR and economics have relied primarily on a combination of geography, administrative designations and economic factors such as trade patterns, currency use, and/or capital or labor flows to define regions. In general, they have ignored scholarship from the humanities and more "interpretive" social sciences. As a result, the definition of "regions" and "regionalism" remain problematic for many social scientists (Feld and Jordan 1994; Deutsch 1969), because important changes in collective perceptions and identity are largely ignored.

Early analysts of regionalism, such as Lewis Mumford (1938) did pay attention to social and cultural factors in their discussions of the creation of regions. Recently, a few scholars of the "new regionalism," such James Mittelman (2000), have (re)turned to such influences. Mittelman's work moves beyond the primacy of economic factors found in much of the recent regionalization (and globalization) literature—much of which simply treats regionalism as a step toward further neoliberal globalization. Mittelman's new regionalism includes interactions among "(1) ideas and their ties to institutions, (2) systems of production, (3) labor supply, and (4) sociocultural institutions, all undergirded by power relations" (pp. 111–112). Mittelman argues that power relations, particularly among nation states, and social institutions beyond those associated with economic exchange are ignored in much contemporary scholarship on regions.

Mittelman's rejection of the narrowly economic notions of regionness and his attention to social institutions hearkens back to Mumford's (1938) work. Mumford saw human activity and the natural environment as deeply interconnected. Because environments are not uniform across regions and social institutions are embedded within environments, social institutions also vary across regions. For Mumford, economic factors do not construct regions because economic factors are driven by social and environmental factors—not vice-versa. Natural landscape is simultaneously an economic and cultural resource: "As the cultural heritage increases, a larger part of the environment becomes useful and meaningful: *the natural conditions of a region, so far from being nullified by the increases in culture and technical skill, are actually magnified.*" (Mumford 1938, p. 313). In other words: For Mumford, natural conditions are at the root of regional ecological and social differentiation.

Benedict Anderson's (1991) understanding of nations as "imagined political communities" offers one way to pull together various approaches to the study of regions. If one understands regions as imagined transnational communities, then one might begin to ask how and why people come to identify with a particular regional construction. One advantage of Anderson's view is his focus on the mechanisms of communicating "imagined" connections (see also Jasanoff 2001). Anderson (1991, pp. 163–185) originally viewed print capitalism as most significant in the production of national identity. In his later writing, he posited "three institutions of power" which changed the nature of colonial state power and collective identity in the colonial world: census, map and museum. As we will see, similar institutions and processes have striking parallels within regional environmental protection regimes.

Attention to the role of political imagination and to mechanisms for constructing and communicating imagined connections between people offers a framework for understanding the role of scientific and technical experts in regional environmental regimes. Regional solidarity, politics and, perhaps, identities are being imagined through international regime activities around the Baltic Sea and European air pollution. In Mary Douglas's (1986) terms, regional "cognitive communities" are being constructed around issues related to environmental protection.

Scientific and technical experts are particularly important interpreters of "regionness," because they frame their research and understandings of the natural world in regional terms. They study and define regional environmental processes and represent them in data sets, modeling exercises and images. While Anderson's treatment of nationalism pays little attention to science, regime participants with scientific and technical training play a large role in the creation of regional identity because they are a major source of knowledge about "regional level" connections between people and nations. Their work, and representations of it, help people to think (and discuss policy options) in new "regional" terms. It simultaneously frames collective understandings of shared environments, environmental problems and potential multilateral policies to address these "shared problems."

Regionally framed scientific and technical research and assessment helps to create and reinforce cognitive foundations for "regional" policy-making institutions. Like modern states (Ezrahi 1990; Jasanoff 1990), the environmental protection regimes for the Baltic Sea and European transboundary air pollution have relied on scientific and technical knowledge to justify their policy-making and administrative authority. Since the late 1970s, both regimes have expanded their organizational structure to support the production and use of scientific and technical knowledge to support the regimes' substantive scope and legal authority. Civil society actors such as environmental NGOs also play a part in stabilizing regional identity—in part by incorporating information produced by "regional" scientific bodies into their policy advocacy and public awareness campaigns. In this way, knowledge making within international environmental regimes helps to create new, in this case "regional," notions of community and communal space.

Air Pollution Politics: From Détente to Brussels

The issues of transborder air pollution and acidification emerged on political and scientific research agendas in the late 1960s.[2] Initially, participating researchers and state officials framed their debates in terms of pollutants traveling across national borders—particularly the borders of those states seen to be "exporting" pollutants to "downwind" states that were often characterized as victimized by pollution. Gradually, a more transnational, pan-European notion of regionality came to dominate policy making around long range transboundary air pollution. As outlined below, the concept of "critical loads" and the "RAINS model," which simulates pollution transport, deposition and damages on a continental scale, played critical roles. The model produced images of a pan-European regionality. States and peoples across the European continent were seen to share air masses, pollutants and existing and potential pollution damages—in short, a shared "European environment."

In the view of the LRTAP Secretariat: "The [LRTAP] Convention was the first international legally binding instrument to deal with problems of air pollution on a broad *regional* basis" (emphasis added). The LRTAP Convention has spawned a large and growing body of literature—most of it drawing attention to the roles of scientific and technical expertise in negotiations, in policy making, and in assessment organizations (Connolly 1999; Darst 2001; Levy 1993; Selin 2000; Tuinstra, Hordijk, and Amman 1999; Wetstone and Rosencranz 1983; Wettestad 2002). While much of this literature analyzes the influence of scientific advice and knowledge on international policy making, none of it examines the role played by participating scientific and technical experts in altering collective notions about Europe as an environmentally and politically salient regional entity.

Acidification science and politics, and formal assessment efforts prior to the establishment of LRTAP, were driven by Scandinavian nationals concerned that their countries' environments were victims of transboundary pollution. These initial concerns prompted international assessment efforts and participation patterns that framed European transboundary air pollution discourse in terms of acidification. The most active "early movers" around transboundary air pollution and acidification were Swedish scientists and public officials (Cowling 1982, Bäckstrand and Selin 2000). Scientists, including Svante Oden, argued that links existed between increasing levels of pollution in precipitation and environmental damages observed by others in fields such as limnology, atmospheric chemistry, forestry and agriculture (Oden 1967 1968; Cowling 1982; McCormick 1997). Once preliminary scientific studies suggested that acidifying substances could (and did) travel long distances, "downwind states" introduced acid rain issues to the international agenda, calling for multilateral research, data gathering, analysis, and policy making.

Early assessment efforts included the OECD-sponsored Air Management Research Group (AMRG) in the late 1960s, the preparatory case studies for the 1972 United National Conference on the Human Environment (UNCHE) in Stockholm, and two simultaneous efforts organized under the OECD and the Norwegian Interdisciplinary Research Programme (the "SNSF Project") (VanDeveer, forthcoming (a)). These multinational research and assessment efforts raised awareness among West European policy makers and publics and helped delegitimize denials of the occurrence of transboundary pollution transport. For example, a preliminary OECD report stated: "One conclusion which is certain is that pollution travels between countries to a greater or lesser extent" (Reed 1976). Wetstone and Rosencranz noted that "it was OECD's groundbreaking research and monitoring work that made many national and international policy makers aware, for the first time, of the extent and importance of transboundary air pollution in Europe" (OECD 1983, p. 135).

These arenas of thickly connected scientific and political cooperation facilitated the creation of expert networks connecting scientific researchers and state air pollution officials and helped to stabilize discourses for acid rain and air pollution control (OECD 1968, 1977). Surveys were conducted among air policy officials; international working groups, lead countries and scientific and technical research agendas were established; and a multilingual glossary of air pollution terminology was prepared (OECD 1968, p. 6). The glossary, apparently the first of its kind, began to standardize terminology across borders and languages in order to facilitate data communication and information exchange. As one example, the group appears to have coined and brought to prominence the term "long-range transboundary air pollution" or LRTAP. Linguistic standardization, in turn, was necessary for methodological standardization.

Ten years of scientific research and debate effectively reframed air pollution as a transboundary, rather than a primarily "local" or "national" concern. For example, OECD-sponsored monitoring, data gathering and assessment activities resulted in a publication (OECD 1977) that "confirmed the idea that pollutants are transported long distances and showed that the air quality in each European country is measurably effected from all other European countries" (Cowling 1982, p. 116A; OECD 1977).[3] Scandinavian scientists and policy makers organized international conferences and assessment activities that expanded the network of researchers and broadened scientific consensus regarding acidification (Schneider 1986, 1992). These shifts in collective understanding had similar, far-reaching implications for both scientific research about the natural environment and environmental policy making. If pollution is transboundary, with effects on lakes, soil composition and forests, then policy makers and scientific research both had to cooperate across borders to practice their crafts.

Initially, in accordance with traditional IR framings, the international politics of acid rain was framed in terms of pollution among a group of nations. Scientific researchers and state officials both framed the acid rain issues in these "*inter*-national" terms. Svante Oden, for example, spoke of acid rain as a "chemical war" among "the nations of Europe." Throughout the 1970s, acidification research, like the politics around the issue, focused most on transboundary pollution thought to be traveling from the United Kingdom and parts of continental Europe toward Finland, Norway, and Sweden. The notion that transboundary air pollution was a pan-European challenge developed slowly. Furthermore, researchers and officials Central and Eastern European nations were largely (often entirely) absent from the early forum for international cooperation around air pollution (VanDeveer, forthcoming (a)).

States pushing for an international treaty designed to address transborder air pollution problems selected the United Nations Economic Commission for Europe (UNECE) as the host of LRTAP negotiations, largely because it was the only international organization with both environmental and economic interests that included national members from both East and West. East-West membership was considered essential for air pollution policy making because the ongoing international acidification research and assessment activities concluded that parts of Central and Eastern Europe were significant exporters of pollution. Formally, the decision to negotiate the LRTAP Convention under UNECE auspices largely defined the initial notion of the "region" under discussion, because UNECE's membership included the countries of Europe (including the Soviet Union) plus Canada and the United States. In practice, however, the initial 10–15 years of LRTAP Convention activities focused almost exclusively on acidification concerns in the Northern half of the Europe—largely because scientific research framed these as the critical areas vis-à-vis acidification. Exactly what constituted the LRTAP region thus remained undefined for over a decade, as differences persisted between formal UNECE membership and the geographic focus of acidification science and politics.

Since the LRTAP Convention's entry into force in 1983, state parties have negotiated eight protocols covering such issues as funding for the "EMEP" monitoring and data calibration programs and emissions cuts for sulfur, nitrogen, volatile organic compounds (VOCs), heavy metals, and persistent organic pollutants (POPs). A large organizational structure has grown up around LRTAP designed to facilitate information sharing and joint analysis and provide state representatives with "state of the art" consensual knowledge about the environment and various tools to assess environmental conditions. (See figure 1.) Areas of scientific and technological inquiry are delineated across a combination of disciplinary (and some explicitly interdisciplinary) lines and areas of functional policy interest. These are hierarchically organized so that scientific and technical information flows "up" to the official state representatives at the top of the structure. Mandates and questions from policy makers are intended to flow downward to researchers. In practice, there is considerable interaction along both horizontal and vertical dimensions.

The LRTAP committee structure orders complex information about the natural world in ways that are intended to provide useful, relevant information to state officials. Such structures impose order on scientific and technical advice by establishing boundaries between "policy making" and "scientific" activities such as assessment (Jasanoff 1990) and by organizing scientific and technical advice and assessment into the "boxes" in figure 1. The LRTAP structure includes groups associated with effects of air pollution, abatement techniques, EMEP's data gathering and calibration, and "political" international negotiations and policy making (which take place in the Working Group on Strategies). (See figure 1.) This structure helps to maintain boundaries between explicit negotiations over policy between state officials in the Working Group on Strategies, and the scientific and technical knowledge production that takes place in other "boxes" within the LRTAP structure. The technical bodies rely on traditional processes of scientific inquiry, including the application of various professional criteria to determine participants and the use of peer review. State officials retain a degree of control over what issues and questions are assessed in the science and technology bodies. In practice, however, the boundaries between policy makers (i.e. state officials negotiating about policy) and assessment participants tend to be quite fluid and porous (Farrell, VanDeveer, and Jäger 2000).

During the 1990s, LRTAP activities shifted away from the near exclusive focus on acidification issues seen in the 1980s. Pushed again by officials from Northern European countries, state representatives negotiated LRTAP protocols on emissions of heavy metals and POPs (both signed in 1998) and developed a "multi-effects and multi-pollution" protocol on acidification, eutrophication, and ground-level ozone (signed in 1999). Scientific researchers and assessment groups argued that, by simultaneously

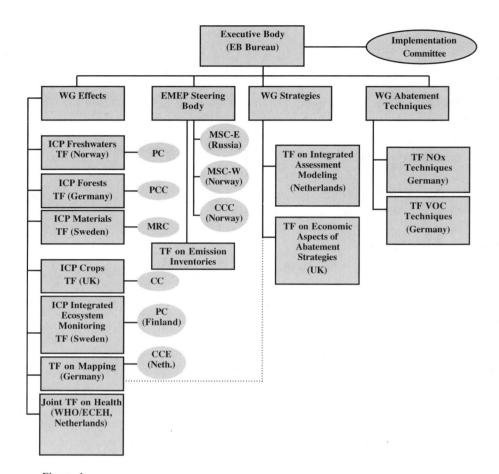

Figure 1
Organizational structure of LRTAP. ICP: International Cooperative Program. PC: Program Center. PCC: Program Coordination Center. MRC: Main Research Center. CCE: Coordination Center for Effects. MSC-E: Meteorological Synthesizing Center East. MSC-W: Meteorological Synthesizing Center West. CCC: Chemical Coordinating Center. WHO: World Health Organization. Unless otherwise indicated, centers are located in ICP host country. Source: UNECE web site.

addressing eutrophication, acidification, and ground-level ozone pollution at the regional (pan-European) level, policy makers could take advantage of potential synergies associated with tackling multiple related environmental policy objectives in a coordinated manner.

Beginning in the late 1980s, participants in LRTAP assessment bodies became increasingly interested in the concept of "critical loads" and its potential applications in international environmental policy making. The concept of critical loads denotes attempts to establish a threshold—or critical level—below which no ecologically harmful effects of pollution occur. It suggests that pollution regulation should be guided by these levels, limiting pollution deposition or concentrations below the critical level. Advocates of the critical loads approach posit it as an effects-based, cost-optimized strategy, which permits emission reductions to be divided among countries on a regional basis in an attempt to minimize the costs for the region as a whole. The 1988 Nitrogen Protocol was the first LRTAP agreement that recognized the validity of the critical loads concept. It was used as a basis for actual reduction schemes in the 1994 Second Sulphur Protocol, and it was used again in the development and negotiation of the 1999 multi-pollutant, multi-effects protocol.

Critical loads for pollutants are determined by assessing ongoing environmental research, applying it on a continental scale to data gathered from the EMEP regional monitoring system, and incorporating this information in the Regional Air Pollution Information and Simulation (RAINS) model developed at the International Institute for Applied Systems Analysis (IIASA), in Austria. The RAINS model generates maps of pollution emissions, transport patterns and deposition across Europe. It generates maps of geographic areas where pollution levels exceed and/or fall below critical levels. The related data sets, models, maps illustrate the "regionality" of air masses in Europe. The RAINS generated maps graphically illustrate the argument that air pollution can no longer be understood as a geographically "local" or "national" phenomenon. Rather, European states and public are seen to share the continent's air masses and pollutants. This suggests that air pollution policy can no longer be left exclusively to local or national level authorities. Rather, it is a regional pan-European phenomenon that must be addressed through regional or continental policy making.

The RAINS model, like all modeling exercises, simplifies empirical reality by reducing the number of causal variables and their interactions

(Jasanoff and Wynne 1998). The model, developed and redeveloped at IIASA, has grown in term of the scope of variables and environmental issues it addresses and its technical complexity over time. The early RAINS model focused on acidification processes while later versions attempt to capture multiple pollutant/multiple effects dynamics. In recent years, the larger and more complex model has been used in assessment and policy-making processes within the European Union (EU) and the European Environment Agency (see, e.g., EEA 1999).

The use of the critical loads approach and the RAINS model helps to con-struct and maintain the "region"—meaning the European continent—as the appropriate scale at which to frame particular air pollution problems and policy solutions. RAINS and its maps are aggregated representations of millions of pollutant sources and receptors across the European conti-nent. These maps illustrate continental patterns of pollutant emissions, deposition and transport, as well as soil pH and critical loads exceedence. (See Alcamo et al. 1990.) The increasing scope and complexity of the model also illustrate the seemingly ever-increasing list of ecological connections across the whole of Europe—producing dense environmental networks from the Atlantic to the Ural Mountains and from Scandinavia to the Mediterranean Sea.

The critical loads approach underlying the RAINS model also frames particular environmental issues as management problems best addressed via scientific and technical solutions (Bäckstrand 2001). For example, the seminal text on the RAINS model, *The RAINS Model of Acidification: Science and Strategies for Europe* (Alcamo et al. 1990), is full of maps illus-trating emissions reductions and increased environmental protection that would be gained if policy makers chose the "best available technology option." The book's very title suggests that the RAINS model is intended to produce policy relevant findings, and its stated "four main goals" are, in a sense, explicitly co-productionist: "(1) To provide scientific docu-mentation for the RAINS model. . . . (2) To record [their] methodology. . . . (3) To report on scientific findings. . . . (4) To report on policy findings using the model. . . ." Options for international policy makers are com-pared, assessed and (sometimes) justified via the RAINS model, even as the book simultaneously legitimizes the model and its use by subjecting the work to greater scrutiny and peer review.

The RAINS model and the maps produced in association with it exemplify Latour's (1987, 1990) concept of "immutable mobiles," but these historical artifacts, in turn, are embedded in standardized actor perceptions and practices. In this way, the RAINS representations, stabilize networks of individuals and organizations around regional (pan-European) data gathering, analysis and interpretive practices within a discourse of long-range transboundary air pollution. Of course, this work demands human agents. IIASA staff explicitly worked to promulgate the RAINS model and encouraged its use by national and international scientists and policy makers. IIASA staff members traveled widely in Europe—East and West—demonstrating the model's utility and arguing its scientific, technical and environmental policy-making benefits.[4] They also organized demonstrations for state officials at LRTAP negotiating meetings and Geneva and, later, for EU officials in Brussels. Copies of the model were distributed and made available upon request—free of charge—in order to encourage its use. Later, in the 1990s, much of the model and its functions were made available for use via the Internet. IIASA staff, their activities and the network of researchers and modelers that has grown up around them are instruments of the coproduction of knowledge in a hybridized science/policy sphere.

As the IIASA staffers involved with the RAINS model adopted, adapted and promulgated the critical loads concept and developed the RAINS model and its associated maps they built credibility and legitimacy within various scientific, technical, and policy-making communities. They submitted aspects of the RAINS modeling work to peer-reviewed publications and they held conferences and workshops at which "outside" experts were shown the model and invited to critique it. At some of these workshops, RAINS was compared to other models. The model's capabilities were demonstrated in national capitals and in Geneva (at LRTAP meetings) and Brussels (for EU officials) to show policy makers that it could adapt to their requests, producing useful and timely information. As such, new "institutionalized ways of knowing" (see Jasanoff, forthcoming) and new ways of representing knowledge were coproduced within LRTAP.

Since the mid 1990s developments in European air pollution politics have paralleled those in European politics generally. The "center" of the continent's air pollution politics has been moving away from the Geneva-based

LRTAP toward Brussels and the European Union (Selin and VanDeveer 1999; Wettestad 2002). LRTAP's knowledge producing bodies are now increasingly interwoven with EU policy-making processes, producing—below the images of regional ecological connectedness—new asymmetries of material resources and political power. With the shift in air pollution policy making toward the EU has come a parallel shift in the focus of scientific and technical research and advice. Researchers and modelers at IIASA, whose RAINS model has been used by LRTAP negotiators for years, now design their models in response to feedback from staff at the EU Commission in Brussels. Air pollution knowledge is being reframed consistent with European integration and EU policy.

Certainly LRTAP's assessment and regional policy-making activities are not the only producers of regional, pan-European environmental assessments, images and policies. The "project" of building an increasingly integrated Europe though EU institutions produces regional images in abundance. Until the 1990s, however, such EU activities focused almost exclusively on EU member states. LRTAP's activities spanned the Cold War's East-West divide, producing data sets and images at a continental scale. As the EU's environmental policy authority grew in the 1990s and the number of EU member states and applicants increased, EU policy makers and environmental protection advocates have taken a more pan-European outlook. In contemporary European policy making, the prevailing notion of the relevant region for air pollution policy is the whole of continental Europe. In fact, LRTAP's (and IIASA's) pan-European critical loads approach and RAINS modeling exercises have become the basis for EU transboundary air pollution policies (Selin and VanDeveer 1999; Wettestad 2002).

In Central and Eastern Europe (CEE) countries—not members of the EU until 2004—all of this means that policy making remains reactive to policies in Western Europe. This reactive position is consistent with most CEE participation in LRTAP policy making and scientific and technical research and assessment since the inception of the regime (VanDeveer, forthcoming (b)). As figure 1 illustrates, for example, almost all of LRTAPs various centers of expertise and data calibration are located in Western Europe. Among CEE scientific and technical advisors, the research agenda continues to be driven by international forces. Thus the coproduction of regions remains embedded in European power dynamics.

Saving the Baltic Sea: From Inter-State Technical Cooperation to Baltic Europe

Prevailing ideas about Baltic regionality have changed over 25-plus years of international policy making designed to protect the Baltic Sea from pollution damages. Like LRTAP, the initial 1970s notion of the Baltic region was based largely on a group of nation-states with coastline on the Baltic Sea—the seven Baltic Sea littoral states (Denmark, Finland, East Germany, West Germany, Poland, Sweden, and the USSR). Over time, environmental and technical assessment and "regional" images produced and used within these processes played important roles in altering the collective definition of the Baltic region toward one based on the total watershed or "catchment area" of the Baltic Sea. This development, together with the ongoing processes of EU-centered European integration resulted in a conception based more on ecological/hydrological notions of a Baltic region within the larger European environment.

Participants in the Baltic Sea environmental protection regime have engaged in regional standardization of environmental monitoring, data gathering, assessment and state regulation since its inception in the 1970s. Scientific study of the Baltic Sea, much of it organized by international scientific groups, began in the early twentieth century (Dybern 1980). Regional international cooperation focused on environmental problems identified by scientific researchers and environmental activists, including increasing toxins and nutrients, declining oxygen levels and threats to biodiversity (see, e.g., Zmudzinski 1989).

Twice, representatives of the Baltic Sea littoral states gathered in Helsinki to sign relatively comprehensive environmental protection treaties: first in 1974 and again in 1992. The 1974 Helsinki Convention is often cited as the first "regional" international agreement limiting marine pollution from both land and sea-based sources, whether air or water borne. It was negotiated among the (then) seven Baltic littoral states as a response to growing concern about the state of the Baltic Sea environment following the 1972 Stockholm convention. The agreement was possible only with the easing of Cold War tensions and the resolution of the diplomatic impasse produced by many states' refusal to recognize two German states (Rytovuori 1980). The 1974 Convention established the Helsinki Commission (HELCOM) as the regime's secretariat and central organization. It also excluded coastal waters from much of its coverage, treating these areas not as shared (eco-logically, legally, or otherwise), but as national territory. The Baltic Sea envi-ronmental protection regime operated across the ideological and strategic divide between East and West, becoming a model for other regional envi-ronmental protection regimes and conventions.

Scientific and technological discourses and "experts" dominated partic-ipation and activities during regime formulation and in the structure and operation of HELCOM for most of its 20-plus years of operation (Haas 1993; Hjorth 1992, 1996; VanDeveer 1997). In 1992, the representatives from the (by then) nine Baltic littoral states agreed on a new Convention, greatly revising, expanding and strengthening the 1974 version. The 1990s witnessed dramatic changes in both the character of Baltic regional envi-ronmental protection and the over-arching political contexts around the Baltic Sea. With the collapse of Soviet state socialism in Poland and Germany in 1989 and the break-up of the Soviet Union in 1991–92, regional inter-state and transnational cooperation changed dramatically.

Like the LRTAP structure, HELCOM is organized partially to maintain boundaries between scientific assessment and policy making. For example, HELCOM issues non-binding environmental policy "Recommendations" with unanimous support of the state parties. State representatives with rel-evant scientific, technical and legal expertise work out recommendations in committee. Thus, HELCOM "recommends" common (regional) envi-ronmental policy standards and procedures to participant states. These HELCOM recommendations, over 200 of them, are based on the work of the scientific and technical advisory bodies described below and on state practice and regulatory experience. They recommend environmental policy content and practice to member states of the regime. The full Commission meets annually to administer the Convention and pass recommendations. Since decisions are taken by consensus at all stages, disagreements from working groups and committees do not progress to the Commission. The fact that recommendations to the full Commission must pass out of the per-manent committees of experts helps to maintain the appearance of a sepa-ration of scientific and political spheres, by relegating disagreements to further work between these "scientific experts" instead of passing them along to the "more political" Commission. This adds legitimacy to deci-sions because, ostensibly, the direct representatives of states at the level of the Commission do not tinker with scientific recommendations during political meetings. In reality, of course, plenty of "politics" goes on within the scientific and technological working groups.

Participants in HELCOM's technical assessment bodies generally have frequent formal and informal links to international and domestic policy makers (they are sometimes the very same individuals, in fact) (Farrell, VanDeveer, and Jäger 2000). HELCOM helped to build a broad network of leading scientific and technical institutions around the region, studying many issues and linking them to state bureaucracies and to some industry researchers. The organization helps to coordinate regional cooperation and collaboration among scientific and technical experts, NGOs, multilateral development banks, domestic policy makers and international assistance programs (Gutner and VanDeveer 2001). It also organizes periodic high-profile regional Ministerial Conferences that attract media and political attention, assess progress toward environmental goals, and address continuing and/or new environmental challenges. HELCOM assessments include state and non-state experts from all of the Baltic littoral states and additional states within the Baltic watershed. Individuals from wealthier states constitute a majority of participants, but post-communist states and expert communities rarely lack representation.

As HELCOM's organizational structure and activities expanded, it became the center of both regional "scientific" and "policy-making" activities and expectations concerning environmental protection of the Baltic Sea (VanDeveer 1997). For most of its history, HELCOM had three permanent committees as well as numerous working groups of experts. Subsidiary groups, usually committees, formulate recommendations and proposals for adoption by the full Commission. In the 1990s, a standing Program Implementation Task Force (PITF) was also created to encourage and assess HELCOM implementation in the region's states. Figure 2 presents the recently expanded organizational structure. Information is collected, assessed, and interpreted within various functional areas.

HELCOM activities produce periodic comprehensive pollution load compilations, large bibliographies of scientific and technical research focused on the Baltic Sea, guidelines for data gathering, monitoring and analysis in the region, and periodic assessments of the state of the Baltic environment. Within HELCOM activities, scientific and technical information and practices have become increasingly standardized around the region. HELCOM-centered cooperation has promulgated principles and

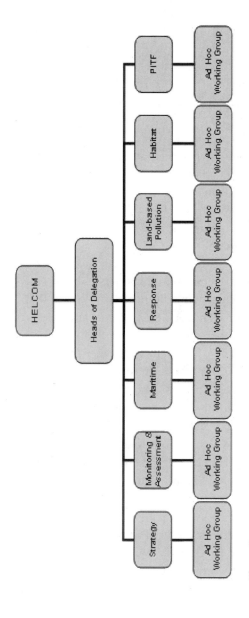

Figure 2
Organizational structure of HELCOM.

norms for state environmental policy making around the region, including emissions standards, best available technology standards, the precautionary principle, and the polluter pays principle (VanDeveer 1997). HELCOM recommendations attempt to regionally standardize state regulations for a long list of industrial processes and state permitting and licensing systems.

HELCOM assessment participants and secretariat staff (these two categories generally overlap) produce copious images designed to represent and communicate environmental knowledge about the "Baltic region." The preferred "regional" maps are those that show the total watershed of the Baltic Sea ecosystem (and often the international river watersheds). In these maps, the watershed area is shaded and boldly delineated. State boundaries, when shown at all, are delineated in softer tones. The sections of the states outside the watershed simple fade away into nothingness at the edge of the maps. Such images position the Baltic Sea and its watershed as the central feature of the region being defined. The sea and watershed, in these images, connect states and societies around the Baltic Sea.

The use of "regional" watershed maps has helped to redefine what actually constitutes the Baltic region. While only the Baltic Sea littoral states (and the EU) are parties to the 1974 and 1992 anti-pollution treaties, the watershed area also includes portions of the territory of non-littoral states (Belarus, Czech Republic, Norway, Ukraine). HELCOM encourages officials (and various types of experts) from these states to become involved in its activities—for example, by facilitating international funding for environmental assessments and investments within the Baltic watershed.

Variants of the Baltic regional map layer additional information over the watershed map to illustrate the shared and interconnected nature of particular environmental problems and to order scientific research and policy making. For example, many of HELCOM's programmatic activities in the 1990s revolved around identifying, assessing and (partially) addressing the worst environmental "hotspots" around the Baltic Sea. Each Baltic littoral state identified a number of its worst environmental "spots" around the sea. Officials from the non-littoral states also lying within the Baltic Sea watershed also did so. Initially, no common criteria were used among the states for the identification of these areas and problems. HELCOM representatives wanted identified spots in all littoral states (and from the non-littoral former communist states), to illustrate that all countries contributed to Baltic Sea environmental degradation. This shared responsibility of littoral states was immediately represented by a widely distributed regional map with all hotspots labeled. The hotspot map was used by HELCOM staff to illustrate that these many local pollution sources necessitated a regional policy response—in the form of HELCOM's Program Implementation Task Force. "De-listed" hotspots—those in which major pollution sources have been addressed—are denoted on subsequent iterations of the map and used to illustrate the environmental achievements of regional cooperation.

Though technical expert discourses have traditionally dominated the Baltic marine environmental protection regime, HELCOM has become increasingly interested in promoting "sites of common heritage" around the region. These "museums" of regionally shared social and ecological history are reminiscent of Anderson's interest in museums as a central institution in the creation of national identity. Images and discourses of Baltic regional connectedness and integration are not monopolized by HELCOM, of course.

Other regionally framed programs espouse "ecological" understandings of the interconnectedness and interdependency of the regions' peoples and environments. For example, on-going transnational education programs and curricula have been developed which (re)read the histories of the region's peoples, highlighting "regional history." Academics from Swedish and Finnish Universities have compiled a multi-session course, with materials in English, entitled, "The Baltic University: Peoples of the Baltic." This cooperative project, coordinated by Uppsala University in Sweden, involves over 100 universities in all of the countries within the Baltic basin. HELCOM participants are involved with the programs, as they are with other associated coalitions of Baltic environmental non-governmental organizations, a Baltic regional Agenda 21 process, and various public and scholarly discussions around notions of "Baltic Europe" (Serafin and Zaleski 1997; Gutner and VanDeveer 2001). All of these international programs take up and redeploy the technical knowledge—and the images that represent it— produced by HELCOM bodies.

Contemporary definitions of the Baltic region used within HELCOM increasingly combine the watershed area with themes associated with European integration. By the end of the 1990s, a HELCOM-coordinated multi-billion-dollar joint implementation effort was underway and EU influence on policy had grown dramatically. Sweden and Finland, having joined the EU in 1995, had already "harmonized" much of their environmental legislation and regulation. Furthermore, Estonia, Latvia, Lithuania, and Poland are all applicants to the EU. As such, they too are attempting to harmonize their policy with that of the EU. HELCOM recommendations and many of its monitoring, data gathering and assessment processes are being "harmonized" with those of European Union policies and programs.[5] As a result, the reinterpretations of the region discussed in this section reposition the nations within the region both in terms of their "Balticness"—their shared Baltic environment and history—and in terms of their "Europeanness" within the context of a more integrated and united Europe.

Ordering Knowledge, Coproducing Regions

The environmental regimes discussed here, LRTAP and the Baltic Sea, illustrate the deeply interrelated dynamics between policy making and scientific and technical knowledge—realms commonly treated as conceptually and empirically distinct in much international relations scholarship. Within both regimes, formalized scientific and technical assessment processes impose order and discipline on complex information about the natural world, rendering it useful and relevant for policy making. Scientific and technical expertise are not only marshaled in service of environmental policy making; they are central forces in defining the nature of particular transnational environmental "problems" and their causes and potential solutions. In each regime, scientific and technically grounded images shape policy maker and societal notions of the "region" under discussion. Maps and other visual images aggregate a vast amount of data from research, which are used by regime participants to illustrate regional environmental functions, connections, problems, and solutions.

In these complex hybrid science/policy domains, there remain tremendous social pressures to maintain or reassert the "purity" of both science and policy (Latour 1993; Jasanoff 1990). These pressures are articulated through discursive practices, "immutable mobiles," and the negotiated boundaries around the bureaucratic structure of scientific and technical assessment and policy making within each regime. Within international environmental cooperation regimes, scientific and technical experts organize knowledge for use in policy making and for use in attempts of advance their collective understanding of nature (their research agendas). As such, the chapter shows that the construction of regionality taking place in international environmental regimes cannot be properly understood or interrogated by scholarly approaches to the study of "regionalism" based primarily on economic patterns or formal membership in international organizations.

One change in HELCOM and LRTAP activities over time illustrates that the construction of regional identities does not take place in isolation. Regionality in both regimes is increasingly negotiated with EU actors and institutions. "Regional" and EU actors and institutions increasingly work in tandem to construct and standardize the roles and structures of assessment (HELCOM 2001; Selin and VanDeveer 2002). The relationships are complex. For example, the EU takes up various forms of knowledge from the regional cooperation regimes, even as regional and state actors seek to harmonize their standards and practices with those of the EU. Such processes "Europeanize" states within the LRTAP and Baltic environmental protection regimes, altering their laws, bureaucratic structures and practices. Regional international environmental cooperation around the Baltic Sea and LRTAP are now embedded within regional and pan-European identity construction.

Knowledge making within the LRTAP and Baltic Sea environmental regimes has repositioned states and nations within new regionalities and helped to reframe these notions of regional space and community within the emergent EU-centered notion of European integration. The emergent regionalities and the three types of order constructed by expert participants—of technical information, regional definition, and collectively sanctioned policy options—help to construct greater harmony between natural and social spaces as they build social institutions and social order around conceptions of regionally shared environments. Coproduction processes do so even as they (re)produce new power imbalances by contributing to the concentration of power within West European dominated EU bodies.

Notes

1. An international regime, according to the oft-cited definition in international relations scholarship, refers to "sets of implicit and explicit principles, norms, rules

and decision-making procedures around which actor expectations converge in a given area of international relations" (Krasner 1983, p. 2).

2. In this chapter, "acid rain," "acid deposition," "acidic deposition," and "acidifying deposition" are used interchangeably.

3. The OECD program was given organizational standing independent of the OECD in 1978 as the Cooperative Program for Monitoring and Evaluation of the Long-Range Transmission of Air Pollution in Europe (EMEP). EMEP, as noted below, was later formally established in international law within a protocol to the LRTAP Convention.

4. This discussion relies heavily on my interviews with Leen Hordijk, former IIASA project director and leader of LRTAP's integrated assessment task force (various dates, 1998–99, Laxenburg, Austria, and Cambridge, Massachusetts) and with Marcus Amann, current project director of the IIASA Transboundary Air Pollution project (various dates, January and February 1998).

5. Author's interviews of Christine Full and Kaj Forsius, HELCOM Secretariat Offices, Helsinki, June 2002.

References

Alcamo, Joseph, Roderick Shaw, and Leen Hordijk, eds. 1990. *The RAINS Model of Acidification: Science and Strategies for Europe.* Kluwer.

Anderson, Benedict. 1991. *Imagined Communities,* second edition. Verso.

Bäckstrand, Karin. 2001. What Nature Can Withstand: Science, Politics and Discourses in Transboundary Air Pollution Diplomacy. Doctoral dissertation, Lund University.

Bäckstrand, Karin, and Henrik Selin. 2000. "Sweden—A Pioneer of Acidification Abatement." In *International Environmental Agreements and Domestic Politics,* ed. A. Underdal and K. Hanf. Ashgate.

Chossudovsky, Evgeny. 1989. *"East-West" Diplomacy for Environment in the United Nations.* UNITAR

Connolly, Barbara. 1999. Asymmetrical Rivalry in Common Pool Resources and European Responses to Acid Rain. In *Anarchy and the Environment,* ed. J. Barkin and G. Shambaugh. State University of New York Press.

Cowling, Ellis B. 1982. "Acid Precipitation in Historical Perspective." *Environmental Science and Technology* 16, no. 2: 110A–123A.

Darst, Robert G. 2001. *Smokestack Diplomacy: Cooperation and Conflict in East-West Environmental Politics.* MIT Press.

Douglas, Mary. 1986. *How Institutions Think.* Syracuse University Press.

Dybern, Bernt I. 1980. "The Organizational Pattern of Baltic Marine Science." *Ambio* 9, no. 3–4: 187–193.

European Environment Agency (EEA). 1999. *Environment in the European Union at the Turn of the Century.* European Environment Agency.

Farrell, Alex, Stacy D. VanDeveer, and Jill Jäger. 2001. "Environmental Assessments: Four Under-Appreciated Elements of Design" *Global Environmental Change* 1: 311–333.

Global Environmental Assessment (GEA) Project. 1997. *A Critical Evaluation of Global Environmental Assessments: The Climate Experience.* CARE (Calverton, Maryland).

Gutner, Tamar, and Stacy D. VanDeveer. 2001. "Networks, Coalitions and Communities: Capacity Building in the Baltic Sea Region." Presented at Annual Convention of International Studies Association, Chicago.

Haas, Peter M. 1993. "Protecting the Baltic and North Seas." In *Institutions for the Earth*, ed. P. Haas et al. MIT Press.

Hajer, Martin. 1995. *The Politics of Environmental Discourse.* Oxford University Press.

Harding, Sandra. 1991. *Whose Science? Whose Knowledge? Thinking from Women's Lives.* Open University Press.

HELCOM. 2001. Harmonization of HELCOM Recommendations with EU Directives and OSPAR Decisions and Recommendations. Final report.

HELCOM. 1998a. The Third Baltic Sea Pollution Load Compilation (PLC-3). Baltic Sea Environment Proceedings No. 70. Helsinki: Helsinki Commission.

HELCOM. 1998b. Final Report on the Implementation of the 1988 Ministerial Declaration. Baltic Sea Environment Proceedings No. 71. Helsinki Commission.

Jasanoff, Sheila. 1990. *The Fifth Branch: Science Advisers as Policymakers.* Harvard University Press.

Jasanoff, Sheila. 2001. "Image and Imagination: The Formation of Global Environmental Consciousness" In *Changing the Atmosphere*, ed. C. Miller and P. Edwards. MIT Press.

Jasanoff, Sheila. Forthcoming. *States of Knowledge: The Co-Production of Science and Social Order.* Routledge.

Jasanoff, Sheila, and Wynne, Brian. 1998. "Science and Decisionmaking." In *Human Choice and Climate Change*, Vol. 1: *The Societal Framework*, ed. S. Rayner and E. Malone. Batelle.

Krasner, Stephen D. 1983. "Structural Causes and Regime Consequences: Regimes as Intervening Variables." In *International Regimes.* Cornell University Press.

Latour, Bruno. 1987. *Science in Action.* Harvard University Press.

Latour, Bruno. 1990. "Drawing Things Together." In *Representation in Scientific Practice*, ed. M. Lynch and S. Woolgar. MIT Press.

Latour, Bruno. 1993. *We Were Never Modern.* Harvard University Press.

Levy, Marc. 1993. European Acid Rain: The Power of Toteboard Diplomacy. In *Institutions for the Earth*, ed. P. Haas et al. MIT Press.

Miller, Clark A., and Paul N. Edwards, eds. 2001. *Changing the Atmosphere: Expert Knowledge and Enviornmental Governance.* MIT Press.

Mittelman, James. 2000. *The Globalization Syndrome: Transformation and Resistance*. Princeton University Press.

Mumford, Lewis. 1938. *The Culture of Cities*. Harcourt Brace.

O'Riordan, T., and Jill Jäger. 1996. *The Politics of Climate Change: A European Perspective*. Routledge.

Rytovuori, Helena. 1980. "Structures of Détente and Ecological Interdependence: Cooperation in the Baltic Sea Area for the Protection of Marine Environment and Living Resources," *Cooperation and Conflict* 15, no. 2: 85–102.

Schneider, T., ed. 1986. *Acidification and Its Policy Implications*. Elsevier.

Schneider, T., ed. 1992. *Acidification Research: Evaluation and Policy Applications*. Elsevier.

Selin, Henrik. 2000. Towards International Chemical Safety: Taking Action on Persistent Organic Pollutants (POPs). Linköping Studies in Arts and Sciences no. 211.

Selin, Henrik, and Stacy D. VanDeveer. 1999. "A Tale of Two Cities: Geneva, Brussels and Attempts to Combat European Air Pollution." Presented at Annual Meeting of American Political Science Association, Atlanta.

Selin, Henrik, and Stacy D. VanDeveer. 2002. "Hazardous Substances and the Helsinki and Barcelona Conventions: Origins, Results and Future Challenges." Presented at Policy Forum *Management of Toxic Substances in the Marine Environment: Analysis of the Mediterranean and the Baltic*, Javea, Spain.

Serafin, Rafal, and Jerzy Zaleski. 1997. "Baltic Europe: Environmental Management in Regional Context," In *Saving the Seas*, ed. L. Brooks and S. VanDeveer. Sea Grant Press.

Tuinstra, Willemijn, Leen Hordijk, and Markus Amman. 1999. "Using Computer Models in International Negotiations: Acidification in Europe." *Environment* 41, no. 9: 32–42.

VanDeveer, Stacy D. Forthcoming (a). "European Politics with a Scientific Face: Framing, Asymmetrical Participation and Capacity in LRTAP." In *The Design of Global Environmental Assessments*, ed. A. Farrell and J. Jäger.

VanDeveer, Stacy D. Forthcoming (b). "Assessment Information in European Politics: East and West." In *Global Environmental Assessments*, ed. R. Mitchell et al. MIT Press.

VanDeveer, Stacy D., and Geoffrey D. Dabelko. 1999. "Redefining Security Around the Baltic: Environmental Issues in Regional Context." *Global Governance* 5, no. 2: 221–249.

Victor, David G., Kal Raustiala, and Eugene B. Skolnikoff, eds. 1998. *The Implementation and Effectiveness of International Environmental Commitments: Theory and Practice*. MIT Press.

Westone, Gregory S., and Armin Rosencranz. 1983. *Acid Rain in Europe and North America: National Responses to an International Problem*. Environmental Law Institute.

Wettestad, Jørgen. 2000. "From Common Cuts to Critical Loads: The ECE Convention on Long-Range Transboundary Air Pollution (LRTAP)" in Steinar Andresen, Tora Skodvin, Arild Underdal, and Jørgen Wettestad. *Science and Politics in International Environmental Regimes*. Manchester University Press.

Wettestad, Jørgen. 2002. *Clearing the Air: European Advances in Tackling Acid Rain and Atmospheric Pollution*. Ashgate.

Zmudzinsk, Ludwik. 1989. "Environmental quality in the Baltic region." In *Comprehensive Security for the Baltic*, ed. A. Westing. Sage.

Conclusion
Knowledge and Governance

Sheila Jasanoff and Marybeth Long Martello

Globalization as articulated in preceding chapters reveals itself as a far more subtle and complex phenomenon than a simple crescendo in the quantity or quality of transactions among the peoples of the world. Environmental globalization, in particular, involves new ways of making sense of the human condition on Earth; it involves changes in systems of meaning, not merely measurable increases in the number, diversity, intensity or extent of human impacts on planetary ecosystems and natural resources. Slowly but surely, it appears, the forces of environmental science and politics are making people conceive of the Earth as a single, unified, and limited habitat, calling for responsible standards of stewardship and globally accountable institutions of governance. Yet, as we have also seen, this grand convergence of perspectives has had the paradoxical effect of renewing commitments to locally specific ways of knowing and responding to environmental problems. The period of arguably the most heightened global awareness in history has also brought with it the sharpest rise in claims on behalf of the vitality and legitimacy of the local.

The clearest marker of the rediscovery of the local is the formal admission of local and indigenous knowledge into many global environmental regimes (Martello 2001); both such knowledge and the people who hold it have thereby gained higher status in a wide variety of environment and development projects. In this respect, environmental treaties and accords have again provided a precursor and model for other areas of international cooperation, confirming that how people know their own ways of life must be reckoned with in building the new global order.[1] Knowledge, moreover, is correctly seen as a more expansive category than science pure and simple. By including diverse knowledges, global regimes can defer to different cultures and forms of life while generating support for overarching norms such as precaution, sustainability, and global governance.

Forward-looking as this development has been, it continues the modernist tradition in distinguishing science, treated as a universal public good, from knowledge, which is seen by contrast as particularistic, indigenous or local. The essays in this volume have sought to refine this picture in three ways: by showing, first, that there is nothing essential or predetermined about the *global* and the *local*, but that each category is constituted through the beliefs, actions, and practices of relevant actors; second, that the legitimacy of both formations depends on *situated* knowledges, whose capacity to travel beyond their initial context of production depends on multiple factors; and third, that effective governance requires dynamic interaction between global and local forms of life. Localization, in consequence, demands the same kind of critical attention from social scientists as does the more widely acknowledged phenomenon of globalization.

In this final chapter, we reaffirm the need to take the mechanisms of knowledge production centrally into account in evaluating the institutions and processes of global governance. We then reiterate the reasons for emphasizing the local perspective in designing global environmental governance arrangements. We conclude with some observations about how to insert the local viewpoint more effectively into decision making for environmental sustainability on supranational scales.

The Salience of Knowledge

It is not surprising that knowledge has emerged as a salient theme in projects of environmental governance. The role of science in environmental decision making has long been recognized, although for many years the relationship between science and policy was thought to be linear. Environmental decisions, it was assumed, could invariably be improved by securing more and better inputs of scientific knowledge. Science would educate decision makers and raise public awareness, and this awareness in turn would lead to informed and rational policy choices—so conventional wisdom asserted. Environmental research budgets accordingly grew in most advanced industrial nations, as did a vast array of advisory and assessment bodies charged with translating complex scientific information into terms that policy makers could use as a basis for decision making. With the advent of global environmentalism, a similar explosion of research and expertise occurred at supranational levels of governance.

By the 1990s, however, empirical observations began to undermine the validity of the simple linear model. Science and scientists played pivotal roles in discovering and publicizing the ozone hole, identifying global warming, and propelling biodiversity onto the global policy agenda. But more science, as indicated by a wealth of case studies, did not necessarily lead to quicker or more certain decisions (Collingridge and Reeve 1986; Graham et al. 1988; Nelkin 1992). Instead, waiting for "better" science proved to be a favorite tactic for stalling decisions on a range of issues, from toxic pollution and acid rain to climate change (for historical evidence, see Social Learning Group 2001). Protracted controversies focused as often as not on the deconstruction of scientific claims, and closure, when it came about, resulted from resolving the normative differences that produced divergent interpretations of scientific evidence (Jasanoff 1986, 1987; see also Richards and Martin 1995). In the international arena, it was not scientific knowledge alone, but rather coalitions of normatively and discursively united actors who brought about collective solutions to environmental problems (Haas 1990; Litfin 1994; Hajer 1995; Keck and Sikkink 1998). By contrast, the "same" scientific knowledge often led to divergent regulatory decisions in countries that were economically and politically similar (Brickman et al. 1985). None of these findings denigrated the importance of scientific research in support of environmental policy, but they did indicate that more sophisticated analysis of the links between knowledge and policy was greatly overdue. Such an exploration was bound to have profound consequences for the institutions and practices of environmental governance.

From the standpoint of environmental policy, we can look at the decade of the 1990s as a long march toward doubt and uncertainty. In place of confidence in the power of science to silence controversy, awareness grew in many quarters that science is neither complete nor univocal (EEA 2001), and that its ability to bridge deep ideological and normative divisions is correspondingly limited. In place of certitude that science, unlike all other forms of social activity, is subservient only to its own unique norms (Merton 1973 [1942]), recognition mounted that social interests and relationships are every bit as critical in the formation of scientific consensus as in any other domain of human activity (Jasanoff et al. 1995; Collins 1985).

Through focused historical and ethnographic investigations of scientific practice, sociologists of scientific knowledge demonstrated that mundane processes of negotiation and trust-building are essential to the production of credible scientific knowledge (Collins 2001; Shapin 1994; Latour and Woolgar 1979); these processes closely parallel those involved in producing democratically accountable political decisions. These studies led to the unavoidable conclusion that natural and social order are co-produced through intertwined intellectual and social processes (Jasanoff 2004; Latour 1993; Shapin and Schaffer 1985). Accordingly, the expectation that politics can be legitimated by appeal to an autonomous, free-standing, "independent" science proved to be untenable. Instead, it became imperative to reanalyze—and if possible reform—institutions of governance built on outmoded assumptions about the independence of science from politics. This was one guiding objective of the contributors to this book.

Bringing the Local Back In

As long as it seemed that answers to the basic questions of environmental governance could be found through science, there was little need to make room for local or "situated" (Haraway 1988) knowledges, politics or values. But the discovery of science's limitations—particularly uncertainty and ignorance—as well as mounting recognition of the social dimensions of knowledge production provide strong justification for bringing local perspectives back into processes of environmental governance. Once admitted to these forums, local actors can benefit enormously from the resources offered by global scientific and political institutions.

Drawing on concepts and findings from science and technology studies, the contributions to this volume reaffirm the need to expand the range of knowledge sources in global environmental governance and supply several additional reasons for endorsing knowledgeable conversations between the local and the global. One after another, the cases demonstrate, to begin with, that "science" itself is a form of powerful but situated knowledge, whose reductions and constraints can be overcome only by supplementing it with perspectives that were formerly regarded as "merely local" (e.g., Fogel, Goldman, Gupta, Iles, Lahsen, Scholz). Once marginalized local and indigenous viewpoints are now viewed as incorporating tacit, historical, cultural, and place-based knowledges that do not easily lend themselves to verification by conventional scientific means. Ironically, it is this kind of knowledge that appears in the global context as more truly reflective of complex environmental realities. Based more often on experience and trial and error than on laboratory experiments, and refusing to abide by *a priori* distinctions between the social and the natural, local knowledges offer useful counterpoints to the reductionist, though indispensable, contributions of orthodox science.

A second reason for reintroducing the local that emerges forcefully from earlier chapters is to counteract the simplifying and erasing role of science-based environmental standards. When science is used for predictive or diagnostic purposes, as so often in environmental policy making, its limitations may lead to overlooking some causes or to framing problems too narrowly. The consequences can be even more dire when science is used—without more—for managerial purposes, as in standard-setting for example: standards not only oversimplify, and in that sense misrepresent, the worlds they seek to regulate (Bowker and Star 1999), but they tend to do so in ways that systematically overlook unorthodox, marginal or non-scientific viewpoints. Enlarging the scope of environmental governance from nation-states to the supranational has entailed precisely such simplifications, as noted in several chapters (Goldman, Fogel, Forsyth, Jasanoff, Miller, among others). In all these cases, the efficiency of the global issue framing was achieved at the cost of eliminating some people and their needs and interests from the managers' purview. If these are the costs of global governance, then it is not surprising, in the poignant words of a Brazilian witness before the World Commission on Environment and Development, that "these people that still live don't want to reach down to the level of survival" (WCED 1987, p. 40).

A third point that the cases drive home is the intimate link between nature and culture that characterizes local or situated environmental perspectives, as well as the risks of abandoning such holistic thinking in the name of science and technology. One of the clearest cases in this respect is Martello's account of the Makah whaling controversy, where the cultural survival of a marginal population depended on its ability to defend its construction of what was "natural." Another illuminating example is Lachmund's account of the development of Berlin ecology, a *science* that had to accommodate deep within its practices the *social* particularities of a devastated and memory-burdened postwar metropolis. But other stories in the book also underscore the need that many feel to bring scientific assessments into dialogue with cultural commitments beyond those incorporated within the practices of science itself. Cross-regional scientific exchanges reveal, at times painfully, the extent to which scientific means of understanding nature have embedded within them highly particular and locally specific ways of knowing (Beck, Gupta, Lahsen, VanDeveer). Thus, scientists working across national or disciplinary boundaries frequently discover that their assessments of causes and consequences differ from those of counterparts in other countries and fields. Differences in their historical experiences, intellectual priorities, standards of proof or definitions of safety lead to interpretive disagreements. Invoking a univocal, and supposedly value-neutral, science to resolve such deep-seated and consequential divergences is a recipe for discord rather than harmony.

Fourth, and finally, the cases considered here suggest that making room for local knowledges may serve to shape new, more environmentally aware social identities, thereby increasing support for robust management practices.[2] Particularly interesting in this regard are Lachmund's treatment of urban ecology in Berlin and VanDeveer's demonstration of new regionalisms emerging around environmental issues and resources in Eastern Europe; the latter are supported by both scientific and political representations of what the people of these regions hold in common. Scientists involved in environmental negotiations may, in the best of cases, serve as cultural diplomats, reflexively aware of their own standpoints and able to build stronger platforms from which to negotiate their differences with equally "situated" experts from other localities. Too often, however, the rhetoric and hidden ideology of a universal science stand in the way of such normative and reflexive awakening (Fogel, Forsyth, Goldman, Gupta, Jasanoff, Miller).

For local perspectives to prove effective in global contexts, however, more is needed than a formal entry ticket for local activists. Negotiation and interactivity, we have argued, are crucial. Indeed, as many of our studies show, it is not only the local that contributes to the enriching of the global, but also the global that provides means for local entities to gain access to, engage with, and draw benefits from global forums and discourses (Fogel, Iles, Lachmund, Martello, Miller, Scholz). For example, in Scholz's account, a bioprospecting enterprise in Panama provides training, equipment, career opportunities, and other resources to local residents. Lachmund's ecologists draw upon global concepts like biodiversity to anchor and legitimate their urban projects. The historically conservative chemical industry, as Iles demonstrates, empowers local people to enter new domains of governance by cautiously broadening its narrow notions of expertise. Miller shows how global climate forecasters attempt (though not without problems) to share useful information, practices, and technologies with Peruvians. And indigenous peoples in Fogel's and Martello's case studies crucially rely on the global indigenous rights movement in advancing their claims on behalf of local cultures and knowledges.

Guideposts for Governance

Armed with these insights, we now turn to the last of our three objectives: reviewing the implications of our theoretical program for the pragmatic challenges of environmental governance. How does the analysis of local-global dynamics offered in this book bear on the design and conduct of governance arrangements? A few general remarks are in order.

First, our studies have underscored the need to stop regarding globalization as a natural or unidirectional phenomenon, unstoppable in its homogenizing thrust. We recognize it instead as a social achievement, painstakingly built by human agents using the material and institutional resources at their command. Institutions of global governance do not merely implement policies that are "naturally" global but serve as construction sites, or signaling stations, for sorting out the very meanings of the global and the local. Thus, a variety of international policy forums constructed climate change as a global problem and local knowledge preservation as a global goal while also producing worldwide CFC phase-outs, whaling moratoriums, and transnational networks to combat desertification. In these cases, cooperation to save the fragile Planet Earth resulted from successful exercises in globalization, mediated by national and international research programs, expert bodies, NGOs, and negotiating forums convened under varied environmental regimes (see also Miller and Edwards 2001). Concurrently, however, these same actors and forums also worked to define and delimit the rights and prerogatives of the local. Through their efforts, global environmental protection and economic development goals were translated into arrangements to address the problems, needs, capacities, and objectives of communities in particular ecological and political settings. Mitigating and adapting to (global) climate change, for instance, called forth behavioral changes at the local, even individual, level. The bio-diversity regime deferred to nation states for its worldwide implementa-tion. And development funding, when effectively dispersed, often resulted in projects at municipal or community levels.

Second, the processes of globalization and (re)localization are political to the core: they frame policy problems and set political agendas, with signifi-cant consequences for legitimacy, power, and voice. Whether an issue is framed as local or global can help determine whether and in which forums it will be taken up and who may speak for it. Biodiversity conservation and land degradation, for example, are considered global problems deserving supranational attention, while wetlands conservation and tropospheric ozone pollution remain national or regional concerns. In the 1970s, a young United Nations Environment Program played a central role in characteriz-ing desertification as a global problem amenable to scientific solutions (Martello, forthcoming). In contrast, water scarcity, long considered a local or regional concern and addressed at these levels of governance, is only now beginning to emerge as an international issue. These dispensations and their political consequences may seem natural to observers after the fact, although they were in practice contingent on particular historical circumstances.

Third, policy forums do not merely naturalize ideas of the local and global; they are important sites of meaning-making, and hence should be viewed as localities of political significance in and of themselves. Institutions such as the IPCC (Beck, Fogel, Lahsen), the IRI (Miller), the World Bank (Goldman) or the IWC (Martello) create and embody particular cultures with their own languages, practices, and standards. They offer ready entry to some actors while consciously or unconsciously erecting barriers against others. Institutionalized policy discourses (e.g., those of "sound science," "precaution" or "indigenous knowledge") may be aimed at facilitating global cooperation or at securing the participation of diverse interests and communities. But however neutral or technical such discourses may appear on the surface, they are also normative in the ways that they join together, reach across, circulate through or obstruct passage between spheres that are held to be local or global.

These observations are reflected in the prescriptions we offer below. We advance our conclusions in all modesty, recognizing that if our collective analysis is well founded then no set of prescriptions can possibly do justice to the infinite plasticity of the forms of governance in a globalizing world.

These conclusions should be seen at best as moveable guideposts, not as a finished architectural blueprint. We group them under three headings that are crucially important to the success of *all* governance arrangements, regardless of their scope or substantive focus: *institutions, expertise,* and *democracy.* All three, however, have special resonance in connection with representing the local in global environmental regimes, and vice versa.

Institutions

Institutions are absolutely central to the story lines of globalization and (re)localization. They define what counts as global or local; in addition, they both *have* politics and *make* politics. Accordingly, the normative and organizational structure of global environmental institutions is of the greatest importance to the growing world polity. What can we say about institutional design on the basis of the foregoing explorations?

Perhaps the most important recommendation to flow from this book is that there is an enormous need for institutions of global governance to become more aware of their active role in constructing the processes of globalization and localization. Such a sea change in the mindset of ruling institutions will not come easily. The dominant epistemic orientations of most global institutions remain those of naturalism and scientific or technological determinism. That is, institutions take for granted that some problems are global or local by their very nature, failing to see their own hand in the creation of these categories; these institutions also subscribe to notions of scientific and technological inevitability. Their presumptions are no less strong for being, mostly, inexplicit and inchoate. They tend to be embedded in routinized practices, such as methods of assessment and standardization, whose intellectual and normative foundations are not ordinarily subject to radical questioning or critique. It is this imaginative blockage that has to be countered, using instruments that will not in their turn rapidly fall victim to similar rigidity or paralysis.

Improved means of creating openness and transparency may go a considerable distance toward producing the environment of enhanced self-reflection that we advocate. While these are not panaceas and should not be treated as such (Strathern 2000), the need to hold oneself accountable to external critics acts as a powerful motor of self-regulation. Transparency is an essential step in the practices of global (and regional; see EU 2001) governance. Institutions should also consider adopting best practice guidelines for subjecting their methods of technical analysis, advice-seeking, and review to regular criticism. Such practices will necessarily be extremely diverse and must be carefully tailored to the capacities of particular governing institutions. Relevant practices might include the maintenance of historical data bases recording past successes and failures, routine analysis of the likely distributive and socioeconomic impacts of decisions or programs, follow-up studies to monitor these exercises, and methods for soliciting minority and dissenting opinions on major proposed actions.[3]

Mechanisms are also needed to force institutions, at regular intervals, to reflect on the rationale for accepted problem framings and alternatives to them. "Why" questions should gain greater prominence at the expense of the "how to" questions that currently enjoy pride of place in most policy implementing agencies. Global institutions should find ways of analyzing their own role in making (and frequently erasing) particular meanings of the local. For example, global regimes for climate change, biodiversity loss, whaling, and desertification all seek to shape beliefs and behaviors among local communities and individuals. The ways in which global institutions conceptualize "local knowledge," "subsistence hunting" (of whales for instance), "natural products" or "climate change impacts" have important implications for how people may act in a variety of local contexts— whether these be scientific disciplines, rural villages, expert advisory bodies, or transnational networks of indigenous activists.

Expertise

Institutionalized expertise is one of the most powerful instruments for creating boundaries between global and local governance arrangements for the environment. Who counts as expert, whose knowledge is deemed relevant, and who participates in advisory and negotiating bodies are all critically important choices in the development of environmental regimes. Historically, expertise kept company with globalism—scientifically trained and technically skilled individuals carried with them the standardized, delocalized perspectives of their professions and disciplines. Lay knowledges, by contrast, were not ordinarily thought to confer expertise. It is no accident that the discourse of contemporary environmentalism refers to "holders" of indigenous or local knowledge; lacking formal training, such holders are by definition not considered experts, even if the knowledge they bear is occasionally deemed valuable for management purposes.

The cases considered in this book warn us to be wary of such asymmetrical distinctions and of unquestioningly importing them into policy processes. Instead, a robust finding of many of the studies is that claims of expertise in global forums are themselves valid only within particular "situated" frameworks of presumptions and practices. These expert claims, no less than unorganized claims of local knowledge, should be regularly subjected to criticism and review so as to challenge their founding assumptions. Particularly needing scrutiny are long-term, highly routinized, standard-setting bodies which tend to develop their own insular analytic practices and discourses without accountability to skeptical scientific or civic audiences. Not restricted to the natural sciences alone, such bodies often concern themselves with social, economic or engineering standards whose social and political implications, and even whose claims to technical validity, are gradually lost to view under layers of administrative routine.

Another point at which there may be both a need and an opportunity to build improved critical capacity is during the emergence of new domains or cultures of expertise. In the global arena, for example, there has been a near-explosion of new analytic techniques: environmental economics, integrated assessment, general circulation models, sustainability science, and others. To the extent that these endeavors provide opportunities for systematic reflection, particularly across traditional disciplines, their representatives deserve to be greeted positively. Yet, given the prominence of mundane reasoning and negotiation in the formation of any branch of expertise, these new advocates for the global environment should be required to account for themselves in lay as well as expert arenas and to submit their "universalist" framings to diverse external critics.

A third modest institutional improvement that could yield major dividends is the creation of forums where lay knowledges could be routinely critiqued and assessed by members of relevant scientific communities. What our studies support is *not* the standardization of local experiences according some universal template of data coding (as, for example, in the practices of the World Bank; see Goldman), but rather the informed uptake of local epistemologies by scientific communities—and the possible incorporation of holistic environmental insights into disciplinary research agendas. As yet, most expert-lay dialogue is oriented toward exposing experts to public questioning through hearings, inquiries, and the like. Reversing the relations of epistemic power implicit in such arrangements could promote, as several of our chapters have shown, the importation of relevant local knowledges into global policy domains. The absence of forums to facilitate such discussion has led in the past to serious policy failures, on both epistemic and normative grounds (Jasanoff 1997; Wynne 1989).

Democracy

Along with the rise of globalization fear has grown of a global "democratic deficit." The worry is that, as centers of power shift further and further away from people's immediate control, out of their communities and nation-states, the opaque administrative routines of *governance* will take over from the relatively transparent processes of *government*. People will then be left without voice, without remedy, and even without certain knowledge of where the controls on their liberties are coming from. This inchoate but deeply felt anxiety is no doubt responsible for the intensification of anti-globalization sentiments around the world and for the rise of various forms of protest politics, such as the resurgence of the far right in recent European elections. Supranational organizations frequently assert their commitment to democracy—who, after all, would say "no" to democracy?—but how to go about delivering on that promise is another question. Our analysis suggests some concrete, if cautious, answers.

The acknowledgment that local or indigenous knowledge and its holders deserve a place at international negotiating tables makes explicit one of the principal contentions of this book: there cannot be a meaningfully accountable, let alone a democratic, global order without making room for voices and epistemologies organized at levels much below the global. Engaging with local viewpoints (or those seen to be local), however, has to be a continuing commitment, demanding institutional and procedural reform. We have argued that the line between global and local is fluid and socially achieved, a conclusion that militates against once-for-all determinations of what are valid "local" inputs. Incorporating standardized packages of "local knowledge" into complex and contested decision-making processes simply will not serve as a substitute for repeated mutual questioning between global and non-global actors.

Democratization of global governance ultimately calls for more than formal invitations to dialogue. The new institutions that have sprung up to manage the global domain produce, as we have seen, their own parochial cultures, with distinctive rules of participation and deliberation. It takes considerable "local knowledge" to penetrate these closed institutional preserves, knowledge that first-time players and other disadvantaged groups rarely possess. It makes little sense to hold global forums open to the world's heterogeneous populations without providing adequate support for their interventions. Environmental NGOs and indigenous peoples' organizations have sprung up to perform some of the spadework of representation, but global policy forums should seek proactively to lower the barriers to participation. In this context, notions of capacity building should be broadened so as to include the expertise needed to represent one's cause more competently in global forums.

Final Reflections

Through the long course of human history, attempts to understand how the world works have led to untold innovations in science and technology and, many would add, to steady material and social progress. So uncontroversial is this statement that modern governing institutions unhesitatingly accept that there can be no progress without science and technology—indeed, that policy cannot be made without first "getting straight" the facts about nature. Only in recent years have we begun to realize how profoundly developments in knowledge and technological capacity are linked to human self-understanding and social relations. To discover new facts about nature, we must routinely revise preexisting categories and habits of thought, and accompanying material practices, often in quite salient ways. In changing nature we change ourselves. To build on "natural" facts without taking stock of associated social orders is risky business. This book has sought to show how these newly reflective and critical orientations are finding their way into the practices of environmental governance—albeit slowly, partially, and not without resistance.

In making room for local knowledge, environmental regimes have learned a lesson that other globalizing institutions would do well to assimilate. Politics in the global order requires taking on board the divergent ways in which the world's peoples have chosen to make sense of nature and the environment. In applauding the move from science to knowledge, the contributors to this book have *not* suggested that lay or indigenous knowledges are better than science or that all knowledge claims, regardless of their source, are entitled to equal respect. Rather, we have made the case that all *disciplined* ways of knowing nature, as well as conceptualizing human-nature relationships, have their strengths and limitations. Knowledge gained from historical experience, ancestral myths, long-established social practices, and lay experimentation are not the same as knowledge acquired through lab experiments, formal models or methodologically disciplined empirical observations. It is the complementarity of diverse ways of knowing that provides richness and offers safeguards against the perils of a too enthusiastic scientific reductionism.

We have also called attention to science itself as a form of localism, a perspective that is not yet adequately reflected in the practices of global environmental institutions. Scientific and expert bodies, we have suggested, should (with help from friendly critics) look in upon themselves so as to become more sensitive to possible blind spots and constraints of imagination underlying their global and universal orientations. There are many concrete steps through which such reflexivity could be gained and nurtured. We have proposed a few that might enhance the quality of dialogue between perspectives deemed to be global and those held to be local. In the end, however, it is the *ideology* of global governance that we wish to influence more than the design of specific institutions or processes. For this larger purpose, we have argued throughout, practice needs to join hands with theory and close empirical studies must ground themselves in deeper conceptual analysis. This book, we hope, will serve as both a model and an invitation.

Notes

1. To distinguish the approach to knowledge and governance adopted in this book from standard political science analysis, it is instructive to look at the commentary generated in connection with the European Commission's recent white paper on governance (EU 2001). Schmitter (2001) usefully distinguishes governance from representative democracy and advances a number of "modest proposals" for achieving more democratic governance in the European context. European governance arrangements, in his view, are directed toward specific issues and may require for their success "a good deal of 'local knowledge' about those affected" (ibid., p. 9). Knowledge is here seen as a resource to be instrumentally mobilized for purposes of governance. Although Schimitter is keenly aware of the need to secure a "common understanding" of the matter to be governed (ibid., p. 13), he evidently does not recognize the critical role of governance institutions in creating the very knowledges that they then apply to policy problems. The authors in this volume, by contrast, generally subscribe to a co-productionist view in which knowledge making and social ordering proceed in tandem (Jasanoff 2004).

2. On this point, the authors diverge from the conventional accounts offered by students of common pool resources, who treat the management institutions around the resource as independent of the resource itself (Ostrom 1990). Our view, rather, is that ways of organizing management institutions inevitably reflect, and reflect on, the meaning of the resource to users and managers. Equally, our cases suggest that social identity plays an important role in the efficacy of environmental regimes, and that the construction of such identities is related to meanings that communities accord to their shared resources.

3. Many practices of these kinds were historically incorporated into national policies for environmental impact assessment. However, these have sometimes fallen into disuse and lost their critical function as bureaucracies have become more confident, complex, and resistant to external supervision. For the most part, such requirements of transparency and pre-action assessment have not been generalized to the level of global governance.

References

Bowker, Geoffrey C., and Susan Leigh Star. 1999. *Sorting Things Out: Classification and Its Consequences*. MIT Press.

Brickman, Ronald, Sheila Jasanoff, and Thomas Ilgen. 1985. *Controlling Chemicals: The Politics of Regulation in Europe and the United States*. Cornell University Press.

Collingridge, David, and Colin Reeve. 1986. *Science Speaks to Power: The Role of Experts in Policy Making*. Pinter.

Collins, H.M. 1985. *Changing Order: Replication and Induction in Scientific Practice*. Sage.

Collins, H. M. 2001. "Tacit Knowledge, Trust, and the Q of Sapphire." *Social Studies of Science* 31, no. 1: 71–85.

European Environment Agency (EEA). 2001. Late Lessons from Early Warnings: The Precautionary Principle 1896–2000. Environmental Issue Report 22.

European Union. 2001. European Governance: A White Paper. COM(2001) 428 final. Brussels: Commission of the European Communities.

Graham, John D., Laura C. Green, and Marc J. Roberts. 1988. *In Search of Safety: Chemicals and Cancer Risk*. Harvard University Press.

Haas, Peter M. 1990. *Saving the Mediterranean: The Politics of International Environmental Cooperation*. Columbia University Press.

Hajer, Maarten A. 1995. *The Politics of Environmental Discourse: Ecological Modernization and the Policy Process*. Clarendon.

Haraway, Donna J. 1988. "Situated Knowledges: The Science Question in Feminism as a Site of Discourse on the Privilege of Partial Perspective." *Feminist Studies* 14, no. 3: 575–599.

Jasanoff, Sheila. 1986. *Risk Management and Political Culture*. Russell Sage Foundation.

Jasanoff, Sheila. 1987. "Contested Boundaries in Policy-Relevant Science." *Social Studies of Science* 17, no. 2: 195–230.

Jasanoff, Sheila. 1997. "NGOs and the Environment: From Knowledge to Action." *Third World Quarterly* 18, no. 3: 579–594.

Jasanoff, Sheila, ed. 2004. *States of Knowledge: The Co-Production of Science and Social Order.* Routledge.

Keck, Margaret E., and Kathryn Sikkink. 1998. *Activists beyond Borders: Advocacy Networks in International Politics.* Cornell University Press.

Latour, Bruno. 1993. *We Have Never Been Modern.* Harvard University Press.

Latour, Bruno, and Steve Woolgar. 1979. *Laboratory Life: The Construction of Scientific Facts.* Princeton University Press.

Litfin, Karen. 1994. *Ozone Discourses: Science and Politics in Global Environmental Cooperation.* Columbia University Press.

Martello, Marybeth. 2001. "A Paradox of Virtue?: 'Other' Knowledges and Environment-Development Politics." *Global Environmental Politics* 1, no. 3: 114–141.

Merton, Robert K. 1973 [1942]. "The Normative Structure of Science." In *The Sociology of Science.* University of Chicago Press.

Miller, Clark A., and Paul Edwards, eds. 2001. *Changing the Atmosphere: Science and the Politics of Global Warming.* MIT Press.

Nelkin, Dorothy, ed. 1992. *Controversy: Politics of Technical Decisions,* third edition. Sage.

Ostrom, Elinor. 1990. *Governing the Commons: The Evolution of Institutions for Collective Action.* Cambridge University Press.

Richards, Evelleen, and Brian Martin. 1995. "Scientific Knowledge, Controversy, and Public Decision Making." In *Handbook of Science and Technology Studies,* ed. S. Jasanoff et al. Sage.

Schmitter, Philippe C. 2001. What Is There to Legitimize in the European Union . . . and How Might This Be Accomplished? No. 75, Political Science Series, Institute for Advanced Studies, Vienna.

Shapin, Steven. 1994. *A Social History of Truth.* University of Chicago Press.

Shapin, Steven, and Simon Schaffer. 1985. *Leviathan and the Air-Pump: Hobbes, Boyle, and the Experimental Life.* Princeton University Press.

Social Learning Group. 2001. *Learning to Manage Global Environmental Risks.* MIT Press.

Strathern, Marilyn. 2002. "The Tyranny of Transparency." *British Educational Research* 26, no. 3: 309–321.

World Commission on Environment and Development (WCED). 1987. *Our Common Future.* Oxford University Press.

Wynne, Brian. 1989. "Sheepfarming after Chernobyl." *Environment* 31: 11–15, 33–39.

Contributors

Silke Beck
Institute for Technology Assessment and Systems Analysis

Cathleen Fogel
University of California, Santa Cruz

Tim Forsyth
London School of Economics and Political Science

Michael Goldman
University of Illinois

Aarti Gupta
Wageningen University

Alastair Iles
University of California, Berkeley

Sheila Jasanoff
Harvard University

Jens Lachmund
University of Maastricht

Myanna Lahsen
Harvard University
University of Colorado, Boulder

Marybeth Long Martello
Harvard University

Clark A. Miller
University of Wisconsin, Madison

Astrid Scholz
Ecotrust

Stacy D. VanDeveer
University of New Hampshire